THE ROLE OF AGRICULTURE
IN ECONOMIC DEVELOPMENT

UNIVERSITIES–NATIONAL BUREAU
CONFERENCE SERIES

The Role of Agriculture
in Economic Development

A CONFERENCE
OF THE UNIVERSITIES–NATIONAL BUREAU
COMMITTEE FOR ECONOMIC RESEARCH

Erik Thorbecke

IOWA STATE UNIVERSITY

Editor

NATIONAL BUREAU OF ECONOMIC RESEARCH
NEW YORK 1969
Distributed by COLUMBIA UNIVERSITY PRESS
NEW YORK AND LONDON

National Bureau of Economic Research

Relation of National Bureau Directors
to Publications Reporting Conference Proceedings

Since the present volume is a record of conference proceedings, it has been exempted from the rules governing submission of manuscripts to, and critical review by, the Board of Directors of the National Bureau.

(Resolution adopted July 6, 1948, as revised
November 21, 1949, and April 20, 1968)

CONTENTS

THE ROLE OF AGRICULTURE
IN ECONOMIC DEVELOPMENT

Introduction

ERIK THORBECKE

IT HAS BECOME INCREASINGLY EVIDENT in the last few years that the conception of both economists and policy-makers regarding the role of agriculture in economic development has undergone an important evolution. Whereas in the past, agriculture was often viewed as the passive partner in the development process, it is now typically regarded as an active and co-equal partner with the industrial sector.

During the 1940's and 1950's there was a resurgence of interest in analyzing the determinants of economic growth. The economics profession turned its attention to the study of economic development to better understand the anatomy and physiology of the growth process and to formulate prescriptions for appropriate development policies and strategies. It was widely believed during this period that industrialization was the unique key to development and that the industrial sector, as the advanced sector, would pull with it the backward agricultural sector. More specifically, industry, as the leading sector, would be a source of alternative employment opportunities to the rural population, would provide a growing demand for foodstuffs and agricultural raw materials which it would process for domestic consumption or export, and would begin to supply industrial inputs (e.g., fertilizer) to agriculture.

It became fashionable to use as an analytical and planning framework one-sector models of the Harrod-Domar types which, because of their completely aggregative and simple production functions, with only investment as an element, emphasized at least implicitly investment in infrastructure and industry. The one-sector, one-input nature of these models obviously precluded any measurement of the sectoral production effects of alternative investment allocations and of different combinations of factors (since it was implicitly assumed that factors could only be combined in fixed proportions with investment). In the absence of either theoretical constructs or empirical information on the determinants of agricultural output, the tendency was to equate the modern sector with high productivity of investment (and vice versa for the backward agricultural sector) and thus direct the bulk of investment to industry and industrial infrastructure.

With the advent of two-sector models economists continued to assign to subsistence agriculture an essentially passive role as a potential source of "unlimited labor" and "agricultural surplus" for the rest of the economy. Not only was it assumed that the farmers could be released from subsistence agriculture in large numbers without a consequent reduction in agricultural output, but also that they could do so while carrying their own bundles of food (i.e., capital) on their backs. One popular policy prescription to encourage the above transfer of labor and of the agricultural "surplus" was to turn the terms of trade against agriculture. The trouble with this approach was that the backward agricultural "goose" would be starved before it could lay the golden egg.

As the dual-economy models became more sophisticated and realistic it was increasingly recognized that the functions which the agricultural and industrial sectors must perform in order for growth to occur are totally interdependent. On the one hand, the agricultural sector had to release resources for the industrial sector, which in turn had to be capable of absorbing them. On the other hand, the release of resources, by and of itself, and the absorption of resources, by and of itself, were not sufficient for economic development to take place. It was felt that growth could result only if these conditions occurred simultaneously and that this release-cum-absorption of labor and capital resources was, in fact, the key to development. Recognition of this active interdependence was a large step forward from the naive industrialization-first prescription, because the above conceptual framework no longer indentified either sector as leading or lagging.

Even though two-sector models did provide important insights into the interaction between the agricultural (backward) and industrial (advanced) sectors, there were at least two fundamental points that they did not address explicitly: foreign trade and the determinants of agricultural output. The foreign trade sector was eliminated—a closed economy being selected as the frame of reference rather than the open economy. A better understanding of the determinants of agricultural output—both in micro- and macroeconomic terms—is essential if agriculture is to play an active role as a supplier of resources.

The relationship between agriculture and foreign trade can be scrutinized at the national level or at the global level. The majority of the developing countries are largely dependent on primary exports as their major source of foreign exchange. The import capacity of the typical developing country is based, to a large extent, on the flow of agricultural and mineral exports that it can sell to the rest of the world. Since the balance of payments is generally the binding constraint to further growth, the role of the agricultural sector as a provider of foreign exchange through exports or as a saver of foreign exchange through import substitution (particularly through increased domestic production of foodstuffs) is a crucial one. In many less developed countries, the agricultural subsector producing for exports tends to be highly commercialized in contrast to the subsector producing foodstuffs for domestic consumption. In such cases, the backward linkages of agricultural exports may be quite small. In other countries, particularly in Africa, the distinction between the commercialized (export) and the subsistence sectors is much more difficult to draw.

At the global level the dependence of the developing world on agricultural exports creates many problems. World demand for these products tends to be both income and price inelastic. As a result, for many crops, of which the supply is also inelastic in the short-run, the growth rate of export earnings is held to a relatively low level and prices fluctuate. Efforts at diversification and commodity stabilization can be successful only if undertaken under viable international agreements. Empirical evidence on the terms of trade of the developing vis-à-vis the developed countries leaves at least a presumption that they are not improving. In most developing countries the level of receipts from traditional exports —determined as it is by exogenous forces—is largely outside of the control of the country; large output and efficiency gains are often negated by perverse price effects. Under these circumstances, the planning of agriculture and over-all development cannot be done through the simple aggregation of independently prepared national plans and projections that are likely to be mutually inconsistent. What is required is that the prospects for agricultural exports and their contribution to development be evaluated through the projection of supply and demand by regions and by commodities within a general and spatial equilibrium setting. National projections need to be aggregated, and differences in planned global and regional output and demand reconciled, before a rational (efficient) production and trade pattern can be established.

The possibility, or even (in the light of very high rates of population growth) the necessity of concentrating directly on increasing agricultural productivity and output tended to be somewhat overlooked during the period of infatuation with industrialization. Once the key role of agriculture was recognized, the knowledge gained from years of experimentation with seeds, fertilizer, and other inputs by foundations, universities, and the private sector began to be applied on a larger scale and more systematically. In the last few years a much better understanding was obtained of the function of industrial inputs as almost the *sine qua non* of agricultural development. Specific and detailed quantitative information became available on production functions—at both the farm and aggregate levels—revealing the complementary relationships between various inputs and the desirability of following a "package-approach." As the effects of the interaction between technical, economic, and social factors on agricultural development became clearer, the last tended to be conceived of increasingly as a system within which analytical questions and policy recommendations could be examined and resolved.

The question as to the form of the production function and the choice of technique within agriculture is fundamental. Because of the limited capacity of the industrial sector to absorb labor productively and because of the very low efficiency and residual nature of employment opportunities in services, a labor-using technique to alleviate the unemployment problem appears called for in a majority of the developing countries. With respect to land, the question is less clear-cut. In Africa land is still abundant and output can continue to increase through land expansion. In parts of Latin America and Asia, the bringing under cultivation of new land areas entails very large capital resources in infrastructure (e.g., irrigation) and thus yield-increasing techniques may be more efficient. In any case, the macroeconomic implications, in terms of employment creation and income distribution, of different techniques and combinations of inputs should be analyzed carefully to determine the possibility of conflicts that might arise in the pursuit of static economic efficiency, on one hand, and long-run economic and social development, on the other. This comparison is further complicated by the discrepancies that exist between the shadow and market prices in the factor market.

In 1965 the Universities-National Bureau Committee decided that the time was ripe to organize a conference on the role of agriculture in economic development. Much had already been accomplished in the areas previously reviewed: the theoretical literature had extended the dual-economy approach to at least three sectors with the introduction of foreign trade; the FAO and other international agencies were analyzing the production, consumption, and trade patterns for the major agricultural commodities on a multiregional basis. In addition, significant new attitudes—both public and professional—were becoming apparent.

First, the public was increasingly concerned about the world food problem (i.e., the widening gap between projected desirable nutritional requirements in the light of the very high population growth rate in the developing world and the extrapolation of dismal historical food output trends); and second, optimism was spreading in knowledgeable circles as to the capacity of technology to cope with the world food problem through an attack on both the food-production and population-control fronts, a strategy which, it was believed, would ultimately solve the problem. Indeed, by the middle 1960's a few key countries such as Taiwan, Korea, Pakistan, and Turkey appeared to be either on the verge of or had already made an agricultural take-off, if sudden and sustained acceleration of growth in agricultural output are any indication. The promise of a "yield explosion" created by new "miracle seeds" combined with other inputs seemed to be capable of realization in the not-too-distant future. At least these countries provided evidence that food output in the developing world could be substantially increased given the appropriate set of policies and input combinations.

In retrospect, it appears that over the last four years many events have further vindicated the judgment of the Universities-National Bureau of Economic Research Committee. The pendulum has swung back in the last twenty-five years from a development strategy emphasizing industrialization at almost any cost to a much more balanced approach in which agricultural development is attacked directly from the supply side instead of indirectly through generation of increased effective demand in nonagriculture. The 1960's will not be remembered as the hoped-for "development decade" but conceivably this period may someday be recalled as the beginning of the "green revolution."

A planning committee consisting of Karl A. Fox, Bruce F. Johnston, Max Millikan, William H. Nicholls, and Gustav Ranis, in addition to myself, was asked to prepare the agenda for the conference. It was obvious from the start that it would be utopian to expect such a conference to cover all aspects of agriculture's role in economic development. We decided, therefore, to emphasize three main themes: agriculture in the world economy, the relationship between agriculture and other sectors, and national studies analyzing the transformation of traditional agriculture.

With respect to the first topic above, we felt that the work already initiated by the FAO on the Indicative World Plan would provide the skeleton of a conceptual framework within which both the over-all prospects for the agricultural exports of the developing countries as well as the internal national effects and linkages of a given level of agricultural exports on the structure of output could be estimated. We asked Louis M. Goreux and J. A. C. Brown, two of the early architects of the methodology of the Indicative World Plan, to address themselves to the above two questions respectively. Goreux reviewed the various trade projections which UNCTAD and FAO had prepared. His analysis brings to light the desirability of increasing trade between developing countries and exports of nonagricultural commodities in view of the bleak outlook for traditional exports from the less developed to the developed world. Goreux discusses some of the implications of present urbanization trends in the less developed countries for the accuracy of projections. He also considers the increasing international inequality of export earnings that would follow for the developing world from a continuation of present export trends.

The Brown paper is an attempt at identifying, within a framework combining input-output and national-income accounting information, the relationship between agricultural and over-all growth and the impact of trade and aid on development. The approach suggested calls for the above data to be consolidated in terms of a number of relatively homogenous regions (e.g., West Africa), which could ultimately be incorporated into a world model. The design of such a model would make it possible, in turn, to investigate the effects of changes in such variables as capital movements and foreign exchange earnings on the whole system, and ultimately to ascertain the prospects for agricultural development in the developing world. In fact, the Brown paper provides an early blueprint for FAO's Indicative World Plan.

Karl Fox goes beyond the already ambitious approach followed by Brown, formulating, in an exploratory outline, a policy model of world economic development with special attention to the agricultural sector. World development is defined in a very broad sense as a function of material and nonmaterial factors. The identification of policies to achieve it requires the application of a comprehensive social science and "the integration of units of observation from psychology, sociology, and economics." Fox provides an analysis of the urbanization process and of its impact on individual and over-all welfare. Building upon the Brown model, he develops the broad outline of a multiregional model in which each region would be further broken down into a set of "functional economic areas." A bridge is thereby constructed between, first, the national and the subnational (regional) effects of agricultural development and, second, between the purely economic and the more general noneconomic effects of development on welfare. The major question with respect to both the Brown and Fox models is the extent to which they can be made operational, in view of the almost insatiable appetite of these models for data, on the one hand, and the scarcity and dubious quality of existing statistics on the other.

The second set of papers is devoted to the relationship between agriculture and other sectors, taking the country as the unit of observation. Fei and Ranis build a rigorous theoretical model of development based on a historical sequence. Agricultural development is described as proceeding through four stages: (1) the agrarian society, (2) the open agrarian society, (3) the dualistic society, and (4) the industrially mature society. The transition is affected by the formation of the export sector and by consequent changes in the relationships between agriculture, services, export production, and the foreign sector. W. Arthur Lewis questions the realism of the assumptions underlying the above model, particularly the presumed relationships between (1) population and productivity; (2) the internal and external terms of trade, and (3) the neglect of the possibility of the capitalists' importing food and labor.

The Thorbecke-Field paper is an attempt at analyzing the relationships within and between the agricultural, industrial, services, and foreign-trade sectors in the development process. The major technological (e.g., input-output), income, and price relationships are identified and a general conceptual framework is formulated to analyze the growth process within the four-sector breakdown. This general model is applied for illustrative purposes to Argentina and in a more limited way to Peru. The behavioral relationships (e.g., the sectoral production and consumption functions) are statistically specified for Argentina, and the model is used to derive certain tentative policy implications with respect to the sectoral allocation of investment, sectoral pricing policies, and other measures. Clark Reynolds, while going along with the over-all conceptual framework and analyses on the national level, expressed reservations about the form of some of the quantitatively derived functions in the Argentine model and brings out some of the limitations inherent in using the model for policy purposes.

Sandee selected as his frame of reference a strictly dual economy, designing a hypothetical programming model. He shows that the introduction of "dual" targets and policy instruments increases realism and modifies conclusions reached with a "one sector" macromodel. The effects of changes in instrument variables on the system are clearly illustrated by means of simple quantitative manipulations. Jorgensen endorses the approach and describes some further uses for this type of programming model, while bringing out one real weakness, the model's failure to include the effects of monetary policy.

The third group of papers incorporates studies of four countries, high-lighting the transformation of traditional agriculture in different parts of the world. Karcz undertakes a comparative study of this transformation in centrally planned economies, namely, the Soviet Union, Eastern Europe, and mainland China. He identifies three separate stages in the transformation process common to all these countries: the redistribution of land, the collection of farm surpluses under a "command farming" system to sustain an ambitious industrialization program, and finally the stage of decompression of command farming characterized by an in-creased flow of resources to agriculture and the substitution of incentives for coercion. Montias suggests that a case can be made for fitting Karcz's broad historical stages into a Fei-Ranis-type two-sector model. By imput-ing to the planners of a Soviet-type economy a welfare function calling for the maximization of some combination of industrial output and non-agricultural employment, a number of analogies between the theoretical Fei-Ranis phases and Karcz's historical stages are brought to light.

The Japanese pattern of modernizing traditional agriculture is the sub-ject of the Ohkawa-Johnston study. There are three basic characteristics of the Japanese model: (1) agricultural output grew within an un-changed small-scale farming system; (2) the increased productivity was associated with the use of improved varieties, fertilizers, and other cur-rent inputs; and (3) agriculture and industry moved forward together in a process of "concurrent" growth. The major theme of the paper is that the Japanese model is transferable to other Asian countries in part, because of the similarities in a number of initial conditions prevailing in Asia today to those that existed in Japan at the beginning of its mod-ernization process—with one major difference: the population explosion that Japan did not have to face. Lee argues strongly that there are serious limitations to the transferability of the Japanese experience to other Asian countries. Using Taiwan as a counter-example, he shows that its agricultural development proceeded successfully along different lines and in a different sequence. Thus, for example, heavy investment in irriga-tion took place at the beginning of the transformation process in contrast to Japan. Furthermore, the organizational changes required to adapt the Japanese model might be incompatible with the "heritage and basic convictions" of East Asian countries.

The Nicholls paper addresses itself to the transformation of agricul-ture in a semiindustrialized country, namely Brazil. The study embraces four parts: (1) a detailed long-range historical review of the Brazilian economy; (2) the rise of São Paulo since the turn of the twentieth cen-tury; (3) the role of the industrial-urban development in transforming

Brazilian agriculture in the 1940's and, finally, (4) a survey of Brazilian agricultural development since 1950. Industrialization, particularly in the state of São Paulo, is given credit for agricultural development. In a concluding parable, São Paulo is compared to a locomotive which in the past had pulled twenty freight cars (the other states). Unfortunately, half the cars came uncoupled (the north and northeast) "and their contents removed and used to fuel the industrial locomotive." Nicholls believes that another industrial locomotive should be found to pull along the depressed north and northeast freight cars. It is clear that in Brazil industrialization was associated with agricultural development. What is still in doubt is the direction of the causality. Schuh takes issue with Nicholls' view that agricultural growth resulted from progress in the industrial sector and suggests an opposite hypothesis: that the dynamic growth of agriculture contributed heavily to the development of the industrial complex of São Paulo through a large transfer of capital. (The case of Brazil illustrates well the importance of the interaction between these two sectors in the growth process.)

The final paper by Van de Wetering consists of a detailed description of the structure of Peruvian agriculture and of the agricultural planning process in that country. The structural and institutional bottlenecks are identified and the conflicts between policy objectives (e.g., efficiency and equity) are made explicit. The whole set of policy measures both direct (e.g., public investment) and indirect (e.g., price policies) is analyzed and the effects of these measures on the major policy goals estimated. Moving back and forth between a positive and a normative approach, Van de Wetering explains the factors that affected the planning decisions and attempts to estimate in terms of goal achievement the opportunity costs of certain policy decisions and public investment allocations. The author illustrates how difficult it is, first, to design a conceptual framework within which the transformation of traditional agriculture can be planned and, second, to implement the forthcoming policy recommendations given the prevailing institutional rigidities. Falcon expresses concern for the strong demand orientation in the agricultural planning process and the emphasis on national and even regional autarky in food production. It is suggested that instead of taking the relatively very low historical share of the national budget allocated to agriculture (about 3 per cent) as given, it would have been interesting to analyze what a 5 or 10 per cent allocation might have meant for agriculture and other macrovariables.

There were a number of areas on which a consensus seemed to emerge among the participants in the conference.

At the sectoral level, the desirability of attacking agricultural development directly from the supply side through the increasing use of improved inputs, appropriate price policies, and other measures, was recognized. At the same time it was generally agreed that a meaningful analysis of agricultural development can only be undertaken within a multisectoral framework bringing out explicitly the price, income, and technological relationships within and between the agricultural, industrial, services, and foreign-trade sectors. The very different conditions existing in developing countries preclude the formulation of a unique and universally applicable agricultural development strategy. The transferability of any given successful experience, such as Japan's, is bound to be relatively limited. Certain elements and policies may be transferable, but ultimately the planning and implementation of agricultural development must be tailored to the situation in each country.

Finally, it was clear to us that a worldwide framework, consisting of regional groupings further subdivided into countries, and even conceivably into "functional economic areas" within countries, was essential to an exploration of the mutual consistency of national agricultural and trade policies. The gap between the microanalysis of production functions in agriculture and the global approach of the Indicative-World-Plan-type is extremely broad. The conference, which was held at Princeton, N.J., on December 1–3, 1967, made a modest contribution to bridging this gap.

Agriculture in the World Economy

Prospects for Agricultural
Trade of Developing Countries

LOUIS M. GOREUX

INTERNATIONAL BANK FOR RECONSTRUCTION
AND DEVELOPMENT

IN THE *first* section of this paper the methodology followed in the FAO projections is summarized, and some of the problems arising from the introduction of prices in the projection model are discussed with particular attention to tree crops. In the *second* section, the trade prospects of the lesser-developed countries (LDC) are reviewed for a number of commodities. A broad distinction is made between the commodities for which the major limiting factor is export outlets and those for which the main limiting factor is the expansion of production in the LDC. In the *third* section the export outlets of the LDC are considered by destination: developed, socialist, and LDC.[1] Emphasis is placed on the limited scope

NOTE: This paper is based mainly on work carried out by the author during the preparation of the agricultural projections for 1970 and 1975 published by FAO in 1962 and 1967. (The author was the main compiler of the FAO projections for 1970 published in 1962 and a major contributor to the projections for 1975 published in 1967.) The results of the UNCTAD projections for 1975 are utilized to provide an over-all trade perspective for the agricultural export prospects of the lesser developed countries. The paper was written while the author was with the IBRD. The views expressed herein are the sole responsibility of the author; they do not commit any of the agencies mentioned above.

The author benefitted greatly from the thoughtful comments made by Bela Balassa on an earlier version of this paper at the time of the U-NBER conference. Many of the points raised by Balassa are incorporated in this version. [Editor's note: Balassa's comments do not appear in this volume since they have been largely taken into account in the present revision of the original paper.]

[1] Following the usage of the UN the nations of the world have been classified in three groups: (1) Developed countries with market economies—North America,

for expanding the net agricultural exports from LDC to developed countries and on the need to investigate more fully the scope for expanding
trade between developing countries in future decades. In the *fourth* section, the prospects for LDC exports are compared for agricultural and
nonagricultural products. This section is concluded by an analysis of
the effect of the sharp decline in agricultural exports' share of the distribution of export earnings between the LDC. The increasing factor of
unequality in the distribution of export earnings among LDC is illustrated by Lorenz curves for 1950, 1955, 1960, and 1965.

Annex I deals with sectoral demand projections in countries with
rapid urbanization. It analyzes the conditions under which projections
based on national averages lead to biased estimates. The method is based
on the covariance analysis of stratified household surveys and is illustrated by data for the USA and for Madagascar. Annex II analyzes the
relation between growth of exports and gross domestic product (GDP)
in a number of developing countries. Within countries the direct elasticity between GDP and export earnings is generally significant, but once
the time trend is eliminated, the relation between the deviations from
the trend is weak. Between countries the correlation between the average
rates of growth of GDP and of exports is low. To reach a better understanding a distinction is drawn between the "accounting" effect of an
increase of export earnings on GDP and the "induced" effect, the first
being felt immediately and the second with a time lag. The hypothesis
of an "induced" lagged effect appears consistent with the data available
in several countries.

METHODOLOGY

The methodology followed in the FAO projections for 1975 [2] does not
differ basically from the one used five years earlier in the projections
for 1970; [3] however, the analysis was carried out more systematically

Western Europe (including Yugoslavia and Turkey), Japan, Australia, New Zealand and South Africa; (2) Countries with centrally planned economies—(European) Eastern Europe and U.S.S.R.; (Asiatic) mainland China, Outer Mongolia,
North Korea, and North Vietnam; (3) Developing countries with market economies. These three groups are often referred to as follows: Group 1, "Developed";
Group 2, "Socialist"; Group 3, "LDC." The nations of the world may also be
classified by income groups: Group 1 together with Group 2 European comprise
the "high-income countries"; Group 2 Asiatic together with Group 3, the "low-
income countries."

[2] United Nations Food and Agriculture Organization [FAO] *Agricultural Commodities Projections* for 1975 and 1985, Rome, 1967.

[3] United Nations FAO, *Agricultural Commodities Projections* for 1970, Rome,
1962.

and in greater depth. Demand, production, and trade were projected to 1975. The demand projections were extended to 1985 to provide a basis for the subregional studies of FAO's Indicative World Plan (IWP).

The main steps may be summarized as follows: formulation of population and income assumptions; demand projections by commodity (and commodity groups), with consistency checks by country regarding nutritional intakes; projections of production by commodities, with consistency checks by country between the growth of total agricultural production and GDP; confrontation of world exportable supplies and world import demand by commodities.

FAO intends to proceed at a later stage to the reconciliation of the commodity approach at the world level with the subregional approach, in which the emphasis is on production problems. This reconciliation is an important step in the formulation of an indicative plan for agricultural development.

The UNCTAD projections,[4] on the other hand, result from the combination of the country and commodity approaches. Detailed country studies based on an econometric model were conducted for about twenty-five developing countries, while estimates were made for the remaining LDC. World commodity studies were undertaken in various degrees of depth for the major LDC exports. For agricultural commodities the UNCTAD projections drew heavily on the FAO study. For petrol, iron ore, nonferrous metals, and textiles original studies were made. Their results are presented as provisional, pending more detailed analysis by the UNCTAD Commodity Division. Adjustments were made between the results obtained in the country and commodity approaches so as to reach consistent projections of exports and imports leading to an estimation of the LDC trade gap.

Population and Income Assumptions

The FAO and UNCTAD assumptions are about the same for population but differ somewhat for GDP. First, the range between the high and the low GDP assumptions is twice as large in the FAO as in the UNCTAD study. Second, the average growth rate for the LDC is higher in the UNCTAD than in the FAO assumptions (see Table 1).

The comparison between the assumptions selected in 1961 in the FAO projections for 1970 are compared with actual developments up to 1965 in Table 2. Population growth appears to have been underesti-

---

[4] United Nations Conference on Trade and Development [UNCTAD] *General Survey of Trade Prospects and Capital Needs for Developing Countries.* To be published.

TABLE 1

Population and GDP; Assumptions for
1965-75 Compared With past Trends
(in percentage per annum compounded)

	Developed Countries With Market Economies	LDC
Population		
1950-62	1.3	2.3
1965-75	1.1	2.6
GDP		
1950-65	4.1	4.5
1965-75		
FAO	3.5 – 4.8	3.6 – 5.5
UNCTAD	4.2 – 4.7	5.2 – 6.1

mated by 0.1 per cent a year in both developed and developing countries. The GDP growth up to 1965 fell within the range assumed. But
for the LDC, actual growth was closer to the low assumption than for
the developed countries. For the period 1958–65 a country-by-country
comparison between GDP assumptions and actual performances shows
that the dispersion between country rates was greater than assumed.
Under the high FAO assumption to 1975 the rate of GDP growth falls
between 4 and 7 per cent a year for 90 per cent of the countries, but
actual dispersion will probably be much wider.

Demand Projections

Per capita demand was projected at constant prices on the basis of the
assumed growth in per capita private consumption. The growth rates of
private consumption and GDP were assumed to be the same as those
under the low assumption. But in the LDC the former rate was taken
as lower than the latter so that the high assumption would reflect the
rising share of investment in GDP associated with an acceleration of the
rate of economic growth. Thus, for all LDC for which the assumption
of growth in per capita private consumption was high, the average growth
rate of total private consumption was only 5.2 per cent a year, compared
with 5.5 per cent for GDP.

TABLE 2

*FAO Growth Assumptions, 1958-70, Compared With
Actual Growth, 1958-65*

(in percentage per annum compounded)

	Developed Countries With Market Economies	LDC
Population		
1958-65	1.3	2.5
1958-70	1.2	2.4
GDP		
1958-65	4.5	4.3
1958-70	3.9 – 5.0	4.1 – 5.2

Four types of demand functions were used: log-log, semilog, log-inverse ($\log y = a - \dfrac{b}{x}$) for commodities likely to reach a saturation level, and log-log-inverse ($\log y = a - \dfrac{b}{x} - c \log x$) for cereals and roots in the LDC to allow for an increase in per capita consumption in a first stage and for a decline in a second stage. For each country per capita demand was projected by commodity and for aggregates, e.g., demand for all food valued at farm prices, total caloric intake, total protein intake. Since the accuracy of the projection was generally higher for aggregates (e.g., consumption of total calories in the U.S.) than for individual commodities (consumption of calories from pork, beef, etc.), consistency was reached mainly by adjusting projections for certain individual commodities downward.

The values of the elasticity coefficients and the type of demand function were originally selected mainly on the basis of a survey-analysis of households, using time-series analysis as a check whenever possible. A number of adjustments were made on the basis of nutritional considerations. For example, in the demand for all caloric intake, the average caloric requirement in a given country was used to check the value of the parameter of the log-inverse function characterizing the level of the horizontal asymptote, i.e., the saturation level in terms of calories. Nutritional factors were taken into account for checking the values of the parameters characterizing the maximum level reached, for example, for all cereals, with the log-log-inverse function.

For major changes in the food consumption pattern the relationships between the principal classes of those nutrients that reflect physiological needs are generally more stable than the relationships between the classes of foods that reflect consumer tastes. One of the original features of these demand projections is the systematic combination of the statistical analysis of the nutrients contained in the food items with the classical econometric analysis by Engel curves. This combined approach proved particularly fruitful in providing an econometric basis for the analysis of nutritional policies.

With commodities such as coffee, cocoa, tea, and sugar, the emphasis was placed on time-series analysis, because fairly reliable data are available for the postwar period. The estimation of the price elasticity permitted assessment of the impact of a price change on demand. For the agricultural raw materials no uniform method was followed. Whenever possible, the analysis was made by end-uses.

During the preparation of the projections for 1975, those made in 1961 for cocoa, coffee, tea, sugar, and oils were compared with actual developments during the last five years. Using the demand function selected in 1961 for the various countries, consumption was calculated on the basis of actual changes in population, GDP, and prices. The relative difference between calculated and actual consumption for the five-year period is shown on Table 3. For the developed countries as a group as well as for the developed and developing countries together, the accuracy of the demand projections was good, especially if account is taken of the amplitude of the price changes (−37 per cent for cocoa, −12 per cent for coffee, and −10 per cent for tea).[5] As might be expected, the accuracy was lower for developing than for developed countries. The small differences for broad groups conceal, however, substantial differences for a number of countries.

It can be argued that projections of demand based on national averages are not very meaningful for developing countries. National averages conceal major differences between the rural population living mainly in a subsistence economy and the urban population living in a market economy. In a country with rapid urbanization projections based on national averages could therefore be misleading. Since data for sectoral projections are not often available, it was considered worth-

[5] Average import unit value for importing countries, and retail price for producers. The price elasticity coefficients used for cocoa were those given in *Agricultural Commodities Projections for 1970;* for coffee and tea, those given in *Agricultural Commodities in the UN Development Decade, 1963,* were used. No price adjustments were made for sugar and oils.

TABLE 3

LDC and Developed Market Economies:
Comparison between Consumption Growth as Projected by FAO
for 1970[a] and Actual Growth over a Five-Year Period.
(in average percentage per annum compounded)

	Coffee	Cocoa	Tea	Sugar	Fats and Oils
Developed Market Economies					
Projected[a] – increase	3.8	4.7	2.1	2.4	1.5
Actual increase	3.7	5.3	1.6	2.1	2.2
Difference	0.1	-.6	0.5	0.3	-.7
LDC					
Projected[a] – increase	5.2	6.9	4.7	4.3	4.4
Actual increase	7.4	3.9	5.3	3.9	3.3
Difference	1.8	3.0	-.6	0.4	1.1
Totals					
Projected[a] – increase	4.1	5.1	2.7	3.4	2.6
Actual increase	4.5	5.0	2.4	2.9	2.6
Difference	-.4	0.1	0.3	0.5	0

Source: United Nations Food and Agriculture Organization, *Agricultural Commodoties Projections 1975-85,* Vol. I, table 8, p. 176; Vol. II, tables I.22-I.25, pp. 51-54, Rome, 1967.

[a]On the basis of selected demand functions adjusted for actual population and income increase and in the case of coffee, cocoa, and tea–for actual price change.

while to analyze the conditions under which the global projections lead to substantial bias. This analysis is presented in annex I.

Production Projections

Trends over the period 1950–63 were taken as the starting point. The historical analysis was carried out for about thirty-five individual commodities, for groups of commodities, and for all agricultural output. For crops, area yields and output were projected separately.

The systematic analysis of past trends was supplemented by a review of national development plans and projection studies carried out by

TABLE 4

All LDC: Growth Rates for the Agricultural and Nonagricultural
Sectors, 1962-75, Projected Under Two Assumptions

(in percentage per annum compounded)

	Low Assumption	High Assumption
Agricultural sector	2.8	3.5
Nonagricultural sector	4.2	6.0
GDP	3.8	5.2

various institutions. The FAO production projections utilize information from various sources; the reasoning underlying the derivation and selection of the figures can best be shown on an ad hoc basis in the detailed commodity notes.

For developed countries a single projection of agricultural production was made. This seems justified in view of the tenuous link between the growth of the value added in the agricultural and in the nonagricultural sectors. This single projection was associated with each of the two GDP assumptions. Therefore, for the temperate zone products as well as for the noncompeting tropical food and beverages, the net import demand of the developed countries is systematically larger in the high-GDP-assumption category than in the low. In short, the projections of production in the developed countries reflect the expectations of the commodity specialists.

For the LDC two projections were made for agricultural production. The low-production projection was associated with the low-GDP assumption and the high projection with the high GDP assumption. A complementarity was assumed between the growth of the agricultural and non-agricultural sectors as shown in Table 4. Because of this assumption,[6] the net import demand for a number of commodities—cereals in particular—was lower under the high-GDP assumption than under the low.

In practice, two production projections were made for each commodity (except for some tree crops). The low projection was "conservative." The high projection was "optimistic," implying the success-

[6] A similar assumption of complementarity has been made between the growth of cereals production and GDP. See the recent USDA study on the LDC cereals gap, "World Food Situation," USDA FAER N.35 Washington, Sept., 1967.

ful implementation of a number of measures reviewed in the commodity notes. The projections by commodities (or commodity groups) were then aggregated for each country to measure the growth for the whole agricultural production and were then compared with the GDP assumptions. When the relative rates of growth implied for the agricultural and nonagricultural sectors were not considered compatible, the production projections were adjusted for the principal commodities.

Undoubtedly a substantial element of subjectivity is attached to the production projections. This margin of subjectivity can only be reduced by a systematic analysis of the factors influencing production. Time series in developing countries are generally not accurate enough for this type of analysis. It is therefore necessary to exploit more systematically the findings of cross-section studies. The field missions undertaken within the framework of the tripartite coffee study, as well as the subregional studies carried out for the IWP have shown that a substantial amount of material could be collected. But the systematic analysis of this material is a delicate and lengthy task.

Trade Projections

The growth coefficients projected for domestic production and utilization by country or country groups for the period 1962–75 were applied to the world commodity balance sheets established for the base period 1961–63. This led to a balancing item for 1975, which has to be interpreted as the first approximation of the potential net import requirement or net exportable supply for any given country and, of the tendency towards surplus or shortage for the world as a whole. This, together with the analysis of past trends in imports and exports, provided the basis for the analysis of the commodity prospects.

Obviously, if we ignore the effect of statistical inaccuracies, world imports and exports will ultimately balance each other for each commodity through a series of adjustments in production and consumption and eventually through changes in the levels of stocks. For the commodities produced mainly for exports, such as cocoa and coffee, such an adjustment could be made on a commodity basis. But, for the basic food items that loom large in the import bill of the LDC, it could not be made without reference to the balances of payment of the importing countries, since these will also ultimately have to be in equilibrium. Since the analysis of the balance of payments falls far outside the scope of the FAO study, an equilibrium between imports and exports was not forced in the commodity balances for 1975.

It should also be noted that the method followed (projection of domestic demand and production) led to a first approximation of the *net* import or *net* exportable supplies for a commodity in a given country and not of the *gross* imports or *gross* exports. For a well-defined primary product such as rice or peanuts, the concept of net import is the most relevant to agricultural planning in a given country, since re-exports—which generally account for the major part of the difference between gross and net—have little to do with agricultural activities. For a group of countries, the concept of net trade may, however, be misleading. An increase in the exportable oil surplus of West Africa may not be offset by an equivalent increase in the potential deficit of India. India may not have the foreign exchange to import from West Africa. Its effective imports may be lower than its potential demand; and it may restrict them to purchases under concessional terms. Therefore, to analyze the trade problems of the LDC the net exports of the net-exporting countries and the net imports of the net-importing countries were summed separately for each type of commodity. The growth rate of the sum of the net imports of the deficit countries provided a proxy for the growth rate of gross imports; the growth of the sum of the net exports of the exporting countries provided a proxy for the growth of gross exports. However, it would have been preferable to project gross and net imports simultaneously to avoid confusion. Statistics are usually published in terms of gross imports and exports, and the net trade deficit of a country is usually projected by subtracting total gross exports from total gross imports rather than by adding up the sum of the projected net imports for each commodity.

The approach followed by UNCTAD was not the same, since a major objective was to arrive at the "capital needs of developing countries." The required capital flow was taken as equal to the deficit of the current account balance of the LDC, assuming no monetary movement such as changes in reserves or IMF drawings. The deficit of current accounts was estimated as the sum of the deficit in three balances: import-export of commodities, invisibles, and investment income.

The UNCTAD study had therefore to come out with one figure for the "import-export gap," which was reached through appropriate adjustments at the country and commodity level for each of the high- and low-GDP assumptions. The trade projections were expressed in terms of gross exports and gross imports. While the FAO study attempted to project the net import demand mainly as the balance between projected domestic demand and production, using the trends in imports mainly as a check, the UNCTAD study relied primarily on the relationships between gross imports by commodity groups and major economic indicators.

The Problem of Prices

The weakest point in the projection model is the absence of prices. As previously noted in the FAO projections published in 1962 and 1967 as well as in the UNCTAD projections, prices were introduced through the back door and often in a qualitative manner. This deficiency can be explained by two considerations. First, a major purpose of the FAO projections published in 1967 was to provide a first approximation of the demand for food as a starting point for the study of production programs to be carried out in the subregional studies of the IWP.[7] Second, projecting price trends a decade ahead or more is a risky exercise. Rather than a clear time trend, the historical price series generally show substantial fluctuations with some kind of periodicity. This suggests that the price-forecasting problem has to be approached from an autoregressive angle, taking into account lagged supply responses, rather than purely in terms of trends. An attempt is made below to consider some of the problems connected with the introduction of prices in the projection model.

The main difficulty is the limitation of our knowledge of the response of production to prices. Although a number of econometric studies deal with the subject, they are generally restricted in the developing countries to the impact of prices on the land area devoted to a particular commodity. Few econometric studies deal with the impact of prices on yields and with the impact of average farm prices on the level of total agricultural output in the LDC. We shall not consider here the general problem raised by a price projection model for agriculture as a whole including direct and cross-price elasticities, since the problem is intractable at the world level with the data presently available. We shall limit ourselves to the consideration of a single-commodity model relating to a typical export crop and assuming all cross-price elasticities equal to zero. Further, we shall initially assume prices to producers and consumers to vary proportionally with world market prices; this assumption together with that of constant elasticity is very convenient for expository purposes.

If there is no lag in demand and no lag in production responses to

[7] The committee on commodity problems, for which the projections were prepared, stressed that price adjustments should be introduced only after completion of the subregional studies.

prices, the change in prices needed to bring a balance between demand and supply projected at constant prices is:

(1)
$$\log \frac{P'}{P} = \frac{1}{b_{2,o} - b_{1,o}} \log \frac{D}{S}$$

where

P = price level in the reference period,
P' = projected price level to clear the market,
D = demand projected at constant prices,
S = production projected at constant prices,
$b_{1,o}$ = short-term price elasticity of demand,
$b_{2,o}$ = short-term price elasticity of supply.

Although response of demand to price is generally somewhat higher in the long term than in the short term, the assumption of no lag in response to price might be considered as an acceptable first approximation for demand. But for production, this assumption is, *a priori,* not acceptable. For most agricultural products, tree crops in particular, the supply response is much higher in the long than in the short term.

In the simplest commodity model, the demand and supply functions can be written with time lags in the form of equations 2 and 3, assuming c_1 and c_2 constant [8] throughout the projection period.

(2)
$$\log D_t = a_1 + \sum_{j=o}^{k} b_{1,j} \log P_{t-j} + c_1 t + U_{1t}$$

(3)
$$\log S_t = a_2 + \sum_{j=o}^{k} b_{2,j} \log P_{t-j} + c_2 t + U_{2t}$$

with
$$E(U_{1,t}U_{1,t-\theta}) = E(U_{2,t}U_{2,t-\theta}) = o \text{ for } \theta > o$$
$$E(U_{1,t}) = E(U_{2,t}) = o$$

Similarly, the reduced form of the price equation can be expressed in relation to a trend factor by:

(4)
$$\log P_t = \alpha + \gamma t + x_t$$

[8] In practice c_1 and c_2 will not be constant. Demand is generally not projected on the basis of constant elasticity and world demand results from the aggregation of country projections. If the projections imply an acceleration of productivity growth, the rate of production growth will generally increase through the projection period either smoothly or by steps.

The level P_t, which will clear the market, will be such that:

$$\gamma = \frac{c_1 - c_2}{b_o}, \text{ where } b_o = b_{2,o} - b_{1,o}$$

(5)
$$x_t = \sum_{j=1}^{j=k} b_j x_{t-j} + \epsilon_t$$

with:
$$b_j = b_{2,j} - b_{1,j}$$
$$\epsilon_t = \frac{U_{1t} - U_{2t}}{b_o}$$

If all the roots of equation 6 are smaller than unity in absolute value, the process x_t is stationary.

(6)
$$\sum_{j=o}^{j=k} b_j x^{k-j} = o$$

The variance of x_t can be decomposed in two elements as shown in equation 7: the variance of the purely random term ϵ_t and the variance due to the lagged responses:

(7)
$$\text{Var}(x_t) = \text{Var}(\epsilon_t) + \sum_{1}^{\infty} a_\tau^2 \, \text{Var}(\epsilon_t)$$

The coefficients a are derived from the b_j coefficients by:

$$a_\tau b_o + a_{t-1} b_1 + \cdots + a_o b_\tau = o \quad \text{with } b_\tau = o \text{ for } \tau > k$$

The autocorrelation coefficients and the spectral density can be derived from the a_t coefficients; the analysis of the spectrum provides a convenient way to assess the periodicity of the autoregressive process x_t generated by the parameters b_j of equation 5.

The system can be simplified, if the short- and long-term responses to price are concentrated at specific points of time. For example, for cocoa during the postwar period, the simplest distributed lag model providing a satisfactory statistical fit can be constructed by introducing, together with a current response to prices, an eleven-year lag reflecting the impact of prices on the size of plantings. Equation 5 characterizing the autoregressive process can then be written:

(5')
$$x_t = -\frac{b_o}{b_{11}} x_{t-11} + \epsilon_t$$

with
$$E(\epsilon_t \epsilon_{t-\theta}) = o$$

The model will be stable only if the elasticity in the current year b_o is higher than the lagged elasticity b_{11}. The crucial parameter is therefore:

$$\beta = -\frac{b_o}{b_{11}}$$

Equation 7 can be written:

(7') $\mathrm{Var}(x_t) = \dfrac{1}{1 - \beta^2} \mathrm{Var}(\epsilon_t)$

If β is equal to 0.3, only 10 per cent of the variance of x_t is explained by the lagged responses to price; the system is strongly convergent. For all forecasting purposes the lagged response can be ignored and x_t approximated by ϵ_t; the projected price change can then be computed from equation 1. The price trend can be expressed in the form of equation 4. For example, if production at constant prices were to rise by 3 per cent a year and demand by 2 per cent, the price would decline by 2.5 per cent a year for $b_o = b_{2,o} - b_{1,o} = 0.4$.

If β is equal to 0.7, half of the variance of x_t is explained by the backward linkage. Prices a decade ahead have to be projected by recurrence.

If β is equal to 0.9, 80 per cent of the variance of x_t is explained by the linkage. The pronounced cyclical influence appears from the spectral density (0.05, 0.1, and 19 respectively for zero, $\dfrac{\pi}{2}$ and π). Ignoring the backward linkage would therefore have generally led to considerable forecasting errors.

If β is higher than unity, the system is explosive. In practice, the system does not explode since prices cannot become negative. It is therefore necessary to introduce into the model a number of constraints reflecting, in particular, the reactions of the market when prices fall below a given level.

When prices are above the long-term equilibrium level, the short-term production response to price is very low; in the case of cocoa, it did not appear statistically significant. But once the producer's price falls below the marginal variable cost, the short-term production response rises very sharply; in the case of cocoa it seems that the low prices prevailing about 1965 reduced supply significantly. Without government intervention the floor price in a downswing would largely depend on the level of the variable production cost and its distribution among producers. Since the variable production cost is low for tree crops, governments often intervene before this limit is reached, by cutting subsidies on fertilizers and pesticides and by withdrawing part of the production from the market through various measures. The high short-term supply response when prices fall below a given level, together with the accumulation of stocks, act to dampen the price trough although they extend its duration.

In the price upswing little can be done to increase supply in the short run once the reserve stocks have been exhausted, although the price decline in the subsequent decade can be reduced by raising export taxes. In the short term the price increase can be reduced only if the consumer's response to a price increase becomes stronger once a given price level has been exceeded. The reaction of U.S. consumers to the peak coffee price of 1954 gives some support to this hypothesis. But on the whole the reaction of the market against a price boom is weak in the short term. This asymmetry in the short-term response of the market is reflected in the shape of the price cycle, with its sharp peaks and dampened but prolonged troughs. Since 1892, the period of the coffee cycle has varied between fifteen and twenty-five years with an average of twenty years, and the length of the upswing has been only about a third that of the downswing.

In view of the variability in the length of the trough, direct analysis of the past price series is of limited forecasting value. What happened in 1900 has obviously little relevance to what will occur in 1975. For forecasting purposes we have to start from the structural equations 2 and 3, with elasticity coefficients that are for all practical purposes estimated from the postwar period. If the ratio between the variance of x_t and ϵ_t computed for the postwar period is comparable to the theoretical ratio given by equation 7 (assuming no error in the specification of the model and in the estimation of the parameters), the model, despite its imperfections, will be useful in explaining the nature of price variations.

In the case of cocoa the impact of prices on the consumption of grindings and on the demand for stocks can be estimated from postwar data with reasonable accuracy. For consumption the accuracy is improved by the introduction of lags, which suggests that all of the price impact is not felt during the current year. For stocks the accuracy is improved by introducing future prices. Changes in future prices are expressed as a function of the expected changes in supply and demand, and stocks are expressed as a hyperbolic function of the difference between future and spot prices. Although the quantity produced can generally be taken as unaffected by the current price, the system is not recursive because of the interdependence between the demand for grindings and the demand for stocks. This problem can be dealt with by two-stage least squares.

A serious problem of estimation arises with the production function. The increase in cocoa output depends on the combination of two factors:

(1) the size of the plantings by age groups, which is correlated with producers' price lagged seven to thirteen years; (2) the yield per tree by age groups, which is correlated with time because of the introduction of improved varieties and the improvement of cultural practices with wider use of pesticides and fertilizers. Because of the lack of data on plantings, lagged prices have to be used as a proxy for plantings. But in view of the length of the cycle, the price lagged is correlated with time during the postwar period. It is therefore not possible to disentangle precisely the relative weights of the lagged price response and of the technological progress in the production growth recorded during this period. Unfortunately, the level of the price projected for 1975 is very sensitive to the relative weights given to these two factors. Placing too much weight on technological improvements would lead to a declining price trend in the 1970's. Placing too much weight on the response of production to lagged prices would give a very sharp uptrend in the same period. One way to resolve this dilemma is to estimate the impact of technological progress from other sources, in particular from agronomic data on the likely impact of fertilizers, pesticides, and improved varieties. From this estimate, the price response can be measured by conditional regressions.

Although strong reservations are necessary concerning the accuracy of the production function, the results of various experiments suggest that the module of some of the roots of equation 6 may be as high as unity. It is therefore essential to introduce into the system stabilization constraints, such as a short-term production response when the world market price falls below a given level (22 cents a pound is a likely figure) and government interventions. To provide valuable long-term price forecasts, the econometric model has therefore to reach a fairly high level of sophistication. From an operational point of view, the problem is to know whether a sophisticated model will provide more valuable answers than a less formalized approach leaving more room for informed judgment. This obviously depends on the nature of the questions that have to be answered by the model.

If the primary objective is to provide guidelines for the production policy or even to reach a reasonable forecast of LDC export earnings, it is doubtful whether the construction of a series of commodity models would, in the short term, substantially improve the quality of the final forecast. If the primary objective is to assess the relative merits of alternative schemes for stabilizing the market and increasing LDC earnings, the model approach is a worthwhile investment. It compels specification of assumptions and provides a way to assess the feedbacks.

In the FAO projections for 1970 the demand curve was projected at three alternative price levels, 18, 24, and 30 cents per pound.[9] The lowest price of 18 cents was taken as the level below which production would react in the short term, although it was not easy at the time to say whether the trough would be over by 1970. The price range selected in 1961 was not unreasonable; six years later a price range of 21 to 29 cents was taken as the basis for the negotiation of a cocoa agreement that should have covered the year 1970. In the projections for 1975 prepared in 1967 it was indicated that the trough would be over by 1975 and that prices around 1975 would be higher than in 1963–65.

In the price stabilization study initiated by the IMF and the World Bank the author felt much more strongly the need for the model approach. The emphasis was not on forecasting, but rather on assessing the genuine stability of the market without intervention, as well as the relative merits of various types of interventions. Since buffer stock was an important issue, attention was given to stochastic processes, with the impact of various policies simulated on a series of samples generated from the post-war data by the Monte Carlo method.

EXPORT PROSPECTS FOR THE MAIN AGRICULTURAL COMMODITIES

To assess the export prospects of developing countries for agricultural commodities it is convenient to draw a distinction between two main groups: (1) the traditional LDC export commodities, for which the major problem is outlet; and (2) cereals, livestock, and wood products, where the major problem for the developing countries is to increase their production. In 1961–63 the LDC had a net export surplus of 8.5 billion dollars for the first group of products but a net deficit of one billion dollars for the second.

Of the first group (coffee, cocoa, tea, bananas, tobacco, oils, sugar, rubber, and fibers), the major portion of world exports is accounted for by developing countries, half of whose production is exported, with the bulk of these exports going to high-income countries. The growth prospects for developing countries' exports are dominated by the rate of expansion of the import demand in the high-income countries. For developing countries as a whole, a marginal increase in the quantities of most tropical food and beverages exported leads, all things being equal, to a reduction of export earnings. This reflects the combination of the dominant position of these countries in the world export of these commodities with the low price elasticity of world import demand for them.

[9] *Agricultural Commodities Projections for 1970.*

More precisely, these commodities' share of world exports usually exceeds the absolute value of the price elasticity of the world import demand for them.

Of the second group of commodities (cereals, livestock, and forest products), developing countries are marginal suppliers in world markets; if rice is excluded, hardly 5 per cent of world exports originate in developing countries. These exports are marginal in relation to the production of the developing countries and to the consumption of the high-income countries. For this group of commodities world trade has expanded rapidly during the last decade, increasing twice as fast as for the previous group.

Unfortunately, production in the LDC increased more slowly for the second than for the first group of commodities, and only a few developing countries were able to take advantage of the rapidly expanding markets. The share of the LDC in the quantum of world agricultural exports declined steadily since 1950. Moreover, between 1959–60 and 1965–66 average unit value of agricultural exports [10] improved by 8 per cent for the developed countries but did not show any increase for the LDC. In part this reflects the superiority of the developed over the developing countries in regard to adaptability of the production pattern to a rapidly changing world demand. In the 1960's, developed countries succeeded in controlling the volume of their agricultural production better than the developing countries; but many of the latter have not yet succeeded in reallocating their agricultural resources to take full advantage of the rapidly expanding domestic or foreign markets.

First Commodity Group

The level of the import demand in the high-income countries is the most important limiting factor to the expansion of LDC exports. The projection of the net import demand of the high-income countries therefore provides the starting point for assessing the potential export growth of the LDC.

TROPICAL NONCOMPETING COMMODITIES (COFFEE, COCOA, TEA, BANANAS)

The import demand of the developed countries, or more specifically their quantity-price demand schedule, can be projected fairly accurately. If we assume a 10 per cent yearly demand growth in Eastern Europe,

[10] General Agreement on Trade and Tariffs [GATT], *International Trade 1966*, table 14, p. 45, Geneva 1967. (Study excludes Israel from LDC).

and if we use the high GDP assumption for the developed countries, the total import demand of high-income developed countries for coffee, cocoa, bananas, and tea, at constant prices, may not increase by much more than 2.5 per cent a year during the next decade. The remaining tariffs and special taxes in developed countries should be eliminated, but the impact of such measures will be small. The major problem is the price level.

The price elasticity of the import demand in the high-income countries is low. The long-term elasticity is somewhat higher than the short-term elasticity but nevertheless, measured at the import level, remains substantially lower than unity. Export earnings of LDC may therefore be raised by restricting supply; the coffee agreement is a case in point.

If, instead of restricting exports, Meade's proposal [11] had been applied, coffee prices might have fallen to half of their present level. To keep foreign exchange receipts of the coffee exporting countries at their present level, an income transfer of the order of one billion dollars a year would have been required. In the prevailing international context it is doubtful that the coffee-producing countries would have received one billion dollars in the form of untied grants in addition to the aid they receive today. In terms of foreign exchange the coffee countries have fared better so far with a policy of restricting supplies.

If, however, exports have been on the whole successfully controlled, the same does not apply to production. Many coffee-producing countries have accumulated useless stocks. The cost in terms of social opportunity of producing these surplus stocks was not negligible. For example, in Guatemala the cost of the imported fertilizer and pesticide applied on coffee can be valued at 3 million dollars *c.i.f.* Without pesticides and fertilizers coffee production would still have exceeded requirements. If output were restricted by acreage quota, the foreign-exchange loss in terms of fertilizers and pesticides would be higher.

The major problem arising from any price-raising scheme is its impact on production. The coffee surplus in the 1960's is largely due to the massive plantings of the early 1950's when prices reached peak levels. The free-market equilibrium in the 1960's would have led to very low prices, since in the short term a substantial curtailment of coffee production would have required a fall in prices below the variable production cost. A very low price in the 1960's could have generated a sharp price upswing in the second part of the 1970's.

[11] J. E. Meade, United Nations Conference on Trade and Development (UNCTAD), Geneva 1964, Proceedings, Vol. 3, Commodity Trade, The International Commodity Agreement, pp. 451–457.

As a means of raising LDC export earnings, an import levy scheme has considerably more appeal than a scheme based only on quantitative export restrictions. To break the cycle, the level of the import levy should be variable. However, in view of the lagged production response the introduction of an import levy scheme during the downward price swing would not permit dispensing with quotas during the initial years.

Let us assume that the price paid by the high-income countries is 30, and that, in a given year, 25 goes directly to the exporting countries and 5 to an international diversification fund. The proceeds collected from the import levy could then be redistributed to the coffee exporters in the form of grants to compensate the producing countries ready to accept a reduction in their export quota. A country with a high opportunity cost would, *a priori,* be more attracted by a grant of a given amount to reduce its export quota one ton, than a country with a very low opportunity cost.

To facilitate rational choice, a study of the relative opportunity costs would be needed. In addition to an analysis of the production costs of the specific commodities subject to an export quota (as carried out in the tripartite coffee study), a general economic survey of the country to assess opportunity costs would be required. For a country to produce so much of commodity A or commodity B in compliance with the directives of an international body of technocrats could be dangerous. But in practice the technocrats would only be asked to produce a study, of which the governments of the countries concerned could avail themselves in deciding whether to accept a quota reduction in exchange for a given grant. One could expect that a country with a high opportunity cost would be ready to give up part of its quota at a given price. The larger the resources of the international diversification fund, the greater would be the flexibility for revision of the quota.

Such grants might be given entirely or partly for specific projects. Within agriculture, the areas that would most often require particular investigation for such projects are livestock, feedstuffs, forestry industries, agricultural processing industries, and production of agricultural prerequisites. But there is no reason for excluding the manufacturing industry proper, if prospects are better there.

TROPICAL COMPETING COMMODITIES (SUGAR, OILS, AND OILCAKES)

Sugar and oils accounted in 1961–63 for 30 per cent of the LDC net export earnings derived from the commodities covered in the FAO study. From 1952–54 to 1961–63, net exports of sugar, oils, and oilcakes from the LDC to the rest of the world increased by about one billion dollars. But the projections give a radically different picture; they suggest a reduction in the absolute level of the net import demand of the high-income countries.

Sugar. The reduction projected for the net importation of sugar into the high-income countries reflects the slackening of the growth of consumption in those countries as per capita intake gets nearer to the saturation level.

As shown in Table 5, the slowdown projected for the developed countries is the continuation of a trend that has already been very noticeable and would have been even more noticeable if figures had been expressed on a per capita basis. In Eastern Europe and the U.S.S.R. the slowdown projected is much more dramatic. The projected consumption level—halfway between the U.S. and the U.K. level—may be too low; however, for physiological reasons, the tremendous rate of consumption growth recorded during the last fifteen years is bound to decline sharply.

In brief, it does not seem that in high-income countries, sugar consumption could increase by much more than 2 per cent a year from 1965 to 1975. On the other hand, sugar production increased steadily by 5 per cent a year in those countries over the last fifteen years, and, from a technical point of view, production could still increase very substantially, mainly because of higher sugar yields. The net import require-

TABLE 5

Past and Projected Trends in the Consumption and Production of Sugar by Volume in High-Income Countries, 1951-75

(in percentage per annum compounded)

	1951-58	1958-65	1965-75
Consumption			
Developed countries	3.5	2.2	1.8
Eastern Europe, USSR	7.6	7.8	2.1
Total	4.4	3.8	1.9
Production			
Developed countries	4.2	4.6	2.8
Eastern Europe, USSR	6.5	5.9	2.7
Total	5.1	5.2	2.8

ments of high-income countries are therefore likely to decline unless there is a basic change in their production policy.

In the LDC gross exportable supplies could increase much more rapidly than gross import requirements. If imports of mainland China do not rise tremendously, a strong surplus situation is bound to prevail on the world sugar market. The burden of the adjustment would fall on the exporting countries, which would have to forego expansion and possibly cut their production, although they are as a rule low-cost producers. Prices do not play a useful role in the allocation of world resources devoted to sugar, because there are so many different prices for sugar. Most importing countries protect their domestic industries with guaranteed prices. Most exporting countries receive preferential prices in domestic or foreign markets for at least part of their production. Consequently, on the residual "free market," prices fluctuate very widely. From an average of 8.3 cents in 1963, prices on the free market fell to an average of 2 cents in 1965. Among agricultural products sugar probably offers the most striking example of resource misallocation at the world level.

Oils. Owing to the variety of products and end uses, projections for oils are very complex and uncertain. Nevertheless, contrary to past performance, the gross exports of high-income countries may increase as rapidly, if not more rapidly, than their gross imports. The reasons for this are as follows: On the demand side—for food uses—the increase in per capita consumption of all oils and fats will slow down, as in the case of sugar, with consumption even in Southern Europe approaching saturation by 1975—for nonfood uses—the competition from synthetics will increase. On the supply side, production of animal fats and soybean oil is bound to increase rapidly following the expansion projected for livestock production. For animal fats the link is obvious; for soybean oil it is explained by the fact that oil is a by-product of soybean cake in great demand for livestock feeding.

Among developed countries most of the increase projected for gross exports is accounted for by U.S. exports of soybean oil, while half of the increase in the gross imports of developed countries would be taken by Japan. For all LDC, the increase in gross exportable supplies (mainly from Africa, the Philippines, and Argentina) could be of the same order of magnitude as the increase in gross import requirements. However, in the past most of LDC exports went to the developed countries and very little to other developing countries. The projected deficit (half of it in India and Pakistan) may be filled partly by concessional soybean oil sales, and the market for LDC with exportable supplies may be very small. In the absence of arrangements to promote trade between LDC the prospects for the developing countries with exportable supplies are not favorable unless the net import demand of the centrally planned countries increases greatly. For oilcakes however the prospects remain favorable.

AGRICULTURAL RAW MATERIALS (COTTON, JUTE, SIZAL, ABACA, RUBBER)

Between 1960 and 1965, the average unit value of LDC exports declined by about 20 per cent for this group of commodities, more than offsetting the increase in the volume of their exports. Prices have declined since 1965 and are expected to decline still further, with a resultant reduction in LDC export earnings. However, the slow expansion or decline projected for LDC exports of raw jute and cotton reflects partly the projected increase in their exports of textile goods. Taking rubber and raw fibers together with cotton and jute goods, export earnings of the LDC might increase slightly. The gain would be even more substantial if account were taken of the reduction of LDC import of textile goods from developed countries.

Among the remedies proposed to improve the competitive position of the natural products versus synthetics are: reduction of short-term fluctuations, research for new uses, and reduction of production costs. A number of experts argue that the production costs of natural rubber with high-yielding varieties could remain competitive with synthetic rubber. If it were possible to insure natural rubber producers of a minimum price five to ten years ahead, even at a substantially lower level of production than the present one, an insurance scheme to promote investment of high-yielding plantings might be considered. This might lead to a better allocation of resources between developed and developing countries in terms of alternative opportunity costs. However, the uncertainty about technological advance in synthetic rubber for the international community may be too great for setting a minimum price level five or ten years ahead.

Second Group of Commodities
(livestock, cereals, wood products and miscellaneous)

Developing countries have a net export surplus only for beef, coarse grains, and round woods. Only a limited number of LDC export these three commodities, and export is directed mainly to the market of the high-income countries. These exports increased rapidly over the last decade and could continue to do so over the next.

Meat. If border trade, which is not accurately recorded, is excluded from consideration, the number of developing countries entering in the world market as significant exporters is small. More than 90 per cent of meat exports from the LDC originate in Argentina, Uruguay, Mexico, and part of East Africa. Of this meat more than 90 per cent is beef.

According to most livestock experts the main bottleneck encountered in increasing output in the developing countries is feed. Emphasis should therefore be placed on higher yield per animal rather than on larger herds. The key problem is how to increase production and improve the sanitary conditions. The possibility of expanding exports, however, depends greatly on the growth in domestic consumption. This growth is illustrated for Mexico, East Africa, and Argentina in Table 6.

In Mexico, beef consumption per capita is only one-fourth of the level prevailing today in Australia and the United States. To keep per capita consumption at its present level beef supplies in Mexico should rise by 3.5 per cent per year. To allow for the increase in per capita demand generated by higher personal income, supplies should rise by 5.3 per cent per year. Such a rate appears enormous as compared with past performances of countries with a dynamic livestock economy. Thus, in Australia and New Zealand, beef production increased on an average only 3.4 per cent per year during the decade 1951–53 to 1961–63. This rapid increase took place as a result of large investments stimulated by the favorable prospects on the world beef market. During the same decade the production record of 5 per cent growth per year was held by the Common Market countries. But this was achieved only by using up a large part of the existing calf reserves.

In East Africa the situation is somewhat more favorable than in Mexico because population is expected to increase by only 2.2 per cent instead of 3.5 per cent a year. Nevertheless, total domestic demand is projected to increase by almost 4 per cent per year at constant prices. A substantial increase in exportable supplies could be achieved only if the control of animal diseases were coupled with a policy of high beef prices to reduce the increase projected for the domestic demand as well as stimulate local production. At present more than 80 per cent of East African meat exports consist of canned meat, because their chilled meat or live animals are generally unable to meet the strict health requirements of most of the importing countries. Since most meat-exporting countries use only the low cuts for canning, price for canned meat will remain low

TABLE 6

Beef and Veal: Trade and Domestic Consumption in Selected Countries

| | 1961-63 | | | 1962-75 Projected Annual Growth in Domestic Demand (per cent) | | |
	Exports (thousands of metric tons)	Trade/ Production Ratio (as percentage)	Annual Per Capita Consumption (kilograms)	Population Effect	Income Effect	Total
LDC						
Argentina	606	25	85	1.6	0	1.6
Uruguay	72	24	85	1.2	0	1.2
Mexico	75	14	12	3.5	1.8	5.3
East Africa	74	10	9	2.2	1.9	4.1
Developed countries						
United States	-715	10	44	1.4	1.0	2.4
Australia	358	42	45	1.7	0	1.7
All	-622	4	24	1.1	1.5	2.6

Source: See Table 3.

on the world market. As long as East African exports remain restricted to canned meat, the export sector will not provide the necessary price incentive to build up a dynamic livestock industry. But if animal diseases could be controlled through large-scale eradication programs, the export sector could be oriented toward the chilled beef market and could offer to local producers the high prices needed to expand production rapidly. A large fraction of the high cuts of beef could thus be exported; and with the price differential, domestic consumption would be reoriented to low cuts of beef and other types of meat.

In Argentina and Uruguay per capita beef consumption today, is almost twice as high as in Australia or the United States. There does not appear to be any need for increasing this exceptionally high level of consumption. Population growth is relatively low: 1.6 per cent per year in Argentina and only 1.2 per cent in Uruguay. To maintain per capita domestic consumption and total exports in Argentina and Uruguay at the 1961–63 level would therefore require a yearly increase of only 1.3 per cent in domestic production between 1962 and 1975. Therefore, if a policy of high beef prices aiming at restricting consumption and stimulating production were politically acceptable in Argentina and Uruguay, these countries could increase considerably the volume of their beef exportable supplies. On the demand side, part of the reduction in domestic beef consumption could be compensated by an increase in the consumption of poultry and of pork, both of which are low at present. On the supply side, with the existing natural resources and high beef prices to producers, production might perhaps rise at rates comparable to those recorded in Australia. But the complete elimination of the foot and mouth disease is essential, if Argentine beef is to enter the U.S. market.

Only a few developing countries are expected to enter the world market as significant exporters over the next decade. In most cases, output will lag behind demand; but only in those countries with adequate foreign exchange reserves—the oil countries in particular—will this potential meat deficit materialize into an effective import demand.

Cereals. The LDC have been rapidly increasing their exports of coarse grains (maize and sorghum) to high-income countries. Argentina has kept the lead, but the emergence of Thailand as an important exporter to Japan and the recent increase in the exports from Mexico and Brazil are interesting features. Further expansion of LDC exports in the next decade and entrance of additional countries, in particular Kenya, Uganda, Tanzania, and Indonesia into the world market is quite possible.

The prospects are less favorable for wheat, since, with the important exception of Japan, the import demand of most high-income countries may shrink during the next decade. Argentina, which is a low-cost producer, is the only significant exporter among the LDC today. Some other countries could increase their production sufficiently to export—Mexico is a case in point—but at a cost generally higher than for the traditional high-income exporters.

The development that recently attracted world attention was not the increase in exports of maize and sorghum from a few developing countries but the increase in wheat imports to the LDC. This rapid rise in imports, at a time when the U.S. surplus stocks disappeared, caused concern. Some economists predicted an over-all world cereal shortage in the near future. The projections, however, do not support this alarming view.

Under the assumptions made in the FAO projections, the increase in the net exportable supplies from the high-income countries could cover the increasing deficit of the LDC, if net imports into China were to remain at about their present level. But this projected increase is far from representing the maximum cereals surplus that could technically be mobilized in the high-income countries. If all available cereal land in North America and Australia were put into cultivation, the exportable supplies of the high-income countries could increase by a further 50 million tons by 1975. Therefore, unless these figures are completely off the mark, by 1975 the high-income countries would still have the physical capacity to fill the cereals gap [12] of the developing countries, even with the most pessimistic assumptions as to the growth of cereal production in those countries during the next decade.

The same conclusion was reached in a recent study [13] of the USDA. The study was based on four assumptions regarding the growth of cereal production in the LDC. The most pessimistic extrapolation over the 1965–80 period of the trend recorded between 1954 and 1966 gave an increase of 20 million tons in LDC net imports. But it was estimated that, if acreage restrictions were discontinued in the United States, the U.S. exportable supplies would rise by 70 million tons between 1965 and 1980. The combination of the two would result in a world surplus of 30 million tons.

It seems, therefore, that for the developed countries with a reserve potential, in particular the United States, the problem in the next decade

[12] Defined as the economic demand and *not* the difference between nutritionally desirable consumption levels and domestic availabilities.

[13] "World Food Situation."

will remain management of supplies. A sufficient reserve stock should be maintained to avoid temporary shortages, since it is not possible to project the net grain deficit of the developing countries with the accuracy required for operational purposes.

The margin of error involved in projecting the net cereals deficit of the LDC is illustrated by the range of projections corresponding to the varying assumptions in the FAO and in the USDA studies. In the FAO study the net deficit of 10 million tons in 1961–63 could either disappear or increase to 25 million tons by 1975, depending on whether the assumption is optimistic or pessimistic. In the USDA study the projected net deficit of the LDC ranges from 6 to 39 million tons in 1980. This wide margin reflects the marginal character of the net deficit (4 per cent of total LDC production in 1961–63), the uncertainty regarding the rate of adoption of improved techniques, and the impact of government policies (price and food aid policies in particular) on production in the LDC.

In regard to the marginal character of the deficit, a difference of 10 million tons in the projection for 1975 under the high FAO assumption would correspond to the difference between an average production growth of 2.7 and 2.5 per cent a year in the LDC, for a given level of demand. Anyone familiar with agricultural statistics in the LDC will recognize that a difference of 0.2 per cent is within the margin of error of the estimation of past trends; it is well within the margin of error of any projection.

Wood-products and miscellaneous. The prospects for exports from LDC to high-income countries are good for round wood and wood panels and for oilcakes, fishmeal, and a variety of miscellaneous items such as off-season fruits and vegetables and various tropical fruits still largely unknown on Western markets. The small miscellaneous items are often those with the most dynamic growth, but none is important enough at present to merit a review of its prospects in a paper of this scope.

MAJOR EXPORT MARKETS FOR THE LDC

In the following section we will analyze the prospects for agricultural exports of LDC by main areas of destination.

Developed Countries with Market Economies

Taking all agricultural products together, developed countries import from the rest of the world more than they export. Their net imports—

TABLE 7

Trends in the Volume[a] of Gross Agricultural Imports and Exports
1952-54 to 1961-63 for Developed and Developing Countries

(average percentage per annum compounded)

	Developed Countries with Market Economies			LDC		
	Gross Imports	Gross Exports	Net Imports	Gross Imports	Gross Exports	Net Exports
All Agric.						
Commodities	3.3	5.5	1.1	5.3	3.4	2.4
Food & feed	4.5	6.1	-.1	5.8	3.9	-.1
Tropical						
beverages	3.5	1.4	3.5	5.2	3.7	3.6
Agric. raw						
material	1.8	4.0	-.4	3.4	2.9	2.8

Source: *Agricultural Commodities Projections 1975 Vol. II,* table
III.9, p. 306, Rome, 1967.
[a]Weighted at 1961-63 prices.

excess of gross imports over gross exports—increased very slowly in the
postwar period. This is illustrated in Table 7 showing the trends in the
volume of trade between 1952–54 and 1961–63. During that period,
gross agricultural exports from developed countries increased rapidly
(5.5 per cent a year). Gross imports into these countries, despite the
intensification of intraeuropean trade, progressed more slowly (3.3 per
cent a year) reflecting an apparent elasticity of 0.8 in relation to GDP.
Net imports into developed countries from the rest of the world increased,
in volume terms, by only 1 per cent a year for all agricultural products,
by 3.5 per cent for coffee, cocoa, and tea under the stimulation of declining prices, and by 1 per cent for sugar, oils, and oilseeds; for agricultural
raw materials, net imports declined slightly.

An accurate picture of the imports into developed countries from developing countries can be derived from the UN trade data systematically
recorded in recent years by origin and destination. The trends over the
period 1960–65 are illustrated in Table 8 for the main commodity
groups.

TABLE 8

Trends in Gross Imports from LDC to the Rest of the World, 1960-65

(average percentage per annum compounded[a])

	World Outside LDC-Current Value				Developed Countries With Market Economies-Volume			
	All Countries	Developed Countries	E. Eur./ U.S.S.R.	Asian Communist Countries	All Countries	North America	Western Europe	Japan
All commodities	7.0	6.4	13.7	12.7	6.4	3.9	6.5	13.8
Agricultural commodities	3.6	2.3	12.0	14.5	2.3	0.1	2.4	9.0
Temperate food	⎱ 6.0	6.6	⎱ 26.0	⎱ 37.0	3.7	4.2	2.2	16.8
Competing food	⎰	0.6	⎰	⎰	-0.5	-0.3	1.0	3.4
Noncompeting food and beverages	3.4	2.8	13.7	38.0	2.8	0.4	4.0	32.0
Raw material	0.4	-0.5	4.1	4.2	2.7	1.7	1.7	7.1
Nonagricultural commodities	10.5	10.3	27.0	-0.2	10.1	7.0	10.9	18.0
Mineral other than fuel	5.6	5.4	21.0	0	2.4	0.3	1.3	10.4
Fuels	10.7	10.7	—	—	11.5	5.7	13.7	23.0
Manufactured gas	19.4	19.2	30.0	-0.2	19.2	19.5	18.8	46.0

Source: Data derived from internal IBRD paper prepared by B. Balassa.
[a]Computed From ratio between terminal years.

The rapid economic expansion of the developed countries during the first half of the 1960's led to a remarkable expansion of their imports from LDC. But the high rate of growth of gross exports from LDC to the developed countries (6.4 per cent a year) between 1960 and 1965 resulted from the combination of two different developments: a very fast increase in the volume of nonagricultural exports (10 per cent a year) and a slow expansion in the volume of agricultural exports (2.3 per cent a year). The impact of GDP growth in developed countries on their import demand from LDC can be expressed in two components: the population effect (1.2 per cent a year) and the income effect measured by the elasticity of imports per capita relative to GDP per capita. The apparent income elasticity thus calculated on a per capita basis amounts to barely one third for agricultural commodities, compared with two and a half for nonagricultural commodities.

The growth of agricultural imports into developed countries during the first half of the 1960's is compared in Table 9 with the FAO growth projections for 1970. In this study, the projections were confined to exports of tropical food and beverages and agricultural raw materials from the LDC to the developed countries. Exports of temperate-zone food (cereals and livestocks) were not included because *en bloc* the LDC are a net importer for this group of products. The average unit value of LDC agricultural exports did not show much change between 1960 and 1965, and the actual GDP growth of the developed countries in this period was close to that of the high-income assumption (5 per cent a year). Therefore, in Table 9 the annual percentage growth in the volume of imports from 1960 to 1965 was compared to the average percentage growth projected under the high-income assumption without any adjustment.

The trends recorded between 1960 and 1965 are well in line with those projected under the high assumption. The most important discrepancies appearing in Table 9 are for sugar and oils in the commodities group, and North America in the importing areas group. However, the declines recorded between 1960 and 1965 under these two headings reflect the 22 per cent reduction in the volume of U.S. sugar imports from LDC associated with the Cuban crisis. This reduction, due to particular circumstances, does not provide a basis for extrapolation over a twelve-year period. If the volume of U.S. sugar imports had remained constant between 1960 and 1965, most of the discrepancy would have been removed (see note Table 9).

Since 1965, the rate of economic expansion of the developed countries has been slackening and this has been reflected in a reduction in the

TABLE 9

Growth of Volume Imports to Developed Countries from LDC of Tropical Food and Beverages and Agricultural Raw Materials; Comparison of FAO Projections for 1970 and Actual, 1960-65

	FAO Projections 1958-70 (high GDP assumption)		Actual 1960-65
	Index 1970 (1957-58 = 100)	Per Cent Per Year Compounded	Per Cent Per Year Compounded
By commodity group			
Sugar, oils, oilseeds	102	0.2	-1.0[a]
Coffee, cocoa, tea	136	2.6	2.5
Agricultural raw materials	138	2.7	2.7
Total (including citrus)	127	2.0	1.75[a]
By importing area			
North America	116	1.2	-.2[a]
Western Europe	123	1.75	2.1
Japan	175	4.8	6.4
Total (including Oceania)	127	2.0	1.75[a]

Source: Index 1970 — *FAO Commodity Projections for 1970,* table 17 p. 1—35, Rome, March 1962; percentages for 1958-70 derived from index projections; percentages for 1960—65 from unpublished IBRD study by B. Balassa.

[a]If the volume of U.S. sugar imports from LDC had been the same in 1965 as in 1960, -1.0 for sugar and oils would have been replaced by +.4, 1.75 for the total by 2.1, and -.2 for North America by +.8

growth of their imports from the LDC. In the second half of the 1960's the growth in the developed countries might therefore be closer to the low than to the high assumption in the 1970 projection (low, 3.9 per cent; high, 5 per cent).

The 1970 projections of the import demand in developed countries for the agricultural products of developing countries were considered gloomy at this time. The analysis carried out in 1966—67 for the preparation of the 1975 projections did not give a more favorable picture. This pessimistic view resulted from a combination of four main factors in the developed countries: (1) slackening in the rate of population growth; (2) per capita consumption moving toward saturation for sugar, oils and fats, and tropical beverages; (3) increasing replacement of agricultural raw material by synthetics; and (4) continued tendency for food output to increase faster than demand for food.

In developed countries food consumption—valued at farm prices—is projected to increase by 1.7 to 1.9 per cent a year. Food production increased on the average by 2.5 per cent a year since 1950, the rate of growth showing no sign of slackening towards the end of the period. Food production is therefore likely to move ahead of food consumption in developed countries, and maintaining income parity between farm and nonfarm occupations will remain a major problem. Since the share of purchased inputs in gross food output will continue to increase, the value added by the agricultural sector is not expected to show much progress. Consequently, much of the improvement in per capita farm income will have to come from further reductions in the size of the farm labor force.

In this context reducing domestic production (that of sugar beets for example) substantially to allow for larger imports from LDC will be politically difficult. Moreover, with the increasing flexibility in the production pattern, restricting production of one commodity may stimulate production of others with a consequent reduction in imports of the latter.

On the whole, the FAO projections for 1975 give an unfavorable picture.[14] Excluding wheat, dairy products, and forestry products, for which LDC are, and will remain, major net importers, the net import demand in developed countries for agricultural products (coarse grains, feedingstuff, and meat included) of undeveloped countries is not projected to rise by more than 2 per cent a year even under the high-income assumption. This represents a significant slowdown in relation to past trends.

The price of tropical noncompeting food and beverages could be maintained and in some cases improved by appropriate international action, but such action would in all likelihood be more than offset by the decline in the price of agricultural raw materials. On the whole, the margin for maneuver appears rather limited.

The decline in the growth of net agricultural exports from developing to developed countries partly reflects the increasing disparity between these two groups of countries in respect to agricultural land available per

[14] The main agricultural products not included in the FAO trade projections for 1975 are: starchy roots, pulses, vegetables, fruits other than bananas and citrus, and fish.

capita. The following figures quoted by Kristensen [15] in this regard are quite impressive. In 1965 there was, on the average, twelve times the agricultural land per head of the agricultural population in the developed countries that there was in the Far East (excluding mainland China). In the year 2000, the corresponding ratio could be 50 to 1, that is four times that of today. Kristensen notes that a sharp reduction in the size of agricultural holdings will not facilitate the adoption of modern technology, and he stresses the need for a modification of the traditional trade pattern between developed and developing countries.

Socialist Countries

Agricultural exports from the LDC to countries with centrally planned economies increased very rapidly in the first half of the 1960's. Between 1960 and 1965 this flow of trade to Eastern Europe and the U.S.S.R. increased by 12 per cent a year and that to mainland China increased even more rapidly (see Table 8). It is very difficult to make any forecast for mainland China, but there are good reasons to believe that the 12 per cent yearly rate of growth registered by Eastern Europe and the U.S.S.R. in the past will be very substantially reduced during the next decade.

Agricultural imports from LDC to Eastern Europe and the U.S.S.R. comprised two major groups: basic foods and agricultural raw materials, which accounted for $650 million each in 1965, and tropical fruits and beverages, accounting for only $240 million. The very rapid increase in basic food imports during the first half of the 1960's was heavily weighted by the large sugar imports from Cuba. This is a one-time effect that should not be extrapolated. For agricultural raw materials, imports increased only by 4 per cent a year between 1960 and 1965, and future growth is uncertain. In 1965, production of synthetics in the U.S.S.R. was surprisingly low, reaching only half of the U.K. output. The production of synthetics may increase sharply during the next decade. Because of the heavy emphasis placed on petrochemical synthetics such an increase might further reduce import needs for natural products in this sector. The past rate of import growth could be maintained only for noncompeting food and beverages—per capita consumption remaining very low. But in 1965 noncompeting tropical food and beverages accounted for only 15 per cent of agricultural imports to Eastern Europe and the U.S.S.R. from LDC.

[15] Organization for Economic Cooperation and Development [OECD] *The Food Problem of the LDC,* 1967, Chapter 4.

Developing Countries

Since the possibilities of expanding LDC agricultural exports to high-income countries are severely limited, it is of particular importance to investigate the scope for expanding trade between the developing countries themselves. Today, about one-third of LDC food exports (including beverages and tobacco—sections 0, 1 and 4 and division 22) goes to other developing countries. After a period of stagnation during the 1950's, this flow of trade expanded substantially in the 1960's. From 1961 to 1965 LDC food exports to other developing countries increased in percentage terms more rapidly than LDC food exports to the rest of the world.

The expansion of agricultural trade between the LDC raises questions on both the demand and supply sides of the trade picture. First, how fast are LDC import needs likely to rise, and which part of these needs could materialize in an effective demand? Second, could the exportable supplies of the needed commodities increase rapidly enough in a number of developing countries to allow for the expansion of such intratrade in addition to LDC agricultural exports to high income countries?

On the demand side, the needs for agricultural imports are bound to increase more rapidly in the LDC than in the high-income countries. As previously noted, between 1952–54 and 1961–63, gross agricultural imports into the LDC increased on the average by 5.3 per cent a year. During the same period the volume of gross agricultural imports into developed countries increased by only 3.3 per cent a year, and this was due in part to a rapid expansion of intraeuropean trade. During the first half of the 1960's, despite an exceptionally high rate of economic growth, gross agricultural imports into developed countries from developing countries increased by only 2.3 per cent a year.

During the next two decades population will increase twice as fast in the developing than in the high-income countries and per capita consumption of most commodities will remain far from saturated. Demand for food valued at producer prices is projected to increase twice as fast in the LDC as in the high-income countries. Urbanization will be the key factor in the increase in LDC food imports. Between 1962 and 1985, the urban population might increase by 580 million in the developing countries (excluding mainland China) as compared with only 140 million in the developed countries. The urban population of the developing countries, which was smaller than that of the developed countries in 1962, would be 70 per cent larger in 1985.

In view of the differences in natural endowment, it would be uneconomical for each developing country to aim at self-sufficiency. If food aid is not used indiscriminately, these import needs should largely materialize in a commercial demand. Among developed countries with market economies the most rapid increases in food imports in recent years have been recorded in southern Europe and Japan. On the basis of the high FAO income assumption, thirty developing countries will reach or exceed by 1985 the average income level recorded for southern Europe and Japan in 1960. The high FAO income assumption is certainly optimistic, but the dispersion in the rates of growth between countries will be much wider than assumed in the FAO study. Preliminary estimates indicate that in 1966 at least fifteen developing countries with a per capita GNP ranging from $200 to $600 have recorded a rate of growth higher than 5 per cent.

On the supply side, the availability of exportable supplies from developing countries is not as easy to predict. It is sometimes argued that developing countries are in the position of having mainly cocoa and coffee surpluses to offer to other developing countries that have little need for them. The actual situation, however, is quite different, as illustrated in Table 10.

The scope for cereal trade between developing countries may be smaller than suggested by the figures in the table, because a large part of the import requirements would be for food grains and a large part of the exportable supplies in the form of feed grains. But for oils, sugar, and tea the scope is very substantial. There is also scope for expanding meat trade between bordering countries. West Africa, where more cattle could be exported from the savannah zone to feed the rapidly growing urban population of the coastal countries, provides an example.

The greatest scope for expanding trade between developing countries might be in processed and manufactured products. For example the largest potential market for cotton textiles is certainly in the developing countries themselves. Notwithstanding this, a modern textile industry already established in several such countries continues underutilized. The same is true of fertilizers and pulp and paper, for which a demand exists in developing countries. With fast-growing species of trees in semitropical climates, several developing countries have the natural resources to expand production considerably. In many cases production costs could be kept low if the size of the mill were large enough. This is true in Chile, for example. In 1962 that country had one integrated Kraft paper mill (sulphate pulp) producing 60,000 tons a year. Half of this production was sufficient for the needs of the domestic market; the other half was

TABLE 10

Projected Expansion of LDC Gross Imports and Exports^a for Selected Commodities, 1962-75,

Under Two GDP Hypotheses

(millions of metric tons)

	Import Needs			Export Availabilities		
		Increase 1962-75			Increase 1962-75	
	1961-63	Low GDP	High GDP	1961-63	Low GDP	High GDP
Cereals	22.0	28.0	6.0	13.0	13.0	16.0
Oils (fat content)	0.8	1.8	1.5	3.2	1.3	2.3
Sugar (centrifugal)	3.4	0.5	0.3	13.3	2.1	8.2
Tea	0.13	0.06	0.08	0.52	0.26	0.23

Source: See Table 3.

^aGross imports is defined as the difference between total consumption and total production in the developing/ importing countries. Gross exports is defined as the difference between total production and total consumption in the developing/exporting countries.

exported. If the capacity of the mill had to be limited to the domestic market, the capital investment per ton produced would have been almost twice as high. Tripling the capacity of the mill to reach a production of 180,000 tons—at present under consideration—would almost halve the capital investment per ton. Since only eleven developing countries have a GDP equal to or higher than that of Chile, a policy of self-sufficiency for pulp and paper in most developing countries would be the negation of efficiency.

According to OECD estimates,[16] developing countries would require by 1980 $5 billion foreign exchange for fertilizers (in the form of products or raw materials) compared with $870 million in 1964–65. Some developing countries with oil resources are in an ideal condition to take advantage of this rapidly expanding market. The raw material to produce ammonia could be obtained at a very low cost from gas which is often just burned; energy would be cheap and foreign exchange available to import the machinery. Here too, as with pulp and paper, economies of scale are very important. By international standards an efficient ammonia plant should produce at least 200,000 tons a year in terms of nitrogen; this corresponds to half the consumption of Africa and one-third of the consumption of India in 1966. Some of the oil-rich countries of the Arabian peninsula could make a most useful contribution to agricultural development by providing cheap ammonia to other developing countries less favored by nature, receiving from them in return food or manufactured goods (for example, meat from East Africa, irrigation pumps from India, etc.).

In the manufacturing field a number of developing countries—including some that are relatively highly industrialized such as India, Brazil, Argentina, and Mexico—seem to have reached the economical limit of import substitution within their national boundaries. An expansion of trade between developing countries is a way of reducing the disadvantages of national policies of self-sufficiency. The foregoing discussion suggests that agricultural products in the raw or processed form could play an important role in the expansion of the trade between developing countries. The gain would result not so much from the comparative advantages in the Ricardian sense, as from economies of scale and from not having to maintain inefficient industries under high protection.

Fortunately, the importance of trade between developing countries seems to be progressively more recognized. During the first UNCTAD conference in 1963, this problem did not raise any interest and was quickly disposed of. But the Algiers charter, adopted by seventy-seven

[16] OECD, *Supply and Demand prospects for Chemical Fertilizers,* Preliminary Report, April 1967.

countries in October 1967 in preparation for UNCTAD II, devotes an important section to the problem of trade expansion between LDC. One can also discern an evolution in the attitudes of developed countries and international agencies, such as GATT and IMF in favor of preferential trade arrangements between developing countries. This change in attitudes has already been reflected in the actual trade pattern. The trade between developing countries, which remained rather stagnant in the 1950's, increased during the first half of the 1960's by 6.3 per cent a year, that is, as rapidly as exports from the LDC to developed countries.

AGRICULTURAL EXPORTS WITHIN THE OVER-ALL EXPORT PROSPECTS FOR THE LDC

To assess the implications of the LDC export prospects for agricultural products, it is useful to refer to the UNCTAD projections for 1975. As previously noted, these projections for agricultural products were based largely on the FAO study. To integrate the findings of the FAO study in the UNCTAD projection model, a number of adjustments had to be made, however.

The UNCTAD projections of LDC exports for the period 1960–75 are summarized in Table 11 by main destinations and commodity groups. For some of the aggregates an attempt has been made to break up the fifteen-year projection period given by the UNCTAD into two subperiods, 1960–65 and 1965–75, on the basis of the IBRD data for the single years 1960 and 1965. This breakdown is presented in Table 12, with due warning as to the limitations of the exercise.

Tables 11 and 12 suggest that from 1965 to 1975 the rate of growth of LDC exports to the three main groups of countries should not differ widely. This reflects the considerable implied reduction in the growth rate of export to socialist countries in relation to 1960–65. This has to be interpreted with great caution in view of the limited knowledge regarding future economic policies in these countries, mainland China in particular. Regarding agricultural products, the lowest rate of import growth should be for the developed countries with market economies, and the highest for socialist countries. In view of the very rapid increase in exports of manufactures from LDC during the first half of the 1960's, the projections implied for 1965–75 may appear conservative. Moreover, the average export unit value of agricultural products may decline in relation to nonagricultural products. These two considerations suggest

TABLE 11

Projected Growth of LDC Volume[a] Exports, 1960-75, According to Two GDP Assumptions

(percentage per annum compounded)

	All Countries		Developed Countries		Socialist Countries		LDC	
	Low	High	Low	High	Low	High	Low	High
All commodities	5.0	5.6	5.1	5.5	6.5	8.2	4.6	5.5
Agricultural	2.45	3.1	1.8	2.2	5.6	7.4	3.6	4.6
Food and beverages	2.8	3.5	2.2	2.5	9.4	11.5	4.0	5.2
Agricultural raw materials	1.6	2.3	1.0	1.6	2.4	3.5	2.9	3.4
Nonagricultural	7.1	7.6	7.6	8.0	11.8	13.0	5.2	6.0
Minerals other than fuels	4.3	4.8	4.0	4.6	7.9	8.7	7.1	7.8
Fuels	7.5	8.0	8.8	9.2	–	–	3.9	4.4
Manufactured goods	8.3	9.3	8.7	9.4	14.2	15.6	7.0	8.4

Source: United Nations, Conference on Trade and Development, *General Survey of Trade Prospects and Capital Needs for Developing Countries*, table II, 3. (to be published).
[a]Weighted at 1960 constant prices.

TABLE 12

Projection Period in Table 11 Broken into Two
Subperiods — Developed Countries Only

	1960-75[a]		1960-65[b]	1965-75[c]	
	Low	High		Low	High
All commodities	5.1	5.5	6.4	4.5	5.2
Agricultural commodities	1.8	2.2	2.3	1.6	2.2
Food and beverage	2.2	2.5	2.1	2.4	2.7
Agricultural raw materials	1.0	1.6	2.7	0.4	1.3
Nonagricultural commodities	7.6	8.0	10.1	6.3	7.0

[a]See Table 11.

[b]From Bela Balassa, "Economic Growth, Trade and the Balance of Payments in LDC, 1960-65" (unpublished).

[c]Computed by difference.

that the share of agricultural products in the total might be lower, rather than higher, than indicated. Such considerations fall outside the scope of this paper, however, and the UNCTAD projections will be used to analyze the changes in the export pattern of the LDC.

The modification in the commodity composition of LDC exports on the basis of the UNCTAD projections is shown in Table 13. The modifications are the most pronounced for exports from developing to developed countries. In this particular flow of trade the most striking feature is the evolution of the relative share of agricultural products and of petroleum. The share of agricultural products was about three times that of petroleum in 1950. In 1960 the ratio had fallen to two to one. By 1965 agricultural products exceeded petroleum by less than 40 per cent. In 1975 earnings derived from all agricultural products exported from developing to developed countries are projected at only half of those derived from petroleum. During the first half of the 1960's the increment in export earnings of LDC derived from petroleum was almost three times that derived from all agricultural products. By 1975 the ratio might be five to one.

A reduction of the share of agricultural products in the export earnings of LDC has two important effects:

The first effect is to increase the outflow of investment income as a percentage of the total LDC export earnings. Factor income payments

TABLE 13

Projected Percentage Breakdown of LDC Volume Exports by Commodity Groups, 1960-75, According to Two GDP Assumptions

(volume weighted at 1960 prices)

	All Destinations					Developed Countries				
	1960	1975		Increment 1960-75		1960	1975		Increment 1960-75	
		Low	High	Low	High		Low	High	Low	High
Agricultural commodities	52	36	37	21	25	53	33	33	15	17
Fuels	27	39	38	51	47	26	43	43	59	57
Minerals other than fuels	12	11	10	10	9	15	13	13	11	11
Manufactured Goods	9	14	15	18	19	6	11	11	15	15
Total	100	100	100	100	100	100	100	100	100	100

Source: See Table 11.

generated from an increase in LDC agricultural exports are insignificant; they are limited to some foreign-owned plantations. But the factor income payments outflow resulting from an increase in petroleum exports is large. The outflow is substantial for minerals other than fuels and may not be negligible for manufactured export goods (Hong Kong is an example).

The second effect is to increase the factor of inequality in the distribution of export earnings among the LDC. Almost every developing country has an agricultural sector, and most are in a position to export some agricultural products. This is not the case with petroleum. In 1965 a few oil-exporting countries, which together had only 1.5 per cent of the total LDC population, accounted for about one-fourth of the total LDC export earnings. Likewise, exports of minerals other than fuels are not very widely spread among developing countries, although the concentration is much less pronounced than for petroleum. In future decades the rapid expansion of manufactures exports may be in favor of countries with large population. In the past, however, the picture was different. Between 1953 and 1965 LDC exports of manufactures increased by 170 per cent.[17] One-fourth of the increase went to Hong Kong, and another 15 per cent to Taiwan and South Korea. Between 1953 and 1965 the absolute increase in manufactures exports from Hong Kong was two and a half times that of exports from India.

This widening factor of inequality of export earnings among the LDC between 1950 and 1965 can be seen from Table 14 and Figure 1. The developing countries were ranked according to their level of export earnings per capita for a given year. The first line of Table 14 shows that in 1950 10 per cent of the population of the LDC received 50 per cent of their export earnings, while at the other end, only 10 per cent of the earnings went to 45 per cent of the population. The inequality factor in the distribution also increased steadily from 1950 to 1965. Thus in 1965, as shown in the fourth line, only 7 per cent of the population received half of the earnings (compared with 10 per cent in 1950), while at the other end 57 per cent shared only one-tenth of the earnings (compared with 45 per cent in 1950). If all the typical oil countries, as well as Hong Kong and Singapore are excluded, the picture is a bit more favorable, but the trend is the same, as shown in lines five and six. The fraction of the total population receiving only 20 per cent of the earnings increased from 58 per cent in 1950 to 66 per cent in 1965. It is worth noting that during that period the reverse occurred among the developed countries: there was less disparity in distribution in 1965 than in 1950.

[17] *International Trade 1966,* table 19, p. 56.

TABLE 14

Cumulative Export Earnings Progressively Related to Portion of Population Receiving Them: Developing and Developed Countries with Market Economies 1950-65[a]

	Cumulative Percentage of Total Population Receiving the Following Cumulative Percentages of Export Earnings:								
	20	30	40	50	60	70	80	90	100
All developing countries									
1950	1.0	1.9	4.8	10.0	16.3	23.2	35.0	54.8	100.0
1955	0.7	1.7	3.8	8.3	14.0	21.5	31.2	48.8	100.0
1960	0.6	1.1	3.1	7.1	12.6	20.1	29.7	46.6	100.0
1965	0.9	1.2	3.5	6.9	11.3	18.7	27.9	42.7	100.0
Selected developing countries[b]									
1950	3.1	6.4	10.8	16.1	21.9	30.3	41.8	60.9	100.0
1965	2.9	5.1	8.8	13.7	19.1	26.0	34.4	59.4	100.0
Developed countries									
1950	5.9	10.1	14.8	21.2	29.4	37.7	48.1	61.2	100.0
1965	6.8	11.7	18.1	25.0	32.8	43.9	57.0	69.7	100.0

[a]Computation based on three-year average centered in the year indicated.
[b]Minus major oil exporters—Kuwait, Netherlands Antilles, Libya, Trinidad, Brunei, Venezuela, Iraq, and Iran; major reexporting centers—Singapore, Aden, Hong Kong, and Israel.

Figure 1

Lorenz Curve Illustrating Changes from 1950 to 1965 in the Distribution of Export Earnings by Countries in Relation to their Population

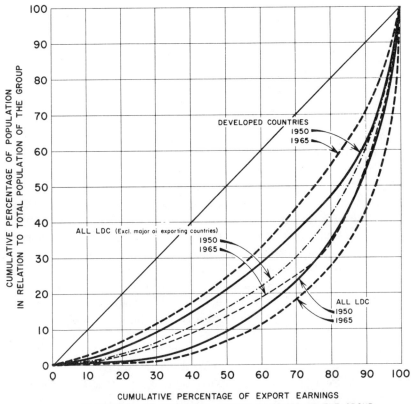

Note: Based on dat in Table 14

The combination of these two effects—greater percentage of outflow of investment income and a wider factor of inequality in the distribution of income among countries—together with the unfavorable growth of the *net* capital inflow go a long way to explain why, despite a higher export growth in the first half of the 1960's compared with the second half of the 1950's, the average rate of economic growth of the LDC declined. Between 1958–60 and 1964–66 the export-import gap of all LDC was reduced by 1 billion dollars. But this over-all reduction concealed an increase of 2.4 billion dollars in the export-import surplus of the developing countries exporting petroleum and an increase of 1.4 billion dollars in the export-import deficit of the other developing countries.

ANNEX I

Impact of Urbanization on the Accuracy of Demand Projections Based on National Averages

In many developing countries, particularly Africa, the rural/urban disparity in per capita income is considerable, and urbanization proceeds at a rapid pace. As a result, the growth rate of the national per capita income is substantially higher than the weighted average of the urban and rural rates. Let us consider a country in which per capita income is three times higher in the urban than in the rural sector and total population, of which 15 per cent is initially urban, increases by 2.5 per cent a year. If per capita income rises by 2 per cent a year both in the urban and in the rural sectors, over a ten-year period the average per capita national income will rise by 2.6 per cent a year. The difference between 2.6 and 2 per cent is explained by the shift into a higher income bracket of the rural population that migrates into urban areas.

Similarly, for a given commodity the growth rate of per capita consumption for the country as a whole will be higher than the weighted average of the sectoral growth rates if the per capita consumption level projected for that commodity is higher for the urban than for the rural sector or vice versa.[18] Whether the weighted average of the sectoral elasticities will be biased and in which direction, depends, therefore, on the relative income and consumption patterns in the urban and rural sectors. Those can be analyzed from nationwide household surveys.

If the same demand function can be fitted to the urban and the rural population, there is no genuine urbanization effect; the difference in the per capita consumption level can be entirely explained in terms of per capita income differentials. The separate projections of the urban and rural demand will then lead to the same result as a direct projection based on national averages (using the weighted average of the sectoral elasticities, provided that if income enters the demand function in the logarithmic form, the percentage per capita income growth is the same in the two sectors). But if the demand functions are not the same for the two sectors, the projection based on national averages is biased.

---

[18] See formula, pp. 65–66.

Figure 2

Positive Urbanization Effect

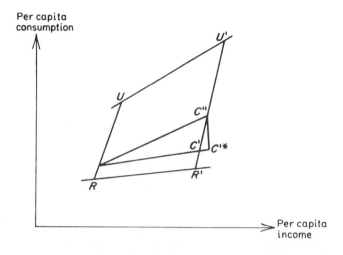

Figure 2 illustrates the case of a positive urbanization effect when the urban regression line UU' lies above the rural regression line RR'. The points R, U, and C are representative of the average per capita income and consumption levels in the base year for rural, urban, and nationwide population, respectively. Points R' and U' refer to the projected year. If the fraction of the urban population in the total were to remain constant ($u' = u$), the average for the country would be at C' ($\overline{RC} = u\overline{RU}$, $\overline{R'C'} = u\overline{R'U'}$). The slope of CC' is the weighted average of the slopes of the urban and rural regressions $[ub_u + (1 - u)b_r]$ when the horizontal projections of UU' and RR' are the same, that is, if the increase in per capita income measured with the appropriate scales is the same for urban and rural population. The point C' is therefore the one that would have been projected from national averages using the weighted average of the sectoral regression coefficients. But, if there is a transfer from rural to urban population ($u' > u$), the average for the country will rise from C' to $\overline{C''}$: as $\overline{C'C''} = (u' - u)R'U'$. The projection based on national averages with the weighted regression coefficient would have led to the point $C'*$. The demand would have been underestimated by $\overline{C'*C''}$.

Figure 3 illustrates a negative urbanization effect. This would often apply to the types of food produced in the subsistence economy; for these, per capita consumption can be as high or higher in rural than urban areas despite the income differential. An extreme example is that

Figure 3

Negative Urbanization Effect

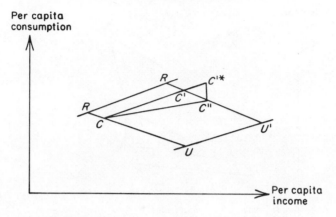

of milk consumption between nomadic and urban populations, when the nomadic population largely fed on milk progressively disappears over the projection period.

For all food valued at farm prices the urban demand curve is likely to lie below that of the rural. In cases of rapid urbanization the projections of total food valued at farm prices may therefore be overestimated. This may partly explain the fact that in some developing countries, despite an increase in per capita national income, per capita food consumption hardly rose.[19] More commonly the tendency would be to overestimate the demand for the commodities produced in a subsistence economy and to underestimate the demand for foods not locally produced. In other words, rapid urbanization would stimulate demand for imported foods rather than for those traditionally produced in subsistence economy.

In the covariance analysis of household surveys the total variance V of income per capita is the sum of the variance between strata VB and the variance within strata ($VW = \sum_i (VW)i$). The average coefficient within strata can be written:

$$b_a = \sum_i b_i(VW)i$$

[19] It would generally imply that part of the increase recorded in per capita income is artificial and reflects differences of accounting for subsistence and market production.

The coefficient b_o obtained without stratification is the weighted average of the coefficients b_a (within strata) and b_m (between strata):

$$(V)b_o = (VW)b_a + (VB)b_m$$

The coefficient b_m measures the slope of RU in Figure 2, while the coefficient b_a may be close to the slope of CC' especially if b_u and b_R have similar values. Consequently, the coefficient b_o estimated without stratification may not differ much from the slope of CC''; at least it is biased in relation to b_a in the right direction.

This can be illustrated in the case of the United States from the 1955 consumption survey. Households were classified in three groups: rural farm, rural nonfarm, and urban. Demand functions were computed for each group and the difference in the relations were analyzed by covariance. If we call (somewhat pejoratively) the shift, rural-farm-to-rural-nonfarm-to-urban "urbanization," then the urbanization effect on consumption can be characterized by the difference between the regression coefficients b_m (between group averages) and b_a (average within groups). This analysis reveals a positive urbanization effect for: fresh citrus, canned and frozen fruits, vegetables and juices, meat (except beef), fish, margarine, vegetable oils, and coffee powder. It showed a negative urbanization effect for: cereals, potatoes, pulses, sugar, fresh vegetables and fruits (except citrus), eggs, milk products, and cocoa.

Over the period 1955–65 the share of the urban population increased from 61.5 to 68.1 per cent while that of rural nonfarm and especially rural farm declined. About one-fifth of the annual growth in the average U.S. per capita income over this period can be accounted for by this urbanization process. Using the formula presented at the end of this annex, a comparison was made between the elasticity coefficient η^* calculated as the weighted average of the elasticity for each group (corresponding to the regression line CC' of Figures 2 and 3) and the coefficient of elasticity η. which should have been applied to the national average to reflect the urbanization process (line CC''). The results are shown in Table 15 for two commodities: cereals, with a negative urbanization effect, and frozen juice, with a positive urbanization effect. The elasticity η^* (obtained by weighting the elasticity for each group proportionally to the total consumption of the group) does not greatly differ from η_a (average within groups) but does differ substantially from the correct elasticity η (reflecting the urbanization effect). The elasticity η_o (estimated for the entire population without stratifying by group) is closer than either η_a or η^* to the elasticity η reflecting the urbanization process.

TABLE 15

Impact of Urbanization on Demand Projections as Reflected in Elasticities for Two Products, U.S.A., 1955-65[a]

(semilog)

Elasticity	Cereals	Frozen juices
Average within groups,η_a	$-.15(\pm.02)$	$0.98(\pm.11)$
Between group averages,η_m	$-.91(\pm.08)$	$3.20(\pm.21)$
Overall without stratification,η_o	$-.24$	1.22
Weighted average of group elasticities,η_*	$-.07$	1.0
Elasticity reflecting urbanization effect over 1955-65 period,η	$-.20$	1.15

[a]Elasticities originally obtained in survey made in 1955.

A similar computation was made for Madagascar starting from the 1962 survey which included a stratification between urban and rural demand. The computation was made working backwards over the period 1950–62, assuming as previously the same percentage per capita income growth in each group. The results (Table 16) show that the application of a weighted income elasticity would have led to an insignifi-

TABLE 16

Impact of Urbanization on Demand Projections as Illustrated by Comparison of Elasticity Reflecting Urbanization and Elasticity Derived From Weighted Group Averages: Madagascar, 1950-62.

(semilog)

Elasticity	Rice	Vegetable Oils	Fresh Milk	Milk
Weighted of urban and rural,η	0.04	1.15	0.75	0.92
Including urbanization effect 1950-62,η	0.03	1.27	0.73	0.91

[a]Elasticities originally obtained in survey made in 1962.

cant overestimation of the demand for rice, fresh milk, and meat, but to a significant underestimation of the demand for vegetable oils.

Undoubtedly, the ideal would be to project demand separately for each sector. But this would require the knowledge of a separate food balance for each. Due to the lack of comprehensive consumption surveys in most developing countries, one can only measure, in the few countries where data are available, the bias attached to national vs. sectoral projections.

Computational Formula

a_i = population of group (group i refers for example to rural or urban) i as a fraction of total population in base year.

a_i' = population of group i as a fraction of total population in projected year.

x_i = average per capita income of group i over average per capita income of total population in base year.

y_{ij} = average per capita consumption of commodity j for group i divided by average per capita consumption of commodity j for total population in base year.

X_i = ratio of per capita income of group i: value projected over value in base year.

Y_{ij} = ratio of per capita consumption of commodity j for group i: value projected over value in base year.

η_{ij} = income elasticity of the demand for commodity j in group i in the base year.

For the entire population the increase of average per capita income in terms of ratio of projected income over income in base year can be written:

$$X = \sum_i a_i' x_i X_i = X^* + \sum_i (a_i' - a_i) x_i X_i$$

with X^* the weighted average of the sectoral ratio X_i:

$$X^* = \sum_i a_i x_i X_i$$

Similarly for the increase of the average per capita consumption:

$$Y_j = \sum_i a_i' y_{ij} Y_{ij} = Y_j^* + \sum_i (a_i' - a_i) y_{ij} Y_{ij}$$

With a semilog demand function, the relation between increase in consumption and income can be written for group i:

$$Y_{ij} - 1 = \eta_{ij} \log X_i$$

With η_j^* weighted average of the sectoral income elasticities η_{ij}:

$$\eta_j^* = \sum_i a_i y_{ij} \eta_{ij}$$

and η_j elasticity relating actual increments in national per capita income and consumption reflecting simultaneously the pure income effect and the modification in the sectoral composition of the population.

$$Y_j - 1 = \eta_j \log X$$

The relation between the correct elasticity η_j and the weighted average elasticity η_j^* can be written:

$$(\eta_j^* - \eta_j) \log X = Y_j^* - Y_j - \eta_j^* \log \frac{X^*}{X}$$

The two elasticities coincide $\eta_j^* = \eta_j$

if
$$Y_j^* - Y_j = \eta_j^* \log \frac{X^*}{X}$$

This implies that the group averages fall along a regression line of slope η_j^*.

ANNEX II

Impact of an Increase of Exports on GDP—Distinction Between "Accounting" and "Induced" Effect

Export may be thought of mainly as a means of securing the imported goods required for growth. Under this premise the developmental impact of an expansion of exports—or more precisely, of the increase in the import capacity thus generated—will depend on the GDP response to an increase in the import capacity.

During the postwar period the elasticity of imports in relation to GDP has been close to 1.1 for all developing countries together. In individual countries, however, the import elasticity departed substantially from this average. Thus, among the twenty-nine developing countries analyzed in the UNCTAD study, the "historical" elasticity fell between 0.9 and 1.3 for ten; below 0.9 for eleven; and at 1.3 or above for eight. Among the extremes were: Brazil (0.28), Colombia (0.38), Venezuela

(0.39), and Ceylon (0.47) on the one hand; and Nigeria (2.6), Pakistan (2.6), Taiwan (1.86), and Chile (1.82) on the other.

If exports are taken as exogenous, the developmental impact of exports on GDP can be estimated by regressing GDP (at constant prices) on exports (deflated by average import unit value). During the postwar period the elasticity of GDP in relation to exports, thus estimated, was found significant ($t > 3$) for twenty-five countries. The elasticity was equal to 1.1 for one country. It fell between 0.7 and 0.81 for ten; between 0.5 and 0.7 for seven; between 0.3 and 0.5 for three; and below zero for four. If we take 0.7 as the most common value, then a 10 per cent increase in export earnings is often associated with a 7 per cent increase in GDP.

Simultaneity between the increase of exports and GDP does not mean causality. For example, one would not like, a priori, to say that, in the case of the four countries with an apparent negative elasticity, the growth of GDP was due to the decline in exports. When the time trend elements in GDP and exports are removed, either by introducing time as an additional variable or by regressing the first differences, the relation between the fluctuations in export earnings and GDP becomes very weak. Moreover, the correlation between the rates of growth of GDP and export earnings between countries is low. Taking all the thirty-nine countries for which data were available, only 20 per cent of the variance in the rates of GDP growth is explained by variations in the rates of export growth. Eliminating the thirteen countries for which the rates of growth are not significant, only 12 per cent of the variance is explained. The relation between the growth of exports and GDP, therefore, needs to be analyzed in greater depth.

Assuming constant prices; a given increase in exports will generally be associated with a somewhat smaller increase in the value added by the export sector. This difference is due to the deduction of the import content of the incremental export and of the inputs from the nonexport sectors incorporated in the export goods. The net import capacity of the country will rise by the difference between the increase in exports and the import content of the incremental exports. This rise, in the nature of an "accounting" increase, would be very small if the increase in exports reflected mainly an expansion of reexporting activities, or if the country started from full utilization of resources with optimal allocation. On the other hand, if the import content and the production foregone in the nonexport sectors were negligible, the automatic increase in GDP and net import capacity would approximate the increase in exports. In brief, an increase of ten dollars in gross exports will be automatically associated with an increase in GDP and net import capacity of somewhere between zero and ten dollars. This "automatic" increase reflects accounting identities. The problem is to know what will be the impact on the economy of this increase in disposable income and import capacity.

Let us assume an automatic increase of seven dollars. At one extreme, this amount could be absorbed entirely by an increase in domestic consumption and be balanced by an equal increase in imports of consumer goods, without any impact on domestic production. In such a case, the increase in exports during the first round would not induce in subsequent rounds any increase in domestic production and GDP.

At the other extreme, the seven-dollar increase in import capacity could be entirely devoted to the importation of equipment. This might induce an increase in domestic capital formation of more than seven dollars. If the lack of demand and in particular the lack of foreign equipment were holding back production and investment, potential savings previously idle and labor and capital previously underutilized might be brought into motion. The initial gain in export could thus have a large induced effect on domestic production and GDP, but the full effect would not be felt immediately.

To summarize: If a one-dollar increase in export earnings is to generate several dollars increase in GDP, the induced effect has to be large, and most of it will probably not be felt during the same year as the initial increase in exports. It might therefore be possible, through distributed lag functions, to express the response of GDP to an increase in export earnings in the form of two components: a short-term and a long-term elasticity.

Within one year one would not expect that one dollar increase in exports will generate very much more than one dollar increase in GDP since only part of the induced effect could be felt. If, however, within a rigidly planned economy, a windfall in export earnings were the only way to correct misallocation of foreign exchange, for example by importing spare parts, the induced effect could be sizable in the short term; but this is likely to be the exception rather than the rule. One could therefore expect the short-term elasticity to range from zero to somewhat above the ratio of exports to GDP. But the long-term elasticity could be much higher.

The value of the short-term elasticity will depend greatly on the nature of the increase in exports: for example on whether the terms of trade or the volume of exports have been modified or the import content and content of scarce domestic inputs have been incorporated in the additional volume of exports, etc. **The ratio between the long- and short-**

term elasticities will depend largely on the state of the economy, in particular on the existence of bottlenecks, and on the economic policies followed. The nature of the export industry will also influence the induced effect. In the case of minerals, the industry is sometimes more closely integrated with the economy of the developed than with that of the developing countries, and part of the induced effect may be felt in the importing countries. On the other hand, when the export sector is closely integrated with the domestic sector, trade may play a vital role in spreading improved technology throughout the economy; unfortunately this is not generally the case in the LDC.

To conclude, one cannot expect on theoretical grounds to find much uniformity in the relation between GDP and export growth in the LDC. The statistical analysis presented below confirms this lack of uniformity.

In several respects the relation between GDP and export earnings or import capacity is comparable to the capital-output ratio. It is extremely convenient to use and it provides an easy argument for illustrating quantitatively the beneficial impact of trade and aid. It should be used with time lags although it is generally used without them. It is not very reliable and cannot usually provide more than a rough first approximation.

Statistical Analysis

Y_t = GDP in year t at constant prices.

X_t = Export earnings in year t deflated by average import unit value.

t = Year.

Functions Without Time Lag

(1) $$\log Y_t = cst + d_{(yx)} \log X_t$$

(2) $$\log Y_t = cst + d_{(yt)} t$$

(3) $$\log X_t = cst + d_{(xt)} t$$

(4) $$\log Y_t = cst + d_{(yx.t)} \log X_t + d_{(yt.x)} t$$

(5) $$\log \frac{Y_t}{Y_{t-1}} = cst + d'_{(yx)} \log \frac{X_t}{X_{t-1}}$$

The regression coefficients $d_{(yx.t)}$ of equation 4 and $d'_{(yx)}$ of equation 5 can be taken as estimates of the short-term elasticity of GDP in relation to exports. The ratio of the regression coefficients $d_{(yt)}$ of equation 2 over $d_{(xt)}$ of equation 3 can be taken as a first estimate of the long-term elasticity. These coefficients are linked by the relation:

$$d_{(tx)} = \frac{d_{(yt)}}{d_{(xt)}} R^2_{(xt)} - d_{(yx.t)}(1 - R^2_{(xt)})$$

or

$$d_{(yx)} = \eta = R^2_{(xt)}\eta_1 + (1 - R^2_{(xt)})\eta_s$$

The ratio used as a proxy for the long-term elasticity is a poor estimate. If $R_{(xt)}$ is low, exports do not follow a time trend and the coefficient $d_{(xt)}$ has not much meaning. If $R_{(xt)}$ is high, the impact of exports on GDP cannot be precisely dissociated from the time trend.

Function with Time Lag

(6) $\log Y_{(t)} = cst + b \log X_{(t)} + c \log Y_{(t-1)}$

The regression coefficient b is an estimate of the short-term elasticity, the coefficient $\dfrac{b}{1 - c}$ is an estimate of the long-term elasticity.

The results of the statistical analysis, summarized in Tables 17, 18 and 19, suggest the following conclusions:

The function without time lag generally leads to a significant elasticity of GDP in relation to export earnings. However, the value of the elasticity (d_{yx}), and in particular the ratio between the rates of growth of GDP and exports (d_{yt}/d_{xt}), varies rather widely from country to country. When the time trend is eliminated, the relation between the yearly fluctuations of GDP and export earnings appears rather loose $(d_{yx.t}$ and in particular d'_{yx} obtained by first differences do not differ significantly from zero in most cases). In cases where the short-term elasticity is significant, it is generally lower than the direct elasticity d_{yx}, which in turn is generally lower than the ratio of the rates of growth (first approximation of the long-term elasticity). Moreover, the correlation between the rates of growth of exports and GDP $(d_{xt}$ and $d_{yt})$ among countries is low.

The lagged function (equation 6), shows that the hypothesis of an induced effect of exports on GDP is consistent with the time series available in a number of developing countries. As shown in Tables 18 and 19 Thailand provides a good example. Over the period 1950–65, the t ratios

TABLE 17

Regression Without Time Lag

Country	Period	$d_{(yx)}$		$\dfrac{d_{(yt)}}{d_{(xt)}}$	$1-\bar{R}^2_{(xt)}$	$d_{(yx.t)}$	
			(t)				*(t)*
Argentina	1951-65	0.52	(3.9)	0.92	0.50	0.05	(0.6)
Chile	1959-65	-.22	(2.7)	-0.27	0.34	0.064	(7.2)
Colombia	1950-65	0.77	(2.6)	2.47[a]	0.76	0.07	(3.7)
Cyprus	1959-65	0.62	(6.2)	1.43	0.20	0.67	(2.5)
Ecuador	1953-63	1.10	(2.9)	2.62[a]	0.64	0.13	(3.2)
Ethiopia	1961-65	0.36	(10.0)	0.67	0.15	0.06	(0.5)
Greece	1951-65	0.52	(19.8)	0.54	0.04	0.13	(2.2)
Guatemala	1950-65	0.81	(9.1)	0.95	0.19	0.15	(1.8)
Honduras	1959-65	0.38	(6.4)	1.61	0.63	0.11	(2.4)
India	1957-65	0.78	(4.5)	1.75	0.34	0.04	(0.2)
Iran	1959-65	0.75	(8.1)	0.30	0.23	0.28	(2.9)
Iraq	1957-65	0.74	(2.9)	1.38	0.38	0.04	(0.4)
Korea	1953-65	0.54	(2.2)	0.81	0.59	0.20	(2.6)
Malaysia	1961-65	0.79	(2.8)	0.96	0.44	0.09	(1.7)
Nicaragua	1950-65	0.72	(13.7)	0.80	0.18	0.31	(6.2)
Pakistan	1957-65	0.75	(3.9)	1.34	0.44	0.06	(1.0)
Panama	1960-65	0.65	(11.0)	1.73	0.29	0.17	(1.9)
Taiwan	1951-65	0.76	(8.0)	0.92	0.22	0.10	(2.5)
Tanzania	1960-65	0.51	(3.1)	2.55[a]	0.84	0.22	(1.6)
Thailand	1953-65	0.82	(11.5)	0.93	0.04	0.34	(4.9)

[a]Coefficient $d_{(xt)}$ does not differ significantly from zero.

of the regression coefficients *b* and *c* are highly significant (5.3 and 11); the long-term elasticity is about 2.5 times the short-term elasticity.

During the postwar period Thailand consistently followed an export-oriented policy with a minimum of import controls. Since no acute disequilibrium took place, the value of the elasticity may have remained

TABLE 18

Distributed Log Model, Selected Countries

$$(\log Y_{(t)} = a + b \log X_{(t)} + c \log Y_{(t-1)})$$

Country	Period	b		c		Watson Test	$\overline{R}^2$	$\dfrac{1}{1-c}$	$\dfrac{b}{1-c}$
			(t)		*(t)*				
Argentina	1952-65	0.13	(1.5)	0.77	(6.2)	1.99	0.865	4.35	0.57
Dominican Republic	1960-64	0.74	(5.0)	0.49	(4.6)	1.49	0.941	1.98	1.47
Ecuador	1954-63	0.18	(2.4)	0.95	(17.5)	2.32	0.984	20.0	3.6
Greece	1952-65	0.17	(1.8)	0.65	(3.6)	2.48	0.981	2.86	0.49
Nicaragua	1951-65	0.25	(3.2)	0.69	(6.8)	1.97	0.978	3.23	0.81
Pakistan	1958-65	0.20	(1.4)	0.84	(9.5)	2.85	0.981	6.25	1.25
Syria	1957-64	0.63	(2.9)	0.59	(4.9)	3.12	0.841	2.44	1.53
Thailand	1953-65	0.31	(5.3)	0.61	(11.0)	2.62	0.984	2.5	0.77

stable. The export sector was on the whole closely integrated with the rest of the economy, the five main exports being rubber, rice, tin, maize, and kenaf (variety of jute). Maize and kenaf were the two dynamic export commodities (more than 30 per cent yearly growth) that might have acted as the "engines of growth." The fluctuations [20] of the export earnings derived from these two crops, although high (25 per cent for maize and 40 per cent for kenaf), amounted to only 8.4 per cent for total export earnings, 6.2 per cent for all imports and 3 per cent for GDP.

[20] Fluctuations measured as the average absolute value of deviations from a logarithmic trend:

$$\log y_t = \log \hat{y}_t + \log \left(1 + \frac{e}{\hat{y}_t}\right)$$

$$\log \hat{y}_t = a + bt$$

$$f = \frac{100}{n} \sum_t \frac{|e_t|}{\hat{y}_t}.$$

TABLE 19

Short – and Long-Term Response of GDP to Exports

Country	Period	Direct $d_{(yx)}$	(t)	Short-Term Response $d_{(yx.t)}$	(t)	b	(t)	$d'_{(yx)}$	(t)	Long-Term Response $\dfrac{d_{(yt)}}{d_{(xt)}}$	$\dfrac{b}{1-c}$
Argentina	1951-65	0.52	(3.9)	0.05	(0.6)	0.13	(1.5)	0.08	(1.4)	0.92	0.57
Dominican Republic	1959-64	1.03	(1.7)	0.42	(1.5)	0.74	(5.0)	0.46	(2.6)	1.45	1.47
Ecuador	1953-63	1.10	(2.9)	0.13	(3.2)	0.18	(2.4)	0.14	(4.1)	2.62	3.6
Greece	1951-65	0.52	(19.8)	0.13	(2.2)	0.17	(1.8)	0.16	(1.5)	0.54	0.49
Nicaragua	1950-65	0.72	(13.7)	0.31	(6.2)	0.25	(3.2)	0.22	(2.9)	0.80	0.81
Pakistan	1957-65	0.75	(3.9)	0.06	(1.0)	0.20	(1.4)	0.04	(0.6)	1.34	1.25
Syria	1956-64	0.73	(1.2)	0.82	(3.0)	0.63	(2.9)	0.44	(1.7)	3.53	1.53
Thailand	1953-65	0.82	(11.5)	0.34	(4.9)	0.31	(5.3)	0.22	(3.4)	0.93	0.77

A Regional Model of Agricultural Development

J. A. C. BROWN

UNIVERSITY OF BRISTOL

I

Introduction

IN APRIL 1965 the UN Food and Agriculture Organization (FAO) published a study entitled "West African Pilot Study of Agricultural Development 1960–1975," the substance of which was discussed at an international meeting held at Dakar May 24–31, 1965. Essentially the study was an attempt to portray the agricultural economy of the West African region as it would be in 1975 if certain conditions were met. The most important of these related first to external factors over which the coun-

NOTE: The author participated as a consultant in the work on the FAO West African Pilot Study and is similarly participating in the work on its Indicative World Plan. The present paper is an individual contribution, however, and in no way commits the FAO to anything expressed therein. The author wishes however to thank the FAO for allowing the paper to be presented to the Econometric Society and for giving the author full access to material and to discussions with FAO officials. In particular the author gladly acknowledges a personal debt of gratitude to Mr. Louis Goreux of the FAO (now at IBRD) with whom much of the content of the paper has been jointly evolved. The West African study was published in English and French in two volumes with reference WIOA/W/AFR/65/1 and 2, and the report of the Dakar meeting was included in document CCP/65/14/2 presented to the thirty-eighth session of the Committee on Commodity Problems, FAO, Rome, June 1965. What in this paper are called regions are subregions in UN nomenclature.

tries embraced do not have complete control, such as the level of export earnings and the net inflow of foreign capital, including aid; and second to a target rate of growth of the gross regional product of 5 per cent per annum over the period 1960–75. By comparison of the projected picture for 1975 with the actual one for 1960, broad policy conclusions were drawn, which it was hoped would provide guidelines both for individual countries that are members of the region and for organizations responsible for considering regional development projects, including bilateral and multilateral aid-giving agencies. The study itself did not attempt the setting of targets for individual countries, although by grouping these into a number of "zones" within which ecological conditions are similar, it was possible to draw certain conclusions with strong implications concerning the growth and content of intraregional trade in agricultural commodities and of specialization in lines of agricultural production.

The projections and conclusions of the Pilot Study must therefore be considered as provisional in three important respects. First, since the technique was to treat the region as an economic unit and to discuss production and other balances, although disaggregated by commodities, at the level of the region or at most the zone, the regional picture presented in the study will remain viable only if individual national development plans are consistent with it and if the achievements of national economies are harmonious with each other. It may indeed turn out on closer investigation that the regional targets imply inconsistent or unrealistic behavior at the national level and that therefore a revision of the regional "indicative" plan is called for.

Second, the agricultural sectors and those closely dependent on them are dominant in the region, and although the remaining sectors were explicitly treated in the Pilot Study, they were not investigated in as great a detail as were the agricultural sectors. If false assumptions have been made about the remaining sectors in the study, there may again be a need to call for a revision of the study as a whole.

Third, the study was made in comparative isolation from the problems of the other developing regions of the world, some of which may compete to a greater or lesser extent in export markets and in the attraction of capital inflows from the developed countries. At the same time, the successful development of these other regions could lead to market opportunities for the West African region that have not been taken into account in the study. Thus some of the factors that have been treated as exogenous in the Pilot Study would become endogenous if similar exercises were undertaken for other developing regions, and the present assumptions can be taken as a starting point only for a more general approach.

The FAO now in fact proposes to initiate such a general approach as part of its preparation for the Second World Food Congress to be held in 1968. About fourteen regional studies comparable to the Pilot Study for West Africa will be attempted, and the whole will be integrated within a world framework. The main purpose of this framework is to clarify the relations of the agricultural economies of the developing regions with the developed and centrally planned economies and to make sure that the assumptions on which the individual regional studies— especially in the areas of world trade and financial flows—are based, will be consistent.

The purpose of this paper is to set out in computable form the relationships involved in constructing regional projects as described above, taking the West African Pilot Study as the archetype. The second section of the paper is devoted to this task. Since, however, it is not deemed as important to record what was in fact done in the particular pilot study, as to set up what might become the core of future regional models, not all the individual complications of the West African model are included. In the third section of the paper a proposed world model is described in which the regions appear as the elementary units.

Before beginning this discussion, it will be useful to say a few words on the work procedures envisaged, since these have a close bearing on the design of the regional and world models.

The models are designed on the assumption that each regional study will be carried out by a small group of professionally trained people, including economists, nutritionists, and agronomists. Each study will occupy a group for five to six months, and it is expected that a maximum of four studies can proceed simultaneously. Thus, provision must be made for the adjustment of studies begun earlier in the sequence in the light of those began later. The world model will be used to set the basic assumptions for the first group of regional studies to be undertaken, and thereafter to serve as a guide in their continuous revision as the regional studies develop. In addition, the world model will be used in the study of variations in the principal assumptions, for example with regard to the projected magnitude and distribution of capital aid flows and to the total import requirements of the developed and centrally planned regions.

It should be mentioned that in parallel with the regional studies that are the subject matter of this paper, the FAO will undertake commodity studies at the world level, and provision must be made for feeding the results of these into the world model.

It will, therefore, be very useful to have both regional and world models designed as fully computable. In the regional models, however, though it will be necessary to use concepts such as import coefficients and capital-output ratios that are commonly treated as fixed parameters, it must be accepted that the detailed regional studies will be directed, at least in part, to discovering how far these coefficients may be modified in order to achieve the targets of the indicative plans and to meet antici-pated stringencies in the external and domestic capital accounts. Further-more, if a clear accounting framework is used and the general skeleton of the regional model is preserved, it may not be necessary or even useful to work with a model that may be programmed as a whole for an elec-tronic computer. For the world model, on the other hand, it may be useful to have a computer program, since it may be necessary to run a quick investigation of the findings of the regional teams, and the basic model may serve with few modifications throughout the whole process.

II

The Regional Model

The Accounting Framework

In the West African Pilot Study extensive use was made of the account-ing system developed by the Ministère de la Coopération, Paris, for use in the ex-French African territories. This system is described in detail in the series 'Planification en Afrique.' [1] published by the same Ministry, and its principles have been compared with those of the United Nations Standard System by Ady and Courcier.[2] Basically it is an interlocking system of accounts, both real and financial, each divided into sources and uses (*ressources, emplois*), and therefore much more demanding of data than the basic accounts of the Standard System. There is no doubt, however, that something approaching the French system is neces-sary for development planning purposes and especially necessary for meeting the FAO criteria for individual agricultural commodity balances at the regional and world level. It is therefore interesting to note that the Economic and Social Council has prepared a set of proposals [3] for the

[1] *Planification en Afrique,* Volumes I–VIII, Ministère de la Coopération, Paris.
[2] *Systems of National Accounts in Africa,* OECD, Paris, 1961.
[3] A system of national accounts, proposals for the revision of SNA, 1952, UN Economic and Social Council E/ON. 3/320, Feb. 9, 1965. Cf. also adaptation of the proposed SNA for African countries, E/CN.14/NAC/20, UN/ECA, Addis Ababa, Jul. 5, 1965.

revision of the Standard System that go far to meet these needs. The system of accounts described in this paper is in line with the proposed revision.

The basic accounting matrix is given in Table 1. The subdivision of the main classes of accounts is designed to show separately in the table the explicit relationships between agriculture and the rest of economic activity. In the basic table, agriculture is aggregated in production, income/consumption, and capital accounts. Operationally this matrix is backed by a detailed subdivision into (a) monetary and nonmonetary activities, and within these into (b) the separate activities of crop production for regional and export purposes.

Most of the entries in the matrix are self-explanatory and require few comments. These are:

Agriculture production accounts. q_1 is the gross output of agriculture, of which f_{11} is the value of subsistence production, consisting mainly but not entirely of food; sales of agricultural products to other enterprises a_{12} and sales by other enterprises to agriculture a_{21} may not be separately known and may need to be entered net in the base year (an increase in a_{21} may, however, be a condition for raising agricultural productivity); gross investment in agricultural products by agriculture v_{12} includes both the stocking of agricultural commodities and "autoinvestment" by agricultural enterprises; exports outside the region x_{11} are defined as the f.o.b. value of unprocessed agriculture produce; a_{31}, inputs of public services into agriculture allow for the recording of productivity-raising extension services; a_{41} represents trading margins and y_{41} indirect taxes on agricultural products; m_{11} represents the c.i.f. value of imported current inputs such as pesticides and fertilizers.

Other enterprises production accounts. Exports x_{21} will include a component consisting of processed agricultural products, and it is necessary to know this separately.

The income/consumption accounts. The "incomings," r_{12} and r_{22}, from the external accounts represent earnings of regional enterprises located outside the region and remitted to it, while r_{42} represents the level of "current" or budgetary aid where this is relevant. In the "outgoings," the t entries represent, in row 3, the distribution of profits and subsidies to households, and in row 4, direct tax payments. (Subsidies to households t_{34} may be netted against taxes paid by households t_{43}.) Savings s are treated as gross—as no depreciation charges are made in the production

TABLE 1
Accounting Matrix for a Region
(all dollar figures in millions)

Accounts	Production				Income/consumption				Capital				External Goods		Totals
	Ag	OE	PS	OS	Ag	OE	Hh	G	GI	Ag	PuS	Prs	f.o.b.	Other	
Production															
Agriculture		a_{12}	0	0	f_{11}	0	0	f_{14}	0	v_{12}	0	0	x_{11}	0	q_1
Other enterprises	a_{21}		a_{23}	0	0	0	f_{23}	f_{24}	0	v_{22}	v_{23}	v_{24}	x_{21}	0	q_2
Public services	a_{31}	a_{32}		0	0	0	0	f_{34}	0	0	v_{33}	0	0	0	q_3
Other services	a_{41}	a_{42}	0		0	0	f_{43}	f_{44}	0	0	0	0	0	x_{42}	q_4
Income/consumption															
Agriculture	y_{11}	0	0	0	0	0	0	0					0	r_{12}	z_1
Other enterprises	0	y_{22}	0	0	0	0	0	0					0	r_{22}	z_2
Households	y_{31}	y_{32}	y_{33}	y_{34}	t_{31}	t_{32}	0	t_{34}					0	r_{32}	z_3
Government	y_{41}	y_{42}	0	y_{44}	t_{41}	t_{42}	t_{43}	0					0	r_{42}	z_4
Capital															
Gross investment					s_{11}	s_{12}	s_{13}	s_{14}	0	0	k_{13}	0	0	0	k_1
Agriculture					0	0	0	0	k_{21}	0	0	0	0	h_{22}	k_2
Public sector					0	0	0	0	k_{31}	0	0	0	0	h_{32}	k_3
Private sector					0	0	0	0	k_{41}	0	0	0	0	h_{42}	k_4
External															
Goods (c.i.f.)	m_{11}	m_{12}	m_{13}	m_{14}	0	0	n_{13}	n_{14}	0	w_{12}	w_{13}	w_{14}	0	0	e_1
Other	0	0	0	0	n_{21}	n_{22}	n_{23}	n_{24}	0	w_{22}	w_{23}	w_{24}	g_{21}	0	e_2
Totals	q_1	q_2	q_3	q_4	z_1	z_2	z_3	z_4	k_1	k_2	k_3	k_4	e_1	e_2	

accounts—and paid direct into a 'gross investment account' to overcome lack of information on the detailed flow of funds. Of the n entries, n_{13} and n_{14} represent the import of final goods used for private or public consumption, while the second row of n entries contains those that are the obverse of the r entries. This latter group of n entries can, if necessary, be netted against the r entries.

The capital accounts. Domestic savings are represented by the s entries, though it must be remembered that these contain a component r_{42} of current budgetary aid. Gross investment, including imported capital goods (row 1 of the w entries), is financed from domestic sources plus public aid routed through the public sector capital accounts after allowing for capital transfers abroad (row 2 of the w entries). These capital transfers include any repayments w_{23} of previous public aid receipts.

The external accounts. Here a somewhat unorthodox division is made between "goods" and "other," so that the trade gap g_{21} can be shown explicitly. If desirable and if the data exist, the other external account may be split between current and capital. In building up this account from country data the main difficulty is to net out intraregional trade and other flows. It will usually be necessary to construct separate matrices for these, so that they can be treated explicitly in the projection.

The Projection Model

If we write the corresponding capital letter to represent each submatrix in Table 1, the submatrix Y [4] for example is the matrix of income payments. The vector $i'Y$ (where i' is the row vector of units) consists of the income payments of agriculture and other enterprises, public and private services respectively; Yi represents the income receipts represented by the row totals of Y. The scalar quantity $i'Yi$ is the total of all income payments, or the gross regional product measured at market prices. We begin with a target value for this:

$$(1) \qquad i'_t Yi = (1 + \rho)^N \, i'_0 Yi, \text{ where } N = 15 \text{ years}$$

and where ρ is the target annual rate of growth of the gross regional product and $_0Y$ is the base year estimate of the submatrix Y. We have

---

[4] In the ensuing discussion, two-dimensional submatrices will be represented by unsubscribed capital letters which correspond to the letter found in the submatrix. One-dimensional vectors (occurring as "totals") will be represented by different unsubscribed lower-case letters where there is danger of confusion. Thus z represents the "totals" corresponding to Y and e represents those corresponding to X.

also the matrix $_tX$ given by exogenous analysis of world markets (this point is taken up in Section 3 of the paper).

If we knew the input-output coefficient matrices for the target year, which we shall denote by a bar over the symbol for the corresponding submatrix of Table 1, the equations for the production accounts would be

$$(2) \qquad\qquad q = (I - \overline{A})^{-1}(F + V + X)i$$

$$(3) \qquad\qquad M = \overline{M}q$$

$$(4) \qquad\qquad Y = \overline{Y}q.$$

In the West African Pilot Study the initial estimates of the coefficient submatrices were constructed by a variety of means, including time-series and intercountry regressions. These were particularly useful for estimating target-year values of import coefficients and the relation between government and other sector incomes.

The coefficients of the input-output matrix $\overline{A}$ were mainly supplied by agronomists with a knowledge of the region, basing them on a general idea of the increase in outputs required. To fill in the vectors of final demand, first X is exogenously given. The demand equation,

$$(5) \qquad\qquad F = L(Y)$$

was put in as linear relations with provisional coefficients, and V calculated from the scheme

$$(6) \qquad\qquad V = \overline{V}\Delta q$$

$$(7) \qquad\qquad \Delta q = (I - \overline{A})^{-1}(\Delta F + \Delta V + \Delta X)i$$

$$(8) \qquad\qquad \Delta V = 0.$$

Of these equations the last is a simplification based on the assumption [5] of linear growth in final demand from the target year onwards; ΔF and ΔX were calculated analogously to F and X, and the coefficient matrix $\overline{V}$ based on preliminary capital-output ratios. The problem here is that imported capital goods appear in the submatrix W and therefore a provisional split must be made between imported and domestically produced capital goods. In the case of West Africa this was relatively easy, since it could be assumed that all plant, machinery and vehicles would continue to be imported during the planning period, so that domestic capital goods

---

[5] Cf. R. Stone and J. A. C. Brown, Output and investment for exponential growth in consumption, *Review of Economic Studies*, XXXIX, 80, 1962.

consisted mainly of construction, and of stock increases and autoinvestment in agriculture.

By such means the elements of the submatrices representing physical flows can be provisionally filled in, and by means of the estimated submatrix Y and estimates of the growth of income transfers to and from the region (the second column of R and the second row of N) the control vector z for the income/consumption accounts estimated. It should be mentioned that the trade gap g_{21} is implicitly estimated by this stage, since the imports of final consumption goods n_{13} and n_{14} are involved in the demand relations (5). These must be treated as the most flexible of imports in order to arrive at a permissible value for the gap g_{21}, since it is a condition of growth that most of the remaining import coefficients determining M and the first row of W will increase during the planning period. The remainder of the matrix is perhaps best considered under the headings of check calculations which are likely to cause revision of the estimates already arrived at above.

The Check on Sector Incomes

In the West African Study, which may be typical in this respect, agricultural exports were projected to increase at a rate less than the projected growth of the regional produce, and the demand equation used for agricultural products implied income elasticities less than unity. The rate of growth of gross agricultural output was therefore also less than that of the gross regional product, and the proportionate inputs from abroad and from other sectors rose as a function of the projected growth of agricultural output. Thus agricultural incomes necessarily rose at a slower rate than other regional incomes. It is necessary therefore to check that this process has not been allowed to proceed too fast, i.e. faster than the migration of population dependent on agriculture can reasonably be allowed for. In the West African case the most stringent control on this process was felt to be the required level of investment in social capital and infrastructure. To some extent the problem is alleviated by balance of payments considerations, since a policy of import substitution, necessary to check the growth of n_{13} and n_{14} increases the corresponding elements of F faster than the normal demand elasticities would imply. But since in developing countries there is not the scope that exists in developed countries for maintaining the relative incomes of the agricultural population by income transfer, subsidies or protection, the sector-income check is likely to place an upper limit on the projected rate of growth of the regional product.

The Savings and Taxation Checks

If direct taxation rates used to construct T by

$$(9) \qquad\qquad T = \bar{T}z$$

are assumed unchanged from the base year, the domestic savings in S are obtained as residuals in completing the income/consumption column of submatrices F, T, S and N. The implied saving ratios can then be calculated from

$$(10) \qquad\qquad \bar{s}_{1j} = s_{1j}/z_j, \quad j = 1, 2, 3, 4$$

and examined for realism. This of course is not the end of the story since domestic savings with foreign capital inflows must finance the investment program represented in V and W. Anticipating this, and assuming for example that the savings estimates are too low, either imports of final goods or final demand F must be squeezed, and in doing this, account must be taken of sectoral income ratios and the trade gap g_{21}. Pressure will be placed on the taxation ratios of the fourth row of T in the attempt to finance expanded government programs, and the elements of T and S will be in a competitive relationship. In the West African study considerable use was made of intercountry comparisons to determine feasible upper limits to both taxation and savings rates.

The Check on the External Balance

In the second row of W are the capital transfers out of the region, w_{22} and w_{24} relating to transfers made by foreign enterprises (assuming that investments made abroad by domestic enterprises are small) which must be estimated as trends, and w_{23} relates to public transfers which will be largely a function of public loan receipts up to the terminal year of the plan and their repayment arrangements. Similarly h_{22} and h_{42} represent new investments in the region by foreign enterprises, and an assumption must be made as to the extent it is desirable and possible to attract such investments. Public aid h_{32} then appears as the final balancing item and a measure of the ultimate difficulty of achieving the plan targets. This is arranged in the matrix since the balancing item in the savings row is k_{13}, routed through the public accounts, which is merely an accounting device to overcome the deficiency of flow-of-funds information and the difficulties of projecting such flows in detail, whilst these are not essential to the primary purposes of the projection. Once again an unacceptable level of h_{32} implies a fairly fundamental revision of the original provisional projection.

Disaggregation of Agriculture by Commodities

The purpose of constructing the estimated accounting matrix for the base and target year is to provide a control framework, both current and capital, and domestic and external, within which a more detailed study can be made of the agricultural sector and those other sectors closely associated with it.

The main instrument used for this more detailed study in the West African case was the individual commodity balance, and the work was done mainly by agronomists. In the West African study some twenty commodities were treated individually. On the uses side of the account, exports were evaluated by commodity specialists, the direct demand for agricultural products for final consumption by demand equations, and the demand for agricultural products for intermediate use by input-output coefficients. The demand equations were estimated from cross-section and time-series analysis, and with regard to the equations for foods these were checked by computing the aggregate calorific and protein values and the farm-gate value of total consumption. These are very necessary checks in a projection covering fifteen years, and of course are also used by the nutritionist who may wish to achieve a different dietary pattern from that projected on the assumption of free demand at constant base year prices. These modifications of the diet may be achieved by direct means, such as import control, or by use of changes in relative prices, or by educational measures. On the supply side the problem is to balance regional production and imports within the aggregates given in the accounting matrix. In the West African case the limiting factor for regional production was not normally land except for a few cases of specialized crops and livestock production, but more usually the investment required to raise output and the scarce factor of skill to operate more productive techniques. This latter scarce factor is also controlled to a large extent by the allocations made in the accounting matrix for public investment and current outlays on extension services, together with the physical limits of the build-up of trained extension staff at all levels.

At this level of disaggregation, little use was made of simple capital-output ratios based on past performances, but more reliance was placed on best-practice techniques in the regional context. An important factor in determining the capital-output ratios, *ex post,* as it were, is the policy decision for the individual crop as to the extent output should be raised by intensive (increases in fertilizer or pesticide) as opposed to extensive (increases in acreages) methods. Formally the latter would give rise to increases in investment in the accounting matrix V whereas the former would be reflected in increases in current input coefficients $\overline{A}$.

Although the process has been described as though all detailed work were made to conform with the original constraints of the accounting matrix, such detailed work also gives rise to the need for revision of the original matrix, and the processes described above (derivation of the projection model together with the three checks) must be repeated if necessary, though it is hoped that these adjustments would be marginal and relatively easy to make.

Disaggregation by Zones

This process represents an intermediate stage on the way to disaggregation by countries, and the zones were chosen in the West African study to bring out marked differences in the agricultural economies. In principle each zone is a subgroup of countries with strong similarities in ecology and consequentially in dietary habits. There is of course the possibility that each zone should be equipped with a full accounting matrix, and a similar process to that described for the region repeated. The main reason against this is that the ecological grouping is appropriate for the agricultural sector but not necessarily so for the other sectors; also the problem of completely balancing the other sectors at the zonal level becomes increasingly difficult without expertise in industrial projects and without considering interzonal flows of manufactured goods and payments. In the West African study therefore the zonal disaggregation was confined to the agricultural sector, and the treatment was entirely in terms of physical commodity balances. Thus a number of questions were left open. For example, with regard to cotton, the confrontation in the commodity balances of zonal production plans with zonal demands for cotton products gave rise to projected flows of cotton between zones, but it was left open as to whether the cotton would move in raw form or as embodied in textile products, according as to the siting of the processing industries.

The main points then revealed by the zonal disaggregation were: first, the projected structure of agricultural production, particularly as regards the balance between the production of export crops destined for outside the region and the production of food and raw material production for consumption within the region; second, the relative rates of growth of agricultural incomes in each zone; and third, orders of magnitude of interzonal flows in agricultural commodities which would provide a first step towards the evaluation of the infrastructure investment required to sustain these flows. There remains of course the study of the zonal distribution of nonagricultural activities before a final conclusion of the viability of the Indicative Plan can be drawn. It is difficult to see how much further studies by international agencies alone could be taken, since the translation of an indicative regional plan into national policies would necessarily involve negotiation between the countries concerned and with aid-giving agencies. Nevertheless it might be hoped that an operational framework for such negotiations had been provided by the Indicative Plan, and that opportunities had been opened up for faster growth than would have taken place if studies had been made only at the national level.

III

The World Framework

The Accounting Matrix

As mentioned above in the Introduction the purpose of setting the regional studies in a world framework is primarily to achieve consistency between the individual studies and to introduce the key relationships between the developing world as a whole and the developed and centrally planned regions. It is not expected therefore that anything so ambitious as a "world growth model" could be attempted in the sense of a complete set of equations which could realistically simulate the development of the world economy or even of the agricultural sector. Even so, it is difficult to meet the minimum requirements of the world framework, and in many respects, formal completeness and elegance will have to give way before practical statistical difficulties. It is however useful to outline the minimum ideal matrix and operational procedures since, without a simple but firm system continually in mind, control of the regional work may easily be lost.

Table 2 sketches a matrix in which the developing regions are represented by regions 1 and 2, and the other regions by region A, which may be thought of as an aggregation of all those regions. The diagonal matrices represent the domestic flows within each region, and the symbolism is based on that of Table 1, so that the symbol a represents intersectoral flows, f final consumption, v gross investment, y gross income and s gross

TABLE 2

Sketch of a World Accounting Matrix

Accounts	Region 1 Income				Region 2 Income				Region A Income				Totals
	Agr.	Oth.	Consump.	Cap.	Agr.	Oth.	Consump.	Cap.	Agr.	Oth.	Consump.	Cap.	
Region 1													
Agriculture	—	a_{12}^1	f_1^1	v_1^1	—	x_{12}^{12}	x_{13}^{12}	—	—	x_{12}^{1A}	x_{13}^{1A}	—	q_1^1
Other	a_{21}^1	—	f_2^1	v_2^1	x_{21}^{12}	x_{22}^{12}	x_{23}^{12}	x_{24}^{12}	x_{21}^{1A}	x_{22}^{1A}	x_{23}^{1A}	x_{24}^{1A}	q_2^1
Income/consumption	y_1^1	y_2^1	—	—	—	—	y^{12}	—	—	—	y^{1A}	—	z^1
Capital	—	—	s^1	—	—	—	—	h^{12}	—	—	—	h^{1A}	k^1
Region 2													
Agriculture	—	x_{12}^{21}	x_{13}^{21}	—	—	a_{12}^2	f_1^2	v_1^2	—	x_{12}^{2A}	x_{13}^{2A}	—	q_1^2
Other	x_{21}^{21}	x_{22}^{21}	x_{23}^{21}	x_{24}^{21}	a_{21}^2	—	f_2^2	v_2^2	x_{21}^{2A}	x_{22}^{2A}	x_{23}^{2A}	x_{24}^{2A}	q_2^2
Income/consumption	—	—	y^{21}	—	y_1^2	y_2^2	—	—	—	—	y^{2A}	—	z^2
Capital	—	—	h^{21}	—	—	—	s^2	—	—	—	—	h^{2A}	k^2
Region A													
Agriculture	—	x_{12}^{A1}	x_{13}^{A1}	—	—	x_{12}^{A2}	x_{13}^{A2}	—	—	a_{12}^A	f_1^A	v_1^A	q_1^A
Other	x_{21}^{A1}	x_{22}^{A1}	x_{23}^{A1}	x_{24}^{A1}	x_{21}^{A2}	x_{22}^{A2}	x_{23}^{A2}	x_{24}^{A2}	a_{21}^A	—	f_2^A	v_2^A	q_2^A
Income/consumption	—	—	y^{A1}	—	—	—	y^{A2}	—	y_1^A	y_2^A	—	—	z^A
Capital	—	—	h^{A1}	—	—	—	h^{A2}	—	—	—	s^A	—	k^A
Totals	q_1^1	q_2^1	z^1	k^1	q_1^2	q_2^2	z^2	k^2	q_1^A	q_2^A	z^A	k^A	—

TABLE 3

Summary Notation for Table 2

	Region 1	Region 2	Region A	Totals
Region 1	T^{11}	T^{12}	T^{1A}	q^1
Region 2	T^{21}	T^{22}	T^{2A}	q^2
Region A	T^{A1}	T^{A2}	T^{AA}	q^A
Totals	q^1	q^2	q^A	—

savings. The region is denoted by the right superscript. The off-diagonal matrices accommodate trade flows and income and capital transfers between regions. The right superscripts here denote the pair of regions between which the flows take place (see Table 3).

In principle, the entries in such an accounting matrix can be filled in for a base year from national accounting and international trade data. There will be a number of statistical difficulties which will not be discussed here, and only two points will be made which will be useful in overcoming problems of data estimation. First, the accounts for countries represented by region A are required in the present exercise mainly for the flows between these countries and the developing regions.

This makes it possible to use simplifying devices, particularly in the diagonal submatrices for region A, which can overcome for example the differences in national accounting approaches of the developed and centrally planned countries. Second, unallocated flows may be handled by the introduction of a dummy region. This will help in handling the difficulties created by lack of complete knowledge of income and capital flows. We shall proceed for simplicity as though these problems have been completely overcome, and shall discuss the consistency model in terms of the three regions given in Table 2.

Procedure in the Consistency Model

We shall assume throughout the calculations as though the entries in the *columns* relating to region A are given for some target year. This means in particular that the import demands of region A from regions 1 and 2 are given, and also that the income transfers y^{iA} and capital transfers h^{iA} are given. This is not to preclude variations in these quantities, but at least in early experiments, it is best to seek for a solution in terms of the columns relating to regions 1 and 2 on the basis of given columns for region A. Variations for example in h^{iA} may then be introduced as an act of policy designed to discover the variational effects. As in Section 2, a bar over a symbol will denote the input-output coefficient corresponding to the flow denoted by the symbol.

We shall treat the case of region 1 as that of a typical developing region. It would be possible to treat the block of developing regions together and there are some advantages in so doing. However, there are both computing and more general operational advantages in an iterative treatment which would converge under appropriate conditions to the same solution as the simultaneous process. The orders of vectors and matrices will be smaller, and since work on the regional models will proceed sequentially, it will often be the case that the results for some, at least, of the developing regions can be taken as given in addition to the relevant figures relating to region A. An asterisk written as a superscript to a variable vector or matrix will denote that the value is fixed in the above sense during the calculation.

The flow equation for the gross output *vector* $q^1 = q^1$, q^1_2 of region 1 can then be written

$$(11) \qquad q^1 = \overline{A}q^1 + f^1 + v^1 + \overline{X}^{12}q^{2*} + X^{1A*}i$$

$$(12) \qquad \quad\; = \overline{A}q^1 + f^1 + v^1 k^{1*} + \overline{X}^{12}q^{2*} + X^{1A*}i,$$

if k^{1*} be set approximately to achieve a desired rate of growth beyond the target year t. The problem is to obtain values for q^1 and f^1 in equation 11, which will be consistent with the target value of z^1, and achieve balance in the income and capital accounts. The main difficulty is likely to arise from the fact, as it did in the case of West Africa, that the target growth in income of region 1 is likely to be greater than the growth of the region's exports to region A, and if fixed import coefficients were used in matrix T^{41}, the consequential imbalances will be greater than can be met by postulated income and capital transfers between region 1 and region A. Broadly, we can assume that the transfers y^{41} and h^{41} will be fairly rigid in the target year, since their levels will be determined by the past history of investments in region 1. Equally there will be little scope for downwards adjustment in x^{41}_{21}, x^{41}_{12}, and x^{41}_{22}, since these represent current inputs of imported goods necessary to sustain the required growth of outputs, or of x^{41}_{24}, since this represents the import of capital equipment. It must therefore mainly fall on x^{41}_{13} and x^{41}_{23}, imports of final agricultural and other goods respectively, to grow less than proportionately to output and therefore to achieve the required balance in the external and capital accounts.

Let final consumption of agricultural and nonagricultural commodities therefore be linear functions of disposable regional incomes:

(13) $\qquad f_1^1 + x_{13}^{21} + x_{13}^{41} = \alpha_1^1 + \beta_1^1 \ (z^{1*} - s^1 - y^{21*} - y^{A1*})$

(14) $\qquad f_2^1 + x_{23}^{21} + x_{23}^{41} = \alpha_2^1 + \beta_2^1 \ (z^{1*} - s^1 - y^{21*} - y^{A1*}).$

Necessary regional savings are given by:

(15) $\qquad\qquad\qquad s^1 = k^{1*} - h^{1A*} - \overline{h}^{12} k^{2*}$

The totals of the left-hand sides of (13) and (14) are then determined.

If we take imports from region 2 as fixed, to simplify the argument, the split between the f and x^{41} elements operates as follows: If x_{21}^{41}, x_{12}^{41} and x_{22}^{41} are determined by input-output coefficients applied to q^1 and q^2, as x_{13}^{41} and x_{23}^{41} are reduced, f^1 and f^2 increase, and x_{21}^{41}, x_{12}^{41} and x_{22}^{41} increase by less than the reduction of x_{13}^{41} and x_{23}^{41}. Beginning from values of x_{23}^{41} which imply too large a value of the trade gap between regions 1 and A, therefore, reductions of imports of final goods will increase regional incomes z_1^1 and z_2^1 to a point where the implied trade gap is acceptable. This is not necessarily the level where the income accounts balance, namely where the computed values of z_1^1 and z_2^1 are consistent with the value of z^{1*} postulated in (13) and (14). The necessary adjustment must then be made in the propensities to import intermediate products.

Thus, what is envisaged is a calculation of final imports from region A, which, when added to the intermediate imports that are implied by these, fit the required total and an adjustment of intermediate import propensities in order to fit the postulated regional income targets. The mechanism for achieving this result has been deliberately left unspecified, since it is felt that experimental work is required before the most useful form of this mechanism can be worked out. It will however be useful to make such a mechanism algebraically precise, since it will be useful to be able to calculate the effect on the solution of varying such key variables as h^{1A}, the level of capital inflow from the developed and centrally planned economies.

In the foregoing discussion it may seem that the relations between regions 1 and 2 have been treated rather summarily. One reason for this is that the process described has been thought of as a single step in a multistage process, and it might eventually prove useful to operate with groups of developing regions simultaneously. The more important reason is that trade, income, and capital flows between most pairs of developing regions are weak compared with similar flows between developing and region-A countries. The emphasis therefore of any policies of import substitution which may prove necessary has been placed more on intraregional than on interregional developments.

IV

Summary

The purpose of this paper is to outline the social accounting and model-building aspects of a large project which the FAO is undertaking. This project, for which some pilot study work was done, is aimed primarily at identifying the main policy problems for the agricultural sector of the developing world. As an important aspect of the role of the agricultural sector in the general economic development of these countries is its close relation with other economic activities, and as the relations, both of trade and aid, with the rest of the world set conditions for the general pattern of development, the writer has suggested a simple accounting framework for use at both the regional and world levels. The regional accounting frame and its associated projection model is designed to provide a discipline for more detailed studies by commodity experts, nutritionists, and agronomists, working in small teams.

The world frame is designed to provide a frame of control for the regional teams, and also to facilitate investigation in broad terms of the effects of changing basic assumptions concerning capital inflows and foreign exchange earnings vis-à-vis the developed and centrally planned economies. It is envisaged that the world model be evolved, by experiment to the point where it could be fully computerized.

The validity of the approach described, which rests on the decomposition of the world problem to a series of regional models working in an iterative relation with the world model, depends to a large extent on whether a suitable definition of region is possible. If a group of countries show at least potential complementarity in their agricultural patterns, even though their export sectors may at present be strongly competitive in the world markets, the iterative scheme has a good chance of working in the two-stage manner proposed. But the UN subregion of West Africa may have been better from this aspect than some others. The East African subregion for example ranges from Somalia in the north to Basutoland in the south, and the potential complementarity is greater for some of these countries with respect to countries in other UN subregions than with respect to other East African countries. In such a case it may be advisable to construct an intermediate table for the UN region of Africa and to work within this more general frame. This solution is of course inferior to that of using a more meaningful subregional classification.

Comment

KARL A. FOX, IOWA STATE UNIVERSITY

J. A. C. Brown's paper was prepared in 1965 and presented at a session of the First World Congress of the Econometric Society in Rome in September of that year. Its basic intent was utilitarian. It was intended to provide a framework for the Food and Agriculture Organization's studies preparatory to the Indicative World Food Plan, which was to be completed in time for a major FAO conference in October–November 1967. I became acquainted with the paper, and with Brown, in connection with the First World Congress and with a two-day meeting at FAO to discuss proposed methodology for the Indicative Plan, both in September 1965.

At that time I was serving as chairman of the Planning Committee for the present conference (i.e., the Universities-National Bureau Committee conference on *The Role of Agriculture in Economic Development*). It seemed to me that an elaborated and expanded version of this paper would provide an ideal opening for the present conference and the Committee agreed with me.

Brown's model was used in connection with an FAO pilot study for West Africa early in 1965. However, FAO chose not to use such a tightly integrated framework for its studies of the remaining regions of the world, so there was no pressing reason for refining the model beyond its state as of September 1965.

Even so, the Brown model has the virtues of comprehensiveness and consistency. Tentative plans for production, exports, and imports of each agricultural commodity in each world region would confront one another in a closed system. It would be difficult to gloss over prospective surpluses and shortages. Also, each coefficient underlying the demand projections could be varied within a reasonable range to observe its effect on commodity balances and trade.

Brown's model, as befitted the state of the arts in 1965, did not specify the methods by which commodity yields, acreages, and production were to be estimated. These methods would depend upon the data and research bases available in each world region or subregion. They might even depend on the expertise of the particular team of experts surveying a given region, as several different teams were to be used in making the regional surveys preparatory to the Indicative World Food Plan.

My appraisal is that Brown's model was well designed for its purpose. If FAO had used this framework with the help of Brown or anyone else of equivalent competence and realism, the 1965 version of the model would no doubt have been refined and improved. We should also have had a consistent set of data in a format that invited further testing, manipulation and (hopefully) cumulative improvement.

I am in no position to judge whether FAO's decision to use a more eclectic approach in its regional surveys was a wise one, given the considerations of time, personnel, and other constraints it may have faced. In the interest of clarifying certain opportunities for improved policy-oriented models of world economic development emphasizing agriculture, I am contributing the following paper.

Toward a Policy Model of World Economic Development with Special Attention to the Agricultural Sector

KARL A. FOX

IOWA STATE UNIVERSITY

TWO MAJOR VIRTUES of J. A. C. Brown's model are comprehensiveness and consistency. It reminds us very clearly that the world economy is a closed system. The exports of one country are imports of other countries. Inconsistencies among the export plans of different countries can be clearly exposed and quantified only within a complete model which includes all countries (or, as in Brown's model, all multicountry regions).

Except for minor editing, Brown's paper appears in this volume just as it stood in August 1965. If the Food and Agriculture Organization has decided to use this framework for its studies underlying the Indicative World Food Plan, Brown and others would no doubt have enriched and improved the model. As this did not happen, I propose to add some suggestions of my own toward a model of world economic development with special attention to the agricultural sector.

World economic development requires the transformation of agricultural production. It also entails the transformation of both rural and urban social systems. During the development process, such dualism as may exist initially is resolved into monism of the kind reflected in the symmetrical treatment of agriculture and other sectors in an input-output matrix. The rural-urban dichotomy is also resolved into a system of functional economic areas which are essentially urban in character. Hence, I will take a broader approach here than is customary in discussions of agricultural development.

World economic development has implications for every human being. More than a billion persons are now living in villages and are engaged primarily in agriculture. Within two decades hundreds of millions of them will have changed occupations, residences, and ways of life. Increased efficiency of agricultural production is one element, but only one, in the development process. Noneconomic aspects of life may change so drastically that changes in real income per capita will be partial and inadequate measures of changes in human welfare. To guide agricultural development policies on a world scale we need a concept of individual welfare that goes beyond that represented by existing measures. It will require the application of a comprehensive social science and the integration of units of observation from psychology, sociology, and economics. We must also bring to bear the concepts of central-place theory to clarify the nature of the urbanization process and the emergence of a new synthesis of rural and urban society around national (or multinational) systems of cities.

Apart from these innovations, the role of agriculture in world economic development can be expressed by linking several types of quantitative models. These models have generally been applied by different groups of economists in different contexts, and there may be some advantage in spelling out the way in which they could be integrated to form a policy-oriented model of the world economy with a realistic, operational, and computable treatment of the agricultural sector.

I

Toward a Comprehensive Social Science

There are indications that leading social scientists in a number of fields are converging toward a comprehensive social science. In his 1957 collection of essays, *Models of Man,* Herbert Simon tried to set forth "a consistent body of theory of the rational and nonrational aspects of human behavior in a social setting." [1] The essays collected in that volume had appeared in thirteen journals, representing statistics and all the

---

[1] Simon, Herbert A., *Models of Man: Social and Rational,* New York, 1957, p. vii.

social sciences save anthropology. Simon commented wryly on the compartmentalization of readership of these journal articles:

> I am afraid that economists are aware of them chiefly as they impinge upon the theory of the firm, social psychologists and sociologists as they relate to small group theory, learning theorists as they relate to problem solving, political scientists as they relate to the phenomena of power, and statisticians as they relate to the identification problem. The new wine, such as it is, has been safely stored in the old bottles—and I am often complimented, sincerely I think, on the range of my dilettantism.
>
> In assembling these sixteen essays in a single volume, together with some analysis of their mutual relations, I make confession that the compliments were largely undeserved; that what appeared to be scatteration was really closer to monomania. For when these essays are viewed in juxtaposition, it can be seen that all of them are concerned with laying foundations for a science of man that will accommodate comfortably his dual nature as a social and as a rational animal. The unity of the essays lies in that goal and in the fact that, as the foundations began to take shape, they clearly rested on two principal mechanisms—the mechanism of influence and the mechanism of choice.[2]

In his presidential address before the Regional Science Association in November 1966, William Warntz said:

> There is an ever-growing danger that events will come to control men completely. If men of good will and high purpose are to control events, they must be trained to perceive and taught to act in accord with a lawful universe—social as well as physical—and their sympathies must be supplemented by the kind of knowledge that can come only from a well-integrated, pertinent social science.
>
> And, if this kind of social science is to emerge, it must be not only unified and related to all the disciplines but must be global in its pertinence. Moreover, we must recognize that only to the extent that it is a natural science of society does it stand a chance to succeed. Our special plea is that it be a science closely linked to the nature of the very earth itself including its spatial properties. . . .
>
> Social science and physical science are but mutually related isomorphic examples of one generalized logic. In both branches, many and diverse academic specialties can be recognized usefully in terms of content, but when patterns and relationships are investigated in terms of basic categories then the true unity of all knowledge is revealed. The more we learn of any pattern, the more we learn how much it is like some other. . . .

Warntz urges his listeners on to "that next necessary great advance of knowledge, a truly natural science of society," and concludes by

[2] Simon, *Models of Man,* pp. vii–viii.

asking: "And could not this advance be spearheaded by regional scientists and geographers?" [3]

On the applied level, urban and regional planners are becoming increasingly aware of the complexity of the social systems with which they are dealing. Demetrius Iatridis of the Athens Center of Ekistics has this to say:

The increasing acceptance of social planners as full-status members in physical planning teams is the result of several crucial developments. One is the better understanding of the human settlement as an entity in its own right. Another is the increasing tendency to view it and the urban system essentially as individuals, groups, and social institutions in interaction with one another and as aspects of the societal systems. Experts in everyday practice were usually preoccupied with such elements as size, shape, density, stock of buildings or goods. But the recent emphasis on social interaction and social organization—the view that it is really the flow of information, goods, wealth or feelings among human beings in communication which comprises the human settlement—has resulted in an expansion of the physical planner's viewpoint. In practice, the planners' traditional and major foci of inquiry have grown; in addition to size, shape, land use, location and density, they are showing a keen interest in social organization, human interaction, social policy and social change. The study-focus of projects now includes a far greater number and scope of subjects and variables ranging from the political-administrative pattern of the human settlement to the essential behavioral patterns of individuals and groups.[4]

Additional evidences of the approaching convergence of other social sciences and economics are to be found in David Easton's systems approach to political life; [5] Hayward Alker's work on causal inference and political analysis; [6] the papers by Walter and Peter Isard on general social, political and economic equilibrium for a system of regions; [7] and the work of Brian Berry and others on the spatial aspects of human behavior in both urban and open-country environments.[8] The growing

[3] Warntz, William, "Global Science and the Tyranny of Space," *The Regional Science Association PAPERS*, Volume 19, 1967, pp. 7–19.

[4] Iatridis, Demetrius, "Social Scientists in Physical Development Planning: A Practitioner's Viewpoint," *International Social Science Journal*, Vol. XVIII, No. 4, 1966, pp. 474–475.

[5] Easton, David, *A Systems Analysis of Political Life*, New York, 1965.

[6] Alker, Hayward R., Jr., "Causal Inference and Political Analysis," pp. 7–43 in *Mathematical Applications in Political Science*, Vol. II, ed. by J. L. Bernd, Arnold Foundation Monographs XVI, 1966, Dallas, Texas.

[7] Isard, Walter and Peter Isard, "General Social, Political and Economic Equilibrium for a System of Regions: Part I," *Regional Science Association PAPERS*, Vol. XIV, 1965, pp. 1–33. (See also Part II in Vol. XV, published in 1965.)

[8] Berry, Brian J. L., *Geography of Market Centers and Retail Distribution*, Englewood Cliffs, N.J., 1967.

interest in political and social indicators in the United States will almost certainly foster attempts to find (or force) common denominators for measures of economic, social, psychological, and physical welfare.

Research by sociologists and political scientists on power structures in communities of various sizes and types suggests (to this writer, at least) that common denominators may be found for distributions of prestige and influence as well as those of income and wealth. The correlations among these distributions are high but by no means perfect. Power structures and other "mechanisms of influence" are being represented in terms of directed graphs and the corresponding matrices; so are other patterns of human interaction, as in formal organizations (firms, government agencies, and the like). At the level of measurement of individual behavior, the transactional analysis concepts of Berne and others, Roger Barker's concept of behavior settings, and the sociological concept of role playing provide elements ready for a tentative synthesis.

It may be noted in passing that hierarchies of central places (villages, towns and cities of different sizes) almost certainly reflect hierarchical patterns and tendencies within firms, agencies, and other organizations —tendencies that are perhaps too blandly subsumed under the general rubric of increasing returns to scale.

II

Measuring the Impact of Social Change on Individual Welfare

In a broad sense, society consists of patterned interactions among people. It would seem that the nature of an individual's participation in his society could be described partly in terms of the way he allocates his time among different kinds of interactions.

The social psychologist Roger Barker spent a good many years observing the behavior of residents of a small midwestern community of about 830 people. Barker [9] early addressed himself to the question of how the environment of human behavior was to be identified, described, and measured. He concluded that the community environment

[9] Barker, Roger G., Louise S. Barker and Dan D. M. Ragle, "The Churches of Midwest, Kansas and Yoredale, Yorkshire: Their Contributions to the Environments of the Towns," in William J. Gore and Leroy C. Hodapp (ed.), *Change in the Small Community: An Interdisciplinary Survey*, New York, 1967, pp. 155–189; and Barker, Roger G., "On the Nature of the Environment," *Journal of Sociological Issues*, Vol. 19, No. 4, 1963, pp. 17–38.

could be divided into parts or units which he called *behavior settings*. Barker says:

Behavior settings are units of the environment that have relevance for behavior. They provide the primary data of the study to be reported here. We have dealt only with the settings that occur outside the homes of the community, that is, the public behavior settings. The number of public behavior settings in the town is a measure of the size of the town's public environment.

We must emphasize that a behavior setting coerces people and things to conform to its temporal-spatial pattern. This is not an incidental or accidental characteristic. The person or persons who maintain and control the setting (the performers) make a deliberate effort to insure that this is so, and that the setting therefore fulfills its function. This aspect of a setting we call its *program*. Two settings are said to have the same program when their parts and processes are interchangeable. When this is true, two or more settings belong to the same *genotype*. Two grocery stores, for example, could exchange stock, personnel, bookkeeping systems, shelving, and so forth, with little interruption in their operation. They belong to the same genotype. A Methodist and a Presbyterian minister could, and sometimes do, exchange pulpits. The number of behavior setting genotypes in a town is a measure of the variety of the town's environment.[10]

Barker identified about 220 genotype settings in his town of 830 people. Examples include grocery stores, hardware stores, ice cream socials, kindergarten classes, business meetings, religion classes, hallways, bus stops, places of employment, one's own home, and many others.

Elements of Barker's more formal characterization of a behavior setting include the following:

It has a space-time locus.

It is composed of a variety of things and events: people, objects, behavior, and other processes.

The widely different components (of a particular behavior setting) form a bounded pattern, which is easily discriminated from the pattern on the outside of the boundary.

It is an objective unit, in the sense that it exists independently of anyone's perception of it, though not independently of the people who are a part of its pattern.

A behavior setting consists of both behavior and objects; both are essential; the setting is a phenomenon which consists of interdependent objects and behavior.

[10] Barker, *et al.,* "The Churches of Midwest . . . ," pp. 158–159.

An important factor is the space-time boundary; there is a physical boundary (for example, the walls and doors of a church) and there is a temporal boundary (for example, a service extending from 11 A.M. until 12 noon).

Within the boundary of the setting, the behavior of individuals conforms to the pattern characteristic of the setting. This fact is a function of other people in the setting and of the physical arrangement of the setting.

No behavior occurs outside of a behavior setting.[11]

When individual grocery stores, churches, and the like were recognized as separate or *specific* behavior settings, Barker found 884 public behavior settings in his town in 1963–64. He was able to record that the number of daily occurrences of behavior settings during 1963–64 was 53,258, and that the hours of duration of public behavior settings in 1963–64 totaled 286,909. Multiplying the hours of duration of each behavior setting by the number of persons participating in it, Barker obtained a record of "hours of occupancy" of behavior settings, totaling 1,129,295 in 1963–64. As there are 8,760 hours in a year, the total hours of "life lived" during the year by the town's 830 residents was 7,270,800. About 15 per cent of these hours were spent in public behavior settings (not counting, I believe, places of employment); the remaining "hours of living" were presumably spent in private homes, places of employment, and in transit from one behavior setting to another. For formal completeness, of course, we could say that each different kind of transportation between one locationally fixed behavior setting and another was itself a behavior setting (driving one's own car alone, riding with a car pool, walking alone, etc.).

It is tempting to apply the economic theory of consumption to Barker's data on the allocation of time, in the hope that this will lead to a more comprehensive measure of changes in human welfare than GNP.[12] On a purely descriptive level, the extent of the change in living patterns involved when a young man migrates from an agricultural village to a city could be illustrated in terms of the vectors of behavior settings occupied during his last year in the village and his first year in the city. His role in each behavior setting and the temporal rhythm of recurrence of settings are also aspects of welfare which will be mentioned shortly. For the moment, we shall explore the extension of consumption theory to the allocation of time.

[11] *Ibid.,* paraphrased from pp. 157–158.

[12] The present writer suggested this possibility to Barker and others at a symposium on "Change in the Small Community" in Chicago, October 24–25, 1966.

The Optimal Allocation of a Person's Time
among Behavior Settings

How should an individual allocate his time among behavior settings? For a given individual, let

$$(1) \qquad v_i = a_i + b_i t_i, \quad i = 1, 2, \ldots, n$$

where v_i is the value derived per hour of time t_i spent in behavior setting i. Individual occasions (for example, a movie) might be "either/or" affairs, but over a year, the time spent in movies could be regarded as a continuous variable. Let

$$(2) \qquad W = v_i t_i = \sum_i a_i t_i + \sum_i b_i t_i^2$$

be a maximum, subject to

$$(3) \qquad \sum_i t_i = 8{,}760 \text{ hours per year.}$$

Then:

$$(4) \qquad \frac{dW}{dt_1} = a_1 + 2b_1 t_1 - \lambda = 0$$

$$\frac{dW}{dt_2} = a_2 + 2b_2 t_2 - \lambda = 0$$

$$\vdots$$

$$\frac{dW}{dt_n} = a_n + 2b_n t_n - \lambda = 0$$

Thus the conditions for optimal allocation of one's time among behavior settings are formally analogous to those for optimal allocation of a consumer's dollar income among objects of expenditure.

Also, if it costs money, p_i per hour, to occupy behavior setting i, the total money spent for (1) occupying behavior settings and (2) purchasing other services and goods g is subject to the budget constraint

$$(5) \qquad \sum_i p_i t_i + \sum_g p_g q_g \leq y$$

where y = money income. Place of work is included among the behavior settings and one *receives* a payment per hour for time spent on the job. The maximization of W implies an optimal allocation of time between labor and leisure.

For a poor man with expensive tastes, $v_i > p_i$ at the margin for all behavior settings occupied; if his money income were increased, his social income would increase, for he would spend more time in settings costing money. For a rich man, the time constraint would be effective but the money income constraint would not be binding; $v_i = p_i$ at the margin.

The system must include time spent by person j reading books by authors now deceased, painting pictures that may be viewed by persons yet unborn, or watching a specific television program or a category (genotype) of television programs.

In each behavior setting the person has a role—spectator, student, teacher, customer, salesman, committee member, or whatever. Whenever there are face-to-face interactions, mechanisms of influence in Simon's sense will be involved and "transactions" will take place (in the sense of Berne).[13] These micro aspects of interaction influence the amount of satisfaction a person gains per hour and the number of hours he spends per year in any particular behavior setting.

Extending the Time Allocation and Interaction Model to All Human Beings

We are concerned with world economic development and change. The concept of optimal allocation of a person's time among behavior settings could be extended to all human beings alive at a given time.

At present, the world's population is about 3.5 billion. To deemphasize the arithmetic, let us suppose that, world-wide, there are 4×10^9 people and 4×10^9 behavior settings, each home, store, etc. in the world being a different behavior setting. A complete matrix for recording the amount of time spent by person j with person k in behavior setting i, where $j, k, i = 1, 2, 3, \ldots, 4 \times 10^9$, would have 16×10^{18} rows and 16×10^{18} columns. The entries in the vast majority of cells would of course be zeros.

We have, however, a conceptual framework for allocating all the hours lived by 4×10^9 people during 1968 according to behavior settings occupied and persons interacting in each. In principle, we could measure the amount of time spent by each person j in receiving "information" from each other person k in each behavior setting i. However, the role played by person j in behavior setting i may be a more stable and meaningful aspect of his degree of satisfaction in that setting.

[13] Berne, Eric, *Games People Play: The Psychology of Human Relationships,* New York, 1964; and *Transactional Analysis in Psychotherapy,* New York, 1961.

Implicit in the behavior settings and interactions are places of employment and techniques of production, including staffing patterns and administrative organization of each enterprise. The equation system for all persons j could be constructed (or construed) to account for changes in the stock of physical capital, human (individual) capital, institutional and organizational capital ("going-concern" and "good will" values), and informational capital.

If this conceptual framework were used as a guide for economic development planning, additional information would be required, including: (1) attributes of each person, such as age, sex, occupation, education, nationality, language, religion, political party, and others affecting the selection of behavior settings and persons interacted with; and (2) exact geographic coordinates of each behavior setting, including homes, places of work, and "public" settings. These coordinates help to explain the spatial organization of economic and social life. Given 4×10^9 behavior settings, our geographic coordinates would enable us to calculate a matrix of "great circle" distances between settings (containing 16×10^{18} entries in all, or about 8×10^{18} nonduplicated entries). In principle, mileages by actual roads and commercial transport routes (land, water, and air) could be inserted in place of "great circle" distances. Reductions in travel times or travel costs between sets of behavior settings will increase the sizes of the geographic areas which are effectively integrated into communities, labor markets, urban fields, and commodity markets. Travel time and cost reductions will also give greater scope to economies of size in firms and public enterprises, leading to the emergence of hierarchies of central (urban) places that will accommodate larger organizations with more complex labor force structures.

With respect to any person j we may inquire whether the actual value of W_j in 1968 fell short of its potential and if so, to what extent. In other words could W_j have been increased by a different allocation of person j's time among setting-and-role combinations without reducing W_k for any other person k? An increase in the capacity of any person k to give (produce) human values *could* increase the welfare of one or more persons without reducing the welfare of other persons.

The gains from rearrangements within a given year may or may not be large. The potential gains from achieving an optimal pattern of investment in physical, human, organizational, and informational capital between (say) 1968 and 2000 should be enormous as compared with those from the tradition-limited patterns that have so far for the most part prevailed. To what extent can we identify, starting from 1968, a pattern of allocation of all human resources that would be optimal for the social and economic development of all mankind up to (say) 2000 —an optimal deployment of human and physical resources for the achievement of human welfare?

The optimizing approach implies that all human institutions should be plastic and subject to planned or adaptive change to permit the expansion and enrichment of human awareness and interaction. Technological change would be valued to the extent that it made the world "a better home for man."

In the process of world economic and social development, the distribution of roles embodying economic, political, and social influence will undergo sweeping changes. As economists, we have been reasonably successful in measuring distributions of income and wealth. Power and prestige present, for us, novel problems of measurement.

Is there a common denominator for aggregating different kinds of influence? In a social system involving n persons, is there a "stock of influence" to be allocated among individuals according to the rank-size rule or some other regular principle? The rank-size rule would imply that, if the quantum of influence possessed by the most influential person is $I_1 = k$, the quantum of the second-ranking individual would be $I_2 = k/2$, of the third $I_3 = k/3$, and so on down to $I_n = k/n$ for the least influential person. The absolute differences among individuals in the lower half of the distribution would be rather small, ranging from $2k/n$ to k/n, while absolute differences among the top ten individuals would be large. Even granting this assumption, each subsystem in the society (and perhaps each behavior setting) might have its own rank-size rule operating among its own specific members or participants. If considerations of influence affected the utility of a behavior setting, each person would tend to allocate his time among behavior settings in which his situation in this regard was relatively satisfactory.

Eric Berne's concept of *recognition-hunger* seems less clearly asymmetrical as between persons and may be basic to the desire for any or all types of influence: "Each person becomes more and more individual in his quest for recognition, and it is these differentia which lend variety to social intercourse and which determine the individual's destiny. . . ." [14] Our approach in this section implies that an individual's sense of well-being depends partly on his consumption of purchased goods and services and partly on the allocation of his time among behavior settings in which he performs certain roles and receives (or per-

[14] Berne, *Games*, p. 15.

ceives) certain amounts of recognition. The change in the individual's circumstances from one year to the next could be measured in terms both of the goods he consumes and of the behavior setting, role, and recognition combinations which he experiences.

If a man moves from one town to another one at a considerable distance, but works at the same occupation and attends a church of the same denomination, his life pattern in terms of *genotype* behavior settings occupied may change very little. His roles and amounts of recognition in the *specific* new settings may differ from those in his former specific settings. On interview, he might be able to estimate how much money he would be willing to pay (or would require) to exchange each specific behavior setting in the new town for the corresponding setting in his former location, giving a common unit of measure to both the economic and noneconomic aspects of his move.

Arnold Faden has referred to the action of a person who changes (say) his residence but not his place of employment as "partial migration." [15] This term might be extended to any change over time in a pattern of behavior-setting occupancy. A change in role within a behavior setting might be similarly regarded. But if each "partial migration" in this sense can be equated with a compensating money payment, we can add the net gain or loss from "partial migration" to the net gain or loss in purchasing power, obtaining a dollar estimate of the total change in perceived welfare.

Space does not permit much further elaboration. However, a set of photographs of a typical young villager in each of his behavior settings, conveying an impression of his role and recognition in each, might be compared with a set of photographs of a young man of similar background occupying the settings and roles typical of those that the young villager might expect during his first and second years in the city. The technique could be developed to indicate, in film strips, the proportions of time spent in each setting and the sequences in which the settings occur, so that quantitative as well as qualitative differences would be observed.

Typical family adjustment problems could be visualized in this fashion, and so perhaps could the full array of problems of a representative sample of prospective migrants from villages to cities. The effects of alternative development strategies might be simulated in terms of the proportions of persons making specified changes or partially accommodating to change (for example, continuing to live in villages for some years while commuting by bus to factory jobs).

[15] Faden, Arnold M., *Foundations of Spatial Economics*. (To be published.)

III

The Urbanization Process: Rural-Urban Synthesis Around a National or Multinational System of Cities

If we really had all the entries filled in for 1968 in the 16×10^{18} order time allocation and interaction matrix described earlier, we should be able to identify the boundaries of a number of human organizations. The individuals belonging to a nuclear family and living in the same house could be clustered in such a way as to form a block diagonal matrix identifying individual families. Other patterns of behavior-setting occupancy by sets of individuals would identify villages and towns at different levels in the existing central-place hierarchy. Other patterns, very similar, except for the geographical proximity of the behavior settings, would identify neighborhood, community, and "regional" shopping areas within the larger cities.

Each of the human communities identified would be relatively self-contained with respect to a particular set of activities. In mainland China as of 1962 the rural commune was typically coextensive with the traditional administrative village or *hsiang*.[16] The *hsiang* (township) usually covered an area of twenty or thirty square miles, and it would require about an hour's time to walk from the center to the periphery of the area. In the United States as of 1911, C. J. Galpin found what he termed "fundamental agricultural communities" averaging about fifty square miles in area. These areas also required about one hour's time on foot or by horse and wagon to travel from the village center to the *de facto* community perimeter, a radius on the order of five miles.

Galpin described "the actual but unofficial community" which he found in Walworth County, Wisconsin as follows:

Eight of the twelve civic centers of Walworth County are incorporated; four as cities and four as villages. Officially, that is legally, the incorporated centers are treated as communities, each by and for itself. The foregoing analysis of the use of the leading institutions of each center by the farm population discloses the fact, however, that these institutions are agencies of social service over a comparatively determinable and fixed area of land surrounding each center; that this social service is precisely the same in character as is rendered to those people—whether artisans, employees, or pro-

[16] Wang, Tong-eng, *Structural Change and Development in Chinese Agriculture*, unpublished doctoral dissertation, Iowa State University Library, Ames, Iowa, 1966.

fessional persons—who happen to live within the corporate limits of the city or village; moreover, the plain inference is that the inhabitants of the center are more vitally concerned in reality with the development and up-keep of their particular farm land basis than with any other equal area of land in the state.

It is difficult, if not impossible, to avoid the conclusion that the trade zone about one of these rather complete agricultural civic centers forms the boundary of an actual, if not legal, community, within which the apparent entanglement of human life is resolved into a fairly unitary system of inter-relatedness. The fundamental community is a composite of many expanding and contracting feature communities possessing the characteristic pulsating instability of all real life.[17]

When Galpin began his survey in 1911, there were about 600,000 passenger automobiles in the United States. As of 1968 there are more than 60 million—an increase of at least a hundredfold! By 1968, the automobile was the almost universal means of shopping and home-to-work travel in the Midwest. There is conclusive evidence that the American Midwest can be delineated into a set of *functional economic areas* (FEAs) or commuting fields in terms of the patterns of home-to-work commuting from the peripheries of such areas to the central cities of (usually) 30,000 or more population at their centers. The speed of travel is ten times as fast as in Galpin's day; consequently, the radius of the fundamental community of 1968 is about fifty miles (instead of five) and its area is about 5,000 square miles (instead of fifty). Galpin's communities embraced 2,000 or 3,000 people; the functional economic areas of 1968 embrace from 100,000 to 200,000 or more people. Various terms have been used to describe the nature of these functional economic areas, including urban fields, commuting fields, labor market areas, and low-density cities. The functional economic area has also been referred to as "a new synthesis of rural and urban society." [18]

Toward the close of the "horse and buggy" era in 1911, Galpin described only one level of central place; his towns and villages ranged in population from about 500 to 3,000. The FEA in 1968 included at least three levels of fully viable central places, which Brian J. L. Berry has described as towns, cities and regional capitals. The typical populations of such places in western Iowa as of 1960 were about 1,500, 7,500 and 50,000 respectively. Functionally, these same levels can be discerned in

[17] Galpin, C. J., *The Social Anatomy of an Agricultural Community,* Madison: University of Wisconsin Agr. Exp. Sta. Res. Bul. No. 34, May 1915, pp. 16–19.

[18] Fox, Karl A., "Metamorphosis in America: A New Synthesis of Rural and Urban Society," Ch. 3, pp. 62–104 in William J. Gore and Leroy C. Hodapp (ed.), *Change in the Small Community,* New York, 1967.

metropolitan areas in the neighborhood, community, and regional shopping centers, respectively. The villages of less than 1,000 population in the American Midwest are rapidly declining in economic importance, and their Main Street establishments correspond to the scattered convenience shops found in the older sections of metropolitan areas.[19]

What Berry calls a regional capital, I have called the central city of an FEA. Berry recognizes two higher-order categories of central places, namely the regional metropolis and the national metropolis. These various orders of central places form a national system of cities; those of regional-capital (FEA central city) size or larger form the centers of urban commuting fields which, as of 1960, included some 96 per cent of the total population of the United States.[20] There are approximately 350 such FEAs or urban commuting fields in the United States.

The economic development of a large country may be thought of as the development of a national system composed of cities and their surrounding commuting fields. (The boundaries of the commuting fields are determined by the capabilities of the prevailing modes of transportation. In the United States the principal mode is the private passenger automobile. In other countries other modes of transportation range from slightly to vastly more important than in the United States. The boundaries of such commuting fields would tend to be fairly regular in terms of *minutes* of travel time required. In terms of miles, however, they might extend outwards for long distances from the central city along railroad lines, public bus lines, and well-paved highways. If bicycles or slower means of transportation were used from other peripheral areas, the commuting distances in miles would be much less.)

Berry has described the function of the national system of cities in the United States as follows:

1. We live in a specialized society in which there is progressively greater division of labor and scale of enterprise, accompanied by increasing degrees of specialization.

2. There is an increasing diversity of people as producers. But as consumers they are becoming more and more alike from one part of the country to another, consuming much the same "basket of goods" wherever they may live, as well as increasingly large baskets because of rising real incomes.

[19] Berry, *Geography of Market Centers*, p. 15.

[20] Fox, Karl A., "Functional Economic Areas and Consolidated Urban Regions of the United States," *Social Science Research Council ITEMS,* December 1967, Vol. 21, No. 4, pp. 45–49; and Fox, Karl A. and T. Krishna Kumar, "The Functional Economic Area: Delineation and Implications for Economic Analysis and Policy," *Regional Science Association PAPERS,* Vol. XV, 1965, pp. 57–85.

3. The physical problem in the economic system is therefore one of articulation—insuring that the specialized products of each segment of the country are shipped to final consumers, seeing that consumers in every part of the country receive the basket of goods and services they demand and are able to purchase, and bringing demands and supply into equality over a period of time.

4. Articulation requires flows of messages, of goods and services, and of funds. The flows appear to be highly structured and channeled and major metropolitan centers serve as critical articulation points. These flows are as follows: products move from their specialized production areas to shipping points in the locally dominant metropolitan centers; over the nation, products are transferred between metropolitan centers, with each metropolitan center shipping out the specialized products of its hinterland and collecting the entire range of specialized products from other metropolitan centers to satisfy the demands of consumers residing in the area it dominates; distribution then takes place from the metropolis to its hinterland through wholesale and retail contacts. In the reverse direction move both requests for goods and services, and funds to pay for goods and services received, so that the flows are not unidirectional.[21]

The principal railroads and highways planned for a large developing country should connect those central places (present or prospective) that are intended for its regional capitals and its regional and national metropolises. The integration of the presently rural or agricultural population with these regional capitals and larger cities is a problem for local planning and local transport system design.

In the United States each functional economic area or commuting field is currently a relatively self-contained labor market in the short run. The process of attaining maximum agricultural efficiency might be conceptualized as an iterative logical procedure along the following lines:

Starting with the existing labor force and stock of capital in each FEA, we might reallocate these resources within the area (a) to equalize the marginal value products of labor of any given quality among sectors and (b) to equalize the marginal value products of capital among sectors, agricultural and nonagricultural. We may partition agriculture and non-agriculture into as many subsectors as may be required to distinguish significant differences in production functions or processes.

If this initial reallocation were done on the assumption that the FEA is a "point economy," we might next let in real space and allow for the possibility that the marginal value product of labor of a given quality performed at a distance of fifty miles from the central city might be

[21] Berry, Brian J. L., "Approaches to Regional Analysis: A Synthesis," *Annals, Association of American Geographers,* Vol. 54, 1964, pp. 10–11.

smaller than the marginal value product of that labor applied in the central city itself. In other words, within the FEA we would expect to find wage and opportunity cost surfaces for each distinctive kind of labor. These surfaces would have their highest points *at* the central city and would slope downward with increasing distance *from* the central city.

The next logical step would be to compare the marginal value products of labor of given qualities *among* FEAs and also the marginal value products of similar kinds of capital. Then, using spatial-equilibrium concepts we might calculate a pattern for equalizing marginal value products among areas in order to minimize the social and economic costs of migration and capital relocation among FEAs.

Finally, we might consider an optimal pattern of organization in each FEA under present technology and make retraining of the local labor force an alternative to migration. Once again we would equate marginal value products across sectors within each FEA and (globally) among FEAs.

It must be stressed again that an FEA is a labor market area, urban and rural, agricultural and nonagricultural. If the United States should adopt an active labor market policy, it would be logical to try to maintain full employment *in each FEA*. Any worker who could not be employed in a "good" job in the FEA at a given time would be paid while engaged in additional training or retraining. Wages for agricultural workers under such a policy would have to be fully competitive with wages in other sectors of the area's economy at all times.

I mention the existing economic structure of the United States only as it may bear on development planning for countries presently less developed. In the United States the traditional dichotomy between urban and rural has largely disappeared. The city as an economic and cultural entity has surrounded the country. Farmers in most areas must now deal with an essentially urban market for labor, for capital and, increasingly, even for land.

If we refer again to the huge time allocation and interaction matrix we postulated, we may visualize the transformation of the spatial structure of Iowa from 1910 to 1960 as follows:

In 1910, the personal interaction patterns in Iowa's ninety-nine counties would have delineated well over 1,000 "fundamental agricultural communities" of the type described by Galpin. (Iowa has an area of about 57,000 square miles.)

In 1960, the interaction matrix would have partitioned Iowa into approximately twelve commuting fields, averaging about 5,000 square miles each. A careful classification of retail stores and service establishments in towns of different sizes and locations would also have indicated the existence of smaller trade areas averaging about one-fourth the size of the FEA and a set of still smaller trade areas averaging about one-sixteenth. Most of the towns of 1,000 population or less were no longer independent centers of economic activity but served as places of retirement for elderly farm people and as low-cost residential neighborhoods for persons working in larger centers.

In the United States as a whole, the number of "fundamental communities" must have declined from at least 30,000 in 1910 to about 350 in 1960. Transportation revolutions in developing countries may have similar effects. As of 1962, mainland China had about 75,000 rural communes, closely corresponding in number to the administrative villages (townships) of the former regime. Will another thirty years of development reduce the number of relatively self-contained labor markets to less than 1,000?

IV

Modeling Agricultural Production
Within (a) FEAs and (b) Areas Based on Soil and Climate

Potential FEAs or urban fields in the less-developed countries should constitute logical units for forecasting the development of regional population and urban demand for agricultural products. A model such as J. A. C. Brown's could be disaggregated to the level of such urban-oriented areas. The set of areas would have to add up to the (multi-national) regional total; consequently the system would also have to include any areas that represented gaps or interstices between the prospective urban fields. Very sparsely populated mountain and desert areas would be cases in point.

In the United States, total employment in an FEA can be divided into residentiary and export-oriented components. Under present conditions about 60 per cent of the employment in an FEA in the United States is in residentiary activities, such as retail trade, services, and local government. It is this writer's judgment that the residentiary labor forces of two FEAs of equal population are almost perfectly interchangeable. National chains of department stores and other establishments both recognize and reinforce this tendency. Regional and national firms engaged in planning shopping centers, schools, and other facilities also contribute to uniformity.

Export-oriented activities in a national system of FEAs must be defined with respect to typical areas of the FEA size and type. For this purpose, a large metropolitan area must be regarded as equivalent to the close packing of a number of "mononuclear" FEAs each with a population of 500,000 or less residing in the trade area of a regional shopping center. The relation between the locations of the residentiary employment and the export-oriented employment of trade area residents is complicated by the existence of freeways and rapid transit systems.[22]

All agricultural-production activities and all or most manufacturing activities would be classified as export-oriented in an FEA system. Consider an agricultural area covering perhaps 20,000 square miles and having relatively homogeneous soil and climatic conditions. Assume that one corner of this area is included within the commuting field of a rapidly growing city with a relatively high wage and salary structure. Suppose that another corner of the area is included in the commuting field of a city that is growing very slowly and has a considerable amount of low-wage employment. Finally, assume that the two cities are so far apart that the central portion of the agricultural area is at least two-hours' commuting distance from both of them.

Wage rates for hired farm labor (and opportunity costs of the labor of farm operators and their family members) would be high in the neighborhood of the rapidly growing city; lower in the neighborhood of the stagnating city; and considerably lower still in the area remote from both cities. As commuting from the remote area is not feasible, the only alternative to farming would be outmigration, most probably in the direction of the rapidly growing city.

Although soil and climate would permit the same range of agricultural activities in all three portions of the area, the opportunity costs of labor would differ widely. The optimal combinations of agricultural production activities in the three subareas might or might not be sensitive to these differences in the opportunity cost of labor; that would be a matter for empirical determination.

These considerations suggest a two-fold classification of agricultural regions in economic development planning. One set of regions would be distinguished on the basis of such characteristics as soil type, climate, terrain, availability of water, and the like. The other set of regions would

[22] A mononuclear FEA is one in which the commuting field is virtually co-extensive with the major retail trade or shopping area of the central city. See Karl A. Fox, "Strategies for Area Delimitation in a National System of Regional Accounts," paper presented at a joint meeting of the Committee on Regional Accounts and the Committee on Urban Economics, Los Angeles, California, January 23–26, 1968.

be the prospective FEAs or urban fields, with their prospective differences in opportunity costs of farm labor. Where these two types of area boundaries intersect there will be a larger number of segments than are included in either of the two basic sets. These segments could be aggregated within urban fields for some purposes and within homogeneous soil and climatic regions for others. The amount of data gathering and processing necessary to accommodate both sets of purposes should not be much greater than necessary to satisfy either one separately.

Recursive Programming Models
for Homogeneous Agricultural Regions

Richard Day's recursive programming model of an agricultural area in the Mississippi Delta of the United States may well serve as a starting point for agricultural development planning in any subarea that is homogeneous with respect to soil types and climate and is wholly included within an existing or potential urban field.[23]

Day's model defines an array of production activities available for eight kinds of field crops in the Mississippi Delta between 1940 and 1958. With each crop the activities for application of fertilizer at three or four levels and on three different classes of land are defined. The activities are further defined for different technological stages. In the case of cotton, the first technology stage involves share-croppers, mules, and a sufficient acreage of corn to provide feed for the mules. A second stage includes light tractors and a third involves heavy tractors and four-row cultivating equipment. The fourth stage includes mechanical cotton-pickers, flame cultivators, and the use of chemical defoliants.

The model treats the entire cultivable area of the district (1,925,000 acres or 3,000 square miles) as though it were a single profit-maximizing unit. Each new technology comes into the optimal production pattern when it becomes sufficiently profitable relative to existing techniques. For example, as mechanical cotton-pickers were not commercially available before 1946, they were not permitted to enter the solution prior to that year.

Day's model predicts rather well the expulsion of unskilled labor from agriculture in the region, particularly after the advent of the mechanical cotton-picker; it also describes fairly well the year-to-year changes in acreages planted to the different crops.

The first development of such a recursive programming model for a particular agricultural region was a laborious task. The overhead costs

[23] Day, Richard H., *Recursive Programming and Production Response,* Amsterdam, Netherlands, 1963.

of programming and data organization might be reduced considerably if this approach were adopted for a comprehensive set of subareas in a national or multinational region. The initial demands for data may seem excessive in relation to the factual knowledge available in most of the less developed economies. However, the programming model gives a clear indication as to why the data are needed and what level of accuracy would be necessary to make practical distinctions between more and less profitable production activities.

The multinational regions described by J. A. C. Brown are of very large geographic extent, as the total land area of the earth (over 50 million square miles) is to be partitioned into not more than sixteen or twenty regions. The average area of such a region is as large as that of the continental United States. Earl O. Heady and his coworkers have used an exhaustive set of about 150 type-of-farming regions in a linear programming model of the agriculture of the United States. I have not examined the intersections of these 150 farming areas with the 350 or so functional economic areas delineated by Brian Berry. Juxtaposition of the two sets might lead to as many as 500 regions, for each of which a recursive programming model of agricultural production might be formulated.

Spatial-Equilibrium Models of the Agriculture of a Large Country or a Multinational Region

The solutions of such recursive programming models would provide estimates of the production of each agricultural commodity in each subarea, together with estimates of requirements for all inputs. At the same time, a consistent set of demand functions could be formulated for each agricultural commodity in each functional economic area or urban field.

Such a set of demand functions for twenty-four food products was developed by Brandow for the United States as a whole.[24] Because consumption patterns are quite similar over large regions of the United States, the same set of own-price and cross-price elasticities and income elasticities of demand could be applied without much inaccuracy to each of the individual FEAs. For computational purposes, the retail demand functions in each FEA could be approximated by arithmetic straight lines in the neighborhood of the existing price and consumption levels. The estimates of production of each agricultural commodity from the recursive programming models could be aggregated on an FEA basis.

[24] Brandow, George E., *Interrelations Among Demands for Farm Products and Implications for Control of Market Supply*, Pennsylvania State University, Agricultural Experiment Station, University Park, Pa., Bulletin 680, August 1961, see especially pp. 13–18.

If we recognized about twenty different agricultural commodities or commodity groups, we would have at this stage 350 arithmetically linear demand curves for each. We would also have estimates of the quantities of each commodity produced in each of the 350 areas. (Production of some commodities in some areas would, of course, be zero.) To effectuate a spatial-equilibrium model, we would need a 350 by 350 matrix of transportation costs between FEA central cities for each commodity.

If this level of detail for agricultural production planning seems excessive, two points should be kept in mind: (1) For some purposes, the 350 areas could be aggregated into a much smaller number of regions; (2) In a country with clearly marked climatic zones and soil areas, the great majority of the 350 areas will be either consistently surplus or consistently deficit with respect to any particular agricultural commodity for several years at a time. Hence, the structure of interregional price differentials for each commodity is likely to be remarkably stable, though it may be disrupted occasionally by a severe drought or other abnormality.[25]

Given the annual nature of most agricultural production, a set of spatial-equilibrium models within a multinational region could be thought of as a generalized cobweb model in which production in year t was treated as a function of prices in year $t - 1$ and/or support prices and price expectations which were announced or formed toward the end of year $t - 1$. The production of each commodity in each functional economic area in year t would then be taken as predetermined and the values inserted in the FEA demand functions. If the multinational region is considered to be a closed system, the combination of regional production, regional demand functions, and interregional transport costs would determine a set of market prices for all commodities in all regions, along with quantities consumed in each region and quantities shipped between all pairs of regions (again, many of these "shipments" will be zero).

Modeling Interactions between Agriculture and the Rest of the Economy within a Multinational Region

If our emphasis is on the agricultural sector, a highly aggregative model of the other sectors may suffice, as in J. A. C. Brown's scheme.

It is possible to arrange the sectors of an input-output model of the United States economy for 1947 (and presumably for later years) in such a way that most of the direct interindustry commodity flows are

[25] For elaboration of some of these points see Karl A. Fox, "Spatial Equilibrium and Process Analysis in the Food and Agricultural Sector," Chapter 8, pp. 215–233 in Alan S. Manne, and Harry M. Markowitz (ed.), *Studies in Process Analysis,* New York, 1963.

concentrated within four diagonal blocks. Thus, when the twenty-nine-sector input-output table presented by Chenery and Clark is used, the following set of sectors appears to be relatively self contained: fishing, apparel, leather and leather products, processed foods, grain mill products, textiles, lumber and wood products, rubber, chemicals, and agriculture and forestry.[26] Fishing could be excluded from this cluster if desired; the inclusion of lumber and wood products is necessitated by the fact that agriculture and forestry are combined in a single sector by Chenery and Clark.

Similar block diagonal concentrations can be shown for metals and metal products; petroleum and coal products, plus coal mining, petroleum and natural gas; and a group that includes nonmetallic mineral products and minerals, printing and publishing, and paper and paper products (plus industry not elsewhere classified).

The four remaining sectors, electric power, trade, services and transport, provide inputs to all or nearly all of the twenty-nine sectors, including agriculture. In an FEA system, most of the trade and service activities would be included within the residentiary sector, and a good deal of the fuel-based electric power might also be produced and used within the same FEA. Part of the transport activity is of a local character, but a substantial portion is intercity transportation and hence an integral part of the spatial-equilibrium system.

The structure of the input-output matrix just described suggests a number of implications for practical development planning:

(1) The residentiary components of services, trade (particularly retail trade), electric utilities, and local transportation systems should be designed in relation to the development plan for the residentiary sector of each FEA or urban field.

(2) Wholesale warehouses and intercity transport systems should be designed in relation to the planned and emerging system of FEA central cities.

(3) Preliminary development plans might be made for agriculture and forestry and for a set of closely related output-processing and input-supplying industries without too much regard for other industrial sectors.

(4) The preliminary plans for the agricultural and forestry complex could be brought into balance with preliminary plans for the other major industrial complexes in a second-stage calculation or planning operation.

(5) Although the major industrial complexes mentioned are relatively independent of one another as far as interindustry flows are concerned, they are definitely competitive for primary resources such as labor and

[26] Based on rearrangement of matrices in Hollis Chenery and P. G. Clark, *Interindustry Economics,* New York, 1959, pp. 220–230.

capital, and for foreign exchange to pay for imports. Levasseur, for example, has outlined a model in which the levels of output in each industrial sector, generated through an input-output model, are translated into demands for labor by occupation and skill category and the matrix of labor requirements then translated into a set of demands upon the educational and vocational training system.[27]

One could, of course, supplement an input-output flow matrix for a multinational region with a set of capital coefficients, as has been done by Adelman and others.[28]

The proposed recursive or dynamic programming model of agricultural production lends support to the notion of giving a mathematical programming formulation to the multinational economy as a whole. Programming models of national economies have been demonstrated by Adelman and Sparrow,[29] Hollis Chenery, Michael Bruno, and others.

The time-allocation and interaction matrix with which we introduced this paper also seems to call for a normative model of economic and social development planning with an objective function that has not as yet been satisfactorily specified. The "social indicators" movement in the United States and presumably in other countries is pressing social scientists to quantify such an objective function. As an intermediate step an objective function for a multinational region might be defined to include gross regional product, employment (or unemployment), a weighted combination of incomes of various occupational groups, an estimate of the increase in value of "human capital" resulting from education and training, and a (somewhat more speculative) measure of improved access to cultural and recreational services. The quality of life would be measured in part by the per capita forms of these variables.

V

A Model of the World Economy

For our present expository purpose, we will use one element of the objective function to stand for all of its components.

[27] Levasseur, Paul M., *A Study of Inter-Relationships Between Education, Manpower and Economy,* paper prepared for the U.S. Office of Education Symposium on Operations Analysis of Education, Washington, D.C., November 19–22, 1967 (mimeo.).

[28] Adelman, Irma and Frederick T. Sparrow, "Experiments with Linear and Piece-Wise Linear Dynamic Programming Models," in Irma Adelman and Erik Thorbecke (ed.), *The Theory and Design of Economic Development,* Baltimore, 1966, pp. 291–317. See also the comment by Karl A. Fox, pp. 317–326.

[29] Adelman and Sparrow, "Experiments . . ."

We assume that the world economy is divided into sixteen regions. We assume further that region A consists of the centrally planned economies (other than mainland China), region B consists of the industrialized economies not centrally planned, and regions 1–14 consist of regional groups of developing countries. Regions A and B are expected sources of grants, loans, and technical assistance to the other regions and, of course, are related to these regions through trade.

Possible objective functions for regions 1–14 as a group might be

$$\text{Max}\Delta U = \sum_{i=1}^{14} \lambda_i \Delta Y_i, \quad \text{Min}V = \sum_{i=1}^{14} \gamma_i (Y_i - Y_i^*)^2$$

subject to:

$$Y_A \geq k_A$$

$$Y_B \geq k_B$$

$$Y_i \geq k_i, \qquad i = 1, 2, \ldots, 14$$

where Y_i is the gross regional product (GRP) of region i; λ_i is a weight attached by a world policy-making body to a dollar of (increase in) GRP in region i; γ_i is a weight attached by a world policy-making body to squared deviations of actual GRP in region i from a growth path Y_i^* specified as optimal by that body; k_A, k_B and k_i represent minimum permissible levels of the GRP of the respective regions at any given time.

Time indexes and discounting factors are omitted from our notation; however, the variables and constraints should be regarded as applying to a target year (say 1978) or to each year t in a planning period of n years. For example:

$$_{1978}k_A = (1 + e)^{10} {}_{1968}Y_A,$$

where e is the minimum acceptable annual growth rate for the GRP of region A.

Bases for Allocating Total Foreign Assistance among Regions

Assume for expository purposes that the increase in domestic investment-plus-foreign aid required to achieve a planned increase in the GRP of region i is a linear function of that increase in GRP:

$$(I_1^* + H_1^*) - (I_i + H_i) = b_i(Y_i^* - Y_i) \qquad i = 1, 2, \ldots, 14.$$

Suppose also that

$$I_i = c_i Y_i \quad \text{and} \quad I_i^* = c_i Y_i^*.$$

Then

$$(H_i^* - H_i) + c_i(Y_i^* - Y_i) = b_i(Y_i^* - Y_i)$$

and

$$(H_i^* - H_i) = (b_i - c_i)(Y_i^* - Y_i) = d_i(Y_i^* - Y_i).$$

In the above expression, Y_i is the expected GRP of region i in the absence of foreign assistance and Y_i^* the desired value specified by a world policy-making body; c_i is a behavioral coefficient relating domestic investment I_i to GRP_i; and b_i is a coefficient depending on the economic structure of region i which relates a desired change in GRP to the total amount of domestic investment funds I_i plus foreign aid H_i necessary to accomplish this change.

If a regional policy-making body in region i applies relative weights w_{hi} to $(H_i^* - H_i)$ and w_{yi} to $(Y_i^* - Y_i)$, we have

$$H_i^* - H_i = d_i\left(\frac{w_{yi}}{w_{hi}}\right)(Y_i^* - Y_i); \quad \text{let } \beta_i = \left[d_i\frac{w_{yi}}{w_{hi}}\right].$$

Then for regions 1–14 as a group we may write

$$H^* - H = B\left[\sum_{i=1}^{14}\frac{\beta_i}{B}(Y_i^* - Y_i)\right]$$

where

$$B = \frac{1}{14}\sum_{i=1}^{14}\beta_i.$$

The relative weights or tradeoffs between an increase in GRP and an increase in foreign aid *might* vary from region to region.

If taken literally, the above formulation implies that the amount of foreign aid required in region i is a function only of the planned change in GRP in region i. As a matter of fact, all sixteen regions are linked through trade, so it appears intuitively that H_i^* will depend not only on Y_i^* but on Y_A, Y_B, and all the Y_j^*'s, where $j = 1, 2, 3, \ldots)i(, \ldots,$ 13, 14. Recognition of these linkages in an operational way is possible only in a model which treats the world economy as a closed system.

Endogenous and Exogenous Variables in a World Model

A two-region example will illustrate the chief difference between an open model for a single region and a closed model for the world economy:

Region 1:

$$Y_1 = C_1 + I_1 + G_1 + E_1 - M_1$$

$$C_1 = c_1Y_1$$

$$I_1 = i_1Y_1$$

$$M_1 = m_1Y_1$$

Region 2:

$$Y_2 = C_2 + I_2 + G_2 + E_2 - M_2$$

$$C_2 = c_2 Y_2$$

$$I_2 = i_2 Y_2$$

$$M_2 = m_2 Y_2$$

In region 1, we may (initially and naively) assume that E_1 (exports) is exogenous; G_1 (government expenditure) is our main policy instrument. Four variables, Y_1 (gross regional product), C_1 (consumption), I_1 (domestic private investment), and M_1 (imports), are regarded as endogenous.

In our two-region model, of course, $E_1 = M_2$ and $E_2 = M_1$, so the export variables become *endogenous* to the closed system, which may be displayed as follows:

"Leading" Endogenous Variable	Y_1	C_1	I_1	Y_2	C_2	I_2	M_1	M_2	E_1	E_2	G_1	G_2		RHS
Y_1	1	-1	-1				1		-1		-1		$=$	0
C_1	$-c_1$	1	0		0									0
I_1	$-i_1$	0	1											0
Y_2				1	-1	-1		1		-1		-1		0
C_2		0		$-c_2$	1	0								0
I_2				$-i_2$	0	1								0
M_1	$-m_1$						1							0
M_2				$-m_2$				1						0
E_1								-1	1	0				0
E_2							-1			1				0

This display is not in conventional matrix form. The vector to the extreme left is simply a list to help the reader identify rows of the coefficient matrix with equations in the models for region 1 and region 2. The vector of ten endogenous and two exogenous variables, normally written as a column vector to the right of the coefficient matrix, is displayed as a set of twelve "column headings," each of which is to be multiplied by the coefficients in its column. Thus, the first row becomes

$$Y_1 - C_1 - I_1 + M_1 - E_1 - G_1 = 0,$$

or, rearranging terms,

$$Y_1 = C_1 + I_1 + G_1 + E_1 - M_1,$$

the first equation in the model for region 1.

In this system there are now ten endogenous variables and only two exogenous or autonomous ones, G_1 and G_2. Because of feedbacks through region 2, the multiplier effect upon Y_1 of an increase in G_1 is larger than if imports M_1 were a genuine and complete leakage from the economy of region 1. For example, let

$$c_1 = c_2 = 0.5, i_1 = i_2 = 0.2, \text{ and } m_1 = m_2 = 0.3.$$

If M_1 were simply a leakage, the multiplier in region 1 would be

$$\frac{\Delta Y_1}{\Delta G_1} = \frac{1}{1 - 0.5 - 0.2 + 0.3} = \frac{1}{1 - 0.4} = \frac{1}{0.6} = 1.67.$$

However, in the two-region system the corresponding multiplier becomes

$$\frac{\partial Y_1}{\partial G_1} = \frac{(1 - 0.5 - 0.2 + 0.3)}{(1 - 0.5 - 0.2 + 0.3)^2 - (0.3)^2} = \frac{0.6}{0.36 - 0.09} = 2.22.$$

If the policy maker in each region understands the structure of the complete system he will presumably take account of the fact that his multiplier is 2.22 rather than 1.67 in deciding by how much government expenditures should be modified.

A four-region model of the world economy opens up the problem of multilateral trade. If we express the G_i (government expenditures in region i) as functions of the Y_i, $i = 1, 2, 3, 4$ we obtain

$$G_1 = k_1 Y_1 - m_{12} Y_2 - m_{13} Y_3 - m_{14} Y_4$$

$$G_2 = -m_{21} Y_1 + k_2 Y_2 - m_{23} Y_3 - m_{24} Y_4$$

$$G_3 = -m_{31} Y_1 - m_{32} Y_2 + k_3 Y_3 - m_{34} Y_4$$

$$G_4 = -m_{41} Y_1 - m_{42} Y_2 - m_{43} Y_3 + k_4 Y_4,$$

where

$$k_i = 1 - c_i - i_i + \sum_{\substack{j=1 \\ (i \neq j)}}^{4} m_{ji}; \qquad i = 1, 2, 3, 4.$$

Or,

$$
\begin{bmatrix} G_1^* \\ G_2^* \\ G_3^* \\ G_4^* \end{bmatrix}
=
\begin{bmatrix}
k_1 & -m_{12} & -m_{13} & -m_{14} \\
-m_{21} & k_2 & -m_{23} & -m_{24} \\
-m_{31} & -m_{32} & k_3 & -m_{34} \\
-m_{41} & -m_{42} & -m_{43} & k_4
\end{bmatrix}
\begin{bmatrix} Y_1^* \\ Y_2^* \\ Y_3^* \\ Y_4^* \end{bmatrix}
$$

or
$$ G^* = (k - m)Y^* $$

where the Y_i^* are desired values of GRP and the G_i^* are the values of government expenditures needed to attain the Y_i^*.

Obviously, this model could be extended to any number of regions forming a closed system—one that includes the entire world economy. If our chief policy instrument is foreign aid, H, and if government expenditure from domestic revenues in each region i, G_i, is assumed to be a linear function of Y_i (say, $G_i = g_i Y_i$), we may write down the matrix equation

$$ H^* = (k - M)Y^*, $$

where

$$ k_i = 1 - c_i - i_i - g_i + \sum_{\substack{j=1 \\ (i \neq j)}}^{n} m_{ji} $$

and n is the number of regions into which the world economy is subdivided (in our opening example, 16).

The representation of international trade in this model is, of course, much too rigid, and the structures of the regional economies much too aggregative, for policy use. Brown's paper suggests the directions, though not the extent, of needed elaboration of the regional models.

A Detailed Model of the Agricultural Sector

We may recapitulate some of our earlier suggestions as follows:

(1) Expand the agricultural sector in each region into (say) twenty commodities or commodity groups; the same set of twenty must be used in all regions. (a) Represent consumer demand in each region by a Frisch-Brandow matrix, so that

$$ f = Bp_o + \alpha + \gamma(y^{1*} - s^1 - y^{21*} - y^{41*}) $$

in each region; p_o is a vector of base-year prices. The variables in parentheses are defined as in equations 13 and 14 of Brown's paper.

(b) Add other domestic demands to household demand and specify a linear (or piecewise linear) function approximating total domestic demand for each commodity or group.

(2) Obtain regional supply functions and production estimates (S_{ij}) by various means depending on the data and research base available; assume the same base-year price vector p_o in estimating the S_{ij} as is used in estimating the quantities demanded for regional use (D_{ij}).

(3) Calculate exports, $X_{ij} = S_{ij} - D_{ij}$, where i ranges over fourteen less-developed regions plus regions A and B, while j ranges over twenty agricultural commodities. Here, S_{ij} denotes quantity of commodity j produced in region i and D_{ij} denotes quantity of commodity j demanded in region i.

(4) Calculate regional imports of *inputs* through an input-output matrix and regional imports of goods for consumption by means of demand functions, as proposed by J. A. C. Brown.

(5) Assume for the moment that exports go into, and imports come out of, a set of world "pools," one for each commodity.

We have discussed in Section IV the detailed structure (within a single large country or region) of a set of spatial-equilibrium models, with each year's supplies of agricultural products determined by means of recursive programming models for subregions. (Dynamic programming models might alternatively be employed for estimating supplies, depending on our purposes.) Also, we commented on the probable stability of the price structure of each agricultural commodity within a large country or region; "price structure" here referring to differentials among the prices prevailing at the different central cities of FEA or urban fields which constitute the emerging national or large-region system of cities.

So far, we have not discussed the possibility of exports from one multinational region to others among the sixteen, or the corresponding possibility of imports, at the appropriate level of detail.

If commodity price differentials between FEAs within each of the sixteen large regions are stable, it means that the price of a commodity in each of $n - 1$ FEAs will be a linear function of its price in the remaining FEAs. If a single currency is used throughout the region, and if transportation charges between all pairs of FEA central cities are fixed, a price increase of 10 cents per unit in one FEA should be accompanied by a price increase of 10 cents per unit in each of the other $n - 1$ FEAs. Also, if the demand function for a commodity in each FEA is linear, the change in the quantity demanded in each FEA is a linear function of the change in price. If the price in every FEAs increases by the same amount, the slopes of the demand functions in all n of the FEA can be added to give the slope of an aggregative demand function for the region as a whole.[30]

If such stability of price structures prevails within each region i, we can focus our attention on the prices of the twenty agricultural commodities at an FEA central city which is also a major seaport in region i or a major center for interregional trade by rail or motor transport. We need one such city in each of the sixteen large regions in order to complete our world model with respect to interregional trade.

If the proposed recursive programming models of agricultural production in subareas are realistic, the production response to a set of real base-year prices should make export surpluses available for some commodities in some regions at the base-year prices.

Then, given a set of transport costs between the selected port cities or other transport centers in each region, we could compute an optimal pattern of interregional shipments for each commodity and a resulting structure of price differentials for each commodity among the sixteen port cities. The effects of tariffs, subsidies and quotas maintained by any region or regions could also be taken into account in such a model.

The result (after some iterations) should be a price structure that integrates the internal small-area price patterns in each region with the pattern of price differentials among the sixteen regions, as reflected at their port cities. The sizes we have specified for potential FEAs or urban fields, and hence for agricultural production planning areas, would imply as many as 5,000 to 10,000 basic agricultural production programming units in the complete model of the world economy emphasizing agriculture.

A Two-Level (World and Regional) Model for the Allocation of Foreign Aid and Technical Assistance

In a very different context, Francis P. McCamley has combined the two-level planning model of Kornai and Liptak and the decomposition principle of Dantzig and Wolfe.[31]

For our present purposes, we assume seventeen "teams" of development planners, one each for the sixteen world regions assumed and one representing a world-level policy-making body.

Some of the resources available to each region i are locationally spe-

---

[30] See Fox, Karl A., "Spatial Price Equilibrium . . . ,"

[31] McCamley, Francis P., *Activity Analysis Models of Educational Institutions*, doctoral dissertation, Iowa State University, Ames, Iowa, 1967.

cific to that region and are allocable by policy makers in that region. In any given year, each resource of this type is subject to a capacity constraint. Hence, the set of inequations in a mathematical programming model of each region's economy would lead to sixteen diagonal blocks in a complete model of the world economy. In view of the preceding section, however, the fact that some resources are locationally specific is consistent with the existence of a large amount of interregional trade in the inputs and outputs of production activities in the various regions.

In addition, we assume the existence of a particular set (vector) of resources that are suitable for foreign aid and technical assistance, including assistance in developing the agricultural sectors of all regions. Each of the potential foreign aid and technical assistance resources is regarded as a world pool; each of these resources H_j, $j = 1, 2, \ldots,$ m, is to be allocated among the i less-developed regions, $i = 1, 2, 3,$ $\ldots, 14, and$ regions A and B.

We must ascribe to the team representing a world-level policy-making body an objective function which permits it to "price" units of all outputs in all regions in a common currency. Ideally, this function would include both economic and noneconomic aspects of human welfare, as implied in Section II.

An iterative process could be carried out between the world-level policy-making body and the regional teams. For any *tentative* set of allocations of aid resources H_{ji} to region i, region i would compute optimal internal adjustments and report back to the world-level team. The world-level team would then revise its allocations, and each regional team would again compute its optimal internal adjustments. The final result of the iterative process should be an allocation of foreign aid and technical assistance resources that would equate the marginal value products of each foreign assistance resource among all of the sixteen regions, as viewed in terms of the objective function of the world-level policy-making team.

Relationship Between Agriculture and Other Sectors

Agriculture in the Open Economy

JOHN C. H. FEI

CORNELL UNIVERSITY

AND

GUSTAV RANIS

YALE UNIVERSITY

THE SIGNIFICANCE of agricultural stagnation in the economic development of the less-developed world has been increasingly recognized. Concern with the race between food and mouths and for the resultant need to activate the agricultural sector is so widespread today, not only in the profession but among policy makers, that it need hardly be elaborated on. Nor, as we may be quick to realize, is this insight really new. In fact, it may be said that evidences of a deep concern with this problem are discernible at the very beginnings of economic science. As agrarian stagnation was understood by the physiocrats, the *produit net* of the soil was used to finance the sterile classes outside of agriculture, permitting no marked upward deviation from the circular flow depicted in their *Tableau Economique*. The classicists, especially Ricardo and Malthus, analyzed the course of stagnation more fully in predicting the long-run cessation of progress. Later in the same century the Marxists shifted the emphasis to the petering out of profits in early commercial capitalism as a causal factor, an approach that led to similar somber predictions for the long run. All these essentially pessimistic views went unchallenged for more than a century, without any competing thesis of growth being elaborated. After the Second World War, interest in problems of long-term growth was revived. This renaissance was manifested in the one-sector models of growth for the industrially mature economy (Solow, Swan, Phelps, *et al.*)—with which we shall not be concerned in this paper—and in the theories of development in a two-sector under-developed world (e.g., Lewis, Leibenstein, Jorgenson, Fei & Ranis, *et al.*), with which we are concerned.

The physiocrats, the classicists, and Marx looked for regularities in the performance of the system they were observing, an approach that lends itself readily to the conclusion that ultimate stagnation is inevitable. The modern view of growth as a feature of a vigorous dualistic society shifting its center of gravity tends to be more optimistic, even though concern with the basic problem of departure from quasi-equilibrium continues to predominate. There can be, in short, little doubt that the assumptions as well as the growth-theoretic constructs of each period are imbedded in actual world conditions as seen through the eyes of the contemporary analyst. Thus, from a long-run historical perspective it may be instructive to think of four types of economic systems that occur in historical sequence: (1) the agrarian society, (2) the open agrarian society, (3) the dualistic society, and (4) the industrially mature society.

It is our view that we are witnessing in most of the contemporary underdeveloped world the attempt of countries to make the transition between open agrarianism and dualism. We must recognize as "normal" the condition in which such attempts are being frustrated by the inability to shake off the endemic structural characteristics of agrarianism. It is precisely for this reason that the study of the causes of stagnation in the open agrarian society—a major concern of this paper—is crucial for an understanding of the dynamics of the contemporary less-developed world in its attempt to activate agriculture in behalf of the process of economic development.

In Section 1 we present a brief statement of the causes of long-term stagnation in the closed agrarian system. Section 2 deals with the break-down of the closed agrarian system under the impact of penetration of foreign trade and the consequential restructuring of the economy. In Section 3 the essential economic functions that must be performed in open agrarianism will be analyzed. Section 4 describes the propellant forces that dictate the performance of the open agrarian economy over time. Finally, in Section 5, the forces of stagnation that continue to grip the open agrarian economy will be identified and the conditions for successful transition to dynamic dualism elaborated.

SECTION 1

Causation of Agrarian Stagnation

Let us begin with some of the basic notions of the eighteenth century physiocrats, who envisioned a circular-flow mechanism between two sectors of the economy: a preponderant agricultural sector and a smaller service sector. As shown in Figure 1, the total output of food (Q-units) of the agricultural sector either flows back to that sector to be consumed by the farmers (H-units) or moves to the service sector (R-units) to be consumed by the workers in that sector. In turn, the output of the service sector T either flows back to the agricultural sector (in the form of con-sumer goods or subsidiary productive services) to sustain agricultural productivity (A-units) or is "consumed" by the nobility, the church, and the aristocracy (C-units) to sustain their cultural, religious and military activities. While, to the eternal credit of the physiocrats, the regularity and stability of such a circular-flow system is identified, it was left to the classicists, about sixty years later, to give, in their positive theory of stagnation, a causal explanation of the same phenomenon.

From our point of view, the most important analytical contribution of the classical economists is the understanding of the role of labor and the problem of the existence (at least implied) of a labor surplus. Sup-pose the total labor force of L units is allocated to two sectors in such a

Figure 1

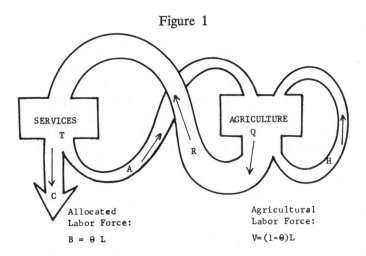

SERVICES
T

AGRICULTURE
Q

R

A

H

C

Allocated
Labor Force:

$B = \theta L$

Agricultural
Labor Force:

$V = (1-\theta)L$

way that θL units are workers in the service sector and $(1 - \theta)\ L$ units remain as farmers. Then

(1) $\theta = R/Q$ (or $R = \theta Q$).

This indicates a basic fact of agrarianism: food must be allocated to the agriculture and service sectors in the same proportion as population is distributed.[1] It follows that the expansion of agricultural productivity leading to the availability of R as an agricultural surplus (to sustain the workers in the nonagricultural sector) is a prerequisite to the emergence of the service sector and the expansion of its size θ relative to the total labor force. This physiocratic idea of an agricultural surplus is indeed a powerful tool for the analysis of growth phenomena for all economies with an agricultural base. It should be noted, moreover, that the agricultural surplus defined in this way is quite independent of whether or not the marginal product of labor in agriculture is zero, a question on which, in our view, all too much energy has been expended.

The basic arithmetic of an agricultural surplus can be summarized with the help of three indicators, namely θ, p, and c, where θ is the surplus labor ratio, i.e., the fraction of L in the service sector, $p = Q/L(1 - \theta)$ i.e., the remaining farmers' average productivity, and $c = Q/L$, i.e., the per capita consumption standard in the economy as a whole. From (1) we have

(2) $p\,(1 - \theta) = c$ (or $1 - \theta = c/p$)

demonstrating that the farmers' fraction of the total $1 - \theta$ must be equal to the consumption standard as a fraction of agricultural productivity (c/p).

The relationships within this triplet θ, p, c can be quickly summarized in Figure 2a in which the vertical axis is used to measure p and c and the horizontal axis (measured to the left) is used to measure θ. Let the distance oo' represent *one* unit (i.e., if the value of θ is given by point "m" then $o'm$ is $1 - \theta$). Suppose points p_o and c_o (with $c_o < p_o$) are indicated on the vertical axis. Let point q_o be the point of intersection of the straight lines $o'p_o$ and $c_o c$ (horizontal line); then the distance $q_o c_o$ is the equilibrium surplus labor ratio θ and $c_o/p_o = 1 - \theta$. (This is easily seen from (2). Thus, when p increases (as in p_o, p', p'', p_e . . .), the value of θ will increase (as in q_o, z', z'', z_e . . .) *if c remains constant* at c_o. On the other hand, the value of c will increase (as in q_o, q', q'', q_e . . .) *if θ remains constant* at θ_o. It is economic common sense

---

[1] Under the simplifying assumption of no wage gap or consumption standard differential between the two sectors. The (likely) existence of a real world differential could easily be accommodated.

that higher agricultural productivity p will lead either to a higher fraction of the population allocated to the service sector θ or a higher standard of consumption c. These two alternative ways of using the increased agricultural surplus may be referred to as the labor allocation adjustment (when c remains constant) and the consumption adjustment (when θ remains constant).

Figure 2

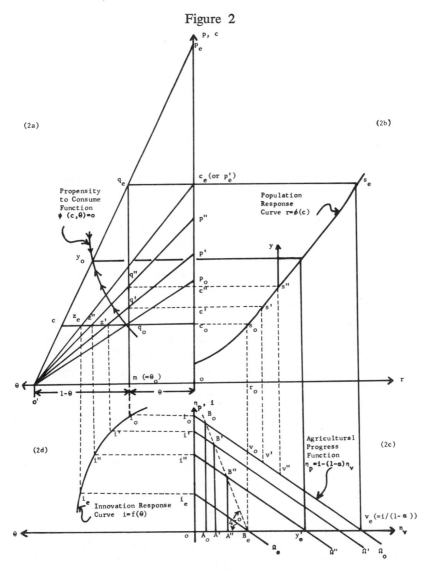

The above arithmetic of agricultural surplus can be the starting point for developing a thesis of agrarian stagnation. First, the very phenomenon of agrarian stagnation itself must be defined in terms of the long-run stability of the triplet θ, p, and c. Using a Cobb-Douglas production function (with fixity of land),[2] we may relate the rate of technological change "i" (i.e., the intensity of agricultural innovation) and the growth rate of agricultural population $\eta_v = \eta_{(1-\theta)L}$ [3] as follows:

(3a) $Q = e^{it}v^{\alpha}$ (v is agricultural population)

(b) $\eta_p = i - (1 - \alpha)\eta_v$ where

(c) $p = \dfrac{Q}{v}$.

Equation 3b is represented by the negatively sloped straight line (the line labeled Ω_o) in Figure 2c in which η_p is measured on the vertical and η_v on the horizontal axis. This curve may be called the agricultural progress function and reflects the struggle between innovation and the law of diminishing returns. Thus, for a given value of innovational intensity, "i" (represented as the vertical intercept of the Ω_o line), the rate of increase in agricultural productivity declines as the population growth rate increases. The point v_e (where $v = i/(1 - \alpha)$) on the horizontal axis is the point of "long-run stagnation" as p and v take on stationary values (since $\eta_p = 0$ along the horizontal axis). Any thesis of long-run agrarian stagnation must explain how such an equilibrium point on the horizontal axis is reached in the long run.

It is frequently argued that any initial productivity gain in agriculture is bound to lead to upward revisions of the consumption standard. When the increased agricultural surplus is used entirely for such consumption adjustment, to assume the extremal case of this alternative, we have the Jorgenson-Classical thesis of stagnation.[4] For this thesis a population response curve can be postulated by

(4a) $r = \phi(c)$ (population response)

where

(b) $r = \eta_L$ (rate of growth of *total* population),

[2] If land is not entirely fixed, this can be treated as an additional component of innovational intensity.

[3] Where $\eta_x = \dfrac{dx}{dt} / x$, i.e., the rate of growth of x.

[4] See D. W. Jorgenson, "The Development of a Dual Economy," *Economic Journal*, LXXI, 1961; also his "Testing Alternative Theories of the Development of a Dual Economy," in I. Adelman and E. Thorbecke (ed.), *The Theory and Design of Economic Development*, Baltimore, 1966.

and is represented by the positively sloped curve in Figure 2b. This relation simply states that the population growth rate is "controlled" by the consumption standard c (measured on the vertical axis in Figure 2b) and leads us to the conclusion that the operation of a "consumption adjustment" mechanism is likely to culminate in ultimate stagnation.

To illustrate this, let us start from our initial values of p_o, c_o, and θ_o in Figure 2a. We can then determine point s_o on the population response curve in Figure 2b. In case no relative reallocation of labor occurs, i.e., if θ is constant, $\eta_v = r$.[5] Thus we can obtain point v_o on the agricultural progress function in Figure 2c. Since η_p is positive at v_o, the value of p will increase to say p', in the next period (Figure 2a), and the value of c will increase to c'. This, via points s' (Figure 2b) and v' (Figure 2c), further depresses the rate of increase of p (i.e., from v_o to v'). Nevertheless, since v' is still positive, p continues to increase following the sequence p_o, p', p'', ... The long-run stagnation equilibrium position is then given by the triplet p_e, c_e, and θ_o corresponding to the points s_e on the population response curve and v_e on the agricultural progress function. (Conversely, starting from an initial value of p greater than p_e, p will decrease to p_e in the long run.) Thus, according to the Jorgenson-Classical mechanism, the long-run stability of p_e, c_e, and θ_o, as well as r, is due to the fact that the population growth rate is controlled by the consumption standard in such a way as to suppress or encourage labor productivity gains when consumption and productivity levels are too high or too low respectively.[6]

The above represents a modified version of the Jorgenson-Classical thesis of stagnation. The modification comes about through our postulation of the coexistence of two sectors—a point strongly emphasized by the physiocrats, but generally neglected in the classical writings. We have thus shown that, under the assumption of the constancy of θ (the labor surplus ratio), the salient features of the Jorgenson-Classical thesis apply equally well to the two-sector economy.

On the other hand, if the increased agricultural surplus is "used" via a labor reallocation adjustment, we have a possible alternative thesis of

---

[5] $\eta_v = \eta_{(1-\theta)L} = \eta_{(1-\theta)} + \eta_L$. Thus $\eta_v = \eta_L$ if θ is constant.

[6] To be more precise, this is the Jorgenson "trap" case. Jorgenson, unlike the classicists, also presents a "take-off" case according to which population growth is no longer responsive to increases in the consumption standard while η_p is still positive. For example, if the population response curve in Figure 2b has the shape $s_o s'' y$, the rate of growth of per capita output η_p will stabilize at level v'' (Figure 2c), and continued growth, rather than stagnation, will result.

stagnation.[7] For this thesis the essential assumption is that the innovation intensity "i" is inversely related to θ, a relation described by

(5) $i = f(\theta)$ with $f'(\theta) < o$,

and represented by the negatively sloped "innovation response" curve, in Figure 2d. The justification for this relation lies essentially in the fact that a part of the labor force in the agricultural sector is engaged in investment in overhead capital in the agrarian economy and that its presence in that sector is necessary to sustain technical progress. Such progress involves long-term improvements in crop practices, many of which are barely perceptible over the centuries. But even this progress is possible only where terracing, irrigation, and drainage networks, for example, are kept from falling into disrepair. In fact, however, many a keen observer has noted with Ester Boserup that, "besides revenue, they (feudal landlords and kings) need servants, bodyguards and soldiers, and these requirements set an upper limit to the investment activity they are willing to organize. . . . Feudal landlords and government are likely to reduce the village population too much in their desire for soldiers, servants and luxuries." [8] It is the use of labor in maintaining the agricultural infrastructure from one period to the next that may thus be measured. If too much labor is drawn out of the farm sector by the food surplus, the intensity of innovation in agriculture declines.

The technology-adjustment mechanism works as follows: starting again from the initial position at p_o, c_o and θ_o or point q_o, we determine the point i_o (on the innovation response curve), and the point i_o on the vertical axis of Figure 2c. For this i, as we have seen, the agricultural-progress function, labeled Ω_o in Figure 2c, is determined. On the other hand, given the initial value of c_o, we can determine the total population growth rate at the point r_o (on the horizontal axis of Figure 2b) or point B_e (on the horizontal axis of Figure 2c). Since θ is no longer constant, r_o, the rate of increase of *total* population and η_v, the rate of increase of *agricultural* population, are different, and must satisfy the relation $\eta_v = r - \eta_p$.[9] To achieve this, let us construct, from the point B_e, a 45-degree line B_eB_o obtaining the point B_o on the agricultural progress function. It should be noted that $A_oB_o = A_oB_e = \eta_p$ by virtue of the 45-de-

---

[7] See Fei and Ranis, "Agrarianism, Dualism and Economic Development," in Adelman and Thorbecke, *op. cit.*, for a more systematic critical evaluation of the Jorgenson-Classical thesis.

[8] Ester Boserup, *The Conditions of Agricultural Growth*, Chicago, 1965, p. 96.

[9] This follows directly from $\eta_v = \eta_{(1-\theta)} + \eta_L$ (as $v = (1 - \theta)L$) and $\eta_p + \eta_{(1-\theta)} = 0$ (by equation 2, when c is constant).

gree construction. Since OA_o on the horizontal axis measures η_v, it is true at point A_o (and only at point A_o) that $\eta_v = r - \eta_p$. Thus the initial value of η_v is located uniquely at B_o. Since η_p is positive here, p will increase in the next period, assume to p' (Figure 2a), and, *as long as the consumption standard remains constant,* the value of θ will increase (from q_o to z', etc.) in Figure 2a. This calls into action the technology-adjustment mechanism by depressing the innovation intensity (from i_o to i') on the innovation response curve. A new agricultural progress function Ω' (passing through the point i' on the vertical axis) is obtained at a position parallel to the Ω_o curve. Using the same reasoning as before, given a constant r, the new value for η_v and η_p can then be located at B'. In this fashion the rate of increase of p is continuously depressed and the value of θ continuously increased over time. The long-run equilibrium position is then given by c_o, p_e, and z_e with the relevant agricultural progress function Ω_e in Figure 2c intersecting the horizontal axis at B_e at a point corresponding to the fixed population growth rate r_o.

Any explanation of long-run stagnation in the agrarian system which relies wholly on either the consumption-adjustment or the technology-adjustment mechanism is bound to be off the mark. What is clearly called for is a synthesis of the two mechanisms. This is a natural synthesis, because in the real world, any increase in the agricultural surplus will, in fact, be used partly to increase consumption c and partly to induce greater labor reallocation θ. A host of economic, institutional, and political factors such as the necessity for carrying on feudal wars, the nobility's desire for services, pressure from the cultivator, etc., will operate at all times to determine this division, which may be described as a "propensity to consume" function. This function is represented by the equation:

$$(6) \qquad \psi(\theta, c) = o \quad \text{with } d\theta/dc > o$$

and by the positively sloped curve in Figure 2a. All that is assumed is that some of the increase in agricultural surplus will be absorbed by the consumption-adjustment mechanism and some by the allocation-adjustment mechanism. It is easy to see how the twin forces working toward stagnation can be depicted in diagrammatic terms. When labor productivity increases, for example, the increased consumption standard c will induce additional population increase, and the increased labor allocation θ will reduce innovational intensity; both forces operate to put a brake on productivity expansion. In the case indicated in Figure 2, the long-run equilibrium position is reached at some point y_o in (2a) and some point y'_o in (2c) signifying the long-run stability of the triplet θ, p, and c, as well as i and r.[10]

The above, then, represents our analysis of the economic forces that operate to lock the agrarian economy into a state of long-run stagnation. To be sure, the economy is getting bigger (as both i and r are positive). However, r and i are so "regulated" that biological reproduction r and economic progress i compensate each other in such a way that there will be no marked change in the structure of the economy in the long run. A steady stream of surplus labor supported by surplus food is constantly being funnelled into the service sector at a consumption standard c that is often close to the subsistence level.

Long-run stagnation in such an agrarian setting results in the establishment of certain institutional relations essential to the discharge of the basic economic functions of the system. Crucial among these functions are the delivery of the labor force to the service sector and the delivery of food (R in Figure 1) to sustain these workers. These magnitudes are not determined by pure market forces, and the obligation to deliver is not a commercial contract. The most common historical example is that the nobility, which consumes the output of the service sector (C in Figure 1), is at the same time a landed aristocracy—whether it resides on or near the land (e.g., the feudalistic lords of medieval Europe, the daimyo of Japan) or not (e.g., the scholarly landed gentry in Chinese history, the Church in Europe). It is in its landowning capacity under the feudal system that this nobility exacts labor and/or agricultural output as a statutory obligation. The conversion of such a closed agrarian society into open agrarianism under the impact of outside forces must be accompanied by the development of new institutional arrangements to replace the old social order. It is to this aspect of the problem that we shall now turn.

SECTION 2

Transition into Open Agrarianism

For most underdeveloped countries with a colonial heritage—and this description applies to almost all contemporary underdeveloped countries —what may be termed "open agrarianism" appeared as a result of the

---

[10] As a check of the consistency of our reasoning, the four unknowns c, θ, r, and i are solved for simultaneously in 3b [with $\eta_P = o$, and equations 4, 5, and 6] to obtain their long-run equilibrium values.

penetration of the closed agrarian system by a new economic agent, namely, the foreigner. Making his debut typically as a trader, the foreigner takes on successively more important economic functions. He is instrumental in the creation of a new sector in the agrarian society, the export production sector. Thus we now have three domestic production sectors to deal with (see Figure 3): agriculture, services and exports. The export production sector generally relies on the exploitation of a cheap labor supply and/or of natural resources productive of specific raw materials, either agricultural (fibers, tropical fruits) or mineral. Inputs flowing into this sector are food R' produced by the agricultural sector and services produced by the service sector K. The output Q_E, of course, flows entirely to the foreign market, i.e., the foreign sector as indicated in Figure 3.

The role of the foreigner expands steadily from that of trader to that of entrepreneur servicing the export sector or actually taking over the direction of its activities. Progressively, the service sector ministers less to the feudal needs of the nobility or the Church and concentrates more on meeting the demands of the export sector for the services of banking, shipping, insurance, warehousing, etc. At a later stage this sector will also turn to the construction of trade-related social-overhead capital

Figure 3

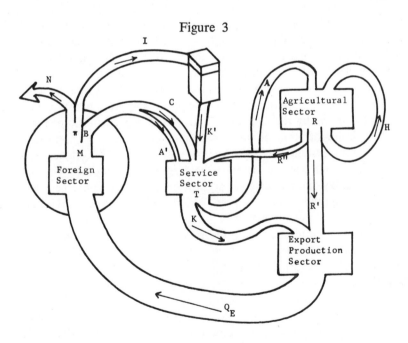

such as electric power, transportation, and housing. Such services flow into the export production sector as an input K.

Another important outflow from the service sector is to the agricultural sector A as an inducement or compensation for the food supply, R' and R'', given up and provided to the workers employed in both the service and export sectors. The principal goods delivered, at least in the early developmental stages, include manufactured goods destined for rural consumption (e.g., cloth, kerosene, candles, sewing machines) which the service sector first imported from abroad A'. Certain domestic services performed by labor employed by the service sector may be added to these goods in the course of the transfer. However, since there is not much value added, for simplicity, we can let $A = A'$.

The economic functions of this "new" service sector thus differ drastically from those of the "old." Instead of serving the interests of the landed aristocracy, its primary function is now to serve the interests of the export-oriented foreigners and their domestic commercial allies. This transition may not occur without a struggle as the feudal aristocracy resists the inroads of the new commercial spirit, and the foreigners attempt to gain adherent allies within the local power structure. The struggle may go on for many decades, even centuries, with the foreigners likely to win out ultimately. Moreover, when the penetration from abroad isn't artificially delayed—as it was in Japan—it is often accompanied by political upheaval. When the new economic order of the open colonial economy is established, the inflow into the service sector will include, in addition to the already referred to food R'' and imported consumer goods A' ultimately destined for the agricultural sector, two other important items. The first is imported luxury consumer goods C for use by the foreigners and by the new domestic commercial class. The importation of these consumer goods may be important for the agrarian system since in the material sense it introduces a completely different way of life into the traditional economy. The service sector thus becomes in essence a "port city," an economic and cultural enclave within the agrarian system. The second is the commercial capital stock K' consisting of inventory, credit in foreign banks, warehouses, transportation equipment, etc., the services of which are used primarily to facilitate the export trade. (Hence in Figure 3, K as well as K' can be identified.) The cause of the addition to the capital stock is "investment" I which consists of the part of the export proceeds M utilized for such trade-oriented capital accumulation.

The establishment of the new service sector introduces into the agrarian economy new agents (the foreigners and a new domestic commercial class), new factors of production (commercial capital stock K'), new production activities (exports), and a new consumption horizon (A and C). What is perhaps most important of all, however, is the introduction and gradual acceptance of a new mode of rational economic behavior. The new life is characterized by an insatiable appetite for economic acquisition which, although taken for granted in contemporary elementary economics textbooks, nevertheless represents a radically different value system from the set of feudal relationships that preceded it. The export goods Q_E are converted into foreign exchange M, which is disposed of as either current expenses B (including A' and C introduced above) or as profits π. Moving out of his exclusive role of trader, the profit-oriented foreigner may take over some of the entrepreneurial tasks in the export production sector itself. Not infrequently he moves into the political sphere as well in order to maintain the necessary minimum levels of government stability and administrative efficiency. All such expansion, the extent of which will vary from case to case, is guided by one primary motive, the enhancement and safeguarding of export-related profits. This maximization of profit is the basic purpose of economic life in open agrarianism. This point is essential for a full understanding of the agrarian system.

Commercial profits π, which are the immediate objective of this activity, can in turn be either reinvested (I leading to the accumulation of capital stock) or repatriated N. The fact that profit repatriation is possible insures that not all the savings generated by the export activity will necessarily be used for capital accumulation within the system. If continuously profitable export potentialities are anticipated, profits are likely to be reinvested in the service or export sector or both. To the extent that such prospects are dim or uncertain, profits will be repatriated and capital accumulation will decline or cease. Thus, it appears that profit repatriation could conceivably be blamed—as it, in fact, has been—as the primary economic evil of colonialism, because it signifies that the foreigner generally regards the economy as an enclave and refuses to invest beyond what is necessary to augment future repatriable profits. Certainly, frustration in the development effort is the norm of performance of this open agrarian system, as observed on the contemporary scene. But as we will see below, this is for reasons quite separate from the phenomenon of insufficient reinvestment. Important as "profit repatriation" may be as a contributing factor, with the vagaries of such exogenous forces as discovery, conditions in international markets, and exhaustion of mineral deposits, it should not be regarded as a primary cause of long-run stagnation. The thesis of long-run stagnation in such a system holds, even if all profits are reinvested. For this reason we shall assume from now on that $\pi = I$ (or $N = o$) which means that all profits are, in fact, reinvested within the open agrarian system.

SECTION 3

The Anatomy of Open Agrarianism

The new organization that we have just sketched is intended to carry out certain essential economic functions in the open agrarian society. There are four types of such functions: (1) acquisition of the labor force, (2) production of exportable goods, (3) successful sale in the export market, (4) accumulation of commercial capital. These correspond to the four sectors of Figure 3. We shall now proceed to discuss each of these briefly in order to elicit clearly the appropriate analytical assumptions that can be postulated for the successful performance of each of the functions.

Acquisition of the Labor Force

The concepts of surplus labor—labor not employed in the agricultural sector—and agricultural surplus—the food consumed by surplus labor—which are important to the closed agrarian economy, remain relevant, and in fact crucial, to the analysis of the open agrarian economy. As in Section 1, let θL be the surplus labor, with θ as the fraction of the total labor force L which is now being employed in the service sector or the export production sector. The total agricultural surplus R in Figure 3 consists of food supply to the service sector R'' and to the export production sector R'. Notice that regardless of the physical location of employment, such allocated labor is used, after a time, directly or indirectly to promote exports, and for all practical purposes, there is no need to distinguish between labor in the service sector and in the export production sector proper. It is quite evident that θL and R—the labor surplus and the agricultural surplus—are the primary means of export production. The export-oriented foreign entrepreneurs are obviously vitally interested in a steady supply of these factors. Barriers to the "free mobility" of these factors are barriers to export expansion. The foreign entrepreneur advocates breaking down these barriers; the physical by such means as road construction and investment in warehousing and in urban social overheads, and the more institutional by laws permitting the transfer of titles to land, commercial codes, etc. However, at any moment in time, the major instrument at the disposal of these entrepreneurs in their effort to induce the desired movement out of agriculture is the delivery of imported consumer goods (A in Figure 3) not previously consumed by the cultivator. The following equation expresses a ratio:

$$(7) \qquad\qquad w = A/L.$$

We will refer to this ratio as the "inducement ratio"—because "A" is used to "induce" the giving up and delivery of surplus labor and food for export production. The inducement ratio is expressed as total imported consumer goods per unit of total population L.

It should be noted that the prognosis for reaching long-run stationary equilibrium, in the sense of a constant per capita consumption standard c and a constant agricultural productivity p, continues to be valid for the open agrarian economy. In other words, the stand-off between the forces of population growth and technological change, as analyzed in Section 1, continues to hold. Thus Figure 4a is a reproduction of Figure 2a, in which the long-run stagnation point is indicated at q_o—corresponding to the stationary triplet θ_o, p_o, and c_o. The question now is whether this stagnation can be broken by the importation of goods from abroad. For example, suppose food grains are imported to the amount $\bar{w}$ per unit of total population, as indicated in Figure 4a on the vertical axis. Then, with fixed values of p_o, and c_o, the equilibrium allocation point shifts from q_o to q_o'' signifying an increase in θ.[11] This corresponds to what we might have expected intuitively: that "food imports" can substitute for "domestic productivity increase" as a factor causing the reallocation of a larger fraction of labor θ. We then readily have:

$$(8) \qquad\qquad \theta = \theta(w) = (1 + (w - c)/p) \quad \text{with } \theta' > o.$$

This simply states that the surplus labor ratio θ is an increasing function of the inducement ratio.

In the more general case, where the initial consumption standard c_o, is sufficiently above caloric minimum to begin with, the larger surplus labor ratio θ can be induced through the delivery of industrial consumer goods—rather than food—to the agricultural sector. In Figure 4b let us assume an indifference map (not shown) of a typical farmer as a consumer. As the farmer's productivity (and hence his income in terms of

---

[11] This is due to the fact that the consumption demand for domestically produced food is now lowered to point c'' on the vertical axis of Figure 4b. The expression in equation 8 (below) is obtained by replacing c with $c - w$ in equation 2.

Figure 4

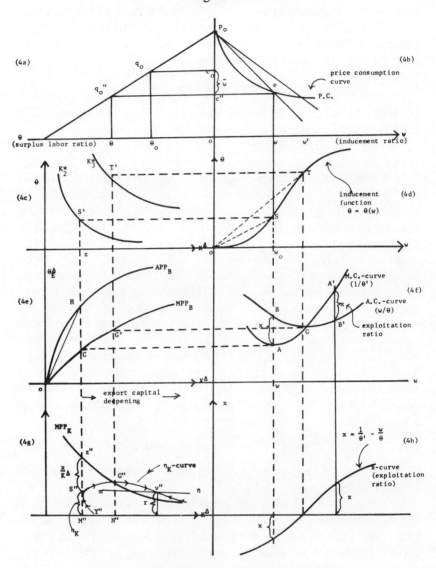

food [12]) is at "p_o" a price consumption curve (labeled P.C.-curve) can then be drawn from p_o. Suppose then that the inducement ratio is w units of *industrial* goods as marked on the horizontal axis. Then the equilib-

[12] Abstracting from the possibility that disposable income may be lower by some fraction due to feudalistic tithe remnants or taxes.

rium consumption point is at e with c'' units of food consumed. Returning to Figure 4a, we see that the new equilibrium allocation point is then established at q'', again signifying an increase of θ. In this way we can see that the surplus labor ratio remains an increasing function of w, the inducement ratio, as postulated in equation 8 when the inducement takes the form of imported industrial goods.

In general, we shall refer to the ratio in (8) as the surplus labor *inducement function*. It is presented in Figure 4d, with w on the horizontal and θ on the vertical axis. This function predicts the manner in which surplus labor (and agricultural surplus) can be induced to leave the rural sector through the delivery of imported consumer goods. On the basis of the above discussion, we may assume that the inducement curve is positively sloped and that, furthermore, the excitement of new goods appearing on the taste horizon has its strongest cumulative effects initially, both in terms of choice between food and industrial goods and between leisure and industrial goods. Finally, we may assume that ultimately a "law of diminishing returns to the seduction process" begins to set in (after some point S).

We may thus legitimately think of θ (measured on the vertical axis in Figure 4d) as a measure of the relative "availability" of surplus labor to the export sector and of w (the inducement ratio) as a measure of the cost to the entrepreneurs in the export production sector. Given this inducement function we can readily formulate two equations. The first defines the average cost of labor (in terms of imported goods per unit of surplus labor induced):

(9a) $$u = w/\theta \quad (= wL/\theta L).$$

The second defines the marginal cost of labor:

(b) $$m = dw/d\theta \quad (= 1/\theta').$$

From the point of view of the export-oriented entrepreneur, the *total* cost of labor is simply the total volume of imported goods used to induce the flow of surplus labor.

Notice that this inducement is strictly a "market phenomenon." If "w" represents the units of imported industrial consumer goods per unit of L, the terms of trade between imported industrial and domestic agricultural goods established in the market are represented by the slope of $p_o e$ (Figure 4b). The total value of consumption (of w units of industrial goods and "c" units of food) of a typical worker, at the established terms of trade, has the same market value as p_o units of food. Moreover, the *total* value of imported goods is equivalent to $\overline{c''p_o}L$ units of food, which value enables the trading entrepreneur to buy $\overline{c''p_oL}/p_o$ units of labor,[13] or, as a fraction of L, $\theta = \overline{c''p_o}/p_o$. (This can be measured horizontally in Figure 4a as $c''q_o''$ or vertically in Figure 4d as w_oS.) Thus, under open agrarianism, labor, for the first time, becomes a marketable *commodity*—a heretofore completely unknown phenomenon. The relevance of this new maximizing calculus to the labor market can be shown more directly by representing varying levels of u and w—the average and marginal cost, respectively, of surplus labor—by an AC (average cost) and an MC (marginal cost) curve in Figure 4e.[14] Comparing Figures 4d and 4f, we see that the MC-curve reaches a minimum point (at A) as the laws of diminishing returns set in (at S) and that the MC-curve crosses the AC-curve at the minimum point of the latter (at G) when the inducement curve has unit elasticity (at T). Intuitively, we expect the profit-maximizing entrepreneur to carry out his "labor seduction" according to a marginal principle. For this reason, let us define the vertical gap between the MC-curve and the AC-curve. This gap can be expressed by the equation

$$(10) \qquad\qquad x = MC - AC.$$

We shall term the ratio defined in this equation, the "exploitation ratio," and shall show that it is an important concept in the open agrarian society. As a function of w, the exploitation ratio is plotted in Figure 4b, i.e., the x-curve, and is positive or negative as the inducement curve is inelastic or elastic, respectively.

Production of Exported Goods

Surplus labor is acquired to provide first, the necessary overheads, roads, warehouses, etc., and then, direct inputs into the production of exportable commodities.[15] It is possible to classify various subtypes of open agrarian economies by differentiating among the production conditions prevailing in specific export activities. For example in the ". . . export-dominated economies of South East Asia, two rather distinct subtypes can be identi-

---

[13] Since p_o is equivalent to the real wage.

[14] At the point w_o in Figure 4d, the slope ow_o/oS of line oS is equal to the height wB in Figure 4f while the inverse slope of the inducement function at point S in 4d is equal to the height wA in 4f.

[15] As Fisk put it, "where external factors, such as the development of European commercial enterprise . . . have brought marketing facilities within reasonable reach of the subsistence units, the labor surplus has been used first to complete the linkage with the markets, and then to increase agricultural production for sale" (E. K. Fisk, "Planning in a Primitive Economy," *Economic Record,* Dec. 1962, p. 472).

fied for the historical pre-World War II period. . . . For one type, export production continued to emphasize traditional, labor-intensive methods applied to an indigenous crop—rice being the outstanding example. For the other type, export production was associated with capital-intensive methods introduced from abroad. Most commonly these were applied to products which were also implanted from abroad—rubber and sugar representing two important examples. . . . Exploitation of mineral rather than agricultural resources for export (e.g., tin and petroleum) may be considered as a variant of the second case." [16] Such further sub-classification of the export production sector undoubtedly has more general applicability.[17] It is obvious that, on the whole, the initial contact of the traditional economy is afforded by—and indeed, the initial growth-promoting force of the open agrarian economy is expressed through—the production of agricultural goods for export—a heritage still apparent in most contemporary underdeveloped economies.

Distinctions among particular types of crops and related organizational configurations are of importance and must be dealt with in any complete analysis of the transition from open agrarianism to dualism. However, for purposes of this paper, these distinctions need not distract us from the basic fact of production, namely, that it is through the joint effort of surplus labor B, and commercial capital K that output for export Q_E is generated. Thus we may postulate a production function of the type

(11a) $Q_E = f(K, B)$ (export production function)

(b) $B = \theta L.$

If the exportable item is derived from an exhaustible mineral source, the production function is subject to the condition of long-run decreasing returns. In that case, it is obvious that stagnation is more likely to occur. But, under the more general (neutral) assumption of constant returns to scale, the productivity of surplus labor, $Q_E^\Delta \equiv Q_E/B$, is an increasing (and convex) function of capital-per-unit-of-surplus-labor, $K^\Delta \equiv K/B$. This production function is expressed by the equations:

(12a) $Q_E^\Delta = f(K^\Delta, 1)$ where

(b) $Q_E^\Delta \equiv Q_E/B$ and

(c) $K^\Delta \equiv K/B.$

[16] D. S. Paauw and J. C. H. Fei, "Development Strategies and Planning Issues in South-East Asian Type Economies," *The Philippine Economic Journal*, 1965, Vol. IV, No. 2, pp. 204–205.

[17] For examples, with special reference to Africa, see Robert E. Baldwin, "Patterns of Development in Newly Settled Regions," *Manchester School*, XXIV, No. 2, May 1956.

The function is represented by the APP_B-curve in Figure 4e. In the same diagram, the marginal productivity of surplus labor is represented by the MPP_B-curve. The marginal productivity of capital, as a function of K^Δ, is shown in Figure 4g by the curve with a negative slope. When K^Δ ($=K/B$) increases (i.e., as more capital is combined with labor), export-sector capital intensity increases; this is referred to as export capital deepening. (The converse happens as K^Δ decreases.) The average-product curve in Figure 4e shows how the law of diminishing returns to capital operates in the process of export capital deepening.

Selling in the Export Market

All exported goods are, by definition, destined for the foreign market. If the terms of trade are t, then the total amount of exported goods Q_E can sell for $M = tQ_E$ units of "foreign goods"—which may be viewed as the revenue in real units of foreign exchange. Thus we have:

$$(13) \qquad\qquad M = tQ_E.$$

A whole set of factors may affect conditions in foreign markets. If the open agrarian economy that is exporting is a major supplier of a commodity (e.g., cocoa for Ghana), "t" is a decreasing function of Q_E. If the economy is a price taker, "t" tends to take on a constant value in the short run. However, in either case, the terms of trade are likely to change in the long run in accordance with patterns of world demand (the availability of natural or synthetic substitutes), and a variety of other considerations that have been discussed at great length in the Prebisch vs. Kindleberger literature. It is therefore rather difficult to come up with any really satisfactory generalization about the likely behavior of "t." Nor is this paper the appropriate place to make the attempt, purely for the purpose of emphasizing the internal logic of open agrarianism independent of these admittedly important exogenous considerations. We make the simplifying assumption of a constancy of "t" through time, an assumption that permits us, through a redefining of the unit of measurement of imports, to let $t = 1$.

Accumulation of Commercial Capital

As is evident from the flow chart of Figure 3, the proceeds from the export sale can be used in three ways: for investment I, for the luxury consumption C of the export-related entrepreneur, and for the importation of incentive consumer goods destined eventually for rural consumption.[18] It may be reasonable (but not necessary) to assume that C is proportional to K (i.e., $C = gK$), because it is obvious that the luxury consumption of foreign entrepreneurs tends to be proportional to the stock of commercial capital managed by such entrepreneurs. Finally, since investment leads to capital accumulation, we can summarize this relation as:

(14a) $$I = M\text{-}A\text{-}C$$

(b) $$C = gK$$

(c) $$\frac{dK}{dt} = I$$

(d) $$\eta_K = I/K$$

where (d) is the growth rate of capital.

We must also recall that in performing the four economic functions just outlined, the open agrarian economy must face certain conditions inherited from the closed agrarian system. One of the most important of these is the persistence of population pressures. Let us assume that population continues to grow at a constant rate:

(15) $$\eta_L = r.$$

We should recall here that the long-run stagnation thesis of closed agrarianism (above) provides us with the stability of the population growth rate r, the consumption standard c, and labor productivity p. As is evident from our discussion, these conditions ensure that a steady supply of surplus labor and of surplus food can be induced to flow into the export sector in the open agrarian setting. In other words, the demographic factors inherited by open agrarianism are such that they are "right" for the open economy in which the labor will be induced to move into the export market. It is obvious that such population pressure must be weighed in terms of the over-all factor endowment of the economy as measured by capital per head K^* ($=K/L$). Thus we readily have:

(16a) $$K^\Delta = K^*/\theta \quad \text{where}$$

(b) $$K^* = K/L \quad \text{(by 11b and 12c)}.$$

[18] If we continue to neglect the possibility of capital repatriation.

These equations show a simple relation between over-all factor endowment K^*, export capital intensity K^Δ and the surplus labor ratio θ. We can imagine that, at any point in time, the economy's over-all factor endowment K^* is fixed. Therefore, as (16a) shows, K^Δ is inversely related to θ, in other words a larger surplus labor ratio θ leads to less capital deepening K^Δ in the export sector. This relationship can be shown in Figure 4c by the system of rectangular hyperbolas—where a fixed rectangular hyperbola represents a fixed value of K^* in (16a).

Figure 4 may now be used to summarize briefly our description of the open agrarian economy up to this point. To begin with, let us suppose that the total stock of capital and the labor force are fixed at any point in time, i.e., K^* is fixed (e.g., represented by the K_2^*-curve in Figure 4c). Using the inducement ratio "w" as an instrument to acquire surplus labor, entrepreneurs tentatively set a "trial" value of w as indicated on the horizontal axis (Figure 4d). This determines the (tentative) values of the surplus labor ratio (i.e., w_oS in Figure 4d), the level of export capital intensity (z in Figure 4c), and the marginal and average productivities of surplus labor (points C and H in Figure 4e). This enables the entrepreneur to calculate his total revenue ($M = tAPP_BB$) in terms of the foreign exchange that can be earned. On the other hand, when "w" is chosen, the entrepreneur can also readily calculate the total labor cost, in terms of the foreign exchange (wL) expended on imported consumer goods. Thus, profits, as the difference between total cost and total revenue, are determined by "w," the inducement ratio.

As we pointed out earlier, the most conspicuous new institutional aspect of open agrarianism is that the society is dominated, for the first time, by the unsatiable acquisitive commercial spirit of the entrepreneurial class. This spirit translates itself concretely into the desire to maximize total profits, or, since at any point in time the capital stock is fixed, the desire to maximize profits per unit of, or the rate of return to, capital. Thus, the entrepreneurs either through calculation or through trial and error experimentation will tend to set w at that level which maximizes total profits at each point in time.

Now let us deduce an explicit expression of the rate of return to capital as a function of w. Notice that investment I in 14a is precisely the definition of profits and that "the rate of growth of capital" η_K in 14d is precisely the definition of the profit rate (i.e., profits per unit capital). The profit rate can be written as:

$$(17) \qquad \eta_K = \frac{tf(K^*, \theta(w)) - w}{K^*} - g.$$

The proof is as follows:

$$\eta_K = \frac{M\text{-}A\text{-}C}{K} = \frac{tQ_E - wL - gK}{K} \qquad \text{(by 14ab, 7, 13f)}$$

$$= \frac{tQ_E^\Delta - w/\theta}{K^\Delta} - g \qquad \text{(by 12bc, 11b)}$$

$$= \frac{t\theta f(K^*/\theta, 1) - w}{K^*} - g \qquad \text{(by 12a, 16a, 8)}$$

$$= \frac{tf(K^*, \theta) - w}{K^*} - g \qquad \text{(by CRTS property of 11a).}$$

Thus we see that for a fixed K^* (t, g) the profit rate is a function of w. To maximize the profit rate, with respect to w, we have, by setting $d\eta_K/dw = o$:

(18) $$tf_B = \frac{1}{\theta}, \quad \text{or}$$

$$tMPP_B = MC \quad \text{and} \quad MPP_B = MC \quad \text{(if } t = 1\text{)}.$$

These equations illustrate the condition of maximization of profits at equality between $MPP_B t$ (the marginal value product of surplus labor in export production) and MC (the marginal cost of surplus labor in terms of imported consumer goods).

It should be recalled that any such equilibrium condition is relative to a fixed value of K^*, the factor endowment of the economy. Under our assumption that K_2^* (Figure 4c) represents the current value of K^*, the equilibrium condition shown in 18 can thus be represented by the "equilibrium rectangle" $S'SAC$, signifying the equality between MPP_B (at point C in Figure 4e) and MC (at point A in Figure 4f).

SECTION 4

Operation of Open Agrarianism

An understanding of the origin of profit which is at once the inducement to capital accumulation as well as the source of investment finance, throws considerable light on the internal logic of open agrarianism. First of all, the optimum (i.e., the maximized) rate of profit can be written as follows:

(19)   optimum $\eta_K = MPP_K + \dfrac{x}{K^\Delta} - g$ or $\eta_K + g = MPP_K + \dfrac{x}{K^\Delta}$

The proof is as follows:

$$\eta_K = \frac{f_K K^* + f_B \theta - w}{K^*} - g \quad \text{(by 17 and CRTS)}$$

$$= f_K + \frac{f_B - w/\theta}{K^*/\theta} - g$$

$$= f_K + \frac{\dfrac{1}{\theta'} - w/\theta}{K^\Delta} - g \quad \text{(by 18)}$$

$$= f_K + \frac{x}{K^\Delta} - g \quad \text{(by 10).}$$

Notice that "x" (the exploitation ratio) as introduced in 10—i.e., the vertical distance AB in Figure 4f—is equivalent to the modern definition of labor exploitation as given by Joan Robinson, "the deviation of the actual wage from the competitive level of the real wage." This we may verify as follows: we know that $wL/B = w/\theta = AC$ (i.e., the distance wB in Figure 4f) is the actual average wage cost (per unit of surplus labor), while the competitive wage cost is $MPP_B = MC$ (i.e., the distance wA in Figure 4f). Hence "x" (defined earlier as the exploitation ratio) represents the tax on (or subsidy of) surplus labor, and the term $x/K^\Delta = xB/K$ can be called exploitation per unit of capital. Notice that x can be negative as well as positive, i.e., labor can be subsidized as well as taxed. Referring to Figures 4d and 4f, we see that when the inducement function is elastic, $MC < AC$, and both x and x/K^Δ are negative, that is there is a subsidy of labor to the left of point G in Figure 4f. When the inducement function is inelastic, $MC > AC$, x and x/K^Δ are positive, i.e., there is a tax on labor to the right of point G.

We can now attempt an economic interpretation of 19. Referring to the underlined expression, we see that the term $MPP_K + x/K^\Delta$ is the "gross income" per unit of capital, which is the sum of the competitive income per unit of capital (MPP_K) and exploitation per unit of capital. On the other hand, the term $\eta_K + g$ is the "disposition of capitalist income." In the case of the equilibrium rectangle $S'SAC$ just described, x is negative, that is, labor is subsidized, and hence the profit rate η_K, which may be indicated by distance $S''M''$ (in Figure 4g), falls short of the MPP_K by the amount $S''Z''$, which is the sum of consumption g and the subsidy per unit of capital x/K^Δ.[19]

Let us now suppose that the factor endowment of the economy as a whole changes in such a way that K^* increases from K_2^* to K_3^*—as represented by the upward shift of the corresponding rectangular hyperbola. The new optimum solution is now represented by the equilibrium rectangle $T'TGG'$ and the new rate of return to capital by the vertical distance $N''G''$ (Figure 4g). Notice that this is the special case when the inducement function (Figure 4d) is of unitary elasticity and the exploitation ratio is consequently zero (i.e., $x = o$ in Figure 4h). For this special case the profit rate is $MPP_K - g$. However, since we have assumed, for simplicity of exposition that $g = o$, the profit rate η_K coincides with MPP_K in Figure 4g. In like fashion, as increasing values of K^* are successively postulated (by a system of rectangular hyperbolas in Figure 4c), the successive equilibrium values of the profit rates η_K will generate a locus of points, such as the curve η_K in Figure 4g passing through the points Y'', S'', G'', V'' . . . as K^* increases.

Obviously there exist many different subcases of open agrarian economies in the real world—both on the contemporary scene and in the historical context. It is our hope that the analysis in Section 3, through the identification of the four economic functions required for execution in an open agrarian economy, will help to make possible the elucidation of subcases by (hopefully empirical) references to how these functions are, in fact, performed. It is then obvious that in accordance with the special characteristics of such subtypes, open agrarianism may exhibit a wide variety of behavior patterns in the process of growth. Specifically, the changes, in certain essential observable characteristics, that take place as the factor endowment of the economy changes (i.e., as K^* increases) may be in different directions. Our model (and Figure 4) has been designed to attempt an answer to only some of the problems that can arise, for example the problem of the impact of change of K^* on other observable characteristics. We shall now briefly indicate some of the comparative static results of our analysis—leaving all proofs to the appendix.

Referring to Figure 4d once again, we see that the two equilibrium rectangles indicated earlier—i.e., $S'SAC$ and $T'TGG'$—correspond to two special cases: where the point of inflexion of the inducement func-

---

[19] We are letting $g = o$ in Figure 4g. Notice that if $g > o$, point S'' will shift downward by the constant amount "g" and our entire analysis below will hold after suitable (easily accomplished) modification. We shall assume for now that $g = o$.

tion (point S) falls; and where the inducement function is unit-elastic, at point T. Corresponding to these two special "land-mark" cases, the points S and G divide the $\eta_{_K}$-curve (in Figure 4g) into three segments: $Y''S''$ (corresponding to falling portion of the MC-curve in Figure 4f), $S''G''$ (portion of rising MC-curve that lies below the AC-curve), and the segment $G''V''$ (portion of the MC-curve that lies above the AC-curve). Keeping these landmark points in mind, we proceed to summarize our comparative static conclusions.

(1) As K^* increases, the value of w increases. This means that in case of over-all capital deepening (i.e., K^* increases), the w set to maximize profits and the inducement ratio always increase. Thus, in case the inducement function is positively sloped, the surplus labor ratio (θ) also increases. Figure 4b shows that the terms of trade (between food and imported goods, for example) tend to move against the entrepreneurs in the export sector.

(2) As K^* increases, the value of K^Δ will decrease (increase) if the inducement function is elastic (inelastic)—i.e., before (after) point S. This is shown in Figure 4g by the fact that the curve $\eta_{_K}$ moves to the left before and to the right after the point S''. The economic interpretation is that there will be capital shallowing in the export sector as long as surplus labor can be pried loose with ease from the subsistence agricultural sector. This turns to capital deepening once the inducement function becomes inelastic. It is intuitively obvious that as the "law of diminishing returns" takes effect in the labor acquisition process, making it increasingly difficult to acquire labor, capitalists will naturally be forced to use less labor per unit of capital in the export production sector.

(3) As K^* increases, $\eta_{_K}$ increases (decreases) if $x < o$ ($x > o$). This is indicated in Figure 4g by the fact that the curve $\eta_{_K}$ reaches maximum value at the point of crossing the MPP_K curve, signifying that the profit rate increases when labor is subsidized and declines when labor is taxed. This is further illustrated by the fact that the vertical gap between the curve $MPP_{_K}$ and the curve $\eta_{_K}$ shrinks to zero before the point G'', signifying that in the process of increasing export capital intensity, the diminishing need to subsidize labor more than compensates for the unfavorable effect of a lower MPP_K produced by the operation of the law of diminishing returns to capital. Conversely, when labor is taxed, the profit rate will decline after point G.

In the above, we have emphasized a reasonable behavioristic pattern of the inducement function as an illustration of the flexibility of our framework of analysis. Clearly other *a priori* hypotheses as to the slope of the inducement function are admissible and would lead to somewhat different conclusions.[20] Moreover, other applications of our framework of analysis are possible; for example, we could identify the behavioral characteristics of the production functions more fully, or make "richer" assumptions in connection with the terms of trade or the value of g.

Let us now turn to the long-run prognosis for the open agrarian system and the requirements for its emergence into vigorous dualism.

SECTION 5

Prognosis for Open Agrarianism

We are now in a position to inquire about the long-run prospects for the type of open agrarian system we have tried to depict. To facilitate this, let us show a horizontal line mn in Figure 4g at the height of the population growth rate r in 15. Suppose the point of intersection of that curve with the η_K curve is at point v''. Then to the left of v'' there must be eventual capital deepening, i.e., a rising K^*, because the rate of growth of capital η_K exceeds the rate of growth of labor r. Similarly to the right of v'' there must be capital shallowing. With a stable equilibrium prevailing at v'', the long-run stationary value of K^* implies in turn long-run stationary values for all the essential economic magnitudes (e.g., K^Δ, MPP_K, MPP_L, θ, and w) with which we are concerned.

It should be noted that this conclusion is valid irrespective of the detailed framework presented earlier. In other words, the prospect for long-run stagnation is independent of the precise transitional stages through which the long-run stationary state is reached. All that is really essential is that the curve η_K (in Figure 4g) decline over the long run, a phenomenon which, as we have shown, can be traced to the fact that the inducement function becomes inelastic for higher values of w. Notice that the inelasticity of the inducement function at large values of w is compellingly reasonable since θ cannot exceed 1. In other words, the attempt by the foreign-oriented entrepreneurs to take advantage of the existing labor surplus in the open agrarian economy ultimately runs up against physical limitations. The stagnant p and c, inherited from the closed agrarian system, cannot be shaken off. The growth that does take place may be substantial, but as long as it is restricted to the export production sector as an enclave in an otherwise stagnant, but still preponderant, agricultural hinterland, the prospects are for ultimate stagna-

---

[20] S. Hymer has pointed out to us that the inducement function may, in fact, not exhibit any range of increasing returns.

tion. This conclusion can be avoided only when the opening up of the closed agrarian system brings with it additional dynamic benefits relating to the advent of technological change as a routinized behavioral pattern. The ability or inability to effect a successful implantation of such technological dynamism is, in fact, what distinguishes stagnant, open agrarianism from vigorous dualism.

In summary, there are a number of reasons why the structure of open agrarianism is closer to dualism than that of the closed variety. First and foremost among these is the advent, for the first time, of profit maximization as the propellant motive force, displacing feudal and kinship relationships. As Georgescu-Roegen put it "from the middle of the nineteenth century, if not before, these [agrarian] countries began . . . to receive the impact of Western capitalism. Increasing trade with the West revealed the existence of other economic patterns and at the same time opened up new desires for the landlords and new ambitions for the bureaucracy. Under this influence the feudal *contrat social* began to weaken." [21] Second, while surplus labor may have been employed to satisfy culturally or religiously important values, open agrarianism succeeds for the first time in making productive use of such labor in the modern sense, that is, commercializing it by mobilization via the price mechanism instead of by feudal edict. As labor mobility results in response to changes in the commodity flow, the foundations are laid for what could eventually develop into a full-blown, intersectoral labor and intersectoral commodity market in the dualistic setting. Third, physical capital formation makes its appearance for the first time in the social and economic overheads servicing the export sector and in the export producton sector proper. Finally, a new class of economic agents —acquisitive foreign entrepreneurs and their local counterparts with whom they form flexible alliances—gradually replaces a reluctant landed aristocracy in positions of economic and political power.

The environment has thus changed markedly under the impact of foreign trade and the workings of the profit-maximizing calculus. There nevertheless remains a considerable gap between the operation of open agrarianism and the workings of a vigorous dualistic system. [22] We have no more than to look about us to see that a considerable number of less developed countries remain trapped in the open agrarian situation.

[21] Georgescu-Roegen, "Economic Theory and Agrarian Economics," *Oxford Economic Papers,* February 1960, p. 33.

[22] As described, for example, by W. Arthur Lewis, "Development with Unlimited Supplies of Labor," *Manchester School,* Jan. 1958, & Fei and Ranis, *Development of the Labor Surplus Economy: Theory and Policy,* Homewood, Ill., 1964.

While the chances for transition into dualism are clearly and substantially enhanced, there remain a number of crucial factors that tend to keep the less developed economy in the grip of stagnation over the long term. Dominant among these is the failure of development in the export enclave to touch the life of the agricultural production sector in any really meaningful or pervasive fashion. Industrial capital formation in the sense of a dualistic or mature economy has not as yet put in an appearance. In this context the required routinized interaction between a small but relatively expanding industrial sector and a large but relatively shrinking agricultural sector has no chance to take hold. As a direct consequence, the ability to count on a dependable, routinized, innovation-inducement mechanism in both sectors (but especially agriculture), is missing. This mechanism is the most important single link in the chain of successful dualistic growth, the growth that has a chance to culminate in economic maturity. There is, as yet, no dualistic entrepreneur with one foot in each sector, making his investment-maximizing and innovative decisions so as to ensure balanced progress. As one observer has aptly put it, "technological change is, itself, one of the more difficult products for a country in the early stages of economic development to produce. In fact, it sometimes appears that an industrial economy is a prerequisite for technological change in the agricultural sector." [23]

The analysis in this paper is thus intended to shed some light on the reasons for the continuance of stagnation as a norm, as well as on the elements that must receive attention if departure from that norm is to be achieved. It will be clear to the reader that the transition to dualism has been substantially eased by the opening up of the closed agrarian economy. A more precise definition of what is needed—in terms of aid, trade, and the flow of technology—to translate open agrarianism, with its enhanced opportunities, into vigorous dualistic growth and ultimately economic maturity is clearly of the utmost importance and the authors hope to take up this matter in a future work.

[23] Vernon Ruttan, "Subsistence Agriculture and Economic Growth," Agricultural Development Council Seminar on Subsistence and Peasant Economies, East-West Center, Hawaii, p. 8. See also the contributions of Nicholls and of Tang, on this subject, including: W. Nicholls, "Industrialization Factor Markets & Agricultural Development," *Journal of Political Economy,* LXIX (1961), 340; and W. Nicholls & A. M. Tang, *Economic Development in the South Piedmont, 1860–1950: Its Importance for Agriculture,* Nashville, 1958.

APPENDIX

The model for the open agrarian economy may be summarized succinctly in the following six equations presented in the text:

(A1 a) $\qquad\qquad \theta \;\; = \theta(w) \qquad\qquad$ (8)

(b) $\qquad\qquad m \;\; = \dfrac{1}{\theta'(w)} \qquad\qquad$ (9b)

(c) $\qquad\qquad Q_E^\Delta = f(K^\Delta, 1) \qquad\qquad$ (12a)

(d) $\qquad\qquad K^\Delta = K^*/\theta \qquad\qquad$ (16a)

(e) $\qquad\qquad \eta_K \;\; = \dfrac{tf(K^*, \theta(w)) - w}{K^*} - g \quad$ (17)

(f) $\qquad\qquad m \;\; = tf_B(K^\Delta, 1) \qquad\qquad$ (18),

which can be used to solve for the six unknowns, θ, w, m, Q_E^Δ, K^Δ, η_K, when K^* is given. Thus conceptually, for any fixed value of K^*, the optimum (i.e., maximized) values can be written as

(A2) $\quad \bar{\theta} = \bar{\theta}(K^*); \quad \bar{m} = \bar{\theta}(K^*); \quad \bar{w} = \bar{w}(K^*), \; \overline{Q_E^\Delta} = \overline{Q_E^\Delta}(K^*),$
$$\bar{K}^\Delta = \bar{K}^\Delta(K^*), \; \bar{\eta}_K = \bar{\eta}_K^{(K^*)}.$$

This merely shows that the optimum values (indicated by the upper bar) are all functions of K^*. The comparative static conclusions relevant to open agrarianism and referred to in the paper are obtained by investigating the signs of the derivatives of the functions in A2. For purposes of the dynamic aspect of our model, we have the additional equation:

(A3) $\qquad\qquad \eta_{K^*} = \bar{\eta}_K - r = \phi(K^*) \quad$ (by 13).

The notation $\phi(K^*)$ simply states that the rate of growth of K^* is a function of K^*. Thus A3 is a differential equation in K^*, the solution of which is the time path of K^*. When this is substituted in A2, the time paths of all the variables are determined. The theorem of long-run stagnation (Section 5) is dynamic and refers to the properties of these time paths. (Notice that in A1, 2, and 3, we have formulated the problem in such a way that only "ratios" are involved and that the absolute magnitudes K, L, Q_E, I, M, . . . are all dispensed with by taking advantage of the constant-returns-to-scale property of our model.)

The model structure defined above is similar, at least from a purely mathematical point of view, to what may be called a socialist "maximum speed development model." [24]

Comment

W. ARTHUR LEWIS, PRINCETON UNIVERSITY

The object of this paper is to explain the stagnation of primitive agrarian economies. Stagnation is not defined as Malthus and the classical economists defined it, namely as a situation of zero population growth. On the contrary, it is defined as a situation with population increasing at a constant rate, productivity constant, and the ratio of farmers to population constant. Since the point of Malthus and the classicists was that a growing population and constant productivity were incompatible in primitive societies if the cultivated area was assumed to be constant, one must ask how our authors achieve their result.

They offer two alternatives. In the first, productivity grows exogenously. As productivity increases, consumption increases, so the rate of population growth increases. Land being fixed and intensively cultivated, average productivity falls endogenously as population grows, offsetting the exogenous rise. When the endogenous fall and the exogenous rise in productivity are exactly equal, we have equilibrium. Thus population can grow indefinitely by 3 per cent per annum if this produces an endogenous fall in productivity of 1 per cent per annum, exactly offset by an exogenous rise of 1 per cent.

The mathematics seems impeccable; it is the assumptions that are odd. Malthus warned that while population increases in a geometrical ratio, production increases only in an arithmetical progression. We laugh at this formulation, but translated into modern terms his warning is essentially that we should not fall into the trap of using a Cobb-Douglas function for large changes in the ratio of labor to land in agriculture, or into the worse trap of assuming a constant percentage growth rate of exogenous productivity. If population increased steadily by 3 per cent, endog-

[24] J. C. H. Fei and Alpha Chiang, "Maximum Speed Development through Austerity," in Adelman and Thorbecke, *op. cit.* Readers interested in detailed proofs of the equations in this appendix are referred to the appendix of this work.

enous productivity would not decline steadily by 1 per cent. What would happen is that the island would be reduced to a desert within a century, for population would multiply sixteen times. In their effort to survive, the people would first reduce the periods of fallow, then they would cut down all the seemingly useless trees and shrubs and turn over every inch of soil. Soon soil erosion would sweep much of the soil into the sea, and much of the island would become uninhabitable.

The other alternative offered us, to produce steadily rising population with constant productivity, is an adjustable rate of growth for exogenous productivity. Here we introduce landlords, who keep the farmers' consumption constant whatever may happen to productivity. This gives a constant rate of population growth, which again, via Cobb-Douglas, reduces productivity at a constant rate. The ratio of consumption per head to farmer productivity determines the ratio of farm to total population. Without exogenous growth of productivity the ratio of farm population would rise constantly, because productivity would fall endogenously; with exogenous growth of productivity exactly equal to the endogenous decline, the ratio is held constant; with still higher exogenous growth the ratio falls constantly. The authors invent a function that automatically brings the exogenous growth rate down to the right level, and so they get stability.

The authors are assuming that the cultivated area is constant. That population can grow with constant productivity if the cultivated area increases is not in dispute. Given a constant area, productivity per head can also be kept constant with rising population if there is also rising effort per head; this is the emphasis of Miss Boserup, who shows how rising population induces harder work and greater investment in land. Fei and Ranis assume both constant area and constant effort per head. In these circumstances, one can expect in primitive societies only very small increases in exogenous productivity, averaging perhaps 10 per cent per century. Therefore the sort of stability they are seeking would be compatible only with very slow population growth and a level of consumption barely above subsistence. If this is their world, they ought to add to their mathematical model constraints which keep all rates of increase fairly close to zero, and this would make it only minimally different from the model of Malthus.

In any case, I am prejudiced against all models that make the rate of population growth a direct function of consumption per head. They clearly do not apply to our times. Yet the authors offer their model as an explanation of the contemporary tropical world. Such models were useful for Malthus's times and before, but they do not explain what is happening in the world today.

So far, we have been analyzing a closed economy. The remainder of the paper deals with an open economy. Now we have an export sector that grows relatively to a subsistence sector from which it is drawing labor and food. Ultimately equilibrium is reached because the local food terms of trade reach a level that gives the same rate of growth to population, farm population, capital per head in the export sector, profits, etc.

One must pay tribute to the geometrical ingenuity that makes it possible to bring so many variables into a stagnant equilibrium. But of course, the value of a model is in direct proportion to its relationship to reality.

Confronted with the stagnation to which the authors have brought their island, one asks, "Why don't the capitalists get out of the terms-of-trade trap by importing food?" The authors state that the external terms of trade are constant, so how can the local-food terms of trade move against the export sector? The answer has to be that food cannot be imported, or is much dearer on the foreign market than it is at home (in which case it should be exported). The assumption that food cannot be imported is contrary to historical fact, for very many export sectors have been developed on the basis of imported food. For that matter, many export sectors were developed on the basis of imported labor, this being the chief reason why there are so many Indians and Chinese all over the tropical world. Then too, there is the earlier forced migration of Africans. But if labor and food can be imported, and the terms of trade are fixed at a reasonable level, as the authors assume, then the only obstacle to export growth is land, which is oddly enough omitted from their production function for the export sector.

The capitalists are smarter than our authors allow. Having decided to develop some export sectors with imported labor, they also decided to build ports, roads, and railways in Burma, Thailand, and Indo-China. These countries soon brought forth a rice surplus and kept the food terms of trade in their favor. This rice was grown and sold by peasants, reminding us that the development of an export sector does not require capitalist plantations hiring labor. Our authors' model, in which exports are from plantations that can import neither labor nor food, is therefore a very special case.

It seems to me more fruitful to work with a model in which the local price of food is so closely tied to the world price as to be identifiable with it. We then have a minimum of three products: food, the agrarian export (call it rubber), and the industrial import (call it steel). Let us assume that these are the only three commodities.

As our first operation we can reduce the number to two. If productivity is constant, as it was in the tropics most of the time up to the end of the Second World War, and if exports are only a small part of tropical agricultural output (also the case) then the prices of rubber and of food are tied to each other, whether these products are grown on plantations or on peasant farms. If the price of rubber exceeds the equilibrium, unlimited supplies of rubber will be put on the market, and if it falls below the equilibrium, rubber will disappear from the market. The terms of trade between rubber and steel therefore depend on the terms of trade between food and steel. Since tropical food production is relatively small, the tropical terms of trade depend on what happens to the terms of trade between food and steel in the developed world. Here is no mystery. The real price of food fell after 1873, as immigration, railways, and horse-driven machinery opened up the great wheat lands in central North America. Prices turned round and rose after 1900 as the American frontier closed. They fell again after 1920, as mechanical traction started a second agricultural revolution; they rose through the Second World War; and fell again in the 1950's as the third American agricultural revolution, based on chemistry and genetics, created new surpluses. The future is no more predictable now than it was in 1873, 1900, 1920, 1939, or 1950, or any other turning point. But what happens to the terms of trade between food and manufactures in the developed world will determine the terms of trade for tropical agricultural products.

Superimposed on this are the effects of changes in productivity in tropical agriculture. A rise in productivity in rubber merely reduces the price of rubber in terms of both food and steel, since if it did not, there would be an unlimited switch of tropical production from food to rubber. Therefore, a rise in productivity in rubber does not benefit the tropical countries. On the other hand, a rise in tropical food productivity would improve both the factoral and the commodity terms of trade for rubber, since a constant rubber yield would buy more food and therefore more steel. Historically, tropical food productivity has remained constant. The standard of living has been rising mainly because the relationship between food and exportable crops has been sufficiently favorable to bring forth ever increasing exports—admittedly more favorable in Asia and in Africa than in Latin America. The stagnation of export production that our authors are seeking to explain has not in fact existed.

One could wish that it did exist. For what we now have is a tropical world producing more and more cocoa, rubber, coffee, and sisal than the world may want, while beginning to mount up a large annual deficit of food. Policy changes that made it more profitable to grow food than to grow unwanted exports would be sound, especially if some tropical countries would grow food to export to other tropical countries that are already overpopulated. We could fruitfully spend much time discussing how to effect this transformation, but this would take us well outside the boundary of the paper before us.

Reply

JOHN C. FEI AND GUSTAV RANIS

Professor Lewis claims that the closed-economy section of our paper neither depicts the situation in contemporary less developed countries nor precisely duplicates the Malthusian theory of stagnation. We agree on both counts, but we never claimed otherwise. Our objective in the closed economy model is to try to understand the causes of stagnation over long historical time periods *before* such agrarian societies were decisively impacted by foreign trade. As we explicitly point out in several places in our paper, we believe that the contemporary less developed world is engaged in the attempt to move from open agrarianism to dualism, and that it is this open economy model that must be subjected to the test of real world relevance.

With respect to the second point, the proper meaning of stagnation over centuries of closed agrarianism, we think that the classical model narrowly defined (i.e., zero agricultural productivity increase and population growth) is, in fact, less relevant than a model that is capable of explaining low rates of productivity increase (not really exogenous, but some unknown function of "learning by doing" from generation to generation) accompanied by low rates of population increase over long centuries of human experience, e.g., in China, Japan, and parts of Western Europe.

Finally, in connection with the theory as to how the society arrives at our version of stagnation, we also are prejudiced against models that lean exclusively on the Malthusian population-response mechanism. It was, in fact, a side objective of our paper [1] to modify what we call the Jorgenson-Classical thesis by proposing that it be married to another hypothesis, the allocation adjustment thesis, and that the combination of these two forces may have the observed long-term results for the closed agrarian system.

Turning now to Professor Lewis' discussion of our open economy model, his major criticism here seems to be that we have neglected the possibility of the capitalists' importing food and labor and thus vitiating our ultimately pessimistic predictions for the open agrarian system. But, we might ask in return, if things went so swimmingly in Lewis' tropical world of the nineteenth and early twentieth centuries, why do we have so many less developed countries to be concerned about at midcentury? The heart of our problem, in fact, is to show why the colonial pattern did not yield sustained development. If food imports— for which, incidentally, we do make allowance—were in fact empirically important, would this really obviate the necessity of involving the stagnant agricultural backyard in the growth process—a necessity that goes far beyond the provision of food and labor to the enclave export sector? We assume constancy of the external terms of trade only for convenience, but we see no reason, given the literature, to expect these to improve historically, thus negating the tendency towards stagnation. What we are trying to explain is not the (nonexistent) long-term stagnation of export production, as Lewis claims, but the (existent) long-term stagnation of economies whose agricultural hinterland has not been pulled into full participation via sustained increases in productivity.

[1] Also reflected in our earlier piece "Agrarianism, Dualism and Economic Development," in *The Theory and Design of Economic Development,* I. Adelman, Erik Thorbecke (ed.), Baltimore, 1966.

Relationships Between Agriculture, Nonagriculture, and Foreign Trade in the Development of Argentina and Peru

ERIK THORBECKE

IOWA STATE UNIVERSITY

AND

ALFRED J. FIELD

UNIVERSITY OF NORTH CAROLINA

THE PRESENT STUDY is an attempt to analyze the economic development of Argentina and Peru in terms of vital relationships within the principal productive sectors and between these sectors and foreign trade.

Section 1 is devoted to the formulation of the analytical framework used in the study. The main elements of the framework are: (a) a sectoral breakdown in terms of agriculture, industry and the service complex, (b) a specification of the major relationships between sectors (e.g., technological, income and price relationships), and (c) the formulation

NOTE: Much of the work on this paper was done under the auspices of the A.I.D. summer research program in 1967. The views expressed herein are the sole responsibility of the authors and do not in any way commit the Agency for International Development.

of a policy framework within which the national performance can be evaluated.

Section 2 applies the above analytical framework as the basis for a review of the experience of Argentina from the beginning of this century to the present. Three phases are distinguished in this review.

Section 3 presents a simple multisectoral model that incorporates a number of the elements of Section 1. The structure of the model and the causal relationships between the relevant variables is discussed before applying the model statistically to the case of Argentina. The model illustrates quantitatively some of the assertions made in the previous part particularly the key role of agriculture as a determinant of Argentina's growth and stagnation.

Finally, Section 4 analyzes the performance of the Peruvian economy during the post-World War II period. Again the function of the agricultural sector is emphasized, but within a very different context than that of Argentina. A comparison of the two countries provides interesting insights into (a) the relationship between agriculture and foreign trade when the balance of payments is and is not a binding constraint, and (b) the contrast between the contribution to developmental objectives of an entirely commercialized agricultural sector (Argentina) and a dual agricultural structure (Peru).

1

The Framework of Analysis

The literature of theoretical economic development has been built largely upon a two-sector model analyzing the relationships between agriculture and nonagriculture and/or between a backward (traditional) sector and an advanced (modern) sector. In a few instances this framework was extended to three sectors by adding foreign trade. Valuable insights into the physiology of the development process were derived from these models and fruitful hypotheses formulated. Yet very few attempts have been made at testing these models empirically.

The present study is a modest attempt at specifying and examining within a quantitative and policy framework the relationships within and between the agricultural, nonagricultural, and foreign trade sectors. Argentina and Peru offer interesting contrasts that will be brought out explicitly by empirical studies.

Sectoral Breakdown

Four sectors are distinguished in the present framework: agriculture, industry, the service complex,[1] and foreign trade.

It is clear that, from the supply side, the first three sectors above undergo, throughout the process of development, certain important changes affecting the sectors' relative importance and interdependence. Note that foreign trade is viewed as a subset of agriculture and industry, not of services. The agricultural and industrial sectors produce either for the domestic or for the foreign market, but the service section is assumed to produce exclusively for home consumption. This assumption would not be valid for every developing country. In some, the service sector can be a major export contributor (e.g., because of tourist receipts), but in neither Argentina nor Peru is it more than a marginal contributor to exports.

From the consumption side, changes also take place. Here again imports can be considered as a subset of the other sectors through their allocation to the sectors of destination (use). Agriculture, industry, and services, then, can be thought of as producing and consuming spheres of home and foreign goods and services.

Figure 1 shows the interrelationship between sectors: A from the supply side; B from the demand side; and C from the supply and demand sides by superimposing A and B. The boxes are drawn approximately according to scale. The industrial complex is broken down into production of consumer and capital goods in the case of Argentina and into fishing, mining, and the rest of industry, respectively, for Peru. The shaded area represents the portion of total sectoral output presently exported or imported. The upper pair A reflects the current sectoral value added. The middle pair B reveals the sectoral destination of imports. It should be noted that final-demand imports (e.g., consumption goods and food) are additional to, not overlapping with, value added. The bottom pair C gives a good picture of the sectoral pattern of foreign trade.

In the case of Argentina, it can readily be seen that the great bulk of exports (about 90 per cent by value in the early 1960's) originates in agriculture. Raw materials and fuel, constituting about 60 per cent of import value, are used mainly for consumption and capital goods production. Only a relatively small proportion of imports is directed to the

[1] This complex of activities which includes, among others, construction and government is to be referred to as "services" in the subsequent discussion.

Figure 1

Sectoral Origin and Destination of Value Added:
Exports and Imports

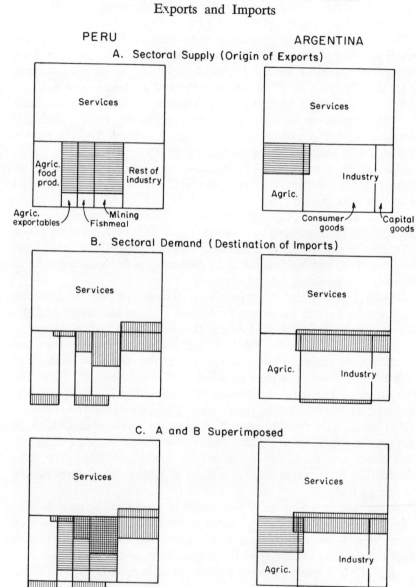

Note: Based on data in Tables 2, 3, 8–10

agricultural sector. The share of capital goods in total imports amounts to about one-third.

In C it can be seen that agriculture provides practically all of Argentina's exports while receiving only a fraction of the nation's imports. The major beneficiaries of imports appear to be the service sector and the industrial consumer goods subsector, as opposed to the capital goods subsector.

The agricultural sector of Peru in contrast with that of Argentina is highly dualistic. As a whole, Argentina's agriculture had, for all practical purposes, reached the commercialization stage by the early 1900's. Peru on the other hand, while it contains a commercialized and highly efficient agricultural subsector on the coast (producing mainly the traditional crops, cotton and sugar) also has a food-producing subsector in both the coast and in the backward (subsistence) region. A meaningful analysis of Peru, therefore, requires a division of agriculture into these subsectors. Currently, about one-fourth of exports originates in agriculture (see Figure 1). The remainder consists of fishmeal, 28 per cent of total exports [2] and of mining products 45 per cent. The relative importance of exports to value added is high and provides, as will be seen, the major stimulus to growth. Imports consist of capital goods, 42 per cent of total; food, 18 per cent; consumption goods excluding food, 16 per cent; and raw materials and fuel, 23 per cent. A considerable share of imports is used by the industrial sectors particularly by the export-producing activities of which mining and fishmeal are the principal. In addition, as illustrated in B of Figure 1, Peru is not self-sufficient in food. Imports of capital goods and inputs (raw material) into agriculture are fairly limited, constituting only 4 per cent of imports.

The Peruvian box in C captures well the sectoral trade structure. One characteristic is a relatively large degree of overlap between the sectoral origin and destination of foreign trade for the fishmeal and mining subsector. A part of this overlap can be explained by the limited linkages between these export activities and the domestic economy. Both the fishing and mining industries tend to spend a large share of export earnings to import capital goods and raw materials required for the production of exports. Agriculture, on the other hand, receives only a very small share of imported inputs and capital goods.

Argentina and Peru present a significant contrast in their sectoral trade structures. In Argentina the balance of payments gap has clearly been the binding constraint on economic development since the early

[2] The percentages refer to 1965. See Tables 7 and 8.

1930's. It can be argued convincingly that the development of Argentina would have been (and in fact may still be) best served by a heavier allocation of imports to agriculture and to exportable consumer goods. Such an allocation would have increased the supply of exportables thereby improving the capacity to import scarce capital goods. The type of import substitution that Argentina followed appears, furthermore, to have impeded the growth of the capital goods subsector by favoring the production of consumer goods. It will be seen later that Argentina's attempt at insulating her economy from that of the world in the early 1930's led to a neglect of agriculture, the country's almost unique source of foreign exchange. At the same time, the import substitution policies strangled the supply of capital goods further by favoring consumer goods. The result was the short-circuiting or interruption of economic growth in an already semiindustrialized country.

Peru offers a very different situation. It is a classic example of a dual economy, with the export sector providing the stimulus to growth. This sector, which is very large (more than one-fifth of the GNP) and highly diversified, is essentially divorced from the domestic economy to which, in fact, it tends to be a kind of appendage. Imports flow into both export activities (with the exception of agriculture) and final demand and yet contribute to a high rate of growth of aggregate income. The economy is truly export led.

Thus, the contrast is between, (a) a semideveloped country that attempted to insulate itself from the world economy and embarked on policies that led to the stagnation of the previously dynamic sector (agriculture) and to curtailed over-all growth, and (b) a less-developed, dual economy whose income (but not development) performance was superior because of a dynamic and diversified export sector assisted by liberal trade policies.

If Argentina might have benefitted from policies favoring agricultural development and the production of exportables—given that the balance of payments was the main constraint to growth—Peru, on the other hand, has been blessed throughout most of the post-World War II period with a strong balance of payments situation that permitted the maintenance of a large capacity to import. The need for import substitution was not felt, and the refusal to resort to this policy had numerous effects, among them, a rise in food imports from $39 million in 1950 to $134 million in 1965. The limited contribution of exports to some of the developmental objectives, such as employment creation and a more equal income distribution, together with the bleak export prospects may necessitate substantial changes in the production and import structure. For example, greater agricultural food output may be required to replace food imports. Graphically, this means that in the Peruvian boxes in B and C of Figure 1 the shaded rectangle representing food imports would have to be replaced by equivalent domestic food production.

Relationships Between Sectors

There are at least three major ways in which sectors are related: (a) technically or technologically, (b) by income, and (c) by price.

A. TECHNICAL RELATIONS

The technical relations determine the sectoral production functions through the input-output framework. Given a certain level of technology, the production functions can be assumed constant. A prerequisite as well as a consequence of economic development is a change in the technical (input-output) coefficients. The process of economic development entails the transformation of an essentially agrarian economy in which labor is abundant, technology traditional, and capital scarce, to a modern technological economy with a high ratio of capital to labor. In the process, labor and capital are transferred from agriculture to industry, and agriculture itself is modernized through increased use of capital. A comparison between the input-output structure of agriculture, industry and services in a developing and a developed country is very instructive.[3] It reveals that in both types of countries agriculture has a high internal requirement and a high requirement for services. There is, however, a significant difference in manufacturing deliveries to agriculture. The per-unit direct and indirect industrial inputs to agriculture are very substantially higher in a developed than in a developing country.[4] As Falcon points out, "This is simply another measure of the long recognized fact that purchased industrial inputs into agriculture are the *sine qua non* of agricultural development." [5] On the other hand, the contribution of agriculture to industry appears to differ less than the converse coefficient.

---

[3] See Walter Falcon, "Agricultural and Industrial Interrelationships in West Pakistan," Development Advisory Service, Harvard University Report No. 70, 1967; Karl A. Fox, "The Food and Agricultural Sectors in Advanced Economics," in Tibor Barna (ed.), *Structural Interdependence and Economic Development*, New York, 1963; and Erik Thorbecke, "The Role and Function of Agricultural Development in National Economic Growth," in *Economic Development of Agriculture*, Ames, Iowa, 1965.

[4] This ratio equals 2.5 comparing the U.S. and West Pakistan, see Falcon, "Agricultural and Industrial Interrelationships. . . ."

[5] *Ibid.*, p. 4.

Often the growth of the manufacturing sector is stimulated by a desire for import substitution in the form of a higher degree of processing for agricultural raw materials, such as textiles and non-durable consumer goods, and an increased domestic production of foodstuffs and of capital inputs for agriculture such as fertilizer.

B. INCOME RELATIONS

A second major way in which these sectors are interrelated is through income. For example, it is clear that the demand for agricultural goods, *ceteris paribus* [6] depends on the rate of growth of GNP and the income elasticity of demand for agricultural goods for the domestic component, as well as on income in the rest of the world for the export component. Thus, the rate of growth of domestic food demand (f) is entirely determined by the rate of growth of population (p) plus the rate of growth of per capita income (y) multiplied by the income elasticity of demand for food (ϵ_y). In symbols:

$$f = p + \epsilon_y y$$

A low rate of income growth means a limited effective domestic demand for food. Likewise, a slow growth of output in the agricultural sector of a developing country translates itself, given the relative importance of agricultural output in total output and income, into a low effective demand for industrial goods and services.

C. PRICE RELATIONS

The third way in which sectors are connected is through prices. At one extreme the price system may be entirely free to operate as an "equilibrating" mechanism for *ex ante* discrepancies between planned supply and planned demand. At the other, the price system can be used as a controlling or planning device to influence sectoral output and demand for home and foreign goods through changes in the internal and external terms of trade. Prices and exchange rates can be controlled, for example, to encourage agricultural production during the stage of "traditional agriculture." By moving the terms of trade in favor of agriculture the adoption of new inputs, such as fertilizer and, to some extent, of more modern methods of production, can be encouraged. On the other hand, after agricultural output and productivity has risen, the terms of trade can be used *against* that sector to help siphon off capital and labor resources and channel them into industry and the service sector.

There exists a very real risk that the terms of trade will be moved

[6] Assuming, among other factors, constant relative internal and external price relationships. The price relationships between sectors are discussed subsequently.

against agriculture (a) too early in the development process, as has happened in a number of presently dualistic economies, or (b) too strongly or for too long a period after the stage of commercialized agriculture has been reached, a situation which, as will be seen, was characteristic of Argentina from about 1930 to 1955.

The relationships in the three basic areas described above are used in a more or less quantitative way (depending on data availability) to examine and describe the intra- and intersectoral performance and links in Argentina and Peru.

Policy Framework and Developmental Objectives

To relate sectoral performance and intersectoral relations (both quantitatively evaluated) to major developmental objectives requires a policy framework. The objectives must be specified to establish a multidimensional norm against which the development performance can be judged and the conflict between objectives better understood.

Economic development is a function of a number of target variables. The most important of these are (a) the level, or rate of growth, of GNP; (b) the distribution of income on a personal, functional, and regional basis (here the criterion may be a minimum nutritional standard or a certain share of wages to national income); (c) internal equilibrium, in terms of maintaining a certain degree of price stability; (d) external equilibrium, in terms of maintaining balance of payments stability; and (e) employment in terms of percentage reduction of the unemployed labor force.

In the Tinbergen tradition, one can assume that the policymaker (the government) is trying to maximize, either implicitly or explicitly, some welfare or preference function that contains the above variables as elements. The policymaker's task is to formulate policies that will maximize this welfare function subject to the constraints imposed by the structural relations described in sections A and B above. It is obvious, however, that conflicting rather than complementary relationships may prevail between the objectives, in the sense that policies designed to achieve a higher level of attainment of some goals, such as high rate of growth of GNP or employment, may worsen the attainment level of others, such as inflation or balance of payments disequilibrium. One good illustration of the problem is the conflict between stabilization and economic growth.[7] Policies designed to achieve economic stabilization à tout prix may be so "successful" that they may preclude growth and

[7] On this point, see Hollis B. Chenery, *Toward a More Effective Alliance for Progress*, A.I.D. Discussion Paper No. 13, 1967.

result in stagnation. Alternatively, policies assigning an unduly high weight to long-term growth may result in balance of payments crises and run-away inflations. The existence of conflicts among targets makes the question of the priority among variables a crucial one. It is fair to say that there is a tendency on the part of policymakers, in both the developed and underdeveloped world, to underestimate the negative side effects of policies directed to the achievement of specific objectives.

The above-described framework will be applied in a general way to Argentina and Peru. In the case of Argentina it was possible to formulate a quantitative model to follow through the sectoral and policy interactions for at least one of the phases of that country's economic development. A similar model could not be constructed for Peru because of the limited sectoral information. Nevertheless, the availability of a previously built aggregate model of the Peruvian economy [8] and of a detailed agricultural sectoral study [9] made it possible to undertake the present analysis.

For both countries an attempt is made: (a) to examine sectoral performance with emphasis on the performance of agriculture compared to the industry and foreign trade sectors; and (b) to evaluate the extent to which price, income, and trade policies, as well as the sectoral allocation of investment, affected sectoral and over-all economic development as defined in terms of the above mentioned objectives.

It is felt that some insight into the role of agriculture at different developmental stages and the importance of the proper policy mix can be obtained from the analysis of these two countries within the above-described framework.

2

Argentina

General Observations

Because of the crucial role that the foreign sector has played throughout the history of Argentina, that country provides an excellent case study in the interrelationship between the foreign sector and domestic development. Argentina, after reaching a relatively high level of de-

[8] Erik Thorbecke and Apostolos Condos, "Macroeconomic Growth and Development Models of the Peruvian Economy," in Irma Adelman and Erik Thorbecke (ed.), *The Theory and Design of Economic Development,* Baltimore, 1966.

[9] Iowa Universities Mission to Peru, *Peruvian Macro-Economic and Agricultural Prospects and Strategy, 1967–1972,* Lima, 1967.

velopment by 1930, has since experienced considerable difficulty in maintaining sustained growth. The connection between economic growth, export promotion, and import substitution is fundamental to any developing country. It is believed that the Argentine experience holds lessons of value to other developing countries facing similar structural problems.

Argentina provides a good illustration of industrialization promoted without a complete understanding of the complex interdependence between the foreign sector and the other principal sectors on both the import and the export sides. The need to induce economic changes in the major sectors in an internally consistent manner was not fully appreciated until it was too late and severe structural bottlenecks had developed. It is ironical that the government policies aimed at reducing external influences resulted, if anything, in increasing the dependence on the external factors. The Argentine experience in recent years demonstrates vividly the problems that arise as a country pursues conflicting short-run targets.[10]

The development of Argentina has evolved through three very general stages.[11] The first stage, ending around 1930, can best be described as a period of export-led economic growth, with the foreign trade sector acting as the proverbial "engine of growth." The second stage, beginning with the Great Depression and ending during the late 1940's is characterized by intensive import substitution, industrialization, and an expansion of the government-service sector. Greater government intervention occurred in all phases of economic activity. The third stage, spanning the period from the late 1940's to the present, exhibits the predominance of sectoral imbalances accompanied by severe inflation and political-economic instability. (Argentina is currently engaged in attempting to reduce the dependence on imports of intermediate goods while altering the sectoral priorities towards agriculture.[12] This policy could lead to a

[10] A good example is the conflict between growth and price stability which has been evident in Argentina in recent years.

[11] The authors relied heavily in their review of the economic history of Argentina on the excellent studies by (1) Carlos F. Diaz-Alejandro, "An Interpretation of Argentine Economic Growth since 1930," *Journal of Development Studies,* Part I, October 1966, Part II, January 1967; (2) Eprime Eshag and Rosemary Thorp, "Economic and Social Consequences of Orthodox Economic Policies in Argentina in the Post-War Years," *Bulletin of the Oxford University Institute of Economics and Statistics,* February 1965; and (3) Javier Villanueva, *The Inflationary Process in Argentina, 1943–60,* Institute Torcuato Di Tella, 1966. The three-stage historical breakdown followed here corresponds closely to the treatment in the second source above.

[12] This is reflected in the National Development Plan. For an analysis of the projections contained in this development plan see the study by Larry A. Sjaastad, "Argentina and the Five Year Plan," multilith paper prepared for Latin American Conference, Cornell University, April, 1966.

new phase.) The growth rates of selected variables for these respective time periods are presented in Table 1. Tables 2 and 3 show the distribution of GDP by sectors and the composition of Argentine exports and imports.

The Pre-1930 Period

During the latter part of the nineteenth and the first part of the twentieth century Argentina experienced a rate of growth in its domestic product that has few parallels for rapidity in economic history.[13] Throughout this period the "engine of growth" was agricultural exports, which provided the means for importing the required capital goods.[14] The success of the rural sector in maintaining its competitiveness in world markets was a direct result of its ability to adapt to changing technology and world demand.

The capital stock of Argentina during this period was employed, for the most part, in economic activity connected directly or indirectly with the foreign sector. Argentine industry was principally concerned with transforming rural inputs into products that would be competitive in world markets. The railroads, built primarily to expedite the transportation of agricultural products to processing plants or exporting centers, together with the capital directly employed in agriculture, accounted for nearly one-half of the total capital stock. It is extremely significant that agriculture became "commercialized" during this period, contributing thereby to the development and industrial transformation of the country.[15]

Argentina experienced throughout the period 1900–29 a high rate of growth of GNP (4.6 per cent per annum) made possible by: (a) expanding exports (which grew at 4.1 per cent in volume terms); (b) a large inflow of foreign capital; and (c) a large rise in the size of the labor force through immigration. The structure of production was oriented towards exportable agricultural commodities.

The Period from 1930 to the Late 1940's

The major goal of the Argentine government during the second major phase was to transform the externally oriented economy, via import sub-

[13] It has been estimated that the pattern and rate of growth before 1900 was not very different to that of the early years of the twentieth century; from 1900 to 1914 GDP grew at a rate of 6.3 per cent. See Diaz-Alejandro, op. cit.

[14] A heavy immigration of labor was also an important factor contributing to the economic growth during this time. From 1895 to 1929 the Argentine population grew at a rate of over 3 per cent per year.

[15] The degree to which agriculture had become commercialized is reflected in the lively market for rural machinery rentals which existed in the 1920's.

TABLE 1

Argentina: Growth Rates of Selected Economic Variables, 1900–69

Variable	1900–04 to 1925–29	1925–29 to 1945–49	1945–49 to 1960–64	1960–69[a]
Gross domestic product	4.6	2.8	1.8	3.6
Agricultural output	3.5	1.2	1.2	3.7
Agricultural exportables	–	0.3	0.2	–
Agricultural nonexportables	–	3.5	3.4	–
Industrial manufacturing	3.6	4.2	3.6	–
Personal consumption	4.3	3.1	1.9	4.4
Gross investment	5.8	1.1	1.7	3.0
Exports (volume)	4.1	−1.2	1.3	4.1–6.2
Imports (volume)	4.4	−1.4	0.7	0.2
Retail price level	n.a.	4.7[b]	25.5[c]	–
Terms of trade				
Internal[d]	n.a.	−1.9[e]	1.0[f]	–
External[g]	0.5	−0.2	−2.2[f]	–
Wages share of national income	n.a.	1.1	−0.3[f]	–
Total capital stock	4.8	1.4	2.4[h]	–
Capital stock in agriculture	3.3	0.4	1.2[i]	–
Labor force in agriculture	2.5	0.5	−1.8	–
Land area in agriculture	4.4	0.4	0.5	–
Domestic consumption of agricultural commodities	3.8	3.0	n.a.	–
Population	3.4	2.0	1.8	1.7

Note: These figures must be looked upon as tenuous because of the questionable quality of the underlying data.

Source: C. F. Diaz-Alejandro, "An Interpretation of Argentine Economic Growth Since 1930," *Journal of Development Studies, October 1966, January 1967;* United Nations, ECLA, *Analisis y Proyecciones del Desarrollo Economico de la Argentina,* Consejo Nacional de Desarrollo, Plan Nacional de Desarrollo, 1965–69, Buenos Aires, 1965; Republica Argentina, Secretaria de Asuntos Economicos, *Producto y Ingreso de la Republica Argentina en el Periodo 1935–54,* Buenos Aires, 1955; L. Sjaastad, "Argentina and the Five-Year Plan," Paper prepared for Latin American Conference, Cornell University,

[a] Target rates included in the National Plan.

[b] 1936–45.

[c] 1945–66.

[d] The ratio of wholesale prices of all rural to nonrural products.

[e] 1926–29 to 1945–49.

[f] 1947–49 to 1962–64.

[g] The ratio of export unit values to import unit values.

[h] 1945–49 to 1962.

[i] 1945–49 to 1955–59.

TABLE 2

Argentina: Distribution of Gross Domestic Product by Sectors,
Selected Years

(value in billions of 1960 pesos;
percentage distribution in parentheses)

	1950	1959	1963
Value added in:			
Agriculture	125.3 (17)	150.7 (16.2)	145.5 (15)
Industry	201.1 (27.2)	274.3 (29.4)	280.9 (28.7)
"Service complex"	412.7 (55.7)	505.2 (54.3)	544.5 (56.2)
GDP	739.1 (100)	930.2 (100)	970.9 (100)
Industrial production			
Investment goods	20.5 (3.9)	52.1 (7.3)	66.8 (9.3)
Consumption goods	293.4 (55.5)	372.3 (52)	349.2 (48.5)
Exports	48.6 (9.2)	50.4 (7)	65.2 (9.1)
Intermediate goods	165.7 (31.4)	241.0 (33.7)	237.7 (33.1)
Total	528.3 (100)	715.7 (100)	718.8 (100)

Source: Presidencia de la Nacion Argentina; Consejo Nacional de Desarrollo, *Plan Nacional de Desarrollo, 1965–1969,* Buenos Aires, 1965.

stitution, to a more balanced economy less dependent upon the foreign sector for both consumption and capital goods. As world trade (and foreign investment in Argentina) dropped off sharply during and after the great depression, the value of Argentine exports suffered a considerable decline and so consequently did the country's ability to import needed capital and raw materials.[16] It is interesting to note, however, that Argentina maintained its competitiveness in world markets throughout the period.[17]

[16] Argentine exports declined 35 per cent in volume over the period 1925–29 to 1935–39 while its volume of imports declined 24 per cent over the same period. See U.N. Economic Commission for Latin America [ECLA], *Analisis y Proyecciones del Desarrollo Economico de la Argentina,* Mexico D.F., 1959.

[17] Ruth Kelly points this out in noting that Argentina's ". . . export performance in the thirties, compared with the rest of the world, may be considered satisfactory. Indeed . . . it gave rise to expressions of optimism concerning the country's future prospects as one of the world's major exporters of agricultural products" (Ruth Kelly, "Foreign Trade of Argentina and Australia, 1930 to

TABLE 3

Argentina: Composition of Exports and Imports, Selected Years
(value in millions of dollars; percentage distribution in parentheses)

	1951	1955	1959	1963
Exports				
Agricultural goods	1100 (94.1)		965 (95.5)	1192 (87.3)
Forest products				
and minerals	46 (3.9)		22 (2.2)	36 (2.6)
Others	24 (2)		22 (2.2)	138 (10)
Total	1169 (100)		1009 (100)	1365 (100)
Imports				
Consumption goods		85 (7.2)	33 (3.3)	46 (4.7)
Raw materials and				
intermediate goods		847 (72.3)	733 (73.8)	558 (56.8)
Capital goods		241 (20.5)	228 (22.9)	377 (38.5)
Total		1173 (100)	993 (100)	981 (100)

The short-run success of the programs during this period is evident when it is realized that real consumption rose at a rate of 2.7 per cent annually from 1925–29 to 1940–44 and that real GDP grew at a rate of 2.2 per cent over the same period in spite of world conditions that caused export volume to decrease.

The manufacturing and service sectors contributed to this income growth, in contrast to agriculture which lagged behind the over-all growth of the economy.[18] In spite of these internal adjustments, Argentina still remained highly dependent upon exports for the financing of needed raw materials and capital goods. This capacity to import was increased during the late 1930's and early 1940's as the terms of trade of, and world demand for, agricultural exports improved.[19] However, the desired capital imports were difficult, in fact often impossible, to obtain as the major industrial suppliers transformed their industry into war production. As a result, Argentine industry could neither expand

1960," *Economic Bulletin for Latin America*, ECLA, Vol. X, No. 1, March 1965).

[18] The use of multiple exchange rates during the 1930's, whereby exchange rates for imports were higher than those for exports, appears to have had a powerful stimulus to industrialization in this period.

[19] The destruction of European agriculture permitted Argentina to negotiate huge intergovernmental contracts at almost exorbitant prices.

nor maintain the level of its capital stock via imports, and with exports at high levels, a buildup of foreign exchange reserves occurred. The capital stock in machinery and equipment fell by 30 per cent between 1938 and 1945.

The Great Depression of the 1930's and World War II did more, perhaps, toward initiating import substitution than any internal political change. However, the political atmosphere in Argentina contributed much to the *degree* to which import substitution was carried out and the extent to which the structural imbalance and economic bottlenecks were allowed to develop. This was particularly true of the early years of the Peron era during which the production of the service complex (e.g., government services, and construction) was stimulated in order to maintain high levels of urban employment and domestic demand. Because the external terms of trade were improving and the foreign exchange reserves were ample, little attention was paid to the possible development of constraints that could impair the growth of the economy in the event of a chronic import surplus resulting from the squeeze on exportables. The first six years of the Peron Administration (1943–49) were characterized by a general economic expansion in which real per capita income increased at a rate of 6.9 per cent per annum.[20] The high rate of growth of the service sector resulted, of course, in an increase in the proportion of national income accounted for by wages. The decline in agriculture's share of GNP, which accompanied this transformation, was looked upon as a necessary evil, inasmuch as a high rate of industrialization required a transfer of labor from the agricultural sector to the industrial-service sectors.[21] Argentine agriculture was already in the commercial stage, however, and the transfer of labor out of agriculture to the other sectors in the economy contributed to a reduction in output, because the labor transfer was not compensated by increased investment in capital goods for agriculture. Such investment might have been stimulated through the normal market processes had agricultural prices not been manipulated. However, the government moved the internal terms of trade against agriculture.[22] The artificial

[20] *Analisis y Proyecciones del Desarrollo Economico de la Argentina.*

[21] In those less developed countries characterized by surplus labor in the rural sector such a transfer out of agriculture would not have had the impact it did in Argentina. Argentine agriculture could not supply enough labor, however, and so the doors were opened to increased immigration. In 1947–51, a net immigration of 460,000 took place.

[22] The policies toward the rural sector were carried out in part to provide foodstuffs for urban workers even at the expense of foreign exchange earnings. In other words, the policy weight attached to a more equal income distribution in the short run compared to other policy objectives such as over-all income growth and external equilibrium was high.

price constraints may have prevented agricultural output from expanding, by removing the normal price incentive. At the same time, the
increase in the industrial labor force and in per capita income resulted
in a larger domestic demand for the relatively inexpensive foodstuffs.
Increased domestic demand, coupled with stagnating agricultural output,
reduced the agricultural surplus available for export.[23] The worsening
of the external terms of trade after 1949 and the drawing down of
foreign reserves altered the economic situation drastically. The structural
imbalance imposed by the stagnating agricultural sector and consequent
decline of Argentine exports began to impose a constraint on domestic
consumption and expansion.[24] The great expansion of social services [25]
and the increased industrialization in the area of consumer goods contributed to the development of a bottleneck in foreign exchange. Diaz
has argued convincingly, that the problem was not simply one of too
much industry and not enough agriculture, but rather, of two few
exports relative to the domestic demand for imports.

In summary, this period was characterized by a major attempt at
insulating the domestic economy from the world economy, a policy
that was initially motivated by the fall in export demand during the
Great Depression. Argentina embarked on import substitution policies,
particularly with respect to consumption goods. The reduction in agricultural output caused by worsening internal terms of trade acted
together with a rise in domestic demand to produce a squeeze on exports.
The rate of growth of GDP (2.8 per cent per annum) was relatively
high given the depression setting of the thirties. The major policy
objectives appear to have been the achievement of income growth and
an improved income distribution in favor of wage earners, entailing a
structural shift away from agriculture.

The Period from the Late 1940's to the Present

The third major phase was highlighted by inflation and shortages of
foreign exchange, symptoms of the structural imbalances existing in the
economy. As W. Arthur Lewis [26] points out, "Growth without inflation

[23] The transfer of labor out of agriculture and the withdrawal of land from
crop production created a domestic food shortage following the severe drought
of 1949–50.

[24] Few efforts were made to expand the volume of exports, while at the same
time the domestic capital goods industries were neglected. This eventually led
to a severe shortage of new machines and equipment.

[25] Massive use was made of central bank credit to finance budget deficits
throughout the boom of 1946–48. Substantial wage increases were decreed also
in the Peron era.

[26] W. Arthur Lewis, *Development Planning*, New York, 1966.

requires either balanced development of industry and agriculture, or a breakthrough in export trade." Increased domestic production of consumer goods did result in savings of foreign exchange. However, these savings were not large enough to compensate for increased demands for raw materials and capital goods. By 1950 it was evident that little further income growth could be attained through additional investment in activities producing consumer goods and/or services, such as construction. What was required was either a more balanced growth of industry and agriculture, increased exports of manufactures, or some combination of both. Argentina at this point had reverted to the stage where its growth was dependent upon its exports. The link between a reduction in agricultural production and the capacity to import badly needed raw materials and capital goods became quite clear during the early 1950's. Consequently, authorities embarked upon a program of encouraging agricultural production via various price incentives. However, the uncertainty surrounding the stability of improved internal terms of trade and the response lag, partly attributable to the prevailing system of land tenure, led to little if any real growth in agricultural output.[27] Thus, instead of stimulating an increase in agricultural production, the primary effect of these government measures was to raise the retail price of food, thereby initiating a wage-price spiral inflation.

To counteract inflation, generally restrictive fiscal and credit policy measures were introduced. The resulting stagnation was made more severe by the fact that the steep fall in imports of raw materials and capital goods curtailed production in such industries as metallurgy, rubber, printing, and furnishings. A fall in aggregate demand followed, and soon other industries were forced to operate far below capacity. Consumer goods industries were particularly affected and some were reported operating at only 50 per cent of capacity.[28]

Following Peron's overthrow more orthodox policies were instituted in an attempt to slow down the rate of inflation.[29] The Peron regime had, however, left the country with a low capacity to transform. This unfortunate state of affairs was further aggravated by a price mechanism so controlled that it had become, as Diaz pointed out, more a method of income distribution than of resource allocation.

Numerous problems arose as Argentina attempted to remove the

[27] The seriousness of the situation is evidenced by the fact that the value of exports in terms of constant prices declined by nearly 50 per cent from 1947–48 to 1951–52.

[28] Diaz-Alejandro, *op. cit.*

[29] There were large devaluations in 1959 and 1962.

economic bottlenecks that were inhibiting its growth and development. The urban unemployment rate began to rise as the economy tried to shift its production away from domestically consumed goods and services towards exportables and domestically produced capital and intermediate goods.[30] The share of wages and salaries in national income fell.

Excessive price fluctuations were also a problem during this third stage following discrete adjustments of the exchange rate and sporadic changes of government-controlled prices.[31]

This third phase can be said to be characterized by an attempt to redress the discrimination against the agricultural sector by moving the internal terms of trade in its favor. Because wages were typically tied to food prices,[32] the relative increase in the latter contributed to a severe inflation of about 26 per cent per annum between the late 1940's and the early 1960's. Agricultural output failed to respond adequately to higher prices partially because of the uncertainty regarding the stability of these prices. Exports grew only marginally and the capacity to import continued to be a limiting factor to growth.

The National Plan

Before leaving the historical analysis, a word must be said about the national development plan for Argentina. The plan provides perhaps the best indication of current attitudes towards economic objectives and the means to be employed to attain them. (The growth rates of selected target variables are presented in Table 1.) The fulfillment of goals under the plan will depend to a great extent upon the capacity of the foreign sector to provide the required raw materials and capital goods. As Sjaastad[33] indicates, the realization of the objectives and projections of the plan depend implicitly upon significant upward shifts in the supply functions of agricultural commodities. Exports will have to show an increase of 18 per cent over the period 1963–69 for the low projection to be met, while the achievement of the high projection calls for a 35 per cent increase in exports. Sjaastad estimates that such an

[30] Starting around 1953–54 attempts were made to stimulate production of machinery and equipment and the intermediate goods required in their production. The *ad hoc* establishment of automobile and tractor industries stimulated increased investment in metal working such that by 1961 significant amounts of steel began to be produced domestically.

[31] The economic instability was intensified by the fact that policymakers chose a few prices to manipulate while leaving others to fluctuate freely.

[32] Villanueva, *op. cit.*

[33] Sjaastad, *op. cit.*

increase in exports combined with an anticipated 17 per cent increase in domestic demand would necessitate an upward shift in the agricultural supply functions of some 20 per cent.

It would appear that these targets are beyond the reach of the economy. The main consideration is that whatever is achieved will depend on the technical progress in agriculture, or will require some sort of breakthrough in the exports of nontraditional industrial products. Sjaastad's conclusion that the realization of the targets in the plan will require some devaluation appears to be realistic. The degree of the devaluation required will depend of course on the elasticity of supply of exportable goods and the timing of the response.

3

A Simple Multisectoral Foreign Trade Model Applied to Argentina

General Observations

It was felt that a more formal presentation of some of the relationships discussed in the conceptual framework presented in Section 1 would prove of value for Argentina. Therefore, an econometric model was prepared to provide a clearer quantitative understanding of the structure and "modus operandi" of the Argentine economy and, hopefully, of changes that would promote its growth and development. The model is designed to describe the interrelationships of the foreign trade and the productive sectors of the economy, investigating sector by sector the effect of policy actions on the structure and levels of current exportables and on the composition and destinations of current imports. The importance of this sectoral follow-through is borne out by the experience of Argentina, where the failure of policymakers to promote exports and (in any meaningful sense) to promote import-competing industries contributed heavily to disequilibrium between the foreign sector, other sectors, and certain targets of growth and development. The Argentine experience demonstrates how, at a given point in time, supply conditions in both the import-competing sectors and the export sector can influence the growth and development of the economy. Short-run policy measures that treat only the symptoms of such a structural imbalance and do not cope with the more basic structural causes may provide temporary relief at the expense of other targets.

This model was built to reflect the Argentine conditions; it appears that the general construct might be applicable, with proper modifications, to other countries as well.

The Model

Numerous theories have been evolved to describe the interrelationships of the foreign trade sector and the major productive sectors of the developing economy, but few empirical studies have been made of the relationship between the foreign trade sector and the productive sectors and/or the import substitution process. Although it is recognized that many of the relationships are typically nonlinear in nature, the model presented is a modest attempt to illustrate the above development process problem within the framework of a set of linear equations.

The general form of the model is given below followed by the list of variables appearing in the model.

(1) $\quad Y_s = V_a + V_b + V_o$

(2a) $\quad V_a = v_a(\overline{L}, \overline{N}_a, K_a, \overline{RF})$

(2b) $\quad V_a = v'_a(\overline{L}, \overline{N}_a, \overline{K}_{a_{-1}}, \overline{RF})$

(3) $\quad V_b = v_b(\overline{N}_b, K_b)$

(4) $\quad V_o = v_o(\overline{N}_o, K_o)$

(5) $\quad C_a = c_o + c_1 Y^d + c_2 \overline{tt}_i + c_3 \overline{y}$

(6) $\quad C_b = c_4 + c_5 Y^d + c_6 \overline{tt}_i + c_7 \overline{y}$

(7) $\quad C_o = c_8 + c_9 Y^d + c_{10} \overline{tt}_i + c_{11} \overline{y}$

(8) $\quad X_o = \dfrac{d_o}{b_o} V_o - C_o - I_o + \dfrac{1}{b_o} (\overline{M}_o + \overline{Ti}_o)$

(9) $\quad X_a = \dfrac{d_a}{b_a} V_a - C_a - I_a + \dfrac{1}{b_a} M_a + \dfrac{1}{b_a} (\Delta \overline{St}_a + \overline{Ti}_a)$

(10) $\quad X_b = \dfrac{d_b}{b_b} V_b - C_b - I_b + \dfrac{1}{b_b} M_b + \dfrac{1}{b_b} (\Delta \overline{St}_b + \overline{Ti}_b)$

(11) $\quad M_b = M_k + \overline{M}_c + eM_{rm}$

(12) $\quad M_a = (1 - e) M_{rm}$

(13) $\quad M_{rm} = m_o + m_1 V_b + m_2 \overline{tt}_e$

(14) $\quad M_k = X_a + X_b + X_o + \overline{I}_f - M_{rm} - \overline{M}_c - \overline{M}_o$

(15) $K_a = \overline{K}_{a_{-1}} + \alpha I_t - \overline{D}_a$

(16) $K_b = \overline{K}_{b_{-1}} + \beta I_t - \overline{D}_b$

(17) $K_o = \overline{K}_{o_{-1}} + j I_t - \overline{D}_o \quad (\alpha + \beta + j = 1)$

(18) $I_t = I_a + I_b + I_o$

(19) $I_a = \Delta \overline{St}_{an}$

(20) $I_o = O$

(21) $I_b = I_d + M_k$

(22) $I_d = i_1 + i_2 \overline{CAP}_{-1} + i_3(V_b - \overline{V}_{b_{-1}})$

(23) $Y^d = Y_s - \overline{T}_y$

It should be noted that through substitution the definition of GDP from the demand side can be obtained:

(24) $Y_d = Y_s = C_a + C_b + C_o + I_t + X_a + X_b + X_o$
$$- M_k - M_{rm} - \overline{M}_c - \overline{M}_o - \overline{T}i - \Delta \overline{St}$$

LIST OF VARIABLES IN MODEL
(all national-income variables expressed at constant prices)

Endogenous Variables:

C_a = consumption of agricultural commodities

C_b = consumption of manufactured commodities

C_o = consumption of "services"

I_a = contribution of agriculture to gross capital formation

I_b = contribution of industry to gross capital formation

I_o = contribution of the service complex to gross capital formation

I_d = value of domestically produced gross investment

I_t = gross investment

K_a = capital stock in the agricultural sector

K_b = capital stock in the industrial manufacturing sector

K_o = capital stock in the service complex

M_a = agricultural imports

M_b = industrial imports

M_k = imports of capital goods

M_{rm} = imports of primary and intermediate goods used in the current production process (raw materials)

V_a = value added in the agricultural sector

V_b = value added in the industrial manufacturing sector

V_o = value added in the service complex (all remaining sectors)

X_a = agricultural exports

X_b = industrial exports

X_o = service exports

Y^d = disposable income

$Y_s = Y_d$ = gross domestic product

Exogenous Variables:

$\overline{CAP}_{-1}$ = capacity in machinery and equipment industry lagged one year

$\overline{D}_a$ = replacement investment (depreciation) in agriculture

$\overline{D}_b$ = replacement investment (depreciation) in industry

I_f = net foreign investment plus any changes in holdings of foreign currency

$\overline{K}_{a_{-1}}$ = capital stock in agriculture lagged one year

$\overline{K}_{b_{-1}}$ = capital stock in industry lagged one year

$\overline{K}_{o_{-1}}$ = capital stock in remaining sectors of the economy lagged ore year

$\overline{L}$ = number of hectares used in production in agricultural sector

$\overline{M}_c$ = imports of consumption goods

$\overline{M}_o$ = service imports

$\overline{N}_a$ = size of labor force in agriculture

$\overline{N}_b$ = size of labor force in industry

$\overline{N}_o$ = size of labor force in service complex

$\overline{RF}$ = index of yearly average rainfall

$\overline{St}$ = over-all change in stocks

$\Delta \overline{St}_a$ = change in stock in agriculture sector

$\Delta \overline{St}_b$ = change in stock in industrial sector

$\Delta \overline{St}_{an}$ = change in stock of livestock $(\Delta \overline{St}_{an} = \overline{St}_{an} - \overline{St}_{an_{-1}})$

$\overline{T}_y$ = direct taxes

$\overline{tt}_e$ = external terms of trade (ratio of the price of imports to the price of exports)

$\overline{tt}_i$ = internal terms of trade (the ratio of agricultural to non-agricultural prices)

$\overline{V}_{b_{-1}}$ = value added in industry lagged one year

$\bar{y}$ = the share of wage income in total income

$\overline{T}_i$ = indirect taxes

The model consists of 23 equations in the 23 endogenous variables listed above. Eight of the equations (numbers 2, 3, 4, 5, 6, 7, 13, and 22) are behavioral, with the remaining 15 definitional or technical. A brief discussion of these equations follows.

The first is the income identity equation relating gross domestic product, Y_s, to the sum of its components. Equation 24 defining GDP from the demand side can be obtained through a substitution process involving equations 1, 8, 9, 10, 11, 12, and 18 and is therefore not an independent relation in the model.

Equations 2, 3, and 4 are the sectoral production functions for agriculture, industry, and services (V_o) respectively. For each sector the value added is posited a function of labor and capital, with the exception of agriculture where, in addition, the quantity of land and the amount of rainfall are assumed to influence the level of output. An alternative equation (2b) relates current agricultural output to the value of capital stock lagged one year rather than to the current level of capital stock. The nature of the agricultural production process is such that, in the aggregate, the net increase in capital stock may not affect output in the same period (e.g., output response to increases in the stock of livestock, the acquiring of new machines after the crop year has begun may not have an appreciable impact for one or more years). It is important to note that agricultural production in contrast to the production process in other sectors, is essentially discontinuous. Such a response lag might well cause investment in the other sectors to appear more desirable from a policy standpoint, inasmuch as the *short-run* impact of investment in the nonagricultural sectors could lead to a higher income response than the same investment in the agricultural sector (assuming a shorter lag in output response to investment in the remaining sectors, a situation that, of course, would not hold true for social overhead capital and the mining sectors where the output lag can be very long).

Equations 5, 6, and 7 relate consumption of agricultural products, industrial manufactures, and services to changes in disposable income, the internal terms of trade, and a variable reflecting changes in income distribution, respectively.[34] The sign of the terms-of-trade variable is usually negative in the agricultural consumption function, reflecting the decline in consumption of agricultural products resulting from an increase in agricultural prices relative to nonagricultural prices, and vice-versa in the industrial consumption function. While the overall impact of improvements in the internal terms of trade upon agricultural production appears to have been slight, a relative increase in price of agricultural products leads to an increase in the potential supply of agricultural exportables by reducing the domestic demand for agricultural products. The impact of an increase in the wage share of income on agricultural consumption (C_a) would normally be positive, assuming that the propensity to consume of wage earners is typically higher than that of nonwage earners.

Exports $(X_a, X_b,$ and $X_o)$ are specified (equations 8, 9, and 10) essentially as the surplus available for export after consumption and investment requirements have been deducted from available supply.[35] This assumes that the foreign demand for Argentine exports is infinitely elastic, an assumption that appears reasonable, at least for the country's major export products. The exports equations are derived directly from input-output relationships. Indeed, we know that gross sector output $(D_i,$ were sector $i = a, b, o)$ is equal to the final demands components $(C_i, I_i, X_i, \Delta St_i)$ and the sum of intermediate demands (Id_i)

(1a) $$D_i = C_i + I_i + X_i - \Delta \overline{St}_i + Id_i \qquad (i = a, b, o)$$

[34] Changes in the income distribution will be assumed to be reflected by the ratio of wage income to total income.

[35] For an application of the exportable surplus concept to Brazil, see Nathaniel H. Leff, "Export Stagnation and Autarkic Development in Brazil, 1947–1962," paper prepared for A.I.D.'s Summer Research Program 1966.

where:

$$D_i = \text{gross sectoral output of sector } i \, (= a, b, o)$$

$$C_i = \text{consumption demand for goods of sector } i$$

$$I_i = \text{investment demand for goods of sector } i$$

$$X_i = \text{export demand for goods of sector } i$$

$$\Delta \overline{St}_i = \text{changes in stocks for goods of sector } i$$

$$Id_i = \text{sum of intermediate demand of sector } i$$

Likewise, gross sectoral income (S_i) is equal to value added of sector i (V_i) plus sectoral imports (M_i) and the sum of intermediate inputs (Ii_i) and indirect taxes $(\overline{Ti}_i)$.

(2a) $$S_i = V_i + M_i + Ii_i + \overline{Ti}_i$$

(3a) $$D_i = S_i$$

There exists a relatively constant relationship between intermediate sectoral demand and the components of sectoral final demand, on the one hand, and between intermediate sectoral inputs and sectoral value added, on the other. Thus, it may be assumed that:

(4a) $$Id_i = a_i^1 \, (C_i + I_i + X_i),$$

and

(5a) $$Ii_i = a_i^2 \, V_i$$

Let $1 + a_i^1 = b_i$ and $1 + a_i^2 = d_i$; then through substitution of the above equations, it follows that:

(6a) $$X_i = \frac{d_i}{b_i} V_i - C_i - I_i + \frac{1}{b_i} (M_i + \overline{St}_i + \overline{Ti}_i)$$

which is equivalent to the sectoral export equations (8, 9, and 10) in the model above. The sectoral parameters b_i and d_i are derived from input-output information.

It is assumed that in the service sector changes in stocks are negligible and imports are given exogenously (see equation 8). As noted previously, total agricultural output increased only marginally after 1930, while domestic agricultural consumption grew substantially. The combined effect of these two forces was a squeeze on exports. Inasmuch as agricultural exports fluctuated between 80 and 96 per cent of total exports throughout this period, the relative importance of industrial and service exports is marginal for Argentina, although these may become more important in the future.

Imports are broken down into their basic categories, i.e., imports of raw materials and intermediary goods M_{rm}, capital goods M_k, and consumption goods $\overline{M}_c$. $\overline{M}_c$ are specified exogenously. The rationale for this stems from the fact that in Argentina, and most developing countries, imports of consumption goods are regulated almost entirely by government import controls. It makes little sense, therefore, to relate this demand to any economic variable in the system when the yearly variations in its size are in fact determined by certain *a priori* government policy decisions. Imports of raw materials (equation 13) are specified endogenously as a function of the level of output in the industrial sector and of their purchasing price as reflected by the external terms of trade. It is recognized that this relationship presupposes that imported and domestically produced raw materials and intermediate goods are more nearly complementary than may be the case in Argentina.[36] The remaining import equation, 14, defines imports of capital goods M_k residually after all claims on foreign exchange earnings have been deducted. This implies that Argentina's capacity to import is always fully utilized and that the demand for imports of capital goods is bounded only by the availability of foreign exchange. The first claimant on foreign exchange will be raw material imports. With the relatively high level of industrial capacity in Argentina, it is obviously necessary to utilize existing capacity to the fullest before applying foreign exchange to the importation of capital goods. Equation 11 defines industrial imports M_b as equal to the sum of capital goods and consumer goods imports plus a share of raw materials imports. The remainder of the latter are agricultural imports (equation 12). It follows from equations 11 and 12 that $M_a + M_b = M_k + \overline{M}_c + M_{rm}$. The proportion of M_{rm} consisting of "industrial" imports ($=e$) is presumed given.

Equations 15 to 17 are self-explanatory. Note, however, the α, β, and j coefficients included in the respective capital stock equations. These are policy parameters that reflect the shares of total investment to be allocated to the three major sectors. (By definition the sum of the three parameters is equal to one.) Apparently policymakers in Argentina did not fully understand the implications of varying these parameters. In general, it is clear that fiscal and monetary policy undertaken to change

---

[36] A certain degree of substitutability between domestic and imported raw materials does in fact exist (e.g., petroleum in the 1960's). In any case there appears to be a justification for such a specification of average import content in the short run.

the size of these coefficients, *ceteris paribus,* could reasonably be expected to have a considerable impact upon the structural development and growth of a less developed country. In the case of Argentina, it is important to note that the supply of exports can only be affected through increases in α, and (less frequently) β.

Equations 18 to 21 provide the definitions of the investment components. Total investment I_t is equal to the contributions of the three sectors to investment demand (equation 18). Agriculture's contribution to investment is assumed to be confined to changes in the stock of livestock, a hypothesis that appears to hold true in Argentina (equation 19). No services are assumed to enter into investment ($I_o = 0$). Finally industrial investment is subdivided into two parts: domestic investment I_d and capital goods imports, equation 21.

A behavioral relationship explaining the output of domestic investment goods as a function of a lagged capacity variable and the annual change in industrial value added is given in equation 22.[37]

Equation 23 defines disposable income. As previously mentioned, the last identity in the model (equation 24) is not an independent relationship. It can be derived by substitution from a set of other equations in the model, thereby providing a check on the equality of GDP from the supply (value added) side and demand side.[38]

Figure 2 presents the causal links between the major variables in the above model. The diagram excludes many exogenous variables for the sake of clarity. The variables listed with a bar are those assumed to be exogenous to the system.

The interpretation of the diagram should be relatively straight-forward. The interdependence of the relationships in the model is essentially an expression of the distribution of total investment among the three pro-

---

[37] Some other forms of the investment demand function were tried. It is interesting to note in this regard that significant results were obtained relating I_d to raw materials imports and lagged capacity:

$$I_d = 64{,}045 + 1.328\ M_{rm} + 738.4\ C\bar{A}P_{-1}$$
$$\phantom{I_d = 64{,}045 + }(4.10) \phantom{M_{rm} + 7}(4.05)$$

$R^2 = .89$

Period: 1950–63   *t* ratios are given in parentheses below coefficients

[38] It is worth noting that in the substitution process, V_a, V_b and V_o are derived from equations 8–10. The sum of the three sectoral value added equals GDP in equation 1, i.e.,

$$\Sigma_i V_i = \Sigma_i C_i + \Sigma_i I_i + \Sigma X_i - \Sigma_i M_i + \Sigma_i \Delta \overline{St}_i + \Sigma_i \overline{T}i_i + \Sigma_i Id_i - \Sigma_i I_{i_i} \quad i = a, b, o$$

The last two terms cancel out since the sum of intermediate demands is equal to the sum of intermediate inputs.

Figure 2

Causal Arrow Diagram: Argentine Model

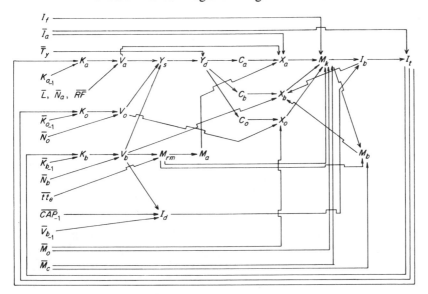

Note: See list of variables, pp. 186–88

ductive sectors. The proportion of total investment destined to each sector is represented by the coefficients α, β and j discussed earlier, the relative sizes of which determine indirectly the static level of equilibrium output in the economy. The supply of investment funds is simultaneously determined by the domestic production of investment goods and the capacity to import capital goods. The capacity to import is determined by the level of agricultural and manufactured output available for export. Since historically the agriculture sector has accounted for 90 per cent or more of total exports, the amount of agricultural products available for export becomes the principal determinant of the capacity to import and, hence, of capital goods imports.[39]

An increase in α would imply the channeling of additional investment into the agricultural sector, thereby increasing agricultural output and in turn the quantity of agricultural products available for export. Exportable surplus could also be increased by reducing domestic consumption of

[39] It must be recognized that expansion of the industrial-manufacturing sector into exportable products could alter the current agriculture domination of the supply side of the foreign trade sector.

TABLE 4

Argentina: Per Capita Consumption of Meat
Compared with United States

Period	Argentina		U. S.		Pounds Difference (col. 1 minus col. 3)
	Pounds (1)	Index (2)	Pounds (3)	Index (4)	
1951–55	222	100.0	151	100.0	71
1956–60	218	98.2	160	106.0	58
1961–63	210	94.6	164	108.6	46

Source: U.N. Economic Commission for Latin America.

agricultural commodities. There is little doubt that such a drop in domestic consumption could make a significant contribution to reducing the foreign exchange bottleneck. In fact, a reduction in Argentine per capita consumption of meat to levels similar to those prevailing in the U.S. would have led to a 60 per cent increase in the value of meat available for export and to a 14 per cent increase in the total value of Argentine exports in 1963 (*see* Table 4).

The restrictive effects of the flow of investment funds into the service sector is also evident. Since this sector does not produce needed capital, intermediary, nor manufactured goods, its expansion neither contributes to a reduction in import demands nor increases the availability of exportables (except in a few countries through tourism). Whereas the other two sectors have the capacity to promote growth and development through exports and/or import substitution, the direct effects of the service sector on trade tend to be much more limited. In fact they are often negative, drawing resources away from agriculture and industry.

The proposed model can also be used to demonstrate why, in the short run, additional investment in nonagricultural sectors is more effective in increasing output and employment than additional investment in agriculture.[40]

[40] If V_a is postulated as being dependent upon the capital stock in the preceding time period, the output response to *current* investment in agriculture is effectively zero. In the other two sectors, in contrast, investment is assumed to be related to current investment. In this case, increasing agriculture's share of

The Statistical Application of the Model to Argentina

In the statistical estimation of the behavioral equations for Argentina a serious handicap was encountered in the form of a lack of reliable and continuous time-series data for many of the variables included in the model. However, by using assorted time periods and several proxy variables, estimates were obtained for eight of the behavioral equations in the model. The results of these estimates are presented below and described thereafter. The remaining equations in the previously presented model are identities, definitional or technical relationships, and form together with the eight estimated behavioral relationships the present model.

current investment (implying a high α) results in smaller increases in *current* over-all (but not future) output than would be the case with a smaller α. Investment in agriculture, in this light, represents a type of short-run investment leakage because of the longer gestation period involved. The upper left-hand corner of the arrow diagram presented in Figure 2 can be redrawn to point out the impact of the above production function (equation 2b) as follows:

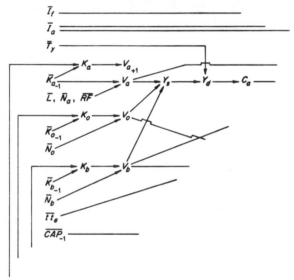

This framework also clearly shows how the transition from a foreign trade sector dependent upon agricultural exports to one more balanced between commodities originating in both agriculture and industry provides another way of breaking out of the structural bottleneck. It is, of course, obvious that the ability to produce competitively manufactured as opposed to agricultural exports grants a developing country a strong advantage because of the higher income elasticity of demand enjoyed by the former.

OLS ESTIMATES OF BEHAVIORAL EQUATIONS—ARGENTINA

(t ratios are given in parentheses below coefficients; equation numbers refer to model in text)

(2a) $V_a = -47,884 + 2.14\,\overline{L} - 57.4\,\overline{W}_{d_e} + 501.2\,\overline{RF} + .247\,K_a$
      $R^2 = .80$ (.80)   (2.19)   (1.38)   (.86)
      Period: 1948–59

(2b) $V_a = -60,381 + 1.45\,\overline{L} - 58.3\,\overline{W}_{d_e} + 510.1\,\overline{RF}$
      $R^2 = .81$ (.36)   (2.05)   (1.30)
                               $+ .34\,K_{a_{-1}} + .247\,I_a$
      Period: 1948–59   (.68)   (.80)

(3) $V_b = -12,983 + .366\,K_b + 283.4\,\overline{W}_{d_e}$
              $R^2 = .80$ (6.01)   (1.53)
              Period: 1948–64

(4) $V_o = 110,439 + .119\,K_o + 75.4\,\overline{W}_{d_e} + 1.07\,\overline{G}$
              $R^2 = .83$ (4.28)   (2.75)   (1.12)
              Period: 1948–59

(5) $C_a = 7,399 + .128\,Y^d - 53.4\,\overline{tt}_i + 365.1\,\overline{y} + 25,654\,\overline{DV}_{40-45}$
      $R^2 = .74$ (3.80)   (.24)   (.42)   (3.05)
      Period: 1935–56

(6) $C_b = -11,052 + .326\,Y^d - 14,341\,\overline{DV}_{50-55}$
           $R^2 = .98$ (9.33)   (2.03)
           Period: 1950–63

(13) $M_{rm} = -12,984 + .366\,V_b - 283.4\,\overline{tt}_e$
          $R^2 = .80$ (6.01)   (1.53)
          Period: 1950–63

(22) $I_d = 64,045 + 1.328\,M_{rm} + 738.4\,\overline{CAP}_{-1}$
        $R^2 = .89$ (4.10)   (4.05)
        Period: 1950–63

The behavioral equations in the first group are estimates of the three production functions. The only time series found for capital stock by sectors was for the period 1944 to 1959.[41] It proved to be impossible to find a reliable time series for size of labor force by sector. Therefore, a

---

[41] The industrial sector was the exception here. ECLA (*Analisis y Proyecciones del Desarrollo Economico de la Argentina*), gives a longer time series of the value of capital stock in the manufacturing sector (1948–64).

proxy variable was used in the place of the size of the labor force. The proxy variable was derived as follows. A study of Argentine development suggests that the principal labor migration throughout the period was out of agriculture and into the manufacturing and services sectors. Much of this transfer of labor was accomplished through the attraction of higher wages in the urban areas. On the assumption that short-run variations in the supply of labor in the three sectors were due, in part, to relative wage differentials, it seemed reasonable to conclude that these differentials could, in some measure, explain changes in output attributable to changes in the size of the labor force. Therefore the absolute difference between monthly wages paid to common labor employed in industry and that of common labor employed in agriculture was selected as the variable $(\overline{W}_{dc})$.[42] In the case of agriculture, an increase in the size of the differential would be anticipated *a priori* to reduce output, since a greater amount of labor would be drawn into the other sectors—hence the negative sign in the agricultural production function (equations 2a and 2b). The opposite would be true for the other sectors. In addition to these two variables, an index of rainfall, $\overline{RF}$, and the quantity of land used in the agriculture sector were included in the agricultural production function.

In 2a the current value of the capital stock is included, whereas in 2b both the capital stock lagged one year and the current level of net investment are used. The resulting coefficients conform to what one would have expected on *a priori* grounds. The lack of statistical significance of three out of the four explanatory variables is not surprising in view of the stagnating character of the agricultural sector throughout this period characterized by little year-to-year variation in total land and capital employed. One possible explanation for the nonsignificance of the rainfall index is that the impact of changes in rainfall have a lagged (delayed) effect upon cattle output and a more immediate impact upon field crops.[43] Correct signs and reasonable values were obtained for the elasticities implied by the regressions for capital and land with regard to their measured value at the means. It must also be recognized that log-linear estimates of the production functions may have better described the production relationships. Because of the limited reliability of the data and because several proxy variables were being used, other possible forms of

[42] Salaries in current pesos converted to constant 1955 prices by deflating through the cost of living index.

[43] However, attempts to disaggregate agricultural output did not turn out more significant results.

the aggregate agricultural production function relationship were ignored.

A reasonable fit was obtained when value added in industry V_b is regressed on the capital stock in industry and the wage differential (equation 3). Value added in the "service" sector V_o can largely be explained by the same wage differential, the capital stock in the sector, and government expenditures $\overline{G}$ (equation 4).

The income variable was significant in both of the OLS estimates of the two consumption functions (equations 5 and 6). Higher coefficients of determination were obtained in both cases by including the respective dummy intercept variables. It seems evident that consumption of agricultural products was abnormally high during the years of World War II.[44] Neither internal terms of trade nor the income distribution variable appeared to be significantly correlated with the sectoral consumption variables.

Variations in V_b and the external terms of trade afforded a relatively satisfactory explanation of imports of raw materials (equation 13). The domestic investment equation was estimated on the basis of the lagged capacity in the domestic production of machinery and equipment and current levels of raw material imports, both of which were significant at the 0.05 level. The impact of current capital imports upon the productive capacity of the investment goods industries appears a priori so slight that it can be left out of the domestic investment equation.[45]

All other parameters appearing in the remaining equations were determined a priori from cross-sectional, historical, or input-output sources. Thus, the parameters b_i and d_i ($i = a, b, o$) in the export equations (8–10) were obtained from input-output information, and the parameter e in equation 11—representing the share of industrial raw materials imports out of total primary and intermediate goods imports—was based on the historical share.

Economic model building is essentially an exercise in specifying the reasonable and the feasible relations between economic variables. It is, of course, impossible to capture the structure of a complex economy in fifteen to twenty equations. However, if the structure of an economy is not mirrored completely, it may be assumed that the interdependence

---

[44] In the case of C_b, the dummy variable is included to show the differing political impact of the Peron and post-Peron governments upon consumption of manufactures. The explanatory ability of the consumption function for agricultural commodities would probably have been higher in the absence of the government's interference with agricultural prices.

[45] This was borne out by the OLS estimate of domestic investment where imports of capital goods were included. In all cases the coefficient carried by capital imports was extremely small and not statistically significant.

between major variables and sectors is sufficiently well reflected to enable new insights and a better knowledge of the economy to be obtained.

The statistically specified relations were incorporated into the model presented in Section 4 with some parameters determined on an *a priori* basis. The system of linear equations solved to derive the reduced form, providing the matrix of multipliers that relate the set of endogenous variables to the set of exogenous variables. The model was run for both versions of the agricultural production function (equations 2a and 2b). Furthermore, two sets of multipliers were obtained corresponding to two sets of values for the sectoral shares of investment. By varying α, the proportion of total investment devoted to agriculture, as well as β and j, the corresponding shares for industry and the service complex, the sensitivity of the system to these policy parameters could be ascertained *ceteris paribus*. When the nonlagged version of the agricultural production function V_a and two sets of investment parameters corresponding, respectively, to the situation existing in 1925–29 and 1955–59 were used, the results proved highly revealing. As previously noted, the sum of the three sectoral investment shares is, by definition, equal to unity. Thus, the multiplier of the lagged capital stock in agriculture (K_{a-1}) on gross domestic income was about 11 per cent higher using a high value for α of .21 (value of β, .11; of j, .68) than when using the value corresponding to the later period, which was .15 (β, .12; j, .73). Likewise, the multiplier relating K_{a-1} to agricultural exports was about 12 per cent higher in the earlier than in the later period as was the impact on capital goods imports and total investment. The above results provide a quantitative indication of the sensitivity of the major variables to investment in agriculture. It seems clear that income, given the model specification, is very responsive to agricultural investment. Two notes of warning should however be sounded: first, given the tenuous nature of the underlying data (or their proxy variables derived therefrom) and the limited statistical significance of a number of the coefficients in the original system (and the fact that a few *a priori* parameter values were used), the multipliers in the reduced form should be taken with more than one grain of salt.[46] Second, the multipliers hold true only over a limited range. For example, if more investment were to be directed to agriculture, the marginal productivity of this investment would drop after a certain level was reached. Conversely, the marginal productivity of investment in the other sectors

[46] This, incidentally, is the reason that the reduced form is not presented here. Efforts to improve the statistical specification of the model are continuing. At this time the most that one can expect from the reduced form is that it provide us with very rough orders of magnitude of the effects of the exogenous variables on the endogenous ones.

TABLE 5

Peru: Growth Rates of Selected Variables, 1950–66

(percentages based on constant 1963 prices)

	1950–52 to 1958–60	1958–60 to 1964–66	1950–52 to 1964–66
Gross domestic income	4.0	6.6	5.2
Exports of goods and Services + terms-of-trade effect	4.6	9.9	6.9
Consumption	4.3	5.3	4.7
Gross investment	3.1	10.1	5.9
Imports of goods and services	5.6	9.3	7.0

Source: Data supplied by Instituto Nacional de Planificacion.

would increase. There is little doubt, however, even in the light of these qualifications that Argentina would have benefited from more investment in agriculture.

4

Peru

The Over-all Structure and Development of the Economy Since 1950

The analytical framework was applied to the Peruvian economy over the post-World-War-II period (1950–66).[47] The main characteristics of the economy are its dualism and the dynamic and diversified nature of its exports with their limited backward linkages. Throughout this period Peru enjoyed a relatively high growth rate of GDI. Between 1951 and 1965, the annual cumulative rate amounted to 5.2 per cent. It can be seen from Table 5 that the rate of growth of GDI appears to be correlated with that of exports. In the first subperiod (1951–59) GDI grew at an annual cumulative rate of 4 per cent, slightly below that of exports

---

[47] The two reasons for limiting the analysis to this period are: first, national income data are simply not available for the preceding period and, second, Peru, in contrast to Argentina, is still essentially in the same developmental phase as it was forty years ago.

Figure 3

Causal Arrow Diagram: Peru Model

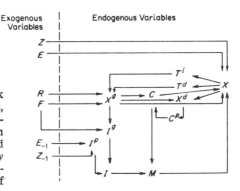

Exogenous Variables | Endogenous Variables

Source: Based on Model C in Erik Thorbecke and Apostolos Condos, "Macroeconomic Growth and Development Models of the Peruvian Economy," in Irma Adelman and Erik Thorbecke (ed.), *The Theory and Design of Economic Development*, Baltimore, 1966. The list of symbols is as follows:

Exogenous Variables
Z = terms-of-trade effect
E = exports
Z_{-1} = terms-of-trade effect lagged one year
E_{-1} = exports lagged one year
R = net revenue from nontax, nonforeign sources
F = net inflow of foreign public investment

Endogenous Variables
C = total consumption
C^p = private consumption
I^p = private gross investment
I^g = public gross investment
I = total gross investment
M = total imports of goods and services
T^i = indirect taxes
T^d = direct taxes
X = gross domestic income
X^d = disposable gross domestic income
X^g = government gross domestic income

(4.6 per cent). In the second subperiod (1959–65) exports grew at an amazing 9.9 per cent annually and the GDI at 6.6 per cent, suggesting that the acceleration in the growth rate of national income after 1959 was generated by activity in the export sector. The ratio of exports (corrected for the terms-of-trade effect) to GDI increased from 16.5 per cent to almost 21 per cent between 1950–52 (average) and 1964–66 (average). These figures reveal that the relative importance of exports in the economy is high and still increasing.

An econometric model of the Peruvian economy explained quite accurately the course of the major macroeconomic variables over the period under consideration. This model confirmed the role of exports in propelling the economy.[48] Figure 3 presents the causal relationships between

[48] Thorbecke and Condos, *op. cit.*

variables in the model. It can be seen that private investment is determined by exports and the terms-of-trade effects lagged one year. Private investment in turn is a major determinant of income, of which private consumption as well as direct and indirect taxes are functions. Finally, imports are explained by consumption and total investment.

It is of particular significance that a foreign-demand-oriented model would describe very accurately the structure and the growth of the Peruvian economy.

There appears to be a near consensus among students of the Peruvian economy that the main growth-generating force was exports, rather than investment *per se*.[49] Actually, as was previously implied, a very good statistical fit was obtained by regressing private investment I^p on lagged exports E_{-1} and the lagged terms-of-trade effect Z_{-1}.[50] Thus I^p is determined completely exogenously through the changes occurring in the export sector. This appears to be a reasonable hypothesis given: (1) the relative importance of the export sector; (2) the highly capital-intensive nature of export industries; and (3) the virtual absence of a domestic capital-goods-producing sector.

In summary, the performance of the export sector contributed to a relatively high rate of income growth and to a strong balance of payments (and a large capacity to import). Furthermore, the favorable balance of payments situation made it possible to maintain relative price stability by allowing imports to compensate for shortages in domestic production of foodstuffs and other consumer goods as demand increased in consequence of rising population and income.

The contribution of the high rate of export and income growth to some of the other developmental objectives, such as creation of employment and improvement of the very unequal income distribution, appears to have been marginal. Most of the export commodities are produced with highly capital-intensive methods (e.g., mining, fishmeal and sugar) and therefore did not provide many new job opportunities either directly or

[49] *Ibid.;* Michael Roemer, *The Dynamic Role of Exports in Economic Development: The Fishmeal Industry in Peru, 1956–1966,* unpublished doctoral dissertation, Department of Economics, Massachusetts Institute of Technology, 1967; and, René Vandendries, *Foreign Trade and the Economic Development of Peru,* unpublished doctoral dissertation, Department of Economics and Sociology, Iowa State University, 1967.

[50] $I^p = 2887 + .773\ E_{-1} + .660\ Z_{-1}\quad R^2 = .90$
$\quad\quad\quad\quad (.077)\quad\quad (.291)$

Sample period: 1950–65.

The standard errors of the coefficients are given in parenthesis. From Thorbecke and Condos, *op. cit.,* and *Peruvian Macro-Economic and Agricultural Prospects and Strategy, 1967–1972.*

indirectly. The income distribution, both personal and regional, appears to be as uneven now as ten years ago. The highly dualistic structure of the Peruvian economy, with the Coast as the advanced export sector and the Sierra as the backward subsistence sector, has not been altered.

Peru has maintained an essentially open economy. The level of tariffs is the lowest in Latin America. There was no exchange control over the period under consideration and the rate of exchange showed amazing stability, remaining constant between 1959 and 1967, in September of which, a worsening balance of payments and a large budget deficit led to a devaluation. The export prospects over the next five years are quite bleak because of supply limitations for fishmeal and mining products and stagnant world demand for cotton and sugar. From a detailed projection of the nine major export commodities it has been concluded that the rate of growth of exports is not likely to exceed 3 per cent annually between 1967 and 1971.[51]

Thus, Peru presents in retrospect a classical example of export-led growth with limited linkages to the production of home goods.

Sectoral Performance

Table 6 indicates the sectoral distribution of gross domestic product (GDP) for 1950, 1959, and 1966. It reveals clearly the sharp decline in the relative share of agriculture in GDP from 25 per cent in 1950 to 16.3 per cent in 1966. This rapid relative drop is not surprising in view of the very modest growth of agriculture (2.5 per cent per annum between 1950 and 1965), a growth that did not even keep up with the rate of population growth (2.8 per cent). The relative loss in agriculture's share in GDP was fully compensated by an equivalent gain in the share of industry, which increased from 20.4 per cent of GDP to 29.2 per cent over the same period. Half of the percentage gain in the share of industry is attributable to two essentially primary export activities, fishing and mining. The growth of the fishmeal industry has been well documented,[52] and provides perhaps the most spectacular case of staple-induced growth since World War II.

It is important to distinguish between two subsectors in evaluating the performance of agriculture: (a) production of industrial crops (cotton and sugar) for exports taking place mainly on the Coast, and (b) production of foodcrops, about 45 per cent of which originates in the Sierra

---

[51] *Peruvian Macro-Economic and Agricultural Prospects and Strategy, 1967–1972.*

[52] Roemer, *op. cit.*

TABLE 6

Peru: Sectoral Distribution and Growth of Gross Domestic Product, 1950–66

| | Distribution[a] | | | Cumulative Rate of Growth, |
	1950	1959	1966	1950–66
Agriculture	11,024 (25)	13,189 (20)	16,409 (16.3)	2.5
Food Crops	–	–	–	3.9[b]
Industrials[c]	–	–	–	.8[b]
Industry	9,004 (20.4)	15,595 (23.7)	29,378 (29.2)	7.7
Fishing	130 (0.3)	590 (0.9)	2,131 (2.1)	19.1
Mining	1,996 (4.5)	3,295 (5)	7,159 (7.1)	8.3
Remainder	6,878 (15.6)	11,711 (17.8)	20,088 (20)	6.9
Service complex[d]	24,083 (54.6)	34,985 (56.3)	54,756 (54.5)	5.3
GDP	44,111 (100)	63,769 (100)	100,543 (100)	5.3

Source: Data supplied by Instituto Nacional de Planificacion.

[a] In millions of constant soles at 1963 prices; percentages of total shown in parenthesis.
[b] 1951–64.
[c] Cotton and sugar.
[d] Includes: construction, energy, commerce, banking, housing, transport, communications, public administration and defense, education, health, and other services.

and is mainly self-consumed.[53] The output of cotton and sugar has stagnated, growing at only 0.8 per cent annually between 1951 and 1964, in comparison with food output, which grew over the same period at an annual rate of 3.9 per cent. Of agricultural output at the present time, about two-thirds consists of food crops and one-third of industrial crops.

Figure 1 (in Section 1) reveals the relative importance of the three sectors and their subsectors) in terms of value added and the sectoral origin of exports. Three subsectors (industrial crops, fishing and mining) provided 99.2 per cent of all exports in 1965. Furthermore, only a marginal share of the output of these subsectors was used domestically. Table 7 illustrates the shift in the commodity composition of exports. The most significant factor is the modest growth of agricultural exports in comparison with the exports of the other two subsectors. Agricultural exports (mainly cotton and sugar) increased at an annual rate of 3 per cent between 1950 and 1965, while the corresponding rates for fishmeal and mining exports were respectively 26 and 9.9 per cent. As a result of the phenomenal performance of fishmeal exports and the spectacular performance of mining products combined with the low growth of agricultural exports, the share of the latter in total exports has declined from 57 to about 26 per cent over the period under consideration. On the other hand, the relative importance of fishmeal exports skyrocketed from 3 to 28 per cent of total exports, while the share of mining exports went up from about 38 to 45 per cent. The low growth rate of agricultural exports was largely the effect of the limited world demand for cotton, sugar, and coffee.

Figure 1B depicts the sectoral destination of imports. It can be seen from Table 8 that the percentage share of capital goods and raw materials has risen, at the expense of consumer goods and foodstuffs.

The great bulk of capital goods and raw materials imports are destined for the industry and service sectors; the amount used by the agricultural sector (mainly by the nonfood sector) is estimated only at about $30 million in 1965. It is impossible, in the absence of an input-output table, to determine accurately the sectoral destination of imports. Nevertheless "guesstimates" would place the proportion of imports of capital goods and raw materials absorbed by the fishmeal and mining subsectors at about 30 and 60 per cent of output, respectively. Final demand imports (food and consumer durables and nondurables), because they do not contribute to value added, appear as rectangles at the bottom of Figure 1B. The bottom diagram in Figure 1 effectively illustrates: (a)

[53] It is estimated that not more than one-fifth of the Sierra's food output is marketed commercially.

TABLE 7

Peru: Sectoral Distribution and Growth of Exports, 1950–65

Exports	Distribution[a]			Cumulative Rate of Growth		
	1950	1959	1965	1950–59	1959–65	1960–65
Agricultural	110 (57.1)	138 (43.8)	172 (25.8)	2.5	3.8	3
Fish and fishmeal	6 (3)	44 (14.1)	186 (28)	25	27	26
Mining	73 (37.9)	122 (38.8)	303 (45.4)	5.8	16.4	9.9
Others	4 (2.1)	10 (3.2)	5 (0.8)	–	–	–
Total	193 (100)	314 (100)	666 (100)	5.5	13.4	8.6

Source: See Table 6.

[a]Value in millions of dollars; percentages of total shown in parentheses.

TABLE 8

Peru: Commodity Composition of Imports, Selected Years
(value in millions of dollars; percentage distribution in parentheses)

Imports	1950	1959	1965
Food and food products	39 (22.2)	63 (19.8)	134 (18.4)
Consumption goods (excl. food)	37 (21.0)	40 (12.6)	119 (16.3)
Raw materials and fuel	29 (16.5)	78 (24.5)	165 (22.7)
Capital goods	69 (39.2)	135 (42.5)	308 (42.3)
Others	2 (1.1)	2 (0.6)	3 (0.4)
Total	176 (100.0)	318 (100.0)	728 (100.0)

Source: See Table 6.

the relatively small amount of imports that go into agriculture (a reflection of the small flow of investment, e.g., farm machinery, into that
sector); and (b) the relatively large amount of food imports.

The large capacity to import that provided the basis of, or at least
a permissive factor in, Peru's income growth is likely to become a
bottleneck, given the bleak export prospects mentioned earlier. The
weakening of the major stimulus to growth combined with the small
size of the domestic manufacturing sector (producing for home consumption) and the limited scope for industrial import substitution are
likely to result in a low growth rate of GDI.[54]

It will be argued that the agricultural sector can play an essential role
in attenuating the undesirable consequences to a number of developmental objectives (e.g., employment creation) that would accompany a
low rate of income growth. Agriculture in Peru, as in many developing
countries, fulfills two major functions. First, the commercialized subsector has historically been an important contributor to foreign exchange
earnings. (The performance of agricultural exports however has been
relatively disappointing as was indicated previously.[55])

The second function of the agricultural sector is to provide food for

[54] Using Model C in Thorbecke and Condos, and plugging in projected values
for the exogenous variables (e.g., exports, terms-of-trade effect, net public investment) we predicted a rate of growth of GDI of about 3 per cent for 1967–71.

[55] Industrial crops grew at less than one per cent between 1950 and 1964, and
the share of agricultural exports in total exports declined from 57 to 26 per
cent over the same period.

TABLE 9

*Peru: Rate of Growth of Agricultural Output
by Crops and by Regions, 1950–64*

	Coast	Sierra	Selva	Republic
All food crops	6.9	1.4	4.7	3.9
Cereals	4.7	0.5	3.8	2.9
Tubers and roots	3.5	1.1	4.6	1.7
Beans and pulses	6.1	2.6	4.2	4.5
Fresh vegetables	8.6	3.3	8.2	6.4
Fresh fruits	10.4	5.4	5.0	8.0
Industrials	0.8	2.2	2.0	0.8
All crops	3.5	1.4	3.7	2.7

Source: Iowa Universities Mission to Peru: *Peruvian Macroeconomic and Agricultural Prospects and Strategy, 1967–1972*, Lima, Peru, 1967.

itself and for the other sectors. Even though the production of domestic food crops rose at 3.9 per cent per annum during the postwar period, it did not rise steeply enough to keep up with the growth of food demand. Consequently, the level of food imports increased substantially from $39 million in 1950 to $134 million in 1965 (see Table 7). The relatively poor performance of agricultural exports and the higher dependence on food imports turned the balance of trade in agriculture from a large positive one to a negative one. Indeed, the excess of agricultural exports over imports of agricultural products and inputs was almost $60 million in 1960. By 1966, this balance had become slightly negative, the agricultural sector having become a drain from the balance of payments standpoint.

It is necessary to examine Peruvian agriculture regionally in order to understand its structure. Table 9 gives the postwar rates of growth for the output of various agricultural crops in the three natural regions of Peru: (a) the Coast (the commercialized export subsector), (b) the Sierra (the subsistence subsector), and (c) the Selva (jungle).[56]

The table reveals that agricultural growth in the Sierra was substantially lower than on the Coast. Practically all the output in the Sierra

[56] The Selva produces less than 5 per cent of total agricultural output.

TABLE 10

Peru: Annual Growth Rates for Urban and Rural Population by Regions

	Coast	Sierra	Selva	Nationwide
Urban	4.8	2.5	5.8	4.1
Rural	2.9	1.0	3.9	1.8
Total	4.4	1.3	4.5	3.0

Source: See Table 9.

consists of food crops that grew at an annual rate of only 1.4 per cent. In contrast, agricultural output on the Coast rose at a corresponding rate of 3.5 per cent, the result of a marginal (0.8 per cent) increase in the production of industrial crops and a large (6.9 per cent) growth in food crops.

Since agriculture is the only productive activity in the Sierra,[57] the rate of growth of food output provides a good approximation of the over-all growth of income. Table 10 indicates the population dynamics by regions. The heavy labor migration from the Sierra to the Coast is revealed by these data. It is also clear that per capita income in the Sierra must have remained stagnant as judged by the equivalence between population growth (1.3 per cent after migration) and agricultural growth (1.4 per cent).

The Contribution of Agriculture to Developmental Objectives

In Section 1, five major developmental objectives were outlined. In this part an attempt will be made to assess the contribution of agriculture to these various targets. It has already been seen that the agricultural sector, as a whole, has recently become a net claimant on foreign exchange, a contrast with its previous status of contributor to the balance of payments. The imports of food products have risen to an alarmingly high level. Of the major food imports—wheat, meat, milk products, rice and oils—meat, milk, and rice offer fairly large scope for import substitution. The existence of a strong balance of payments situation through-

[57] The mining activity in the Sierra is clearly an enclave-type operation with marginal economic linkages.

out the period 1960–66 and the maintenance of a fixed exchange rate between 1959 and 1967 explain the high level of food imports. The export stagnation anticipated for the next few years makes import substitution of foodstuffs essential. This, of course, will necessitate increased domestic food production, but the scope for import substitution in other areas is very limited. (The recent devaluation is likely to provide the price incentive for the import substitution of foodstuffs.)

The contribution of agriculture to over-all income has already been discussed. It was seen that the growth rate of agriculture (2.7 per cent) was quite modest compared to that of GDP. Agriculture has been a lagging sector in an otherwise highly dynamic economy. The agricultural stagnation has important implications from an income distribution standpoint (discussed below), given that almost one-half of the labor force is employed in that sector.

The substantial decline in the relative share of agriculture in total GDP (see Table 6) combined with a much slower reduction in the share of agriculture in the total labor force suggests that income distribution might have become more uneven. This inference is strengthened when income performance in the Sierra is examined. As pointed out above, per capita income probably remained at about the same level over the period 1950–64. The distribution of income between the Coast and the Sierra is therefore bound to have worsened, since GDP per capita grew at more than 2 per cent annually while per capita income in the Sierra remained constant. (At the present time about 48 per cent of the population lives in the Sierra.) The inequality in the income distribution is reflected in sharp regional differences in nutritional standards.[58]

The sectoral and regional income disparities are also reflected, of course, in wide disparities in personal income distribution. Attempts at deriving Lorenz curves reveal not only the above trend toward income inequality over time, but also the fact that Peru's income distribution is considerably worse than that of even Ecuador, Chile, Mexico, and Venezuela.[59]

The traditional role of agriculture throughout the development process is to release labor to the other sectors. However, the capacity to absorb

[58] The daily average and per capita caloric and protein intake have been estimated at 2,248 calories and 59 grams, respectively, for Peru and at 3,140 calories and 73 grams, respectively, for greater Lima (20 per cent of the total, and roughly half, of the coastal population). It follows, therefore, that the caloric intake in the Sierra must be around 2,000 calories per capita per day. (See *Peruvian Macro-Economic and Agricultural Products and Strategy, 1967–72.*)

[59] Republica del Peru, Instituto Nacional de Planificacion, *La Evolucion de la Economia en el Periodo 1950–1964,* Vol. I.

labor in the other sectors is extremely limited. The growing industrial subsectors, especially mining and fishing, have been at best fairly marginal users of labor because of the highly capital-intensive nature of their production functions.[60] The service complex has absorbed some labor, particularly in construction, but tends to be a kind of residual claimant of many disguised unemployed. A factor that further complicates the over-all employment problem is that the coastal agricultural subsector producing industrial crops, chiefly cotton and sugar,[61] has been mechanizing on a wide scale, thereby reducing absolutely the number of agricultural workers in these activities.

These various factors, together with the high migration from the subsistence subsector (the Sierra) to the Coast, combine to create an increasingly serious unemployment problem, against which it is very difficult to devise an effective strategy. It appears, however, essential from the standpoints of both income distribution (e.g., to meet minimum nutritional targets) and employment that some resources be allocated to the Sierra to increase agricultural output, which in that region is synonymous with income.[62]

The final policy objective to be examined is that of price stability and the internal terms of trade. The statistical evidence is that food prices increased at approximately the same rate as that of nonfood prices over the postwar period.[63] However, prices of food imports rose at a considerably lower rate than domestic food crops. The reasons for these differences in trends are (a) that the rate of exchange remained constant between 1959 and 1967, a factor that, combined with a higher rate of inflation at home than abroad, made food imports very attractive from the point of view of price; and (b) that the domestic supply of foodstuffs was fairly inelastic given the prevailing technology and structure. It is clear that the government was aiming for low food prices as a major instrument for improving the income distribution in the urban centers. The latter objective was achieved through a variety of measures, including price controls, subsidies, and a fixed exchange rate. However, it appears evident, in retrospect, that these policies discriminated against the agricultural sector, in general. The stability of the exchange rate reduced the profitability of the export crops and of the domestic import competing crops (e.g., meat, milk, and rice). Furthermore, the avail-

[60] See Vandendries, op. cit.

[61] The sugar industry in Peru is said to be run as efficiently as, or even more efficiently than, its U.S. counterpart.

[62] For an excellent discussion of an agricultural development strategy for Peru see Peruvian Macro-Economic and Agricultural Prospects and Strategy, 1967–72.

[63] Ibid.

ability of low-priced grain (wheat) might have discouraged the production of domestic substitutes (e.g., barley and potatoes) by removing the price incentive.[64]

The above discussion has brought out some of the problems resulting from a lagging agricultural sector within a dynamic export-oriented economy. The further development of Peru appears contingent on improving both the structure and the productivity of its agricultural sector.

BIBLIOGRAPHY

Chenery, H. B., *Toward a More Effective Alliance for Progress,* A.I.D. Discussion Paper No. 13, 1967.

Diaz-Alejandro, Carlos F., "An Interpretation of Argentine Economic Growth since 1930," Parts I and II, *Journal of Development Studies,* Part I, October 1966; Part II, January 1967.

Eshag, Eprime and Rosemary Thorp, "Economic and Social Consequences of Orthodox Economic Policies in Argentina in the Post-war Years," *Bulletin of the Oxford University Institute of Economics and Statistics,* Vol. 27, February 1965.

Falcon, Walter P., *Agricultural and Industrial Interrelationships in West Pakistan,* Development Advisory Service, The Center for International Affairs, Harvard University Report No. 70, 1967.

Fox, Karl A., "The Food and Agricultural Sectors in Advanced Economies," in T. Barna (ed.), *Structural Interdependence and Economic Development,* New York, 1963.

Fienup, Darrell, *Changes in Argentinian Agricultural Production and Productivity over the Past 25 Years,* Institute of Agriculture, University of Minnesota, Minneapolis, 1966.

Iowa Universities Mission to Peru, *Peruvian Macro-Economic and Agricultural Prospects and Strategy, 1967–1972,* Lima, 1967.

Kelly, Ruth, "Foreign Trade of Argentina and Australia, 1930 to 1960," *Economic Bulletin for Latin America, United Nations,* ECLA, Vol. X, No. 1, March 1965.

Leff, Nathaniel H., "Export Stagnation and Autarkic Development in Brazil, 1947–1962," paper prepared for A.I.D.'s Summer Research Program 1966.

Lewis, W. Arthur, *Development Planning,* New York, 1966.

Maneschi, Andrea and Clark Reynolds, *The Effect of Import Substitution on Foreign Exchange Needs, Savings Rates and Growth in Latin America,* Discussion Paper No. 18, Economic Growth Center, Yale University, 1966.

---

[64] The devaluation of September 1967 is likely to provide price incentives for the producers of industrial and food crops.

Maynard, Geoffrey and Willy van Rijckeghem, *Stabilization Policy in an Inflationary Economy: Argentina,* Development Advisory Service, The Center for International Affairs, Harvard University, Report No. 34, 1966.

Naciones Unidas, ECLA, *Analisis y Proyecciones del Desarrollo Economico de la Argentina,* Mexico, 1959.

Papageorgiou, Efstathios, *An Econometric Study of Argentina.* (Master's Thesis, Iowa State University, Ames, 1966.)

Presidencia de la Nacion Argentina, Consejo Nacional de Desarrollo, *Plan Nacional de Desarrollo 1965–1969,* Buenos Aires, 1965.

República Argentina, *Producto y Ingresso de la República Argentina en el Periodo 1935–54,* Buenos Aires, 1955.

Republica del Peru, Instituto Nacional de Planificacion, *La Evolucion de la Economia en el Periodo 1950–64* (Vols. I–IV), 1966.

Roemer, Michael, *The Dynamic Role of Exports in Economic Development: The Fishmeal Industry in Peru, 1956–1966.* (Doctoral dissertation, Massachusetts Institute of Technology, Cambridge, 1967.)

Sjaastad, Larry A., "Argentina and the Five-Year Plan," paper prepared for Latin American Conference, Cornell University, April, 1966.

Smith, John Newton, *Competitive Aspects of Argentine Agriculture,* USDA, Western Hemisphere Branch, Foreign Regional Analysis Division, 1967.

Thorbecke, Erik and Apostolos Condos, "Macroeconomic Growth and Development Models of the Peruvian Economy," in I. Adelman and E. Thorbecke (ed.), *The Theory and Design of Economic Development,* Baltimore, 1966.

Thorbecke, Erik, "The Role and Function of Agricultural Development in National Economic Growth," in *Economic Development of Agriculture,* Center for Agricultural and Economic Development, Ames, Iowa, 1965.

Vandendries, René, *Foreign Trade and the Economic Development of Peru.* (Doctoral dissertation, Iowa State University, Ames, 1967.)

Villanueva, Javier, *The Inflationary Process in Argentina, 1943–60,* working paper of Inst. Torcuato Di Tella, Centro de Investigaciones Economicas, Buenos Aires, 1966.

Comment

CLARK W. REYNOLDS, STANFORD UNIVERSITY

One must applaud the emphasis of this paper on the need for increased public support for agricultural development in Latin America. Not that this extremely important issue has been ignored in the historical and theoretical literature on economic development, only that policy-making institutions (at least in Latin America) have tended to neglect the problem until very recently. The study reveals how much the new focus of U.S./AID and international lending agencies on agricultural development as a *counterbalance* rather than *alternative* to rapid industrialization depends upon more and better research on the conditions of production and demand as essential prerequisites to effective policy formation. Ultimately the partial information derived from such research will be successfully integrated in the form of simultaneous estimating models to determine the internal consistency of the economy and its sensitivity to alternative agricultural development strategies.

The authors' model has two ostensible purposes; one is taxonomic serving to isolate sectoral relationships deemed most important in the analysis of postwar Argentina and Peru. The value of the taxonomy depends on the theoretical basis and historical importance of the disaggregation selected, and there is insufficient space devoted to this issue in the present study to warrant a detailed commentary. The other purpose of the model is predictive. The value of the predictions depends on the quality of underlying data, accuracy of specification of the equations, and statistical significance of the results. Although the monographic literature on which the authors depend for insights into the two economies tends to support their sectoral disaggregation into agriculture, manufacturing, services, and foreign trade, the model is less clear about the functional role of such a disaggregation and is particularly weak in its treatment of the service sector.

I shall limit my specific comments to that part of the paper dealing with the application of the general model presented in Section 3 to the case of Argentina. The policy relevance of the present model is limited owing to its preliminary nature. The estimated relationships add little to the insights derived from the underlying source material. It would improve the present form of the paper if the authors attempted an explicit test of the sensitivity of the system as a whole, and the balance of payments in particular, to changes in instrument variables. For example the authors' highly critical *ex post* analysis of industrialization at the expense of agriculture in Argentina suggests little more than the fact that it is possible to go to extremes in policy formation. The model does not reveal limits for alternative policies; in urging the need to increase investment in agriculture at the expense of manufacturing and services (increasing α versus β and j) the authors cite the "multiplier" effect on income of a shift in the agricultural share of marginal investment from

0.15 to 0.21. This is said to have a positive effect of 11 per cent on GNP in the next period. It would be helpful to show what alternative multiplier effects would be achieved from changes in β or j vis-à-vis α. Furthermore the strategy suggested by the model deals primarily with once-for-all adjustments of levels of income rather than with the more important questions of growth and development. A slight change in the growth rate (a possibility not considered in the paper) could rapidly offset the rather slight multiplier effect of so large a suggested change in the investment coefficient. Moreover there is little consideration in the model of the effect of alternative policies on income distribution, the level and composition of final demand, and aggregate rates of savings and investment.

It is argued that agricultural investment should be stimulated at the expense of other sectors through changes in the internal terms of trade. Such a device may raise food prices relative to manufactures, increase pressure for wage increases in industry (particularly in Argentina), lower rates of return on capital, and squeeze real wages in manufacturing and urban services as well. All of these effects may tend to depress the marginal efficiency of investment in industry and services while increasing political unrest among businessmen and the urban working class. In the absence of agrarian reform this condition would imply the redistribution of income so as to favor traditional landowners, with serious political implications in both countries. Neither in the reduced form of the model nor in the initial set of equations is there a sufficiently detailed specification of alternative policies to change investment shares. Moreover the degree to which policy space is constrained by political factors must be considered in Latin America in weighing alternative development strategies.

It is important to analyze the effect on the consumption function of a shift in the internal terms of trade, because such a shift may well produce perverse effects on the rate of growth by lowering the aggregate investment rate, especially if there is a low price elasticity of demand for foodstuffs in the cities. (That agricultural demand is not as sensitive to relative price changes as the authors' recommendations would lead us to believe is suggested by the fact that the agricultural consumption equation in the reduced form model has an insignificant internal terms-of-trade coefficient.) Under such circumstances a shift in the terms of trade toward agriculture may well increase the share of food consumed at home by raising own consumption on the farm more than urban consumption is reduced. In any case, a clarification of this relationship is essential before the model can be used as a guideline to policy.

This writer would, suggest an alternative method of stimulating agricultural production by an indirect approach similar to that used successfully by Mexico. More and, better intermediate inputs were made available to agriculture by industry (farm equipment, fertilizer, and improved seeds), and service activities such as transportation, commerce, and storage facilities plus rural credit were expanded with government support. Another suggested approach, again found effective in Mexico, is a dual-price policy in agriculture, with supports for the farmer plus state purchase and storage of staple crops that are then sold at subsidized prices to the urban working class. Under this plan the costs are borne by taxes on manufacturing and commerce. The preceding policies have the effect of accomplishing an increase in agricultural production, while at the same time minimizing political opposition to the transfer of resources into agriculture.

A word about the form of the production functions: the authors prefer the relationship of agricultural value-added—rather than of total output—to basic factor inputs plus rainfall. This relationship, without accommodating technical change, ignores the importance of intermediate stages of production with which import substitution policy must continually deal. It is precisely in the area of intermediate inputs that agricultural productivity has been so remarkably influenced in other developing countries such as Japan, Mexico, and Pakistan. Moreover, the use in the reduced form of the model of relative rural-urban wages as a proxy for labor inputs in agriculture and, manufacturing is not appropriate in a country such as Argentina, where the urban labor market is highly imperfect because of the entrenchment of politically powerful labor unions and the use of wage policy to influence election results. Only recently has the Argentine government been effective in limiting the influence of labor union opposition to austerity programs.

The estimation of import demand functions in the model is also problematic since there is an assumption that intermediate imports are complementary rather than substitutable. Capital imports are a residual in an accounting identity (equation 14) although the authors do make use of consumer goods imports as an instrument variable, thereby making the residual subject to policy as well. Because of the specification of the import equation, the model is subject to the confines of present import-substitution strategy, which does not permit the working of comparative advantage at all levels of production. For example, the forced substitution of all final consumer goods at the same time that intermediate components are imported is precisely the kind of industrialization policy that has produced so many problems in other countries. An extreme consequence of this policy is the creation of negative value added. An alternative specification worth testing for traded goods would make import demand a residual of total domestic demand and production. This assumes importables to be competing rather than complementary goods. Such a specification allows sectoral shifts from net importer to net exporter and vice versa without altering the model.

There is much to be said for the authors' courage and imagination in working on the frontier of sectoral growth models for open economies. Their paper is a step forward, although as yet the model adds little to the source material on sectoral development of the respective economies and would, in fact, be dangerous if used in its present form as a guideline to policy. Hopefully this and similar work will continue to advance so that the profession may look forward to significant policy-related model building in the future. In the meantime the authors' reliance on historical and institutional materials on Peru and Argentina underscores the importance of continued research in these areas with particular attention to the complexities and diversities of intersectoral behavior and the importance of political constraints on public policy.

Reply

ERIK THORBECKE AND ALFRED J. FIELD

The main objective of our paper was to present a general conceptual framework within which some of the more important intra- and intersectoral relationships of developing countries could be studied and in some cases quantified. The application and quantitative specification of the general model to Argentina was for illustrative purposes only and was definitely not the central objective of the paper as Clark Reynolds infers it to be by devoting his comments almost exclusively to it. We agree entirely with Reynolds that the quantitatively specified Argentina model is of only limited usefulness for policy purposes. The lack of consistent and continuous time series proved to be a serious obstacle in the estimation of the model. However, the general framework and its application to Argentina did reveal and support quantitatively a number of observations and conclusions drawn by serious students of the Argentine economy. Furthermore, the same framework applied to Peru brought out important sectoral differences and contrasts in the development process of Peru as compared to that of Argentina.

In addition to the general issues discussed above, there are two specific points raised by Reynolds to which we would like to reply. First, he appears to recommend using the model to measure the sensitivity of changes in the sectoral investment ratio (α, β and j) on GNP and other variables. This is in fact what was done by taking two sets of values for these ratios and indicating that a shift of 15 to 21 per cent in α (the share of total investment going to agriculture) would have resulted in a more than 10 per cent increase in gross domestic product in Argentina.

Second, Reynolds questions the use of relative rural/urban wages in the model as a proxy variable for agricultural and industrial labor inputs, respectively, on the ground that these wages are not competitively determined. Indeed the political influence of labor unions tended to favor industrial wages as opposed to agricultural wages. However, our hypothesis that labor inputs in industry are directly correlated with an increase in the ratio of the industrial wage rate to the agricultural wage rate and vice-versa for agriculture is independent of whether or not wages are competitively determined as long as entry is not restricted.

A Programming Model
for a Dual Economy

JAN SANDEE

NETHERLANDS SCHOOL OF ECONOMICS

THE ECONOMIES of most developing countries are "dual" in many senses of the word. Few programming models for such countries take account of this fact, however. The sectoral models can, of course, be said to incorporate certain aspects of duality, because some of their sectors belong largely to one part of the dual economy only. Even so, it is generally production only that is sectored, with consumer or financial behavior being represented for the economy as a whole. Some macro models treat agricultural output exogenously, but this can hardly be said to do justice to dualism.

This paper presents a model that concentrates on dualism but is a macro model in every other sense. It is shown that the introduction of "dual" targets and instruments increases realism, and modifies conclusions reached with a "unitary" macro model.

DUALISM DEFINED

This is not the place to study dualism as it affects the greater part of mankind. We shall only give a brief list of the main traits by which the "modern" sector of a nation's economy is distinguished from the "traditional" sector.

NOTE: The present version of this paper has profited in many respects from remarks made by Prof. Dale W. Jorgenson, Dr. Ahmet Beyarslan and Dr. Louis Goreux.

The "modern" sector has factories and plantations, wage labor, cities, tap water, sewers, manufactured foods, cinemas, taxes, banks, and police. To enjoy all these advantages, people migrate towards the cities. The birth rate in the urban areas remains somewhat lower than in the rural sector. Products of the modern sector are shipped by rail or by sea to destinations within the country, and to the developed areas of the world.

Nearly all these characteristics occur jointly in the modern parts of the economy of all developing countries, and nearly all of them are lacking in the traditional parts. Because the characteristics are highly correlated, a sector may be distinguished by any one characteristic. This enables us to vary the names of the two sectors of the economy as the occasion may require.

THE MODEL ECONOMY

The model is drawn up for a "typical" developing country, where in the base year 30 million people live in the rural areas and 10 million in the cities. It is assumed that a five-year plan is being drawn up and that consistent provisional estimates have already been obtained for the major economic variables in the base year and in the final year of the planning period. These estimates are given in the table on the following page.

In the model, sixteen of these variables are endogenous and nine are exogenous. The meaning of the variables will become clearer when they are described in connection with the model. The variable TTR, however, requires some explanation. This measures, in billions of dollars, the gain to the rural sector of a change in its terms of trade with the urban sector. In the final year, the flows between the two sectors are RCM = $1.29 billion and UCF-FIM = $1.23 billion, or $1.26 billion on the average. A change in the terms of trade by 1 per cent would make TTR = $0.0126 billion.

The natural population increase in the rural areas is put at 1.2 million (i.e., 4 per cent) annually, and without migration rural population would amount to 36 million in the final year. As MIG = 0.5 million annually, this reduces to 33.5 million. Natural population growth in the cities is put at 200,000 (i.e., 2 per cent) annually, which, including migration, leads to 13.5 million in the final year.

Symbol	Description	Base year	Final year
		Billion $	
GNP	Gross national product	6.60	8.52
RPR	Rural product	3.60	4.32
UPR	Urban product	3.00	4.20
SLK	Unused urban capacity to produce	—	—
RCF	Rural consumption of food	2.70	3.09
RCM	Rural consumption of manufactures	0.90	1.29
UCF	Urban consumption of food	0.90	1.23
UCM	Urban consumption of manufactures	1.50	2.13
RAT	Urban food rationing	—	—
FIM	Food imports	—	—
OIM	Other imports	0.50	0.70
INV	Urban productive investment	0.40	0.56
HOU	Urban housing	0.12	0.12
IRR	Irrigation investment	—	—
GOV	Government consumption	0.13	0.20
EXP	Exports	0.45	0.60
SAV	Urban saving	0.60	0.84
TAX	Tax increases	—	—
TRF	Transfers to rural sector	—	0.06
SUB	Food subsidies in urban areas	—	—
TTR	Terms-of-trade gain to rural sector	—	—
FCI	Foreign capital imports	0.05	0.10
		$1000 per capita	
RSL	Rural standard of living	0.120	0.131
USL	Urban standard of living	0.240	0.249
		Millions	
MIG	Migration to urban areas	0.50	0.50

THE MODEL

The model consists of the following sixteen equations, which refer to the final-year values of the variables.

(1) $GNP = RPR + UPR$

(2) $RPR = RCF + (UCF - FIM) + IRR$

(3) $RCM = (UCF - FIM) + TTR + TRF + IRR$

(4) $UPR = (UCM + UCF + TTR) - SUB + SAV$

(5)   SAV + FCI = INV + HOU + IRR + GOV + TRF

(6)   FIM + OIM = EXP + FCI

(7)   RPR = 4.320 + 0.686 TTR + 1.000 IRR

(8)   UPR = 3.600 + 1.072 INV − SLK

(9)   OIM = 0.167 UPR

(10)   RCF = 1.660 − 0.230 MIG + 11.780 RSL − 0.500 TTR

(11)   UCF = 0.501 + 0.228 MIG + 2.470 USL − 0.500 TTR +
         + 0.500 SUB − RAT

(12)   SAV = 0.20 (UPR − TTR + SUB) + TAX − SUB

(13)   RSL = 0.030 (RCF + RCM) + 0.010 MIG − 0.005

(14)   USL = 0.074 (UCF + UCM) − 0.046 MIG + 0.023

(15)   MIG = 4.230 (USL − RSL)

(16)   HOU = 0.171 MIG + 0.034

Observations on each equation follow:
1. Definition of GNP.
2. This definition of RPR assumes that rural output consists entirely of "food" supplied to rural and urban areas but not exported and of the construction of irrigation dams and canals.
3. Purchases by the rural sector from the cities, called "rural consumption of manufactures," are paid for out of the proceeds of food sales to the cities, transfers received, and the remuneration from operation of irrigation facilities which is supposed to be fully paid in money.
4. Income disposal of urban sector.
5. Joint capital and government balance.
6. Balance of payments.
7. Rural supply function. The elasticity of supply with respect to relative price is put at 0.2. As the (UCF-FIM) and RCM flows average $1.26 billion in the final year, whereas RPR = $4.32 billion, the coefficient is determined as $0.2 \times (4.32/1.26) = 0.686$.

If IRR expands linearly from the base year to the final year and a slight time lag occurs between IRR and the corresponding increase in RPR, one unit of IRR in the final year will correspond to two units in the part of the plan period in which it can still contribute to RPR in the final year. We would then have the following pattern of irrigation activities in the plan period:

First year   0.2 units
Second year 0.4 units
Third year   0.6 units
Fourth year 0.8 units
Fifth year   1.0 unit

In the first four years this would total two units, and these might all contribute to agricultural output in the final year. Assuming a capital/output ratio of 2, the coefficient is $2/2 = 1.000$.

As will be explained later, a term -0.323 MIG may be added to this equation to represent the effect of the withdrawal of labor.

8. Urban production function. As with irrigation, one unit of INV in the final year represents two units during the plan period that can already contribute to UPR. The capital/output ratio is put at the wholly imaginary value of 1.855 (there had to be some difference with the COR of IRR). The constant is adjusted to match the final year values of the variables. As in the preceding equation, one term may be added to represent the effect of migration on urban output.

9. The average urban propensity to import is 16.7 per cent.

10. Rural food consumption function. One million more migrants during the final year are considered to correspond to 2.5 million more migrants during the five-year plan period, decreasing the rural population by 2.5 million persons. This is the result of a linear expansion of migration from the base-year level to a final-year level raised by 1 million annually (cf. the treatment of irrigation in equation 7). One million rural persons consume $3.09/33.5 = \$0.092$ billion worth of food annually, and 2.5 million would consume $\$0.230$ billion worth, which explains the coefficient of MIG.

Income elasticity of food demand is put at 0.5, and with RSL $= 0.131$ and RCF $= 3.09$ in the final year, the coefficient of RSL is put at $0.5 \times (3.09/0.131) = 11.780$. It should be remembered that RCM includes all purchases from the urban sector, even fertilizer. It is quite realistic to make fertilizer purchases depend on RSL, but the complement of RCM, that is RCF, will then show a lower income elasticity with respect to RSL. Whether the value of 0.5 adequately represents this argument is a matter of judgment.

The meaning of the term -0.5 TTR may be interpreted as follows. If food sold to the cities fetches 5 per cent more in terms of manufactures than before, $2\frac{1}{2}$ per cent more food will be supplied to the cities, and correspondingly less food will be consumed, apart from the income effect of the price change which is incorporated in the RSL term. Our coefficient thus reflects a supply elasticity out of current output of 0.5, as compared to a supply elasticity of 0.2 for output to be produced additionally (equation 7). The constant is adjusted to fit the final-year value of 3.09 for RCF.

11. Urban food demand. The coefficient of USL represents an income elasticity of 0.5. The coefficients of 0.5 for TTR and SUB are to be interpreted as demand (substitution) elasticities with respect to price. The UCF flow represents the raw food content of food purchases only; imported manufactured foods are entirely excluded from it. This might point to somewhat lower elasticities than the ones used.

12. Urban "saving" equation. The marginal propensity to "save" out of "real" income (UPR − TTR + SUB) equals the average propensity. TAX is an instrument variable designed to increase domestic financing by appropriate government policies. There are no explicit taxes in this model. Such taxes as exist already in the final year may be thought of as incorporated in SAV. Food subsidies SUB, while coupled to food consumption UCF, are treated as negative taxes.

13. Definition of rural standard of living as per capita rural consumption. The 33.5 million rural population explains the 0.030 coefficient. One million migrants more in the final year are considered to reduce the population in the final year by 2½ million, or by 7.5 per cent (2.5/33.5). RSL = 0.131 in the final year, and 7.5 per cent of 0.131 equals 0.01. The constant is adjusted as before.

14. Definition of urban standard of living on same lines as rural.

15. Migration is considered to be proportional to the difference between USL and RSL. The coefficient is derived from the final year estimates.

16. Housing and allied expenditure is considered to be proportional to the rate of increase of the urban population. In the final year, the urban population grew by 0.2 million through natural increase, and by 0.5 million through migration, while HOU = 0.12. Thus the coefficient is 0.12/(0.2 + 0.5) = 0.171. The constant is adjusted as before.

Of the twenty-five variables, nine are made exogenous.

The reduced form of the model is given in Table 1.

As usual, the reduced form shows us how variations in exogenous variables affect the endogenous variables. An increase in TAX by one unit, for instance, increases GNP by 1.455 units.

A PROGRAMMING EXPERIMENT

By means of the model we will now try to improve upon the provisional five-year plan, making a judicious use of some exogenous variables as

TABLE 1

Model for Typical Developing Country Based on Major Economic Variables

(reduced form)

Endogenous Variables	Exogenous Variables								
	EXP	TAX	TRF	FCI	IRR	SLK	SUB	RAT	GOV
GNP	-0.394	1.455	-1.299	1.070	-0.299	-1.366	-0.958	-0.394	-1.464
RSL	-0.036	0.009	0.025	-0.019	0.025	-0.016	0.019	-0.036	-0.017
USL	0.039	-0.004	-0.057	0.088	-0.057	-0.046	0.037	0.039	-0.049
RPR	-0.531	0.129	-0.026	-0.314	0.974	-0.202	0.250	-0.531	-0.217
UPR	0.137	1.326	-1.274	1.384	-1.274	-1.163	-1.208	0.137	-1.247
FIM	0.977	-0.221	0.213	0.769	0.213	0.194	0.202	-0.023	0.208
OIM	0.023	0.221	-0.213	0.231	-0.213	-0.194	-0.202	0.023	-0.208
RCF	-0.110	0.024	0.389	-0.095	0.389	-0.014	0.027	-0.110	-0.015
RCM	-1.194	0.293	0.548	-0.677	0.548	-0.483	0.588	-1.194	-0.518
UCF	0.556	-0.117	-0.202	0.550	-0.202	0.006	0.425	-0.444	0.007
UCM	0.172	0.027	-0.787	0.923	-0.787	-0.701	0.116	1.172	-0.751
INV	0.128	1.237	-1.188	1.291	-1.188	-0.152	-1.127	0.128	-1.163
HOU	0.054	-0.009	-0.059	0.077	-0.059	-0.021	0.013	0.054	-0.023
SAV	0.182	1.228	-0.247	0.368	-0.247	-0.174	-1.115	0.182	-0.186
TTR	-0.774	0.188	-0.037	-0.457	-0.037	-0.295	0.365	-0.774	-0.316
MIG	0.318	-0.055	-0.346	0.452	-0.346	-0.125	0.074	0.318	-0.134

instruments. A survey of the exogenous variables leads to the following list of instrument variables, with upper and lower bounds to their changes estimated from the provisional magnitudes in the final year.

Instruments	Upper Bound	Lower Bound
EXP	—	−0.10
TAX	+0.40	—
TRF	+0.40	—
FCI	—	−0.05
IRR	+0.10	—
SUB	+0.12	—
RAT	+0.12	—

To give one example, TAX was zero in the provisional estimates, and may now vary between zero and 0.4 billion.

As targets we may consider GNP, RSL, or USL. It is desirable that none of these should come out lower than in the provisional estimates. To raise USL without at the same time raising RSL would aggravate the large difference in living standards and would in many countries be considered undesirable. Hence, two targets remain: GNP and RSL, while USL is not allowed to decline.

Table 2 shows the effects of the two "extreme" targets, obtained by means of linear programing:

TABLE 2

Effect on Target Variables of Changes in Instruments

	Target	
	Max. GNP	Max. RSL
Optimal changes in instruments		
TAX	+0.400	+0.400
EXP	—	−0.073
RAT	+0.041	—
SUB	—	+0.120
Resulting change in targets		
GNP	0.566	0.495
RSL	0.002	0.009
USL	—	—

While the model offers little hope of a dramatic improvement in rural conditions as long as urban living standards cannot be lowered with respect to provisional estimates, at least it shows the trade-off between such improvement of RSL as is possible, on the one hand, and GNP, on the other.

Little need be said about migration. MIG would, of course, vary according to equation 15, and in the two extremes mentioned above, it would change by 8,000 and 38,000, respectively, hardly enough to merit further discussion. This aspect of duality is probably of far less importance than food prices, food subsidies, and food rationing.

POSITIVE MARGINAL PRODUCTIVITIES OF POPULATION

It was perhaps rather extreme to assume that increased migration to the cities would not affect rural or urban output at all. In order to show the effect of the extreme opposite assumption in this area migration terms can be added to the two production functions (equations 7 and 8).

For *rural* output it may be assumed that 1 per cent less rural population would mean 1 per cent less rural output or that marginal productivity would equal average productivity. In the final year rural output per head is $129, and with the factor of 2.5 translating migration variations in the final year to population variations in that year (cf. equation 10), the coefficient of MIG becomes −0.323.

For *urban* output it may be assumed that 1 per cent more urban population would mean ½ per cent more urban output, or that marginal productivity would equal one-half of average productivity. As the average urban output per head is more than double the rural output per head, the term to be added to equation 8 becomes +0.389 MIG.

The reduced form is only slightly altered, and the optimal programs even less, as shown in Table 3.

VIRTUES OF AUSTERITY IF FOOD IMPORTS ARE NONEXISTENT

It has been shown that a stiff increase in taxation could speed up growth, even if foreign aid is no longer forthcoming. This is explained by the assumption that food imports will be reduced through higher food prices and food rationing so that other imports become possible. The pro-

TABLE 3

Effect on Target Variables of Rural-to-Urban Migration

	Zero Marginal Productivity		High Marginal Productivity	
	Max. GNP	Max. RSL	Max. GNP	Max. RSL
Optimal changes in instruments				
TAX	+0.400	+0.400	+0.400	+0.400
EXP	–	–0.073	–	–0.058
RAT	+0.041	–	+0.047	–
SUB	–	+0.120	–	+0.120
Resulting changes in targets				
GNP	0.566	0.495	0.561	0.481
RSL	0.002	0.009	0.002	0.008
USL	–	–	–	–

visional-plan estimates themselves, however, show no food imports, and this will be the realistic assumption for most developing countries.

The linear programming exercises can be repeated with a lower limit of zero on food imports FIM. The results are shown in Table 4. Apparently, there remains a possibility of increasing GNP through increased taxation, provided this is reinforced by other measures. The "rural" optimum (target RSL) has so little to say for it that it can safely be ignored. But the first column shows that a moderate increase in taxation and the full use of opportunities for agricultural investment can raise GNP by $123 million, or 1½ per cent (in five years), without any further inflow of foreign capital.

How Bad Is Food Aid?

Apparently the model does not much "approve" of food imports. Food aid naturally increases food imports. How bad, then, is this form of aid, as compared to no aid at all or to untied capital aid?

The answer will depend on the amount of aid considered. Table 5 gives the results for amounts of $50 millions. The target of the optimum

TABLE 4

Effect on Target Variables Assuming No
Reduction in Food Imports

	High Marginal Productivity	
	Max. GNP	Max. RSL
Optimal changes in instruments		
TAX	+0.205	+0.174
TRF	—	+0.060
IRR	+0.100	—
SUB	+0.120	+0.120
RAT	+0.061	—
Resulting changes in targets		
GNP	0.124	0.054
RSL	0.004	0.005
USL	0.002	—

TABLE 5

Effect of Capital Aid, With and Without Food, on GNP
Under High Marginal Productivity

	With Food	Untied	No Aid
Assumed changes			
FCI	+0.050	+0.050	0
FIM	+0.050	0	0
Resulting changes in instruments			
TAX	+0.194	+0.400	+0.205
TRF	+0.034	+0.013	—
IRR	+0.100	+0.100	+0.100
SUB	+0.120	+0.120	+0.120
RAT	—	—	+0.061
Resulting changes in targets			
GNP	0.139	0.465	0.124
USL	—	—	—
RSL	0.006	0.008	0.004

program will be GNP in all cases, and the "high marginal productivity" assumption will be made throughout.

Untied capital aid has a tremendous effect on GNP. This is to be expected, because the urban import-to-product ratio is 0.167 so that each dollar of additional imports allows urban product to rise by six dollars.

If, however, the additional imports have to take the form of food aid, the favorable effect on GNP is much reduced. Compared to the optimal program without additional aid of any kind there is, in fact, hardly any improvement at all.

CONCLUSION

A macro model incorporating the nondual features of the model presented here would have counted five equations. What have we learned from sixteen equations?

First, that migration, housing, and marginal productivities of labor are far less important (for programming) than is often assumed by those who have seen the squalor of "bidonvilles" or "bustees." Within the limits of a five-year plan with minimal social expenditure, little can be done in these fields and little impact on over-all growth is to be expected.

The other conclusions could just as well have been reached if MIG and HOU and equations 15 and 16 had been omitted. Such a reduced model would also have shown the benefits of increasing rural output by means of investment in agriculture, and the benefits of food subsidies, which will increase demand for food, thereby encouraging domestic food production. Where food is being imported, it may be better to reduce such imports by means of urban taxation, the proceeds of which can be used for productive investment. Finally, food aid is at best a means of reducing unpopular food rationing; it is hardly a development aid in itself.

While these conclusions have to be verified for each individual country, they have an average validity that has made it worthwhile to employ a sixteen-equation model instead of a five-equation one.

Comment

DALE W. JORGENSON, UNIVERSITY OF CALIFORNIA

Separate treatment of the agricultural sector is now becoming quite fashionable in both explanatory and programming models of economic growth. Professor Sandee was a leader in this development with his pioneering model of India dating from the late 1950's.[1] To begin my comments I would like to draw attention to two additional features of the model that add realism and relevance to the analysis of economic growth: (1) a very substantial increase in the number of policy instruments explicitly represented, and (2) incorporation of substantial price-incentive effects on both supply and demand sides for the two commodities, food and manufactured goods, treated explicitly in the productive sectors—reflecting empirical evidence from demand analysis and budget studies on the consumption side and studies of agricultural supply response such as those of Dean,[2] Falcon,[3] Krishna,[4] and Stern.[5]

The great advantage of Professor Sandee's model for a dual economy over more elaborate multisector models is that in it the most important differences among sectors in an underdeveloped economy coincide with the split between agricultural and nonagricultural or rural and urban. With relatively few equations the salient features of economic duality may be incorporated into the analysis of alternative economic policies. While smaller models lack realism from a descriptive point of view, the use of larger models for analysis of alternative policies is necessarily limited to purely mechanical manipulation of policy instruments without a clear understanding of the underlying economic mechanism. A programming model of a dual economy is just the sort of artful simplifica-

[1] Jan Sandee, *A Demonstration Planning Model for India,* New York, 1960.
[2] Edwin Dean, *The Supply Response of African Farmers,* Amsterdam, 1966.
[3] Walter P. Falcon, "Farmer Response to Price in a Subsistence Economy: The Case of West Pakistan," *American Economic Review,* May 1964, pp. 580–91.
[4] Raj Krishna, "Farm Supply Response in India-Pakistan: A Case Study of the Punjab Region," *Economic Journal,* September 1963, pp. 477–87.
[5] Robert M. Stern, "The Price Responsiveness of Egyptian Cotton Producers," *Kyklos,* Vol. 12, No. 3, 1959, pp. 375–84; and "The Price Responsiveness of Primary Producers," *Review of Economics and Statistics,* May 1962, pp. 202–7.

tion of economic reality that makes model building valuable for practical policy making.

To enhance the reader's understanding of the economic mechanism underlying the programming of a dual economy, Sandee presents a number of interesting exercises illustrating the use of policy instruments to promote growth. One central conclusion from these exercises is that austerity is a good thing for growth. By increasing taxes and using the proceeds to promote investment, the economy can realize a nice increase in gross national product.

The exercise of increasing taxation illustrates another feature of the model. The main instruments at the disposal of the government—TAX, SUB, TRF, and GOV—are assumed to work independently. If a government opts for TAX, the proceeds are assumed to flow nicely into investment with no leakage into GOV, the level of government spending. In short, the government itself is viewed as entirely exogenous in the model, confronting no internal constraints on its own activity.

To illustrate this point, let us consider a model of the government sector in which every tax increase is accompanied by some leakage into government expenditures. Sandee has considered one extreme possibility —no leakage. To heighten the contrast with his results suppose we consider the opposite extreme—one hundred per cent leakage or, algebraically, GOV = TAX. Then Sandee's Table 2 is replaced by:

	GNP	RSL
Assumed changes in instruments		
TAX	+.400	+.400
EXP	—	−.073
RAT	+.041	—
SUB	—	+.120
GOV	+.400	+.400
Resulting changes in targets		
GNP	−.020	−.091
RSL	−.005	.002
USL	−.020	−.020

The new table of targets and instruments illustrates the result of one hundred per cent leakage. While this assumption is extreme, the conclusions are interesting. The level of GNP falls with a tax increase and corresponding increase in government spending. The rural and urban standards of living also decline. An increase in taxes and government spending accompanied by food subsidies and a decrease in exports raises the rural standard of living slightly, but at the expense of a substantial drop in GNP. These calculations, unlike those of Sandee, are not the result of optimization; but they do illustrate both the underlying economic mechanism and the usefulness of the model in considering various policy alternatives.

A second aspect of the model that deserves further scrutiny is its treatment of fiscal policy. Incentive effects of various forms of taxation are ignored. Even within a model limited to two producing sectors, differential effects of taxes on land, income taxes, business taxes, sales taxes, etc., must be incorporated. In the present model all taxes are imposed on the urban sector. Since rural product is responsive to price, it might be worthwhile to consider taxation of agriculture to pay for investment in irrigation.

Some notion of the effects of taxes on agriculture can be formed by calculating the effects of a negative subsidy on food minus SUB accompanied by IRR, dollar for dollar, to use Sandee's notation. Increasing negative food subsidies has much the same effect on GNP as taxation and investment with no leakage (TAX). However, negative food subsidies or food taxes are especially effective in depressing both urban and rural standards of living while increasing investment and preserving balance of payments equilibrium. A tax on food is the ideal means to implement an austerity program. Increasing irrigation investment dampens the growth in GNP, but raises the rural standard of living while further reducing the urban.

We conclude that a tax on food falls on the urban standard of living and is not a means of taxing agriculture. Again, this hypothetical calculation illustrates the usefulness of the model and suggests one way that the model might be made even more useful—by incorporating additional policy instruments through the calculated incentive effects of particular taxes. This can be done while preserving the characteristic economic dualism of the model. This avenue of development has already been explored by Sandee, but the results suggest that further exploration would be valuable.

Finally, the one real weakness of the model as it stands is the failure to include the effects of monetary policy. For many developing countries, especially in Latin America, the interrelationship between inflation and development is critical in evaluating alternative economic policies. This problem is important largely because of constraints internal to government activity, but it is nevertheless one to be reckoned with. By treating the government as partly endogenous the realism and usefulness of the model can be further enhanced.

In summary, Sandee's programming model of a dual economy is an important step forward. It succeeds in capturing key features of economic duality and policy making in a dual economy. The model is simple enough to be thoroughly understood from the economic point of view. It is complicated enough to provide a measure of descriptive realism and a means of considering a substantial range of alternative policies for promoting economic growth.

Transformation of Traditional Agriculture

Comparative Study of Transformation of Agriculture in Centrally Planned Economies: The Soviet Union, Eastern Europe and Mainland China

JERZY F. KARCZ

UNIVERSITY OF CALIFORNIA

IT IS TEMPTING to consider the transformation of agriculture in our three areas primarily, if not exclusively, in terms of the interrelationship between the farming industry and rapid industrialization drives. Two-sector models on which an analysis of this type could be based are not in short supply, and it is quite true that the total impact of initial periods of rapid industrialization on agricultural performance and organization was very considerable indeed. Yet, we should bear in mind that transformation of agriculture in all three areas has (so far) passed through three separate stages and that each of these may legitimately be described as a transformation of its own. Thus, we have some some reason to inquire into the trends and policies of periods preceding the industrialization drives. This stage of peasant farming includes changes in land tenure as well as some other institutional arrangements. At least

NOTE: The author gratefully acknowledges the financial support of the Project on Comparative Study of Communist Societies, University of California, Berkeley, in the preparation of this paper.

one authority has recently formulated a comparison between the Chinese and the Soviet transformation in which the divergent trends during the precollectivization period play a major role.[1] But it is also possible to argue on other grounds that the influence of this stage on the formulation of Soviet strategy and the course of agricultural transformation was very substantial.

The second stage of transformation remains to be defined. It is the stage associated with the implementation of the initial industrialization drive in the Soviet Union and the corresponding strategy of "surplus collection." In this stage agriculture's contribution to growth is viewed narrowly by the planners: for the most part, farming becomes a direct, rather than indirect, supplier of marketable surpluses and of forced savings as well as of labor. During this stage little is done to increase agricultural productivity, and input supplies tend to be neglected. Farm incomes and prices as well as trends in terms of trade reflect these goals quite accurately.

The strategy of surplus collection leads to the emergence of a set of institutions designed to implement its particular goals. The Soviet collective farm is one such institution, and there are certain others characteristic of the Soviet command economy, such as the system of material technical supply, planning through material balances, and certain types of success indicators. The combined impact of these institutions on agriculture as an industry is sufficiently strong to result in the emergence of what may perhaps be called a stage of command farming.[2]

Actually, it is possible to discern a third stage of agricultural transformation that is not easily contemplated apart from its predecessor. That is the stage of "decompression" of command farming. While growth and industrialization still enjoy a priority, the planners no longer neglect the counterdevelopmental impact of surplus collection on the agricultural sector. Modest increases in living standards and in farm productivity become immediate policy goals. A larger supply of inputs and investment funds is allocated to agriculture, and efforts are also made to eliminate some counterincentive features of command farming.

Both the strategy of rapid industrialization and the socialist transformation of agriculture emerged first in the U.S.S.R., and the duration of each of these stages was considerably longer there than in any other

[1] Alexander Eckstein, *Communist China's Economic Growth and Foreign Trade,* New York, 1966, pp. 78–82.

[2] There is more to command farming than simple imposition of wartime controls. In the Soviet Union, at least, command farming has generated a tradition of its own.

area. The precollectivization stage of peasant farming ended in 1929. The second stage may be said to have come to a close in 1953. Decompression is still in progress, and it is by no means clear yet what the final outcome will be. In Eastern Europe the duration of the first and second stages was relatively shorter, but we do observe two cases of reversibility, as Yugoslavia and Poland return to (largely) peasant-type agriculture in 1953 and 1956 respectively. Here, as well as in the Soviet Union, the introduction of "new economic models" and their agricultural counterparts represents the culmination of the decompression effort to date.

My comments (and detailed knowledge) of developments in China are less extensive than for the U.S.S.R. and Eastern Europe. In mainland China, too, three stages of transformation may be distinguished, culminating in the "agriculture first" policy of 1961–62. Yet, developments in the second stage, in particular, were strongly influenced by differences in resource endowments and the much lower level of per capita food production.

THE EMERGENCE OF SOVIET
DEVELOPMENT STRATEGY

The issue of land holding in Soviet Russia was resolved summarily during the revolution and the civil war: large estates were seized more or less spontaneously by village communities or individual peasants. Just prior to collectivization some 25.6 million households were engaged in farming, with an average crop area of about four hectares per household.[3]

This agriculture of small peasants succeeded to an astounding degree in recovering from the damage brought by six years of war. By 1925/6–1927/8 average gross farm output exceeded the level of 1913 by about 14 per cent. Livestock holdings were also greater than they had been at the end of that year. Peasant productive capital was growing at the annual rate of 5.5 per cent.[4] Per head of urban population the volume of farm marketings was only 4 per cent below the level of 1909–13. While grain marketings were only slightly lower, it proved impossible

[3] Lazar Volin, *A Survey of Soviet Russian Agriculture*, Washington, D.C., 1951, p. 13 and Vladimir P. Timoshenko, *Agricultural Russia and the Wheat Problem*, Stanford, 1952, pp. 101, 127.
[4] *Voprosy ekonomiki*, No. 10 (1966), p. 49.

to reach the prewar level of grain exports.[5] This was due in part to greater consumption in the village and in part to a shift in the structure of output in response to changes in government procurement prices undertaken in 1926. The change discriminated heavily against sales of grain, and producers responded by shifting resources (including produced grain) to the production of livestock products.[6]

All these developments took place within a short period in an environment of a regulated market economy. The tumult of wars and revolution, however, left some lasting scars of distrust on the peasantry and the establishment alike. During the war it had been necessary to requisition food, and peasants replied by curtailing sowings and effectively forcing the introduction of the regulated market in 1921. Two years later, an abrupt, adverse shift in peasant terms of trade produced another crisis, which was resolved largely to the satisfaction of the peasants. Within the government the experience generated an excessive fear of similar seller strikes in the future.[7]

The story of the Soviet industrialization debate has been told elsewhere,[8] and only the briefest summary will suffice here. A strategy of balanced sectoral growth was ultimately rejected in favor of heavy emphasis on industry in general and heavy industry in particular, with special stress on development of key industries such as electric power and steel. Ultimately consumption was to be reduced or held in check by low farm prices and by heavy turnover taxes included in retail prices. Massive collectivization of agriculture was not contemplated initially.

The decision to collectivize was closely connected with a grain procurement crisis of 1927/8. I have argued elsewhere that the crisis was a natural outcome of certain government policies, but the fact remains that the difficulties with grain supplies in 1927/8, although avoidable, were very real indeed. Solution was sought in arbitrary confiscations from peasant stocks. Even though this procedure (which copied the experience of the civil war) was successful, grain exports declined substantially. A year later, similar difficulties reappeared. By this time, the government was committed to a program of rapid industrialization

[5] Jerzy F. Karcz, "Thoughts on the Grain Problem," *Soviet Studies,* April 1967, pp. 408, 409, 411.

[6] By 1927/8, grain procurement prices exceeded production costs by 0.4 of one per cent. *Ibid.,* p. 415.

[7] Although peasant withdrawal from markets could cause difficulties in the short run, it is difficult to visualize withdrawals persisting over a longer run, as long as war-induced shortages and habits of thought no longer dominate behavior.

[8] Alexander Erlich, *The Soviet Industrialization Debate, 1924–1928.* Cambridge, Mass., 1960, is a standard source on this subject.

and to the satisfaction of the resulting heavy demand for imports. More-over, difficulties with food supplies led to the introduction of country-wide rationing.[9]

The difficulties might have been avoided by the adoption of alterna-tive policies, but in the atmosphere of crisis, administrative convenience and past experience with procurements suggested a drastic solution. This was sought in the collectivization drive of 1929/30. By March 1930, over half of the peasant households were in cooperative farms. Although a brief period of relapse followed, by 1936 fully 90 per cent of all households were collectivized.

The Soviet government thus applied an essentially short-run war-economy type policy to the solution of a long-run, structural problem: agriculture's contribution to economic growth.[10] If productivity had not improved, such a policy could not have been followed in the longer run without adverse effects on incentives and the size of herds (through the impact on feed supply). Grain procurements rose, productivity did not improve and the violent upheaval of the collectivization campaign increased the already heavy slaughterings of livestock.[11] By the end of 1932 cattle holdings declined by 49 per cent and holdings of pigs and sheep by 55 and 64 per cent respectively. Output dipped below the 1928 levels and did not regain them until the excellent harvest year of 1937.

But from the standpoint of agriculture's contribution to economic growth, the results were not at all unfavorable.[12] From 1928 to 1932 the nonagricultural labor force increased 55 per cent and by 1939, had increased another 44 per cent. In 1930–31 grain procurements were twice as large as they had been in 1926–28 and grain exports were resumed on an unusually large scale. The maintenance of agricultural exports during 1929–32 enabled the government to finance the entire increase in the value of imports between 1926/7 and 1932.

But total food marketings declined between 1928 and 1932. An index, as yet unpublished, of food marketings shows a decline of 20 per cent during this period. The ensuing difficulties in supply were responsible for the major Soviet famine of 1932/3. This, incidentally, is the only

[9] Moshe Lewin, *La paysannerie et le pouvoir sovietique, 1928–1930,* Paris, 1966, p. 260.

[10] Karcz, *op. cit.,* p. 430.

[11] The decline in herds was due not only to peasant slaughterings just prior to collectivization, but also to shortages of feed, hasty collectivization, lack of structures and insufficient care.

[12] This is based on my paper "Soviet Agriculture: A Balance Sheet," in V. G. Treml (ed.), *The Development of the Soviet Economy,* New York, 1968, pp. 108–46.

period in Soviet history during which a reconstructed index of final industrial product shows a decline.[13]

On the other hand, marketings of major technical crops increased by 36 per cent, reflecting privileged treatment for products of high opportunity cost in terms of foreign exchange.

Finally, we note that the government was able to obtain the bulk of its food supplies at prices that had changed little since 1928. This, together with the high rate of surplus extraction and rising retail prices, enabled the government to divert increased savings to finance the industrialization drive.

There was no basic change in Soviet strategy of surplus collection until the outbreak of the Second World War nor, for that matter, was there any during 1945–52. Some adjustments were made in the institutional structure leading to guaranteed household plots and the introduction of fixed delivery or payment quotas and of the dual-price system in state procurements. Urban markets were reopened in 1931. These measures were aimed simultaneously at the improvement of food supplies through greater marketings and the provision of some undefined real income floor for the individual member of the collective farm. For all practical purposes, these changes completed the transition to the model of "command farming" referred to earlier. This model was subsequently emulated in the transformation of agriculture in both the Eastern European countries and in China, and we shall shortly indicate some key features of its performance. It should be noted that a rising trend in output resulted in an increase in marketings, and food rationing was therefore abandoned in 1935. There was also a temporary improvement in peasant real income. In the prewar period, total factor productivity in agriculture declined. Two independent calculations are available. The first, and the more elaborate, is by D. Gale Johnson, who employed data from his study of Soviet agricultural growth for the National Bureau of Economic Research. The input index is based on series for capital, current purchases, weighted sown areas, livestock, and labor (measured separately in man-days and also in numbers employed). Adjusted 1955 weights were used in calculations for the period 1928–38, which show an increase of 7 to 19 per cent in the input index (depend-

[13] Reference is to calculations of final industrial product by Raymond Powell, "Industrial Production," in Abram Bergson and Simon Kuznets (ed.), *Economic Trends in the Soviet Union*, Cambridge, Mass., 1963, p. 178. The calculation in terms of 1928 prices shows no change in output for 1932 and a decline in 1933. The other two computations (in terms of 1937 and 1950 prices) show declines in both 1932 and 1933. See also Naum Jasny, *Soviet Industrialization, 1928–1952*, Chicago, 1961, p. 114.

ing on measurement of labor in terms of numbers employed or man-days). Productivity indices show a decline of 3 to 13 per cent (with the difference accounted for by the change in the measurement of the labor input).[14]

A much rougher calculation, using official Soviet data for sown area, the size of the capital stock (including livestock), and an independent series for the labor input in man-days, was made by the writer on another occasion. Two sets of weights were used, based on relative factor shares of 1958, but with alternative assumptions as to the magnitude of rent. Between 1928 and 1939 the input indices show increases of 2 to 5 per cent and the productivity index shows declines of 4 to 7 per cent.[15]

Important Characteristics of Command Farming

Details of Soviet farming organization need not detain us here. To summarize, we note that it consists of state farms and collective farms (machine tractor stations, MTS, were abolished in the Soviet Union in 1958). These categories make up the socialized sector. The private sector comprises the household plots of collective farm members as well as those of other citizens and such independent farm units as may still be found in the economy. In the late 1950's, the Soviet private sector accounted for nearly 40 per cent of output.[16]

We now comment briefly on some of the outstanding characteristics of command farming and their impact, intended or unintended, upon the performance of farm units or of the agricultural sector as a whole. These characteristics developed initially in the Soviet Union, but they were also found in those East European agricultures that continued to use the system of command farming.

The farm sector as a whole tended to operate under constant pressure from national planning agencies to satisfy the growing demand for farm products. The rise in this demand was due largely to growing employment outside of the farm sector. Income elasticities of demand for food have been high. At the same time, state demand for exportable produce was also high and at times rising. Inputs necessary for the satisfaction

[14] D. Gale Johnson, "Agricultural Production," in Bergson and Kuznets, *op. cit.*, pp. 214–218.

[15] Karcz, "Soviet Agriculture. . . ," Table 2.

[16] Karl Eugen Wädekin, *Privatproduzenten in der sowjetrussischen Landwirtschaft,* Cologne, 1967, p. 22. In Bulgaria, the private sector accounted for 22–24 per cent of output in 1965. For Hungary, the corresponding figure is close to 40 per cent.

of this demand were not always provided. National planners frequently tended to rely upon the supposed availability of unspecified inputs within agriculture. These pressures tended to place a premium on short-run performance of individual enterprises to the detriment of long-run trends.[17]

Established regulations on output distribution in the collective farms subordinated the return to labor to the task of fulfilling various other obligations to the state and the coverage of material expenses. Thus the necessary level of deliveries or sales to the state was maintained more or less unaffected by harvest fluctuations, but peasant incentives suffered.[18]

Until 1958 almost the entire stock of heavier machinery including tractors was concentrated in the MTS (state farms owned their own machines and tractors). This policy, through which duplication was theoretically avoided, was originally intended to minimize capital outlays and to permit maximum utilization of the capital stock, as well as to increase the size of the surplus through the extraction of payments in kind. Problems arose with MTS because of the low quality of their work and the inability to set up an efficient system of incentives for their workers, as well as because of difficulties in coordinating their operations with those of the collective farms.[19] In general, planning of output as well as of livestock herd composition was carried on not on the farm itself but in the superior administrative agencies. Since these were not directly responsible for the results of their planning, certain inconsistencies tended to develop between various plan indicators. Moreover, specialization was often discouraged, as planning agencies tended to divide the output quotas among a large number of farms in order to minimize the risk of failure for the area as a whole.[20]

Machinery was allocated to state farms and to MTS within the framework of the supply plan. This was also true of other off-farm inputs, such

[17] B. Prouza *et al., Základní problémy soustavy ekonomického řízení ČS zemědělství,* Prague, 1963, p. 12.

[18] On details of these rules see Arcadius Kahan, "The Collective Farm System in Russia: Some Aspects of Its Contribution to Soviet Economic Development," in Carl Eicher and Lawrence Witt (ed.), *Agriculture in Economic Development,* New York, 1964, pp. 251–271.

[19] Lazar Volin, "Agricultural Policy of the Soviet Union," in U.S. Congress, Joint Economic Committee, *Comparisons of the United States and Soviet Economies,* Part I, Washington, D.C., 1959, pp. 297–299.

[20] Jerzy F. Karcz, "The New Soviet Agricultural Programme," *Soviet Studies,* October 1965, p. 147. On discrepancies between planning of feed output and numbers of animals in Bulgaria, see Dimitur V. Kinov, *Efektivnost na proizvodstvenite fondove v selskoto stopansto,* Sofia, 1965, p. 47–48.

as fertilizers, building materials, or spare parts supplied to collective or state farms. The principles of planning material-technical supplies were the same as in the rest of the economy, but in view of the low priority of agriculture, the probability of shortfalls in deliveries to farms was increased. Moreover, administrative allocation of machinery and current inputs often neglected the necessary complementarity between individual items.[21]

As noted earlier, a double-price system was introduced at an early stage in order to stimulate larger sales to state agencies. These sales permitted the maintenance of base delivery prices at low levels for very long periods, but the entire system of dual pricing tended to inhibit rational specialization and to accentuate further the existing differences between the weaker and the more prosperous farms.[22]

The low income paid by farms (a direct result of low procurement prices) caused many farmers to rely on supplementary income from the household plot. This became a source of constant friction between the farmers and the government. Locally, the socialized sector and the household plot competed for labor (during peak activity periods), for feed, and at times for land. The proportion of plot income in total income has been very high—but we should keep in mind that the socialized sector has always been an important provider of feed for the household plots.

With the adopted principles that governed product and income distribution in the collective farm sector (payment in kind to MTS, payment of labor from residue product), calculations for production costs in the collective farms were made very difficult. None were allowed in the prewar period, however, probably because of the embarrassingly low level of delivery prices.[23]

State farms owned machinery directly and paid regular wages, and problems of coordinating the use of inputs with the MTS or of calculating production costs did not arise. Since state farms as well as the MTS did not pay for the machinery in the early period, the distribution of machinery between farms tended to be inefficient. Many of these farms were set up in order to maximize output, with the result that management was seldom cost conscious and heavy subsidization was the rule rather than the exception.

[21] *Plenum Tsentral'nogo Komiteta Kommunisticheskoi Partii Sovetskogo Soiuza, 24–26 marta 1965 g.,* Moscow, 1965, pp. 49–51.

[22] Vladimir Vydra, *Úloha výkupu v ekonomickém svazku dělnické třídy a rolnictva,* Prague, 1963, pp. 120–122.

[23] Nancy Nimitz, "Soviet Agricultural Prices and Costs," in *Comparisons of the United States and Soviet Economies, op. cit.,* p. 241.

Since the rules of the game were often in direct conflict with the personal interest of farm managers and farmers, it was necessary to maintain a large enforcement and control apparatus to regulate procurement and planning. In this manner, a considerable proportion of scarce administrative talent was absorbed in activities that contributed little to increase in productivity.

No explicit rental payments were made, and the state attempted to collect a part of the rent through regional variations in delivery quotas and prices. In practice, grain prices were made to bear the major part of this burden, since prices of technical crops were generally set at higher levels to stimulate production. The result was that grain tended to be consistently undervalued in spite of the fact that it was continuously in short supply for animal consumption.[24]

Nor was there much scope for the supply of those "new factors of production" that are responsible for such a large proportion of the increases in factor productivity. Younger and better trained workers tended to leave agriculture for other occupations providing a more regular income. Many of the specialists trained for agricultural occupations tended to follow suit partly because of the low and at times very primitive living conditions in the villages. The introduction of new strains of crops or better varieties of livestock was often hampered or delayed by changes in procurement quotas that resulted in deliveries of breeding stock or quality seed.[25]

Finally, we should note one characteristic of collectivized, as distinguished from command, farming found in the practice of the Soviet Union as well as elsewhere in Eastern Europe. Although it might have been feasible to leave the livestock sector largely in private hands, as is often done in the case of present day East German and Polish collectives, attempts were made to introduce collectivized animal husbandry. The capital costs of construction were of course considerable, and the problem was accentuated by widespread shortages of materials. Nor was it easy to avoid the spread of tuberculosis or brucellosis under those circumstances. In many instances, livestock suffered from a shortage of stalls.

[24] This was a phenomenon that was encountered in all countries of the socialist camp. If we abstract from the Soviet expansion of grain production in the New Lands, grain acreage tended to decline in all other countries of the camp between 1957 and 1962. Cf. *Ukazatelé hospodářského vývoje v zahraničí, 1965,* Part 2, Prague, 1966, pp. 48–49.

[25] Douglas Diamond, "Trends in Output, Inputs and Factor Productivity in Soviet Agriculture," in U.S. Congress, Joint Economic Committee, *New Directions in the Soviet Economy,* Part II-B, Washington, D.C., 1966, pp. 360–363.

One last problem should be mentioned. In the course of collectivization of agriculture, special efforts were made to publish only those indicators that tended to present developments in a favorable light. It now appears that major decisions on resource allocation between the various sectors of the economy were at times based on information provided by faulty but readily available statistical indicators. In one such case an improperly calculated rate of investment for Czechoslovak collectives showed an increase over a period of four years; actually the rate had declined. Thus, the information problem was often another impediment to efficient farming.[26]

Early Soviet Decompression Since 1953

The first attempts at mitigating the environment of command farming were made in 1953 in the Soviet Union.[27] Emphasis was placed on acreage expansion in the New Lands, but a number of other measures were introduced elsewhere as well. In the short space of five years, the price level was raised by a factor of 2.7, agricultural taxes (imposed on the private plot) were cut by 60 per cent in two years, and the volume of capital in agriculture almost doubled, with allocations of fertilizer rising by 59 per cent. The quality of feed, and in many instances its supply, was increased by the corn program. In response to all this, output rose: in 1953–58 the increase amounted to 51 per cent.

The period was also characterized by sharp increases in productivity. Johnson's calculation (referred to above) shows an increase of 30 to 34 per cent between 1950 and 1959. Another careful study by Douglas Diamond (also based on reconstructed input series and a recomputed index of output) shows an increase of 20 to 22 per cent during the same period. Among the factors that contributed to the increase in productivity, Diamond cites a doubling of real payments to collective farm members between 1953 and 1958. Other beneficial factors include the improvement in the quality of the labor force (through an increase in the share of able-bodied farmers), the rise in the number of specialists in agriculture, permissive policies towards the private plot, and the positive impact of the New Lands and corn campaigns.[28]

[26] Jozef Nikl in *Politická ekonomie*, No. 6 (1963), p. 457, and in *Statistika*, No. 3 (1967), p. 117.

[27] There is by now a large literature on this period. The main titles are given in my "Seven Years on the Farm: Retrospect and Prospect," in *New Directions in the Soviet Economy,* p. 399, n. 41.

[28] Johnson, *op. cit.,* p. 218 and Diamond, *op. cit.,* p. 352. Johnson suggests that his index may be too high because of the likely overstatement of output by Soviet indices in this period.

In 1958, however, priorities shifted against agriculture. Deliveries of machinery declined as did the rate of increase in fertilizer allocations. Prices of machinery and of spare parts were raised, while newly set farm prices were cut. In 1959 and 1960 the real value of earnings per man-day from collective farms declined by 10 per cent. Restrictions on private plot farming caused further reductions. The outflow of labor from collectives increased while the quality of the labor declined.[29]

Though input supplies, including investment allocations, improved after 1962, productivity indices for 1961–64 show a small decline.[30]

TRANSFORMATION OF AGRICULTURE IN EASTERN EUROPE

In Poland, Hungary, and Czechoslovakia inequalities in land holdings were already burning political issues before World War II. Hence, land reforms implemented in the postwar period were also affected by political considerations. In the struggle with the remaining political parties, the Communist parties often sought to neutralize a considerable segment of the farm population through the support of land reforms. They were often very successful.[31]

In Eastern Europe as a whole, land reforms affected almost a quarter of all land used for agriculture and forestry. The state kept about half of the confiscated land. Large-estate farming disappeared completely (except on state farms), and most of the land was given to small peasants. After completion of the reforms, small and subsistence farm units accounted for two-fifths or more of all land in Bulgaria and Hungary and about a quarter of private acreage in Poland and Czechoslovakia. Medium-large and large peasant farms were important only in Czechoslovakia, where they comprised about half of total private land, and in Poland, where they comprised a third. Their share of total private holdings in Bulgaria and Hungary was one-fifth and one-fourth respectively.[32]

It has sometimes been argued that the reforms failed to establish a sound base for commercial-type farming. In retrospect, it seems that

---

[29] Karcz, "Seven Years on the Farm . . . ," pp. 402–410

[30] Diamond, *loc. cit.*

[31] For an excellent study on developments in Poland, see Andrzej Korbonski, *The Politics of Socialist Agriculture in Poland, 1945–1960,* New York, 1965, pp. 67–98.

[32] Nicolas Spulber, *The Economics of Communist Eastern Europe,* New York, 1957, p. 245. The small category comprises holdings of up to five hectares, while the "medium-large" begins at ten hectares.

almost any reform would have led to similar results, since alternative employment opportunities were small. It also seems likely that with the choice of proper technology and inputs the base for more intensive and productive farming could have been laid down.

Nevertheless, after the establishment of Communist regimes, the future of private farming was grim, although the intent to collectivize was initially denied. In the early postwar years there was a flurry of collectivization in Yugoslavia and Bulgaria, but the first major drive came in Yugoslavia in 1948/9. By the end of 1949 nearly a sixth of all land was collectivized. Thereafter, however, progress was very slow, and in 1953 the government formally allowed dissolution. Within a year the share of collectivized land dropped from 17 to 3 per cent.[33]

The campaigns to collectivize in other countries began in 1948/9. Occasionally the collectivization campaigns were preceded or accompanied by campaigns against richer peasants (taking the form of discriminatory variations in tax and delivery rates, confiscation of machinery, etc.). The beginning of collectivization corresponded roughly with the implementation of the first development plans, which contemplated high rates of economic growth, especially in industry.

The progress of collectivization was by no means uniform. By 1953, Bulgaria alone had collectivized nearly half of its land; most of this had been achieved within a single year in a campaign unique for its forced pace. Elsewhere, the progress was slower. Though numerous types of collectives were set up to ease the process of transition, only 26 to 40 per cent of the land was collectivized in Hungary and Czechoslovakia. The corresponding figures for Poland and Rumania were smaller.[34]

During this early period, Soviet planning and pricing practices, including compulsory deliveries and dual price systems, were introduced in Eastern Europe. To facilitate recruitment, quotas for collectives were commonly kept low. Crop prices were reduced in Bulgaria between 1949 and 1953 by about 50 per cent; the intent was to raise the rate of saving.[35]

The year 1953 brought major policy changes in Eastern Europe. The "New Course policies" resulted in general relaxation of the collectivization drive, a reduction in compulsory delivery quotas, changes in prices, and an increase in agricultural investment's share of total investment.

[33] Jozo Tomasevich, "Agriculture in Eastern Europe," *The Annals of the American Academy of Political and Social Sciences,* May 1958, pp. 47–48.

[34] United Nations, *Economic Survey of Europe in 1960,* Geneva, 1961, p. IV-5.

[35] N. Dimitrova in *Ikonomicheska Misul,* No. 7 (1963), p. 33. As late as 1956, the total losses of Bulgarian collectives in sales to the state were greater than total investment in agriculture, state and collective.

Fundamentally, the reason for the New Course was the same as for the Soviet reforms of 1953: stagnation in output. In 1950–53, the level of prewar production was exceeded only in Albania and Bulgaria (where the war damage was small).[36]

Milder goals for increases in farm output characterized the new wave of medium-term plans (introduced about 1955). Higher investment allocations to agriculture began a trend that, with some exceptions, continues today.

The earlier pattern of developments was broken by the events of 1956. In October nearly 85 per cent of Polish collectives were dissolved spontaneously, and no further drives to collectivize were launched thereafter. In Hungary, the revolution of 1956 had a similar effect,[37] though a few months later nearly half of the cooperatives were back in operation.

Collectivization drives were, however, resumed elsewhere. Bulgaria and Czechoslovakia largely completed the process by the end of the decade, and Hungary renewed the drive in 1959. East Germany collectivized nearly half of its land in 1960. Rumania resumed the drive in 1958 and completed it in 1962. In all countries, drastic decline in herds and output was avoided, although periods of stagnation did occur, and there was some decline in herds.[38]

By 1965, the socialist sector (excluding the household plots) accounted for the following percentages of arable land: Bulgaria—89; Czechoslovakia—93; East Germany—95; Hungary—87; Poland—14; Rumania—87; Yugoslavia—15.[39] Most of the lower type, looser collectives have since disappeared and the more advanced ones have been consolidated. The 1959 merger drive in Bulgaria yielded collectives of which the average size in 1965 was 3,910 hectares. The year before, Hungarian collectives averaged about 1,200 hectares. The mean size of Czechoslovak cooperatives in 1965 was 608 hectares.[40]

The state farm system also expanded rapidly, in part at the expense of the private sector (as the state took over land abandoned by indi-

---

[36] *Economic Survey of Europe in 1960*, p. IV-15.

[37] I. S. Kuvshinov *et al.*, *Mirovoe sel'skoe khoziaistvo*, Moscow, 1966, p. 59 and Tomasevich, *op. cit.*, p. 47. See also Korbonski, *op. cit.*, pp. 250, 255 for developments in Poland.

[38] J. M. Montias, *Economic Development in Communist Rumania*, Cambridge, Mass., 1967, pp. 96–97. Large numbers of livestock were purchased by collectives at rather advantageous prices.

[39] U.S. Department of Agriculture, Economic Research Service, *The Europe and Soviet Union Agricultural Situation, Review of 1966 and Outlook for 1967*, ERS-Foreign-185, Washington, D.C., 1967, p. 113.

[40] Kuvshinov, *op. cit.*, p. 59; *Statisticheski godishnik na Narodna Republika Bulgaria 1966*, Sofia, 1966, p. 210; *Statistická ročenka ČSSR 1966*, Prague, p. 314.

viduals) and partly at the expense of weaker collectives. In 1962–64, state farms accounted for between 10 per cent (Hungary) and about 17 per cent (Czechoslovakia) of agricultural land.[41]

Reforms of planning, pricing and institutional practices continued. In most instances (with the exception of total or partial abolition of compulsory deliveries) the Soviet reforms were followed. This was true of the abolition of dual pricing, of the introduction of machinery sales to collectives, as well as of the reforms in planning practices. In many instances, the faults, as well as the advantages of Soviet models, were copied faithfully, e.g., the setting of livestock product prices below the cost of production in Bulgaria, Czechoslovakia, and Hungary.

What was the performance of socialized agriculture in Eastern Europe? The answers depend a good deal on the country and the type of indicator used. Bulgaria and Czechoslovakia each lie close to, or at the opposite ends of, the spectrum. In the former, gross output in 1965 was more than twice as high as in 1932–38. In the same year, Rumanian output exceeded its 1938 level by some 40 per cent. In Czechoslovakia, however, prewar levels of output were not recovered until 1960—in the next five years, gross output index fluctuated narrowly around that level.[42]

The preceding comparisons refer to national indices of gross output. In the same terms, there were substantial improvements between the early and the late 1950's. The increase ranged between 19 and 23 per cent for Hungary, Bulgaria, and Poland; in Czechoslovakia it was 13 per cent. In part these increases reflect greater allocation of investment funds to agriculture. National data indicate that the share of agricultural in total (or state) investment rose during the same period by a factor of about 1.5.[43]

Homogeneous data on trends in the labor input are very difficult to come by. Between 1950 and 1960, however, the decline in total agricultural employment in Bulgaria, Czechoslovakia, East Germany, Hungary, and Rumania (taken together) came to about 16 per cent.[44]

Tractor supplies rose by a factor of 3.4; but since in this period the

---

[41] Kuvshinov, pp. 43–44, 52, 59, 66. In Rumania, state farms accounted for 16.6 per cent of arable land—Montias, *op. cit.*, Chapter 2, Table 1.

[42] *Ibid.*, Chapter 2, Table 6; *Statisticheski godishnik na Narodna Republika Bulgaria 1966*, p. 172 and *Statistická ročenka ČSSR 1966*, pp. 32–33.

[43] *Economic Survey of Europe in 1960*, p. IV-15. On volume of investment see *Ukazatelé hospodářského vývoje v zahraničí 1965*, Part 1, Prague, 1966, pp. 163–170.

[44] *Razvitie sel'skogo khoziaistva i sotrudnichestvo stran SEVa*, Moscow, 1965, p. 101.

number of draft animals declined rapidly, the increase in total draft power availability was smaller. Substantial increases were also achieved in fertilizer applications. Here again, the total increase in the supply of plant nutrients was lower as a result of the decline in the application of manure (probably greater on the socialized than the private fields).[45]

Trends in total factor productivity over this period are not easy to gauge. I presume that, in spite of substantial outflow of labor, the increases in the flow of current purchases and of fixed investment (some of which contributed little to output in the short run) would probably cause a decline in total productivity in the East European countries. This impression is supported by Western estimates of agriculture's contribution to GNP (Western concept) for the period 1950–53 and 1960–63. Here, as elsewhere, performance varied, often drastically, from one country to the next.[46]

In the more recent period, indices of net farm output prepared for the area by the U.S. Department of Agriculture show moderate upward trends for Bulgaria, Poland, and Rumania and more modest increases for other countries. The outflow of labor continued, with the decline in agricultural employment estimated at 11 and 12 per cent for Czechoslovakia and Rumania, respectively, at 15 per cent for Bulgaria and 17 per cent for Hungary. Capital productivity, on the other hand, declined by 15 per cent in Rumania, 24 per cent in Hungary, 29 per cent in Bulgaria and 34 per cent in Czechoslovakia.[47] Since 1961, tractor inventories rose at a fairly uniform rate of 50 per cent, while fertilizer applications registered more spectacular increases, especially in Rumania, Bulgaria, Poland, and Hungary. The last three countries are now approaching the level of application reached by Czechoslovakia in the 1950's (70–75 kilograms of pure matter per hectare of arable land).[48]

All these trends resulted in the continuation of a phenomenon that was already present in the earlier period. Current expenditures for production rose still further. In Bulgaria these expenditures increased by

[45] *Economic Survey of Europe in 1960,* pp. IV-20–IV-21. On the sharp decline in manure applications in Rumanian collectives see Montias, *op. cit.,* Chapter 2.

[46] Maurice Ernst, "Postwar Economic Growth in Eastern Europe," in *New Directions in the Soviet Economy,* Part IV, p. 884. In general, the more industrialized countries have a far worse record than those with more abundant labor supplies.

[47] *Economic Bulletin for Europe,* v. 18, No. 1, pp. 45–47. The index of net output is in *The Europe and Soviet Union Agricultural Situation, etc.,* p. 5.

[48] *Ibid.,* p. 112. See also United Nations, *Economic Survey of Europe in 1965,* Part 1, Geneva, 1966, p. 33 and *Economic Survey of Europe in 1964,* Part 1, Geneva, 1965, p. 27.

44 per cent per hectare of cultivated land in collectives between 1959 and 1964. In Czechoslovakia the increase in cooperatives between 1959 and 1963 was 42.4 per cent. In Rumania material expenditures for agriculture as a whole rose by 31 per cent in the period 1958–64.[49]

The only western index of total factor productivity is that calculated for Czechoslovakia by Gregor Lazarcik. The index of output-input ratio based on 1936 prices (with inputs aggregated geometrically) declines to a postwar low of 63 in 1947, recovers to a level of 92 in 1950 and only surpasses the 1936 level by 1958. In 1962 (a very poor harvest year) the index (1936 = 100) stood at 107.[50]

THE NEW ECONOMIC SYSTEMS

Since 1965 a number of reforms have been introduced in Eastern Europe with the aim of reducing inefficiencies in utilization of resources, stemming from rigidities in planning and reliance on faulty performance indicators. In agriculture, the new systems represent attempts to reduce the impact of command farming on decision making, incentives, and resource utilization by greater use of market type instruments such as changes in prices, taxes, or interest rates.[51] These efforts proceed in several directions.

Greater farm autonomy in decision making is one objective. Indicators of the national or local production plan are no longer binding on farms. In theory, production goals were replaced by sale or procurement quotas after 1955. But in many instances the imposition of procurement goals determined the structure of output almost as effectively as a production plan. Now, the number of quotas is being reduced: in Bulgaria quotas will be distributed for only six products. The only physical quotas remaining in Hungary refer to bread grains, while no quotas are imposed on Czechoslovak farms "in ordinary circumstances." In the Soviet Union

[49] P. Marinov and N. Andreev in *Ikonomicheska Misul*, No. 4 (1966), p. 46; Montias, *op. cit.*, Chapter 2, Table 12; J. Nikl *et al.*, *Problémy vývoje a plánoviteho řízení reprodukce v JZD*, Prague, 1966, p. 208.

[50] Gregor Lazarcik, *Czechoslovak Agricultural Output, Expenses, Gross and Net Product and Productivity, 1934–38 and 1946–62*, Occasional Paper No. 7 of the Research Project on National Income in East Central Europe, Columbia University, New York, 1965, pp. 18–19.

[51] This section is based in part on my paper, "Some Aspects of New Economic Systems in Czechoslovakia and Bulgaria," delivered at the Conference on the Agrarian Question in the Light of Communist Experience, University of Washington, Seattle, August 23–26, 1967. An early publication of the proceedings is expected.

efforts were made to stabilize the size of the quota over time and thus to facilitate farm planning. In Bulgaria the quotas are supplemented by formal investment ceilings and limits on acreage to be diverted to orchards or vineyards.[52]

The extent to which administrative interference in farm planning and management will diminish is still uncertain. In the past, more subtle forms of intervention by administrative officials were devised to circumvent outright prohibitions. Such interference is particularly likely when administrative officials retain power to allocate industrial inputs or even to approve financial or output plans of the farms. They are then able to direct the structure of farm investment or to impose larger delivery quotas in return for permission to implement profitable investment projects. The apprehension about continued administrative interference is evident in all countries, and efforts are being made in Hungary and Czechoslovakia to shift a large part of administrative authority to voluntary associations of farms.[53]

Efforts are also being made to promote vertical and horizontal integration of farming, as such, with input-producing and especially with processing industries. At least a partial duplication of the conditions prevailing in the so-called "agro-business" complexes of the West was sought in 1967 by the merger in Czechoslovakia and Hungary of ministries of agriculture with ministries of food processing and some other administrative agencies.[54] The hope is that the reduction in administrative boundaries will reduce the friction between the farming community and the processing industry that led to much waste in the past. Considerable attention is devoted to the provision of better advisory and technical services, some of which are modeled on extension services. Thus, what is sought is the creation of conditions conducive to the use of new factors of production and more modern production techniques in the farming community. There is, however, no provision as yet for the inclusion of farm machinery producers within this surrogate "agro-business complex."

Simultaneously, greater emphasis is being placed on the allocative function of prices. In all countries introducing new systems there were

[52] This reflects the high profitability of grape and early vegetable production in Bulgaria and the unwillingness of authorities to depend on imported grain.

[53] These associations are to be formed within the framework of the new agro-business complexes described below.

[54] More detailed data are available in *Hospodářské noviny*, No. 13 (1967), insert. The Hungarian reform is mentioned *ibid.*, No. 23 (1967), p. 12. It is described in detail in Radio Free Europe, *Situation Report Hungary*, June 14, 1967 (mimeographed).

considerable increases in farm prices during 1965 and 1966. These increases tended to be reflected in higher prices of grains and cattle—the two product groups that were consistently undervalued in previously effective price structures. The vast majority of agricultural economists in all countries feel that the level of farm prices remains too low and that prices (along with taxes) continue to be used as an instrument through which saving is diverted to the central government. The view that prices will continue to rise in the future is virtually unanimous.[55]

Although marginal cost pricing was advocated by several economists in the discussions preceding the introduction of reforms, it was not accepted anywhere as far as the major products are concerned. The explanation for this is twofold. First, very sharp variations in the level of production costs raised doubts as to the possible counterincentive effect of the very large tax rates necessary to absorb the major part of quasi rents. Second, marginal cost pricing in agriculture as well as further increases in farm prices would be in conflict with the still prevailing objective of stabilizing the existing level of retail prices.

Thus, prices continue to be set more or less at the level of average costs, and the need for subsidization will continue. This is particularly apparent in the state farm sector. In the past, state farms benefited from a number of privileges that were in part designed to offset the financial difficulties connected with the takeover of the land of weak and inefficient collectives. State farms are now being brought into a competitive position with collective farms, but the process will take some time. For example, Czechoslovak farms will pay taxes and insurance premiums out of operating revenues for the first time.[56]

The need for subsidies in Czechoslovakia engendered an unbelievably complex system of prices, premiums, and differential payments, designed to preserve the allocative function of relatively low base prices. It is impossible to say whether the structure of these prices corresponds to the priorities of the long-run perspective plan for development of agriculture, for the excellent reason that the plan has not yet been prepared.

Emphasis is also given to the role of credit. In the past, credit often performed the function of a "tool for the socialization of the village," and whenever the size of repayments relative to farm incomes became too large, the outstanding debts were written off. This happened in

[55] A number of recomputations of agriculture's contribution to the national product has been undertaken recently. One such calculation is described by J. Nikl in *Politická ekonomie*, No. 7 (1967), pp. 545–554.

[56] The result is that only 4 out of 329 state farms in Czechoslovakia are not expected to show a loss in 1967 (interview material).

Czechoslovakia in 1958 and 1967, in the Soviet Union in 1965 (as well as earlier), and in Hungary in 1966.[57] It is now hoped that higher farm prices will make it possible for farms to pay the burden of the remaining debt financing in a normal manner.

The role of the state banks as sources of investment funds has been widened. In 1967, the State Bank of Czechoslovakia will allocate (through its branch offices) about 20 per cent of all investment funds. About half will be self-financed, while the rest will be covered by direct state subsidies. The rates of interest were raised slightly: they now amount to 3 per cent for short-term loans and 5 per cent for long-term loans.

Under the general rules of the Czechoslovak New System, five-year plans for the economy are to show the level and the structure of farm prices, tax rates, and interest rates, as well as the availability of credit, off-farm inputs, and other services. On that basis farm planning will continue. But all this is largely in the future, because of uncertainty with respect to future levels of prices.

Much stress is also placed on the introduction of normal—one is tempted to say fully commercial—relations between the farm as a seller of farm products and purchaser of inputs and the various procurement and supply agencies. In all countries proposals have been advanced (and in many instances permission has been given) for bypassing of ordinary "commercial" channels by farms, or for establishment of direct contacts between the producer and the processor. These proposals reflect uneasiness about the ability of the socialist middleman, accustomed in the past to local monopolies, to alter his stance in accordance with the desiderata of the new systems.[58]

Another objective is further democratization of the collective farm system, through guarantees of secret elections, and the right to discuss and approve production plans, and the like in direct or representative assembly.

At the same time, attention is also concentrated on the matter of peasant income. This comes to about 70 per cent of the level of average earnings in industry (Bulgaria and Czechoslovakia) and some 85 per

[57] Interview material. In Czechoslovakia the write off in 1958 followed a long standing policy of writing off 5 per cent of outstanding collective farm debts annually. For Hungarian data, see Radio Free Europe, *The Hungarian Agricultural Policy After the Ninth Congress of the HSWP*, April 10, 1967 (mimeographed). On the Soviet write off see *Pravda*, March 25, 1965.

[58] The new Czechoslovak approach is explained in V. Eremias *et al.*, *Dodavatelsko-odběratelské vztahy a rozvoj služeb ve zdokonalené soustavě řízení zemědělství*, Prague, 1967.

cent of the real income of workers and employees in Hungary.[59] In the past, peasants fared much worse. Guaranteed farm income was first introduced in Bulgaria in 1962. There are some indications that it led to an inflation of job norms (the state guaranteed minimum income per man-day). A similar system of guaranteed wages at about the level of state farm wage rates was introduced in the Soviet Union in 1966. Pension schemes (which existed in Eastern Europe before their introduction in the U.S.S.R. in 1964) have been revised and benefits raised. In recent years, real income of peasants in most countries rose more rapidly than income of workers and employees. If the 1967 Soviet plan is fulfilled in this respect, real income of collective farmers will have risen by 30 per cent in three years. The new Bulgarian five-year plan foresees a faster rise in peasant income than in that of other citizens, and concern about the persistence of income differentials continues in Hungary.[60]

Concern with the level of peasant income is at least partially explained by labor supply problems. In East Germany and Czechoslovakia, the two most developed countries, labor shortages are frequent: the average age of the agricultural worker in the latter country is forty-seven years. But the problem of attracting the specialist—whether a tractor driver or an agronomist—to agriculture and/or of holding him there against the substantial allurements of urban life is present in all countries, including those in which the availability of unskilled labor is generally not an issue.[61]

The new models are being introduced this year and it would be too early to pass considered judgment on the results. Some skepticism is, however, in order because of the dependence of the agricultural component of the "new model" on the appropriate functioning of its industrial component. Even if—and this is a large if—there were no problems on that score, one would still be entitled to question the wisdom of directing production through prices of the chosen type, as well as the ability to apply unfamiliar tools of economic policy making.

[59] *Szabad Fold,* January 22, 1967, as quoted in *Situation Report, Hungary, op. cit.* For Bulgaria and Czechoslovakia reference is to incomes from socialized sector only. For Czechoslovakia and Bulgaria, reference is to income from the collective farm. With private plot incomes the difference is not large, but labor inputs tend to be 18 to 20 per cent higher than in industry or the rest of the economy.

[60] N. K. Baibakov in *Ekonomicheskaia gazeta,* No. 51 (1966), and *Rabotnichesko delo,* July 30, 1966.

[61] Jiři Karlik *et al., Československé zemědělství a pracovní síly,* Prague, 1967, p. 45. Difficulties in attracting trained specialists to the village are felt acutely in Bulgaria.

At the same time, even a partial implementation of some of the objectives of the new models should result in direct and noticeable improvement in efficiency of resource use. And it should be borne in mind that large-scale investment expenditures, a further expansion of mechanization as well as of irrigated acreage, and increased fertilizer supplies are contemplated under the plans running through 1970. Thus, the change in institutions is also accompanied by a favorable pattern of resource allocation.

Special Cases: Poland and Yugoslavia

In these two countries private peasant agriculture still accounts for about 85 per cent of agricultural land use. Because of limitations of space and Yugoslavia's earlier experiments with market socialism, we will emphasize developments in Poland.

In both countries the important sector of socialist agriculture is the state farm sector. In Yugoslavia, these farms tend to concentrate on crop production, employing modern production techniques, improved seeds, and large amounts of fertilizers. They also acquire land through purchase from the private sector. The Polish state farms are not yet in a position to serve as models of agricultural technology, but their condition has improved very considerably since 1956. As for the socialization of the village, there is as yet no official Polish policy.[62] In Yugoslavia, on the other hand, the socialization of the village has been carried out as a part of the official policy on land acquisition.

Production trends since 1956–59 for these two countries have not been markedly different from those for Eastern Europe as a whole. The net output series for Poland is consistently above the total index for Eastern Europe; the Yugoslav index fell below the area total in three out of seven years. The application of fertilizer per hectare of arable land in Poland is the third highest of the European socialist camp; in Yugoslavia it is much lower but nevertheless more than double the Soviet norms.[63]

Polish peasant farming was incorporated into the centrally planned economy through a combination of administrative and market stimuli. Compulsory deliveries still apply to grains, potatoes, and meat. Norms are moderate, and the main aim is to assure minimum supplies of foods,

[62] Cf. Andrzej Korbonski, "Peasant Agriculture in Socialist Poland since 1956: An Alternative to Collectivization," in J. F. Karcz (ed.), Soviet and East European Agriculture, Berkeley, Cal., 1967, pp. 427–429. See also Joel M. Halpern, "Yugoslav Peasant Attitudes," ibid., 366.

[63] The Europe and Soviet Union Agricultural Situation, etc., p. 5.

particularly of meat. In addition, the state uses free purchases and also a system of contract sales. These have been developed as a method of influencing peasant output decisions and of integrating small-scale production into the larger framework of the industrial sector. The area to which they apply is scheduled to reach 30 per cent of total sowing in 1970.[64]

Farm prices are flexible and usually upward (other measures are generally used to force acreage reduction). Seasonal price variation is a common phenomenon. Since 1957 planning has been based on the over-all principle that the productive capacity of agriculture (rather than requirements in terms of marketings as has been the case elsewhere in the socialist camp) shall be the starting point.

Since 1956 marketings of the small peasant sector rose by 30 per cent. This is less than the 74 per cent increase in the marketings of Polish state farms during the same period, but it compares favorably with a 29 per cent increase in the market output of Czechoslovak command farming. Soviet market output rose during the same period by about 30 per cent.[65]

In both Poland and Yugoslavia there exists an important group of part-time farmers who often derive a considerable portion of their income from nonagricultural activities. This group is a source of concern to the authorities because it is less sensitive to pressure to raise productivity and therefore less likely to modernize its operations. (In Czechoslovakia also, part-time farming affects the supply of effort to the collectives unfavorably.)

A SKETCH OF AGRICULTURAL
TRANSFORMATION OF MAINLAND CHINA

The structure of land holdings in China after the end of World War II is not known with certainty, but many western observers believe that approximately half of the land belonged to the peasants directly. Land reform began in 1950; the first measure was a compulsory reduction of rents. Strict rent control was ultimately followed by the seizure and the distribution of lands. The reform was characterized by apparent leniency towards some of the richer peasants, who were allowed to keep land even if it was worked with the aid of hired labor. Considerable violence

---

[64] On this subject, see Henryk Cholaj, *Kontraktacja produktow rolnych*, Warsaw, 1965, pp. 121–134.

[65] *Rocznik statystyczny 1965*, Warsaw, 1965, p. 219; *Statisticka ročenka ČSSR*, *op. cit.*, pp. 34–35 and unpublished calculations for the U.S.S.R.

accompanied the reform, however, and the landowner class was eliminated from the country-side, while the ruling party gained in popularity
among the peasants. The reform was completed in 1952.

On the average, the distribution amounted to about one-third of an
acre per household and approximately one head of large cattle per 100
households affected by the reform.[66] The economic impact was thus
very small.

Almost immediately thereafter, efforts were made to enroll the peasants into mutual aid teams. Such teams were known in parts of prewar
China: they were now organized for the purpose of enlarging the size
of worked land holdings and also to prevent the peasant, as Professor
Eckstein puts it, "from consolidating his gains"—such as these were.
The teams were generally composed of six to ten households. Even in
this form of loose association, there was further differentiation between
teams formed on a temporary and on a permanent basis. By 1954,
there were nearly ten million teams comprising about 58 per cent of all
households.[67]

Agricultural cooperatives of various types were then formed by merg-
ing mutual aid teams. Less advanced cooperatives worked the land in
common and possessed investment funds. Distribution of income allowed
for payment of rents, and private plots were permitted. The more advanced collectives were modeled more closely on the Soviet type.

Formation of mutual aid teams and of the early cooperatives proceeded while the country was already implementing the first five-year
plan (1953–57). The plan gave a priority to industrial development
and was characterized by rising rates of investment and some growth of
urban population. Thus the problem of marketings arose in China.

Compulsory grain quotas were introduced in 1953 and were shortly
thereafter extended to other crops. Growth in marketings was fairly
rapid in 1954 (13 per cent), but in the next year the rate of increase
declined in spite of high delivery quotas that caused some difficulties
with feed and seed in agriculture itself. The correlation between the rate
of change in agricultural output and that of industrial output is very
high. Thus, in 1955, the government was apparently faced with the
problem of raising industrial output as well as that of increasing market-

---

[66] Marion R. Larsen, "China's Agriculture Under Communism," in U.S.
Congress, Joint Economic Committee, *An Economic Profile of Mainland China*,
Washington, D.C., 1967, pp. 213–214. See also T. J. Hughes, D. E. T. Luard,
The Economic Development of Communist China, 2nd ed., London, 1961, pp.
141–147.

[67] Quotation from Eckstein, *op. cit.*, p.73; figures from Larsen, *op. cit.*, p. 217.

ings. It was, however, unwilling to divert resources from industry to agriculture.[68]

Against this background, the collectivization drive was adopted in 1955–56. Although as announced, the plan called for a relatively slow pace, by February 1956, 85 per cent of households were in collectives and the percentage rose to 96.1 per cent towards the end of the year.[69] This was apparently achieved without mass slaughter of livestock; total output rose in 1956 and 1957. This may have been due in part to the policy, in effect since the beginning of the land reform, of conditioning of the peasants to constant changes in organization and to the introduction of mutual aid teams.

Yet, the basic problem facing the leadership remained unsolved: how to increase farm output without an increase in state investment in agriculture (which would have meant a reduction of resources assigned to industrial development).

The brief experiment with Soviet-type collectives during 1956 and 1957 does not appear to have been particularly successful in this respect. Though output rose, net marketings may have remained approximately the same. Within agriculture, there was some tendency to permit decentralization of decision making and to pay greater attention to individual incentives. Yet, these improvements were small and they were abruptly cast aside in the Great Leap Forward of 1958–60.[70]

During a single year, 1958, all of the 740,000 collectives were amalgamated into some 27,000 communes which took over all administrative functions of government together with responsibility for agricultural production and initiated unprecedented efforts at capital formation through giant "community-type" projects directed primarily towards water management and other land improvement projects. Although the existing internal structure was preserved (brigades—roughly corresponding to earlier collectives—continued within the communes and teams within the brigades), the entire pattern of farm work was drastically changed. As the communes embarked on large scale projects and construction of local industrial facilities—complete with backyard furnaces —they paid less attention to the purely agricultural aspects of their activities. Egalitarianism, inherent in the assumptions of the Leap Forward and ideologically appealing to local leaders, exerted a detrimental

---

[68] Dwight H. Perkins, "Centralization and Decentralization in Mainland China's Agriculture," *Quarterly Journal of Economics,* May 1964, pp. 214–215.

[69] Hughes and Luard, *op. cit.,* p. 154.

[70] Perkins, *op. cit.,* pp. 223–225. On grain procurement statistics and their reliability see Eckstein, pp. 312, 315–316.

influence on rural incentives. Private plots were abolished, food was provided in communal dining halls, and small cash wages were introduced. These latter, however, were not made dependent upon the achieved results—as was the case in earlier collectives—but on the number of hours or days worked. Because of the larger size of the operating unit, the degree to which wages were detached from performance was correspondingly increased.[71]

The level of food crop production is believed to have declined by some 14 per cent between 1958 and 1960, while the drop in total farm output is thought to be considerably greater (number of large draft animals available was approximately halved between 1958 and 1961). The decline in food crop production during this time is likely to have reduced available domestic supplies by 18 to 20 per cent.[72]

Recognition of the seriousness of the problem was delayed—in part because of the considerable damage to the statistical apparatus, and in part because of the euphoria generated by the bumper crop harvest of 1958. As the extent of difficulties became clear, various efforts were made to reduce the adverse impact of communal organization and of community investment projects on agricultural production. Rural markets for farm products were again allowed during 1959 (though there is evidence of local variation in implementation), and private plots were again encouraged. Beginning in 1961, the ownership of land devolved upon production brigades, while various efforts were made to limit the use of labor on construction projects during peak periods of farm work. A year later, further devolution of decision-making authority was implemented as production teams stepped up their activities in planning, performance of tasks, and income distribution.[73]

The decline in output with the concomitant reduction in agricultural exports and the shift to import surplus in grains, eventually resulted in a major shift in developmental strategy. The priority of heavy industry was considerably reduced, while that of industries supplying agriculture and producing consumer goods was raised. The rate of investment was also reduced. The "agriculture first" strategy, then, involved an explicit recognition of the necessity of solving the basic problems of agricultural productivity that defied solution within the framework of traditional formulae involving socialization and "cheap" community projects. A

[71] See Larsen, pp. 217–219, and Gordon Barrass, "Measures of Economic Planning," in Werner Klatt (ed.), *The Chinese Model*, Hong Kong, 1965, p. 78.

[72] Eckstein, and Edwin Jones, "The Emerging Pattern of China's Economic Revolution," in *An Economic Profile of Mainland China*, p. 82.

[73] Perkins, p. 232; Larsen, pp. 220–22.

restoration of per capita farm output is apparently planned for 1970, but this goal is not likely to be met. The key role in this task is now assigned to the so-called "modernizing areas" which will absorb most of the available inputs other than labor.[74]

Thus, China finds itself in a position in which the nature of the industrialization strategy, originally patterned broadly on the Soviet model, had to be basically altered because of stagnation and later deterioration in agriculture. In the process, the collective sector was set back to the position in which it is again found necessary to emphasize production teams (as in 1954–55). Furthermore, more resources must be allocated to agriculture than before in order to eliminate some of the adverse impact on soil conditions of low quality "improvements" instituted during the Great Leap Forward.

CONCLUSIONS

Although the common pattern of three stages of agricultural transformation may be discerned in all centrally planned economies discussed in this paper, there were important variations with respect to timing as well as the context in which the phase of surplus collection was applied in these economies. The most outstanding example is that of China, where the introduction of communes within the framework of the Great Leap Forward resulted in a dangerous disturbance of the balance between food production and population growth.

Alexander Eckstein suggests that "the Chinese Communists . . . relatively successful in the drive to collectivize . . . were emboldened to go beyond the tested forms of agricultural and economic organization under socialism. . . . Their success in agrarian policy lay in the tactical adaptation of a tested model." This is undoubtedly true, because the initial collectivization drive of 1955–56 was not accompanied by a decline in output. Yet a related question is in order. How relevant was the tested model to the particular conditions of China in 1957? Could it perform its functions satisfactorily without a major shift of resources to agriculture? [75]

With the stagnation in government procurements of food crops up to 1957, a negative answer seems indicated. Probably, major shifts in the pattern of investment were particularly difficult to introduce in 1957, the

[74] Larsen, p. 224. See also Jones, pp. 83–84 and Eckstein, pp. 37–38.
[75] Eckstein, p. 81.

last year of the first five-year plan. Apart from the matter of prestige, there must have been considerable complementarity between recent additions to capital stock and investments contemplated in industry within the framework of the second five-year plan. Hence, if the leadership opted for the radical solution of the Great Leap Forward, this could have been the result of failure to visualize meaningful, "second best" alternatives.

The tested model did not perform well for a number of reasons. The difficulties associated with command farming must have been particularly acute in the stage immediately after collectivization, because of the lack of experience. But this is only a partial explanation. More fundamentally, it would have been more difficult for the Chinese to pursue the policy of surplus collection than it was for the Soviets, because of large initial differences in the food supply position of Communist China and the Soviet Union. In terms of caloric or grain equivalent the Russians enjoyed a very considerable advantage over China on the eve of the industrialization campaign. It was this advantage that could be used in the process of surplus collection. The Chinese had little room to maneuver.[76]

Thus, the one lesson of the Chinese experience with the adjusted Soviet model is that if a country is to derive the full advantages of the Soviet development strategy and of surplus collection in agriculture, it must be sufficiently rich in terms of per capita caloric supplies and be able (as were the Soviets under Stalin) to make substantial shifts in diet towards starchy foods.

One could also argue that the adherence to Soviet development strategy and to the policy of surplus collection is a hindrance to speedy acceptance of those patterns of agricultural transformation that had been so successful in raising farm productivity in market-type economies. Command farming is the logical consequence of policies of surplus collection. Furthermore, in the postwar period it was also elevated to the status of the only available model of socialist agriculture. But the environment of command farming is basically hostile to introduction of new technology and to the dissemination of, and receptivity to, information on new techniques. We do know now that emphasis on surplus collection virtually put a stop to studies of production functions and delayed those on specialization and regionalization. As long as national policies fail to emphasize rising agricultural productivity, and the total

76 This has been stressed by Anthony M. Tang in "Input-Output Relations in the Agriculture of Communist China," a paper delivered at the 1967 Conference at the University of Washington, referred to in n. 51.

amount of agricultural investment is severely restricted, the supply of new factors of production, such as better seeds, feed mixtures, and the like, tends to be limited. Even to the extent that they *are* supplied, producers may find it physically impossible as well as unprofitable to introduce them into production. If they are introduced, their impact tends to be reduced by failure to supply complementary factors.

Thus, greater emphasis was placed on the supply of traditional factors of production (primarily structures and machinery). In Eastern Europe, the final collectivization drives were generally carried out in the phase of partial decompression and were accompanied by larger allocations of investment to farming. Although competition for investment funds in centrally planned economies remains strong, the share of fixed investment in estimated GNP (at factor cost) was found to be considerably greater in most Eastern than in Western European countries. In many instances, however, productivity of capital was reduced by neglect of complementarity.[77]

In centrally planned economies progress in decompression of the agricultural sectors has not been rapid. Partial attempts at reform were helpful, but their effectiveness was reduced by the features of command farming that were retained. Among these, irrational price systems—in part a legacy of an early Soviet decision to extract forced saving through prices—are a persisting obstacle to more efficient use of resources.

The introduction of the new economic systems is a vivid testimony to the dissatisfaction with the realized extent of transformation. As noted earlier, this stage is now in progress and it seems best to reserve judgment on the extent of transformation that will ultimately be achieved. If these systems are implemented (and improved), considerable improvement in the use of resources should result. But agricultural reform is being introduced jointly with reforms in planning of industry, and progress in agriculture depends to a large extent upon the improvement in the quality and kind of inputs that industry supplies. Here, too, it seems best to reserve judgment.

One feature of the general pattern of agricultural transformation in centrally planned economies has been a shift in expenditures on agricultural development as such, from an early to a later stage of general economic development. Hence, it is possible to apply resources to other

[77] Maurice Ernst, "Commentary," in Karcz, *Soviet and East European Agriculture,* p. 409. Neglect of complementarity has taken a variety of forms. Farms invested in livestock while the necessary number of stalls was considerably below requirements. Efficient use of fertilizers was often rendered impossible by the lack of appropriate machinery. Irrigation facilities were often unused because the necessary draining ditches were not dug.

sectors of the economy at an early stage. This may be said to be one of the advantages of the Soviet strategy. One opportunity cost, however, represents benefits foregone in the application of new inputs. In advanced market economies the rate of return on agricultural research and extension service activities has been estimated at close to 100 per cent.[78] As we have just noted, these returns were generally foregone by centrally planned economies.

This writer ventures the judgment that in Soviet as well as in Eastern European conditions a less exclusive reliance on surplus collection and greater emphasis on the application of new inputs might have yielded superior results in terms of agricultural productivity and of both the potentially realizable saving and the marketing contributions to growth consequent on such productivity. There is no doubt at all that this would have been the case in mainland China.[79]

Comment

JOHN M. MONTIAS, YALE UNIVERSITY

Professor Karcz tells us at the start of his paper that he will not succumb to the temptations of theory, and indeed his paper hardly swerves from the path of detailed description and historical analysis. The historical role of agriculture in the Soviet developmental process is so little known, and Karcz has learned so much about it in the course of years of research on the subject, that his expertise dictates his comparative advantage along the lines he has chosen to pursue. I, for want of expertise, must seek my least disadvantage in the other direction—toward the theoretical range of discourse if not in theory itself.

To justify his rejection of the model approach, Karcz argues that agriculture in the Sino-Soviet area has gone through three separate stages,

[78] As cited in Wyn F. Owen, "The Double Developmental Squeeze on Agriculture," *American Economic Review*, March 1966, p. 57.

[79] *Ibid.*, pp. 65–67. In his stimulating study, Owen finds only one real advantage to the Soviet (in his terms Marx-Leninist) model over the competing market oriented, family farming (Mill-Marshall) model. This is the virtually automatic transmission of increments of real income in the nonagricultural sector to saving (through the system of turnover and profit taxes). As Owen notes, the problem is primarily one of devising an appropriate tax structure for the market economy.

each of which "may be described as a transformation of its own." The first is linked to the redistribution of landed estates to the peasantry, the second to the collection of farm surpluses to sustain an ambitious industrialization program, the third and most recent to the decompression of command farming, when more resources have been allotted to the sector and an effort has been made to substitute incentives for coercion.

The implication of Karcz's argument is that the objective function of the relevant decision-makers and/or the institutional framework of the system are so altered from one period to the other that no single model can encompass all three.

The merit of this argument depends on our conception of a model and on the questions one might wish to address to the historical facts. But I for one would contend that the type of model Ranis and Fei have built is, to some extent at least, capable of integrating these divergent episodes and of illuminating the causes and effects of the changes that occurred. If these models cannot fully capture the diversity and complexity of the real world, their excessive degree of aggregation is to blame rather than their inability to cope with the broad institutional changes that marked Soviet and East European agricultural development.

In their book-length analysis of the labor-surplus economy, Fei and Ranis [1] focused on the marketable surplus of the agricultural sector in its relation to the supply and demand for off-farm workers on the part of the industrial, or nonagricultural, sector. On the demand side, they found that when wages were fixed at an institutionally determined level, the rate of capital accumulation, the intensity of innovations, and their degree of labor-using or labor-saving bias in the industrial sector were the key factors governing the growth in demand for laborers on the part of the industrial sector at an early stage of development. To meet this demand for labor at a constant wage, however, the agricultural sector has to generate sufficient agricultural surpluses to keep the terms of trade from turning against industry. The growth of the industrial sector, despite a high rate of innovational intensity, is likely to be frustrated when agricultural output stagnates and farm marketings per nonfarm employee decline.

The Soviet and East European experience may fruitfully be analyzed in the context of this model with suitable modifications to fit its institutional peculiarities.

First, we may note that the policy objective implicit in the Fei-Ranis

[1] J. C. H. Fei and Gustav Ranis, *Development of the Labor Surplus Economy: Theory and Policy*, Homewood, Illinois, 1964.

model is not very different from that which can be imputed to the planners in a Soviet-type economy, that is, to maximize some combination of industrial output and nonagricultural employment (although I should expect that the social welfare function Fei and Ranis had in mind would give a higher relative weight to the employment criterion than Communist planners would).[2] But in any event, agricultural output both in the model and in the Soviet scheme of development generates little or no welfare directly. It may be considered an intermediate good, necessary to the production of industrial goods and to the generation of nonfarm employment, both of which enter as arguments in these welfare functions.

Consider the first stage of the evolution described by Karcz. By the early 1920's in the Soviet Union and soon after the end of World War II in Eastern Europe, land reform had been completed, and the independent family farm had become the principal mode of agricultural enterprise. Such surpluses as could be spared from on-farm consumption belonged to the farmers themselves and, after governmental obligations had been met, could be traded directly for industrial consumer goods and services on the one hand, and capital goods on the other. In the absence of rent payments to coax out marketings, one might have expected a marked reversion to self-sufficiency. But as Karcz has shown in his study of Soviet net marketings in 1926–27 and as the prompt recovery of urban food consumption in Poland and Czechoslovakia in the period 1947–49 testify, marketings, in the wake of land reform, need not decline drastically and may in fact keep up with the recovery of output. (In the Soviet Union the recovery took place after the ravages of the civil war (1919–21) and in Eastern Europe after the devastation of World War II and the chaos of the liberation period.) The supply of light industrial products for sale in rural areas rose fast enough to stimulate peasant marketings during the NEP period in the U.S.S.R. and in the late 1940's in Eastern Europe. Both urban and rural food consumption per capita were rising. As a first approximation, it may be claimed that the two sectors grew, or recovered, more or less on a balanced path, neither sector acting as a serious drag on the other, given the rates of capital formation and of industrial growth prevailing

[2] See the discussion in Fei and Ranis, *op. cit.*, pp. 139–141. Industrial employment may enter as a separate argument in the Communist planners' objective function because it helps to widen and to strengthen the power basis of the ruling Party (*cf.* the Rumanian argument in favor of protectionism discussed in J. M. Montias, *Economic Development in Communist Rumania*, Cambridge, Massachusetts, 1967, p. 206).

at the time, rates that were of course much more moderate than in the period that followed.

Accelerated industrialization dominates the second stage in Karcz's scheme. Capital formation was raised significantly and channeled to an unprecedented extent into heavy industry and supporting sectors including transportation, wherever bottlenecks arose. We may, as Karcz and M. Lewin have recently done in their articles in *Soviet Studies*,[3] question whether the Soviet Politbureau in 1928–29 was judicious in choosing its "time limits." By analogy, the discontinuous acceleration in the pace of industrialization in Eastern Europe, starting in 1949–50, may also be taxed as irrational. But if we gauge rationality by planners' preferences, including the planners' time rate of discount—which must have been extraordinarily high at the time of the Soviet Five-Year Plan and in Eastern Europe in the early 1950's—then the instruments for carrying out this policy, at least in the agricultural sector, appear to be in keeping with the logic of these desiderata.[4] For if agriculture was to make its maximum contribution to domestic saving without absorbing more than a fraction of investments in fixed capital, the terms of trade had to be kept favorable to industry and industrial wages had to be repressed. Moreover, to assure the flow of farm laborers into industrial and other occupations, the supply price of farm laborers on the margin of choice between retaining their agricultural occupation and getting a city job had to be held down. These aims were simultaneously achieved by imposing steep schedules of compulsory deliveries to "state funds" for basic farm products and thus turning the terms of trade sharply against the peasants. To offset, at least in part, the blunting effect of these deliveries on incentives, farmers were allowed to sell on the free markets any surplus they wished to dispose of after their obligations to the state had been met. The prices on these markets in the Soviet Union and Eastern Europe were many times higher than the purchase prices paid for by the state for compulsory deliveries and for other forms of more or less obligatory government acquisitions.

A remarkable feature of this first round of intensive industrialization,

[3] J. Karcz, "Thoughts on the Grain Problem," *Soviet Studies,* Vol. XVIII, April 1967; and M. Lewin, "The Immediate Background of Soviet Collectivization," *Soviet Studies,* Vol. XVII, No. 2, October 1965.

[4] In the Soviet case, the logic was probably carried too far. It is hard to believe that any degree of urgency of expanding industrial output could justify the hardships inflicted on the farm population, including widespread starvation in 1932–33 and the massive slaughtering of cattle. The East European Communist leaders learned their lessons from these excesses and followed a more prudent course in their respective countries in the 1950's.

both in the Soviet Union and Europe, was that despite stagnant or even (as in most countries) declining real wages in industry, the capital-to-labor ratio went up in industry itself and, more generally, in the entire nonagricultural economy.[5] These statements jointly imply a "very labor-saving bias" (to use the precise Fei-Ranis terminology) in the aggregate production function of industry.[6] Thus the entire growth of nonfarm employment in the countries that followed the Soviet strategy of development can be traced to the expansion of the capital stock, at least in the industrialization period under consideration.

This capital-using bias in industry may, at first blush, appear counterproductive. But this impression must be modified if we take into account the costs of rural-urban migration—the additional housing capacity and social services that must be provided for new migrants after an initial compression of the average space occupied per urban dweller.[7] The new industrial laborers may well "carry their average agricultural surplus on their back," as in one variant of the Fei-Ranis model, but they can hardly bring their cottage and one-room school house along with them. This may explain why raising the participation of women in the labor force, with the relatively moderate capital outlays that this entailed, seemed a more desirable alternative than stepping up the inflow of farm laborers to city jobs, at least after the overcrowding of existing housing and social facilities in urban areas had reached a certain point. It should also be recalled that the low priority in the development program of service sectors with low capital intensity made for a higher average capital-to-

[5] For the increase in the capital-to-labor ratio outside Soviet agriculture in the 1930's, see Richard Moorsteen and Raymond P. Powell, *The Soviet Capital Stock 1928–1962*, Homewood, Illinois, 1966, p. 255. Official capital-stock series in Eastern Europe are generally undepreciated and based on original value. Nevertheless, even if a generous allowance be made for the overstatement of the growth of the capital stock, it would seem that the capital-to-output ratios rose throughout the area in the early 1950's in industry and, to a lesser extent, in the nonagricultural, nonresidential sectors of the economy taken as a whole.

[6] I assume here that wages are approximately equal to the marginal value product in industry. Then, from Fei-Ranis, *op. cit.*, equation 7.3, and from definition A3.3, we have:

$$H_L = \eta_W - \epsilon_{LL}\, \eta_{K/L} < 0$$

where H_L is the growth rate of the marginal product of labor and the Hicksian labor saving bias, η_W is the rate of increase of wages, ϵ_{LL} is the elasticity of the marginal product of labor with respect to labor (positive by definition), and $\eta_{K/L}$ is the growth rate of the capital-to-labor ratio. If η_W is zero or negative and $\eta_{K/L}$ positive, H_L must be negative.

[7] For a systematic theoretical discussion of this point, see Gregory Grossman, "Some Current Trends in Soviet Capital Formation," in *Capital Formation and Economic Growth*, Princeton University Press for National Bureau of Economic Research, 1955, pp. 188–193.

labor ratio outside agriculture than if these sectors had been allowed to expand at the same pace as in market economies.

But whatever the rational or irrational causes of the bias toward capital intensity, the fact remains that the agricultural working force in the Soviet-bloc countries declined very slowly—more slowly than in most Western European countries—particularly in the Soviet Union, Rumania, Bulgaria, and Poland, the countries where rural overcrowding and hidden unemployment were thought to be the most serious prior to industrialization. To this day the labor force in agriculture in the less developed countries of Eastern Europe makes up a larger share of the total labor force than in most noncommunist countries at a comparable stage of development. Compare, for example, Rumania with a national income per head of 600 to 750 U.S. dollars, and over 50 per cent of the labor force still engaged in agriculture in the mid-1960's, with Spain and Portugal—national income per head 350–400 dollars and 500–550 dollars respectively—and about 35 per cent of the labor force still on the farm.[8]

Whether the Fei-Ranis model can provide a better insight into Soviet and East European agricultural policy than a straightforward historical chronicle hangs on its ability to suggest an economic interpretation for Karcz's third stage, which he summarizes as the "decompression of the command economy." In this stage the terms of trade shift in favor of agriculture, recovering some of the ground lost in the second stage. Mainly through the higher farm incomes resulting from this shift, peasants' living standards improve and the farm sector begins to absorb a significant share of total investments.

The simultaneous inception of the new stage, after the death of Stalin, in both the Soviet Union and in Eastern Europe is certainly no vindication of the model, since one would have thought that, if economic factors alone had been operating, the turning point would have occurred at different dates in countries with more or less surplus labor or which were recovering from greater or smaller war devastation. No doubt dogmatic inflexibility played a role in this timing, and in some countries of Eastern Europe at least the turnabout was delayed after the old strategy had reached a point of no return. But it would be futile to deny that even the most "Stalinist" planners would eventually have realized that the disincentive effects on output of the old strategy had begun to outweigh

[8] For data on the agricultural labor force, see Moorsteen and Powell, *op. cit.,* p. 246 (for the Soviet Union); and Maurice Ernst, "Postwar Economic Growth in Eastern Europe (A Comparison with Western Europe)," in *New Directions in the Soviet Economy,* Joint Economic Committee, 89th Congress, 2nd Session, Part IV, p. 893.

its short-term effectiveness in extracting agricultural surpluses and in getting the swelling urban population fed (at ever so low a standard).

The reversal in the terms of trade and the simultaneous rapid increase in urban real wages that took place after 1953 created a situation akin to the one described by Fei and Ranis, in which a massive industrialization drive is eventually brought to a halt by the failure to expand agricultural output.[9] In contrast to the case they describe, however, the growth of industrial output slowed down as capital formation declined, but did not fall to zero, although it diminished significantly. Most notable is the fact that, in the countries of Eastern Europe that were hardest hit by the New Course, including Rumania, Hungary, and Czechoslovakia, nonagricultural employment virtually ceased to expand during the years following 1953. This shut off the only outlet for the natural increase of the farm population, whose absolute size actually increased during the next two to four years.

Except in Bulgaria, where collective farms occupied about 50 per cent of the country's cultivable area by the time of Stalin's death, it was not until 1958–60 that the majority of peasants were herded into collectives in Eastern Europe (outside Poland, of course, where individual farming has been permitted to hold sway to the present day). In Rumania, the only country I have studied closely in this regard, the improvement in the terms of trade for agriculture ceased about the time of the final collectivization drive.[10] The deterioration that occurred after 1958 seems to have been caused, not by a decline in official procurement prices, but by a curtailment and eventual near elimination of the free market. Yet capital investments in the farm sector kept on rising, in large part through the medium of the machine-tractor stations, which, in contrast to the Soviet Union where they were liquidated after 1959, continued to perform their traditional role as "vanguard of the proletariat" in the Danubian economies. Collectivization provided an added degree of freedom for the economic planners who were in a better position than in the past to force the peasants to reinvest—via the "indivisible fund" of the collectives—a significant share of the gains in real incomes that accrued to them from larger output and sales.

Far from "decompressing command farming," the rulers of Rumania pulled the reins tighter during this period; but they also prudently stepped up the resource flow from industry to the farm sector in the form of fertilizers, insecticides, and machinery. This complex policy mix had yet another dimension: the government now supplied industrial resources

[9] Fei and Ranis, op. cit., pp. 181–182.
[10] J. M. Montias, op. cit., Chapter 2.

in first priority to state farms, which were technically better equipped to absorb modern machinery and chemicals, and which offered the special advantage of marketing the bulk of their production. The Rumanian planners apparently came to the conclusion that a concentration of inputs in this modern enclave of the agricultural sector would yield a larger pay-off in the form of exportable marketings than if they had been spread more evenly (and thinly) throughout the sector. The upsurge in food exports of the period 1958 to 1962, which helped to finance larger raw material and machinery imports and which was therefore partly responsible for the acceleration of industrial output that took place in these years, must have justified this preferential allocation in the eyes of the authorities.

This success story leads me to a broader conclusion: The performance of Soviet and East European agriculture cannot be assessed in terms of diminishing capital productivity, rising material costs, and of other partial indicators. In some countries, like Czechoslovakia, the decision has been made to let food imports fill the consumption gap created by a stagnant agriculture. In others, like Rumania and Bulgaria, exports have bought critical inputs for the industrialization program. The wisdom of Czechoslovakia's decision to adopt a British-type strategy hinges on its ability to increase exports of manufactures *pari passu* with its rising food and material requirements. In the case of Rumania, it depends in part on the external opportunity costs of the resources that have lately been injected into the farm sector. Even if the type of industrialization strategy pursued by the communist states were to lead to a deficit in foodstuffs for the entire bloc—a possibility by no means inconceivable in the light of the divergent trends in the area as a whole between the consumption of foodstuffs and their output—this would not necessarily be catastrophic, nor would it necessarily show the improvidence of the planners' single-minded stress on industry. The outcome of such a trend might be good or bad, depending on the aggregate capacity of the bloc to export non-food raw materials and manufactured goods to the rest of the world, and particularly of course to countries, such as the United States, Canada, New Zealand, and Argentina, which enjoy a comparative advantage in exporting farm products. Peter Wiles and the London *Economist* some time ago advocated such a policy for the Soviet Union. It also makes sense, in my opinion, for the more developed East European countries, if not for the entire Soviet bloc.

Now that Professor Karcz and other specialists have pinpointed the various reasons why agriculture in the Soviet bloc is not as efficient as it might be, further analytical studies of the sector in the wider context of these countries' industrialization problems are in order. Changes in labor productivity in agriculture must be assessed in the light of the efficient distribution of labor and capital between agriculture and the rest of the economy. This allocation in turn hinges on the expansion of the branches of the chemical and machine-building industry that provides inputs for agriculture, as well as on the trading policy of the Communist authorities—on their willingness to let the economy become more immersed in foreign trade, either as importers or as exporters of food products. The Fei-Ranis model, if it can be opened to trade and disaggregated to include some of the variables discussed in the present comments, may provide a useful analytical framework for this wider approach.

Reply

JERZY F. KARCZ

Had I, in fact, succumbed to the temptation of using a two-sector model as the analytical framework for my investigation, it would probably have been of the Fei-Ranis variety. I was, however, charged with the review of the transformation of agriculture in centrally planned economies and not with the analysis of the role of agriculture in their economic development. But even in the latter case, the required degree of suitable modification seems much more substantial than Professor Montias suggests. Leaving aside the knotty problem of excessive aggregation, we must inevitably face the question of the applicability of a model based on the existence of surplus labor for the analysis of a very large and varied area. Even if we ignore the more obvious cases of East Germany and Bohemia, there is the difficult issue posed by the fact that "empirical evidence does not favor the doctrine of an absolute zero marginal productivity in mainland China's agriculture." [1] Nor was the release of agricultural labor a priority objective of Chinese planners. It is also apparent that Fei and Ranis deal with genuine agricultural

---

[1] Lawrence J. Lau, "Peasant Consumption, Saving, and Investment in Mainland China," paper delivered at the Conference on "The Agrarian Question in the Light of Communist and Noncommunist Experience," University of Washington, Seattle, August 1967.

surpluses, while those of centrally planned economies are more appropriately described as "forced surpluses." This is a matter of consequence for the functioning of the farm sector. Under the circumstances, I feel more comfortable within the looser (and unavoidably) less precise framework of my three stages (it will, of course, be understood that they differ conceptually from other, more famous, stages that have at times been used to describe the over-all process of development).

The looser framework also makes it possible to bypass, at this time, the awkward question of the relation of turning points of the Fei-Ranis model to the actual developments in centrally planned economies. As Professor Montias himself implies (p. 271), the major turning point after 1953 was more influenced by issues of dogmatic conformity than by the purely economic factors that rule the Fei-Ranis turning point.[2] From this standpoint, it is futile to speculate whether or not the "most 'Stalinist' planners" would—at some point—have called for a turn of the development strategy. The fact remains that in the crucial and pathbreaking Soviet case they did not choose to do so in spite of the mounting evidence of the negative effects of this strategy on farm output.

It is appropriate to touch, even if all too briefly, on yet another consideration. Professor Montias notes correctly that the Soviet development strategy viewed the agricultural output (if not, indeed, the farm sector as a whole) as an intermediate product: final goods are represented by increases in industrial production and nonfarm employment (p. 268). This view implies that we may ignore the impact of developments within the agricultural sector, including trends in output, as long as the major objectives of the planners' preference function are realized (a formulation that takes us a very long way indeed from the emphasis on increases in agricultural productivity which are stressed by Fei and Ranis [3]).

Yet, it is a truism that the quality of the final product depends, *inter alia,* on that of intermediate goods used in its production. To put the matter somewhat differently while stressing the issue of forced surpluses, we could say that it proved possible to treat agriculture as an intermediate product only at the cost of developing and maintaining the institutions of command farming. In a stimulating book, David Granick has recently suggested that organization may be viewed as a major constituent of a nation's intangible capital," and that organizational changes

[2] John C. H. Fei and Gustav Ranis, *Development of the Labor Surplus Economy: Theory and Policy,* New York, 1964, pp. 264-266.
[3] *Ibid.,* pp. 43 ff., 195–199, 214–219.

"can be treated as representing positive or negative intangible investment." [4]

Viewed in this manner, the institutions of command farming should indeed be considered as a disinvestment (measured by the discounted value of foregone income streams). When we recall that command farming in centrally planned economies also absorbed a very considerable amount of capital in the stage of surplus collection as well as in that of decompression, it is difficult to avoid the conclusion that the transformation of agriculture in centrally planned economies was very capital-intensive (as Professor Montias notes, so was the development of industry). Certainly, trends in capital productivity as well as in material costs are of some consequence in assessing the total impact of a development strategy (an issue to which I did not address myself in the paper).

The attempts at partial decompression as well as the introduction of the new economic systems in agriculture may thus be viewed as an effort to increase the volume of intangible national capital. For a variety of reasons, the gestation period has been—and will probably continue to be—a long one, but it should ultimately lead to improved decision making processes as well as to improved incentives. Both form the economic content of decompression. It is for this reason, of course, that I am not perturbed by the absence of recent terms-of-trade effects in Rumania; the stage of decompression of the Rumanian economy as a whole has barely begun. It is precisely because tangible investments are being made in Rumanian agriculture and especially in its "modern," state farm sector—following the Yugoslav model of seed improvement and fertilizer application in state farms—that I am willing to predict the emergence of a stage of agricultural decompression soon.

In closing, one brief comment is called for. I fully agree with Professor Montias that the emergence of a net, blocwide, food deficit need not be a disaster provided that the bloc succeeds in generating a sufficient volume of good quality exports. (From a different standpoint, the magnitude of the deficit could raise some questions.) Japan succeeded in doing so; but in centrally planned economies this along with other scenes of the final act, must still be written.

[4] David Granick, *Soviet Metal-Fabricating and Economic Development: Practice Versus Policy,* Madison, Wisc., 1967, p. 266. See also Chapter 3. I did not consult this work until after I wrote the paper presented in this volume.

The Transferability of the Japanese Pattern of Modernizing Traditional Agriculture

KAZUSHI OHKAWA

HITOTSUBASHI UNIVERSITY

AND

BRUCE F. JOHNSTON

STANFORD UNIVERSITY

INTRODUCTION

To what extent can the factors and conditions that made the transformation of Japanese agriculture possible be reproduced elsewhere? The attempt to identify unique as well as transferable factors, particularly in terms of development strategies, has been made on several occasions by the present writers as well as other authors.

A consensus seems to have emerged concerning the characteristics of the "Japanese model." Of these characteristics we will emphasize three. First, agricultural output has been increased within the unchanged organizational framework of the existing small-scale farming system. This was possible because of increases in the productivity of the existing on-farm resources of land and labor, and was associated with remarkably small demands on the critically scarce resources of capital and foreign exchange, at least during the long prewar period. Second, the bulk of the nation's farmers have been involved in increases in agricultural productivity associated with the use of improved varieties, fertilizers, and other current inputs; and technological progress of this type has continuously been the driving force in increasing agricultural productivity. This is still true for the postwar agriculture in which small-scale mechanization has developed throughout the country. Third, agricultural and industrial development went forward together in a process of "concurrent" growth. Expansion in the nonagricultural sectors has, of course, proceeded a good deal more rapidly than in agriculture, so that the overwhelmingly agrarian character of the economy has gradually been transformed. But throughout the process of modern economic growth, the interactions between agriculture and the rest of the economy that have been associated with this structural transformation, have had profound implications for growth in both sectors. In particular, the raising of factor productivity in agriculture was a necessary condition for the important net contribution that the rural sector made to financing the expansion of the nonfarm sectors of the economy.

These are mutually interrelated phenomena, and only a comprehensive framework can clarify the mechanisms that produced this pattern of growth. The attempt to formulate such a framework is beyond the scope of this short paper. The present treatment is intended to focus attention on problems relating to the type and speed of technical progress, questions that we believe are of crucial importance in determining the efficient strategy for agricultural development. In pursuing this partial approach we are mainly concerned with the first and second characteristics mentioned above, leaving the third almost untouched.

A comprehensive framework of analysis would provide a basis for identifying the variables and parameters that are most important in assessing the relevance of the Japanese experience to contemporary developing countries. In our partial analysis, which considers this question primarily in relation to other Asian countries, we postulate that the Japanese pattern of development was conditioned by three initial factors that have parallels in Asian countries today, and a fourth factor that points up an important difference. The factors that are similar are: first, an economic structure characterized by the dominant position of agriculture (representing some 75 per cent of the total labor force in the early Meiji period and similar fractions in most of the Asian countries today); second, the dwindling of uncultivated arable land, with the consequent growth of dependence on increase in output per unit area; and third, an organizational framework characterized by small-scale farming systems.

The fourth factor relates to the wide disparity between the growth rates of population and total labor force in contemporary less developed countries and in Japan. The fact that these are much higher in the former countries is very significant. But the impact of these high rates of growth of population and labor force on the development problems and prospects of the Asian nations today accentuates the importance of the three similarities with the Japanese experience. Given the initial conditions—the fact that agriculture weighs so heavily in the total labor force—and given the rapid growth of total population and labor force, the "arithmetic of structural transformation" is such that the absolute size of the farm population will continue to increase for some decades.[1] Hence, even in those countries where the arable frontier is still of considerable importance, the availability of unused land of satisfactory quality is being reduced quite rapidly. And the average farm size, already small (though not as small as in Japan), can be expected to undergo considerable further decrease before the trend is ultimately reversed by a reduction in the absolute size of the farm labor force.

The unchanged organizational framework of the small-scale farming system in Japan and the participation of the bulk of the nation's farmers in the increase of agricultural productivity—these two facts would require explanations in some detail from both an historical and an institutional point of view. The evolution of the initial conditions from which the transformation of agriculture started; the early changes in the land tenure system, among others—these are particularly relevant to the discussions that follow. Again, these matters would deserve separate treatment rather than a hasty, superficial description. We believe, however, that a partial treatment along the lines defined above can be carried out effectively enough. In this paper the conventional input-output approach is applied on a more comprehensive scale than before to the analysis of Japanese agricultural development. The aim is to link the results with the strategy of technological development in agriculture. Regarding the approach, two points seem particularly to deserve mention.

First, much more consistent quantitative data than were previously available are used to test our hypothesis. To investigate the problem stated at the outset of this paper, we believe that a consistent interpretation of the historical experience, though not easily achieved, is an essential requirement. This interpretation in turn depends upon long-term

[1] See the Appendix Note to this paper by John Cownie, and also B. F. Johnston, "Agriculture and Economic Development: The Relevance of the Japanese Experience," *Food Research Institute Studies,* Vol. VI, No. 3, 1966, pp. 267–73.

economic statistics of agriculture estimated within a systematic framework consistent with those of the rest of the economy. The new volume by M. Umemura and others meets this requirement although there are still some important areas of uncertainty and ignorance. (See Table 1 below for the citation.) We will begin by presenting a very compact summary of these data in terms of our phase hypothesis.[2]

Second, in approaching the problem of identification of transferable factors or patterns (i.e., certain combinations of factors), an attempt is made to present them in concrete terms, not only as derived from the experience of advanced economies (Japan in this case), but also with due consideration to the the situation of.the presently developing countries. Regarding the latter, the specific focus is East Asia. Owing to the paucity of available data, we resort to a certain amount of speculation in order to identify the factors and patterns required for efficient development of agriculture. This will be described after presenting an interpretation of Japan's experience.

Our conceptual framework is built on two basic ideas: one relates to the historical phases that condition the process of agricultural development, and the other concerns the characteristics of technology in agriculture, particularly Asian agriculture. The former is formulated in terms of the historical pattern of labor force distribution between the agricultural and nonagricultural sectors and is closely related to the thesis of a "turning point." [3] The latter stresses the significance of an agricultural technology in which new inputs of a biological and chemical nature are crucial, and its economic interpretation will be developed so as to be linked with the general thesis of "borrowed technology."

LONG-RANGE GROWTH PATTERN
OF JAPANESE AGRICULTURE: STATISTICAL
FINDINGS AND INTERPRETATION

To what extent can the experts agree in recognizing and appraising the growth pattern of Japan's agriculture in the hundred years since

[2] The phase hypothesis and supporting data are examined in greater detail in Kazushi Ohkawa, "Phases of Agricultural Development and Economic Growth," in Kazushi Ohkawa, B. F. Johnston, and Hiromitsu Kaneda (ed.), *Agriculture and Economic Development: A Symposium on Japan's Experience* (forthcoming).

[3] See Kazushi Ohkawa, "Agriculture and Turning-Points in Economic Growth," *The Developing Economies,* December 1965.

the Meiji Restoration? With some exceptions, especially in regard to the early period, we have the impression that the data presented in Table 1 command a large measure of agreement among students of Japan's economic history.

The table is prepared to show in a concise way the long-range growth pattern of Japanese agriculture since 1885; for the earlier years available data seem to be rather dubious. Estimates of the average annual compound rates of change in output, inputs, and various input-output relationships and ratios are shown. The estimates are explained in the notes to the table, but the conceptual frame underlying Table 1 needs a brief explanation. It is composed of two dimensions: first, a time dimension that is examined in terms of three periods and second, an input dimension based on a two-way classification of inputs. The time periods—1885–1919, 1919–54, and 1954–61 are based on our observations concerning the pattern of major swings in inputs and output which will not be discussed here. The initial discussion is in terms of those three periods, but later a distinction is made between Phase I, which comprises Periods 1 and 2, and Phase II which refers to the period since 1954. For the most part the estimates for Period 3 (1954–61) are used to characterize Phase II, but in some instances reference is also made to data for more recent years. The average rates in the table do not necessarily reveal their acceleration or deceleration during the demarcated periods. When necessary, timing of acceleration or deceleration will be made the subjects of supplementary comments. For the input dimension a dichotomy is made between inputs of nonagricultural or external origin and those of agricultural or internal origin. Because of data limitations, land and labor are shown in terms of a stock rather than a flow concept.

Let us start with the output performance. Its rate of increase shows sizable differences among the three periods: biggest in 1954–61(Period 3), smallest in 1919–54 (Period 2), and intermediate for 1885–1919 (Period 1). This is true irrespective of whether we choose an output index or a value-added series. One might wonder whether such a big variation is a statistical illusion, perhaps a result of the method of artificially demarcating the periods. The answer is no. The following trend measures, including the earlier years before 1885, and based on the value added estimates, give the following rates (percentage):

1877–1919:1.80   1919–38:0.46   1877–1938:1.39
1919–60:0.51   1877–1960:1.17

TABLE 1

Average Annual Percentage Changes In Output, Input, and Productivity of Japanese Agriculture, 1885-1961
(except where specified, seven year moving averages centered on years indicated)

		Phase I		Phase II
		Period 1	Period 2	Period 3
	Item	1885–1919	1919–54	1954–61
	A. Total			
A1	Total output index[a]	1.96	0.70	4.26
A2	Total input index[a]	0.49	0.56	2.13
A3	Total productivity index (A1 ÷ A2)[b]	1.47	0.14	2.51
	Gross added value			
A4(1)	Using linked deflators	1.60	0.31	2.13
A4(2)	Valued at 1934–36 prices	1.69	0.17	2.46
	Current input			
A5	Total	1.76	3.47	8.16
A6	External	3.47	3.22	9.55
A7	Internal	0.29	0.68	1.90
	B. Land and Labor			
B1	Arable land area	0.62	0	0.30[c]
B2	Labor force (number)	−0.03	0.25	−2.74[c]
B3	Land-labor ratio	0.65	−0.25	2.44[c]
	Partial productivity of land			
B4(1)	A4(1) ÷ B1[b]	1.34	0.70	3.96[c]
B4(2)	A4(2) ÷ B1[b]	1.07	0.17	2.16[c]
	Partial productivity of labor			
B5(1)	A4(1) ÷ B2[b]	1.99	0.45	7.00[c]
B5(2)	A4(2) ÷ B2[b]	1.72	−0.08	5.20[c]

(continued)

TABLE 1 (continued)

Item	Phase I		Phase II
	Period 1 1885–1919	Period 2 1919–54	Period 3 1954–61

C. Capital[d]

C1	Total gross capital stock[e]	0.54	0.54	3.18
C2	Livestock[e]	0.52	1.38	3.52
C3	Trees and shrubs	2.17	0.83	5.25
C4	Equipment	1.45	1.48	8.63
C5	Capital-labor ratio (C1 ÷ B2)[b]	0.57	0.29	5.92
C6	Capital-land ratio (C1 ÷ B1)[b]	-0.08	0.54	2.88

D. Other Ratios and Indexes

	Capital-output ratio[e]			
D1	Total	$3.40-2.30^f$	$2.30-2.63^f$	$2.63-2.91^f$
D2	Excluding buildings	$1.05-1.00^f$	$1.00-1.19^f$	$1.19-1.60^f$
	Relative price index of output			
D3	to current input[g]	2.06	1.01	4.08
	Ratios[h]: agricultural to manufacturing			
D4	Wages[i]	$69.9-73.7^f$	$73.7-37.3^f$	$37.3-42.0^f$
D5	Partial labor productivity	$50.0-44.8^f$	$44.8-28.1^f$	$28.1-19.9^f$

Sources: Except as specified hereafter all the original data are from Part 3 of Mataji Umemura and others, *Noringyo* [*Agriculture and Forestry*] (Vol. 9 of Kazushi Ohkawa, Miyohei Shinohara, and Mataji Umemura, eds., *Estimates of Long-Term Economic Statistics of Japan Since 1868*, Toyo Keizai Shinposha, Tokyo, 1966). This thirteen-volume series is a revised and enlarged version of Kazushi Ohkawa et al, (eds.), *The Growth Rate of the Japanese Economy Since 1878*, Toyko, 1958.

The original data for total gross capital stock in C are from Kazushi Ohkawa and others, *Shihon Sutokku* [*Capital Stock*] (Vol. 3 of the above series) Tokyo, 1966. The ratios of wages and productivities in D are reproduced from Tables 4 and 5 in Kazushi Ohkawa and Henry Rosovsky, "Postwar Japanese Growth in Historical Perspective," in *Proceedings of the Tokyo Conference on Economic Growth, September, 1966* (Forthcoming).

(continued)

TABLE 1 (concluded)

[a]Indexes with different weights have been linked; valued at constant 1934–36 prices.

[b]Indicated computation refers to the original data, not to the percentage increases shown.

[c]A five-year average centered on 1961.

[d]Five-year moving averages are used for all series in all years. Residential buildings are excluded.

[e]In terms of 1934–36 prices.

[f]Initial and final ratios based on five-year average centered on years shown.

[g]The relative ·price index is obtained by dividing the index of prices received by farmers by the index of prices of inputs of nonagricultural origin. Both are linked indexes with 1934–36 = 100.

[h]Agriculture, in the computation of these ratios, includes forestry and fisheries.

[i]For agriculture, average daily wage rates; estimated values of payments in kind are not included.

It is clear that the Japanese experience over almost a century presents not only a period of a high rate of growth (an accelerated process), but also a period of a low rate of growth (or a decelerated process). This suggests that considerable changes must have taken place in the operation of the factors and conditions that determined the growth of output.

Of the complex and interrelated factors and conditions that were operative, only the performance of conventional inputs is shown in the table. And yet these can, we believe, provide a broad indication of the causes of the above-mentioned differences.

As noted in the Introduction, we periodize agricultural development in terms of historical and analytical phases based on the distribution of the labor force between agriculture and nonagriculture. To be more concrete, the turning point of agriculture is placed at the period at which the absolute size of the labor force engaged in agriculture begins to decrease as a trend. The basic reason for this demarcation is that the nature and structure of agricultural production and the character of its changes should differ basically between the period before that point and the period after that point. The former period is called Earlyphasia or Phase I and the latter Middlephasia or Phase II.[4] With this demarcation

---

[4] In introducing these terms, Johnston used the terms Earlyphasia and Middlephasia to describe two hypothetical countries for which fifty-year projections of the growth path of total, agricultural, and nonagricultural labor force were presented based on alternative assumptions with respect to the rates of growth of the total labor force and nonfarm employment. See Johnston, *op. cit.*, pp. 267–70. The Earlyphasia situation assumed that initially 80 per cent of the total labor

in mind we would like first to examine the differences between Period 3 on one hand and Periods 1 and 2 combined on the other, ignoring the differences between the latter two for the time being.

The labor force in agriculture tended to decrease appreciably during Period 3 for the first time in Japan's economic history. A number of repatriated people from the overseas territories contributed to an abnormal increase in the agricultural labor force after the war, so that the real turning point may be found a bit later than 1954. Until this time, even with its high rate of industrialization (top level by international comparison), and with its moderate rate of population increase (some 1.0 to 1.5 per cent), Japan could not decrease its farm population (see B-2 in Table 1). A theoretical definition of turning point along the lines of the Lewis two-sector model would require a test of the equality of labor's marginal productivity as between the self-employed sector, essentially agricultural, and the enterprise sector, of which manufacturing is representative. Here we do not claim identity of the turning point historically identified with regard to agriculture and the theoretical turning point. However, the performance of the wage ratio shown in D-4 can be construed as giving some support to such an interpretation. The ratio of the agricultural to manufacturing wage rate has continued to increase since 1961, reaching 48.6 per cent in 1964. This indicates that agricultural wages are catching up fast. (We are not concerned with the level difference itself.)

Phase II has not run for long enough to make a full comparison of its characteristics with those of Phase I. Furthermore, the period 1954–61 marks the postwar investment spurt in Japan, with its unprecedentedly high rate of output growth of the nonagricultural sector, a growth from whose "induced effects," agriculture must have grown rapidly. With these qualifications, it seems legitimate to call attention to the following characteristics. The much higher rate of output growth in Phase II was to a great extent a reflection of the much higher rate of increase in total inputs (see A-2). This is true with respect to both current and capital inputs (see A-5 and C-1). It is particularly notable in

force was in agriculture whereas in Middlephasia only 50 per cent of the total labor force was in agriculture at the beginning of the fifty-year period. The turning point, as defined in the text in terms of the onset of a decline in the absolute size of the farm labor force, may occur either before or after its percentage share has declined to fifty. For the special case in which the nonagricultural and total labor forces grow at constant rates, with the rate of growth in the former twice that in the latter, the turning point thus defined is reached when the farm labor force has declined to fifty per cent of the total. The appendix note prepared by Cownie clarifies the influence of various factors on the time required to reach the turning point.

the case of current inputs of nonagricultural origin (A-6) and of the equipment category of capital (C-4). The output effects of these enormously rapid increases should be clarified by detailed analysis, but here it is sufficient to note the following points. In Phase II, there are two conditions not present in Phase I beginning to manifest themselves: one is the substitution of material inputs for labor, and the other a renewal in the process of extending the availability of agricultural technology.

The increase in current inputs of external origin was promoted by the introduction of chemicals of new types (e.g., insecticides and herbicides) as well as by the increased use of conventional fertilizers and imported feed. These inputs, which were complementary to a renewed progress in cultivating technology and diffusion of improved seed varieties, undoubtedly contributed to raising output. Some of the inputs, for example chemicals for weed control, had the effect of substituting for labor. However, most of the substitution effects were introduced by means of capital investment, particularly in small-scale mechanization. The unprecedentedly high rate of expansion of capital equipment (C-4) has already been noted and also the rapid increase of agricultural wages (D-4). An econometric analysis by Tsuchiya has clarified the substitution effect of power tillers in rice cultivation, but the output effects have not yet been adequately studied.[5]

Although the capital-output ratio is a simplified and partial measure, it provides a convenient basis for examining the relation between capital increase and output growth by industrial sector. During Phase II, even with its very high rate of output growth, the capital-output ratio tended to increase (D-2). Excluding farm buildings, thereby obtaining a better measure for our present purpose, the rate of increase in the capital-output ratio was substantial and it reached a level much higher than in Phase I.

The last point is, we believe, very important in characterizing the pattern of agricultural development in Phase II. The measurement of agricultural capital is confined to private farms, excluding public investment. We know that the postwar government investment in land improvement and the like was extremely high as compared to prewar outlays. Therefore, the above findings do not mean a substitution of private for public capital formation. We do not mean to suggest that the trend of an increasing capital-output ratio will continue unchanged in the future. We do wish to emphasize, however, that a considerable increase

[5] See, for example, Keizo Tsuchiya, "Economics of Mechanization in Small Scale Agriculture," in Ohkawa, Johnston, and Kaneda, *op. cit.*

of capital use per unit of output is inevitable in Phase II, whereas during Phase I the per unit capital requirement was kept almost unchanged; the relatively high ratio in 1885 shown in D-1 seems to be somewhat exaggerated.

Thus it is our view that the leading role in increasing the postwar rate of output growth has been played by technology, embodying advanced knowledge of a biological and chemical nature. The significance of the enormous increase in fixed capital appears to lie in its substitution for labor, which has come to be in increasingly short supply in rural districts.

Now we turn to Phase I. The year 1919 is taken to demarcate two distinct time segments in terms of output-input relations: Period 1 (1885–1919) and Period 2 (1919–54). This demarcation was prompted by two considerations: first, the factors and conditions that determined the agricultural growth pattern are different enough to be distinguished; and second, throughout each interval they seem to work continuously and distinctively. Period 2 covers the war and the postwar rehabilitation, and the extent to which those abnormal episodes affected the period is open to debate. However, the basic characteristics were apparent in the 1920's as well as in the later years of the period.

Period 1 is characterized by a fairly high rate of output growth with a moderate rate of increase in total inputs (A-2); whereas for Period 2 we see moderate rates for both. This makes a big difference in the increases in productivity and value added (A-3, A-4) in both periods.

Regarding the composition of inputs of Period 1, we note two features: the highest rate of increase was in current inputs of nonagricultural origin (A-6), and the rate of increase in fixed capital was very slow (C-1). The former represented the introduction of new inputs that were complementary with the diffusion of improved varieties and cultivating techniques. Those familiar with Japan's agricultural development have long argued that the combined effect of those changes on farm output was very substantial, and the interesting attempt by Hayami and Yamada to test their importance statistically has confirmed that view.[6] With respect to the second feature, several points may be noted in addition to the decrease in the capital-output ratio. Trees and shrubs showed a notable increase (C-3) as a result of the expansion of tea cultivation and sericulture; and this expansion was supported by notable technological progress, especially in the various aspects of sericulture. The

---

[6] Yujiro Hayami and Saburo Yamada, "Agricultural Productivity at the Beginning of Industrialization," in Ohkawa, Johnston, and Kaneda, *op. cit.*

capital-land ratio was kept almost unchanged (C-6); the area of arable land expanded to a certain extent (B-1) and the increase of capital stock (at just above 0.5 per cent) was at a slightly slower rate.

It must be admitted that two very important quantitative indicators are missing in Table 1: one concerns expenditures for the construction of infrastructure, particularly facilities for irrigation and drainage, and the other is data concerning the rate of utilization of farm land. The historical research now under way on these points will not be completed for some time, and therefore we are obliged to offer some speculations based on scattered data in order to complete our interpretation.

It has often been insisted that the agricultural infrastructure had been built primarily during the pre-modern epoch and that at the beginning of its period of modern economic growth Japan's agriculture inherited these stocks, thus avoiding the need for sizable investments in infrastructure. We are skeptical of this argument, and we propose the hypothesis that the capital formation in land improvement and in water control facilities must have been carried out at an appreciably more rapid pace than during the pre-modern period. It is true that the official record of irrigation and drainage works of large-scale areas (i.e., covering over 500 hectares) does not show us such a pattern. A large number of small-scale works, however, were carried out by farmers and landlords. A great amount of labor input, involving the use of considerable materials (mostly of internal origin), also seems to have been required for the repair and improvement of facilities built in the long past.

With respect to changes in the rate of utilization of farm land, things are less obscure. Meadows and pastures are of little significance in Japanese farming, so that the figures in B-1 are reliable for such changes except that they do not reflect changes in multiple cropping. This is significant because the extent of double cropping of paddy fields is particularly important as an indicator of farmers' attitude toward farming. From 1889, when the statistical recording of the practice began, double cropping increased until 1919, when it began to decrease. The decline, continuing during the 1920's, indicates a change in the attitude of farmers between the two periods.

The last supplementary interpretation of the statistical findings concerns labor input. The figures in Table 1 (B-2) and other related figures do not indicate changes in the actual input of labor. On the basis of such evidence as is available, we judge that the rate of utilization of labor must have been intensified during Period 1. To mention a few items: the expansion of double cropping, the spread of sericulture (and of the technique of producing an autumn as well as a spring crop of cocoons), and the on-farm production of more manures, all point in that direction. It is of interest to note that there are indications that the response of farm households to the conditions of Period 1 involved fuller utilization of the labor time of family members, but unfortunately no systematic knowledge is available at present.

We conclude that the major factors responsible for the fairly high rate of output growth during Period 1 were the increased productivity and fuller utilization of existing land and labor. This was made possible by scientific progress and diffusion of technology of a biological and chemical nature, with only minimum requirements for capital equipment and with modest requirements for infrastructure, especially in terms of public expenditures. The result can be described as capital-saving measured simply in terms of the movement of the capital-output ratio.

Why did the picture change so drastically during Period 2? It is clear that the answer cannot be found in a decrease in total inputs. The rate of increase in fixed capital was maintained at more or less the same level as in the previous period, although its composition changed (C-1, 2, 3, 4). Arable land area did not increase. But the rate of increase in total current inputs was higher, and inputs of external origin now weighed more heavily in the total (A-5, 6, 7). In terms of the input-output relationship, this represented a decreasing return to the increase of inputs, compared with the previous period. We will try to find the explanation for this in differences between conditions in this period and the previous one, although a completely satisfactory empirical test is not possible.

First, the relative prices for farmers were less favorable. The ratio of farm output prices to prices of current inputs moved favorably in Period 1 and it became even more favorable in Period 3 (D-3). Increased imports of rice from Korea and Formosa prevented the rise in the price of domestic rice that might have occurred if the shortage of domestic supplies had not been offset by these cheap imports. Undoubtedly this had an adverse effect on farmer incentives. Second, potentials for technological advance became less promising, perhaps because of two reasons. Technical innovations relevant to the system of cultivation became less accessible, resulting in a tendency toward decreasing returns to increases in inputs. And this worked in combination with the traditional landlordism that now turned out to be an institutional barrier to technological advance instead of a positive factor as in Period 1. Third, the deflationary conditions that prevailed in Japan during much of the 1920's and the early 1930's, together with other factors slowed the rate of increase in nonfarm employment opportunities. Hence the farm labor force did not decline in Period 2 as might have been expected. The weight of agriculture in the total labor force had declined sufficiently by 1919 so that the absolute size of the farm labor force would have declined at an increasing rate if nonfarm employment had increased at the high rate of Period 1 or at the even higher rate of Period 3. The prospect for increasing total factor productivity in agriculture would have been considerably improved if labor inputs had been declining, because such decline would have enlarged the scope for substitution of capital for labor.

To be complete in our historical coverage, we have to say at least a few words concerning the earliest period, 1868–85. Although we take the view that the "transformation" of traditional agriculture became a national objective from the beginning of the Meiji Restoration in 1868, we hesitate to treat this first twenty years in detail for two reasons: first, the quantitative data are still not sufficiently reliable. Second, qualitatively this is the transition period of Japan's modern economic growth, and interpretation of the agricultural changes during that period demand special consideration particularly from the institutional point of view. Here we touch upon a few points that relate directly to changes in farmers' behavior and attitudes and to the diffusion of technical knowledge.

The social and institutional reforms carried out during the transitional period gave a strong impetus to the development of agriculture by striking down feudal restrictions such as those on the sale and cropping of land and on the choice of occupation. In particular, the removal of the Tokugawa restrictions on the movement of goods and people and the creation of a unified nation with a "national" economy had a great influence on farmers' attitudes towards modernization. It accelerated the spread of technological knowledge and spurred the adoption of better traditional varieties. In facilitating the diffusion of the considerable backlog of technical knowledge accumulated during the Tokugawa Era both the central and local governments played an important role, thereby making an undoubted contribution to the initial breakthrough and subsequent development of agriculture in Period 1.

EAST ASIAN AGRICULTURAL
DEVELOPMENT: A POSSIBLE PATTERN

Let us begin by posing the problem broadly as follows. The required increase in the current rate of growth in agricultural output must take place within the framework of basic economic conditions. The most influential of these are: first, a fairly serious limitation on further expansion of the arable land area; second, a high rate of increase in the labor force; third, severe limitations on the supply of capital—limitations that stem not only from its over-all scarcity, but also from the competitive demand for use in industrial expansion.

The extent to which the current rate of output growth should be increased differs of course from one country to another. However, the general consensus is that the difference or gap between the rate that should be realized in the future and the rate realized in the past is not small for most countries in the region. On the contrary, it is sizable, indicating a need for a transformation of the traditional agriculture, a transformation whose effects go beyond the sort of acceleration attainable by the methods through which output increases have been achieved in the past. What is needed are changes in the basic structure of input-output relationships. The seriousness of the limitation on further expansion of cultivation differs among countries, but in general, the most promising strategy for increasing output is to raise per acre yields—this is the pattern that has been evident in Japan, particularly in the case of rice cultivation.

It is generally considered that the effects of the recent population explosion will be felt for at least several decades to come. A 2–3 per cent rate of annual increase in the total labor force is so high as to have no parallel in the experience of the developed countries, including Japan. Even with the most optimistic expectation as to the future increases in employment in the nonagricultural sectors, a trend of absolute increase in the employment of labor in agriculture would seem to be unavoidable in all countries in which the farm labor force still bulks large in the total; and this is true of virtually all of the Asian countries other than Japan. And the magnitude of this increase will be greater than that ever experienced in the modern period of economic growth in the advanced countries.

The "concurrent" growth of agriculture and industry is a particular requirement for countries characterized by economic backwardness. For these late-developing countries both sectors must grow side by side. Agricultural development cannot be a precondition for industrialization in the historical sequence that characterized most of the advanced Western nations. As touched upon briefly in the Introduction, this concurrent development is a particularly relevant feature of Japan's pattern of growth. The well-known problem of the competition for limited resources, especially capital and foreign exchange, between agriculture and industry is thus a serious one. It is generally recognized that the transformation of a traditional agriculture requires an enormous amount of capital, especially for building up infrastructure. But from an economic point of view, it is highly unrealistic to ignore a limited availability of capital resources. Therefore, such limitation should be considered as an important given condition for determining a new input-output pattern, and this pattern should be determined for a sustained expansion for agricultural output, not for a once-and-for-all effect.

With these given conditions, in what direction should the traditional pattern of input-output relations be changed? "Towards a more productive and fuller utilization of land and labor," seems to be the reasonable answer in a broad context. The critical need is for accelerated technical progress that is both labor-using and yield-increasing. Taking this as a hypothetical proposal, let us examine the factors and conditions that make it possible to change the present input-output relations in that direction. We are directly concerned with two factors: the type of technological progress and the attitude and behavior of farmers. Both, in our view, can in principle be examined, at least in a preliminary manner, through measurable indicators of input-output relationships.

Let us begin by describing briefly the past and present pattern of agricultural production in terms of three features: the area of arable land, the land area per farm household, and the yield or farm output per unit of land.

First, the arable land under cultivation, particularly for major crops, tended to expand in most cases. In some cases the expansion has been very rapid, as for land in rice in the Philippines and Thailand. In the former country the average annual rate of increase is calculated as 2.7 per cent for the period 1900–60; in the latter it is calculated at 3.0 per cent for 1910–60.[7] If these statistical records are even fairly reliable, the pattern is quite different from that of Phase I in Japanese agriculture. (During the Tokugawa Era, a sizable expansion of cultivated area took place in Japan.) Second, the cultivated area per farm household is on the average much larger in East Asian countries than in Japan—roughly two to three times as large. This generalization is affected, of course, by differences in family size among countries, as well as by differences in cultivated area; and we should be careful to note exceptional cases such as Indonesia. But, by and large, this feature is notable. With respect to the third feature, fairly reliable data are available for crop yields of individual crops, especially for rice. Japan's present rice yield, for example, is a little more than four times as high as the national average yield in the Philippines and more than three times the yield in Thailand, Burma,

[7] S. C. Hsieh and V. W. Ruttan, "Environmental, Technological, and Institutional Factors in the Growth of Rice Production: Philippines, Thailand, and Taiwan," *Food Research Institute Studies,* Vol. VII, No. 3, 1967.

India, and Pakistan. It is much more difficult to compare total farm output per unit of land, but it can be safely assumed that the differences in land productivity are fairly similar to the differences in rice yields.

With respect to agricultural inputs, the available data are extremely limited, making it difficult to compile time trends. Therefore the "irrigation ratio" is often used as a representative indicator. This is sometimes misleading. We badly need further knowledge on the performance of other inputs. The following comparison (from a study by Professor Ishikawa) is based on 1956–57 data for India and the 1956 national average for Japan.[8]

	Gross Crop Income (paddy equivalent in tons per hectare)	Labor Input (working days per hectare)	Total Fixed Capital Excluding Land (paddy equivalent in tons per hectare)
West Bengal	1.79	109	3.21
Madras	1.31	115	2.92
Japan	5.39	543	7.69

The most notable fact is that the labor input per unit area in India is only about a fifth of that in Japan—an enormous difference. Since the difference in gross crop income between the two countries is less than that, the partial gross labor productivity is higher in India than in Japan although the total annual income per farm worker is much lower in India. Although there is no assurance that these data for India are representative of other East Asian countries, we believe that this order of difference can be accepted as reasonable. As noted previously, time series data concerning actual labor input in Japan are not available so that we cannot make a comparison with Phase I. Our guess, however, is that the postwar figure, even in 1956, may be less than the prewar one. Therefore, the above-mentioned difference is the more decisive; and we believe that it is crucial to understanding the factors and conditions which differ from Japan's case.

A comparison of capital per hectare must be less accurate because of measurement difficulties such as the valuation of capital and the allocation of residential buildings, but it reveals the striking fact that the capital stock per labor input is roughly twice as large in India as in Japan. The same is true of the capital-output ratio, India's ratio being much higher than Japan's. Undoubtedly a big difference in the rate of utilization is the explanation.

[8] The price of crops at the farm level was used in estimating the gross crop income in paddy equivalent. For details see Shigeru Ishikawa, *Economic Development in Asian Perspective*, Tokyo, 1967, Table 3-2, p. 226.

How about current inputs? No data are available corresponding to the comparison made above based on farm accounts data, but with regard to rice cultivation Ishikawa presents suggestive material for the same districts in India.[9] The findings are: (1) the average amount of current inputs differs greatly between irrigated districts and nonirrigated districts (the former being four to five times larger than the latter) but is still very small, only some 10 to 15 per cent of the value of output; (2) according to a comparison, by farm household, with labor input per unit area, the current input has a fairly close association in the former district, whereas in the latter almost no association is seen; (3) paddy yields, however, show a surprisingly small difference between the two districts (1.9 to 2.6 vs. 1.5 to 1.8 tons per hectare).

These findings, though based on limited evidence, suggest important characteristics with regard to the input-output relationships. We interpret them as follows. There seems to be close technical complementarity between current inputs, labor input, and irrigation facilities, so that we can expect that an extremely low level of both labor and current inputs per unit area will be associated with a low level of infrastructure. At the same time, however, increased capital inputs for irrigation facilities and increases in other inputs may have a very small marginal product (increase in yield) under the present technology. The data cited above show that despite moderate difference of various inputs between the irrigated districts of Madras and Japan, a big difference does exist in the rice yields.

This pattern of rather rapid expansion of area, fairly large farm units, and moderately high labor input productivity associated with a very low level of labor input per unit area constitutes a set of input-output relationships that we would like to describe as the "extensive" type of Asian traditional farming. These relationships represent a rational adaptation to the given traditional conditions. The required evolution towards fuller utilization of labor and land demands a breakthrough in the direction of an "intensive" type of farming, represented by historical changes in input-output relationships as described in the previous section on Japan. The traditional extensive type, as seen from the development point of view, implies the existence of rich potentials for intensification. If the very low level of yield, for instance, were associated with a very large labor input and accordingly were accompanied by a very low level of labor productivity, then there would be much less potential for intensification. But the real situation appears to be the opposite of this in most, if not all, countries in East Asia. In particular, we would like to stress the signifi-

[9] *Ibid.*, pp. 219–21.

cance of the fact that the output per unit of labor input under the traditional type of farming shows, under a rather conservative interpretation,
no substantial difference as compared with the intensive farming in Japan.
This suggests that the low yield may not be the result of decreasing returns, but rather the result of a low rate of utilization of resources, particularly labor and land.

How is the rate of utilization of labor and land to be raised? To
answer this question the possible pattern of future growth of farm output
in the countries of extensive type of farming should be considered. The
labor force engaged in agriculture will increase. Therefore under a given
land area, the average labor-land ratio will also increase. The distribution of land-holding and land-cultivated area per farm household or the
land-labor ratio of farm-households will in most cases decrease. If this
pattern should materialize, the magnitude of the changes involved will
surpass anything ever experienced in Asian agriculture. The development of industries of a labor-intensive type to absorb the increased labor
force, as was done in Japan, should to some extent moderate this trend.[10]
However, the previous discussions reveal that the transformation of agriculture, enabling it to employ more labor and to use it productively,
might be possible under certain conditions. The principal conditions
favorable to fuller utilization of labor and land are basically two: progress in relevant technology and the existence of economic incentives to
induce farmers to take advantage of it.

Japan's experience does not exhibit an agricultural development associated with an increasing farm labor force, and in this sense probably
even its Phase I differs from the future path of other Asian countries.
It goes without saying that Japan's Phase II, though we can see only its
beginning, is completely different in its nature. However, as economic
history tells us, one country's experience cannot be reproduced in its
entirety. We believe that the relevance of Japan's approach, in its broad-
est context, is that it demonstrates the potential that exists for increasing
farm output within the framework of a small-scale, labor-intensive Asian
agriculture. More analytically the following are particularly relevant in
both a positive and negative sense in the broad context mentioned in the
Introduction.

First, the historical process of increasing agricultural productivity asso-

[10] This important issue requires far more attention than it has received to
date. It has been examined in a preliminary way by the present authors: Kazushi
Ohkawa, in "Agriculture and Turning-Points in Economic Growth," *The Developing Economies,* December 1965; and B. F. Johnston in "Agriculture and
Economic Development: The Relevance of the Japanese Experience," *Food Research Institute Studies,* Vol. VI, No. 3, 1966, pp. 274–79.

ciated with use of improved varieties, fertilizers, and other current inputs
—an advance in technology based on new inputs of a biological and
chemical nature—represents an enormously important potential for the
contemporary underdeveloped countries.

Second, capital intensification, particularly in terms of mechanization
of field operations, is effective mainly in substituting for labor. Therefore
the limited capital available to the agricultural sector should be used
instead chiefly for building up the infrastructure to the extent that its
technical complementarity is essential to the successful introduction of
technology of the type mentioned above.

Third, economic conditions, particularly the trend of relative farm
product prices as related to inputs, have a great effect on farmers' attitudes toward intensification. Japan's experience during Period 2 deserves
special attention as indicative of a pattern to be avoided.

A STRATEGY FOR TECHNOLOGICAL PROGRESS

Taking up the positive factors among the three just mentioned, we turn
now to the theoretical discussion of their detailed implications, particularly with respect to the strategy for accelerating technological progress.
Generalizations with respect to the choice of an efficient strategy are
obviously hazardous because of the great variation among countries
lumped together as "underdeveloped." This variation stems in part from
the extreme diversity that characterizes agricultural production, conditioned as it is by particular combinations of climate, soil, and topography,
in part from the differences in the educational levels and attitudes of the
farm population, and in part from the differing degree to which existing
institutions impede or foster the capacity to absorb the international
backlog of technological knowledge.

Thus it is essential to frame strategies for technological progress in
terms of the unique characteristics of the farm economy of a particular
country—and of the various farming regions within it. But this does not
mean that each country must approach the task of choosing an efficient
strategy on a purely *ad hoc* basis. That would be a counsel of despair because of the complexity of the process. It is critical to an efficient strategy
of agricultural development that it generate new production possibilities
characterized by a specific type of technological progress, rather than by
technological progress in general. In this context, despite the dissimilari-
ties mentioned above, in the countries characterized by technological

backwardness there is a common need for strategies that emphasize borrowing modern—but labor-using—technologies from advanced countries.

It is a widely accepted view that the greatest advantage for developing manufacturing in the economically backward countries lies in the possibility of borrowing the technologies from advanced countries at a relatively low cost and without much difficulty. However, at the same time, the view seems widely accepted that in the case of agriculture this is most difficult because of the different conditions that affect the borrowing of advanced technologies. We do not share the latter view, however, and would emphasize that the advantage of borrowed technology is the key factor for accelerating the rate of growth of all industries in follower countries. Most of the difficulties in the international transfer of agricultural technology do not prevent implementation of the strategy of borrowing advanced technologies, they only modify it.

Even in the case of manufacturing, most of the success stories tell us that an important feature of the process is the choice and modification of foreign technologies in order to fit them into the domestic economic situation, particularly in terms of the structure of factor prices. When a country has achieved this, it has built an appropriate system for developing its own technology. The situation is the same for agriculture. What is important is first to identify the unique nature of agriculture in each of the follower countries and, second, to find the criteria for the choice and the necessary modification of the advanced technologies so that they may be fitted into the desirable pattern of agricultural transformation in each country. Admittedly, agriculture, compared with manufacturing or other industries, poses particular difficulties, because of its wider range of variation in respect to the conditions mentioned above as well as the very nature of its technologies. On the other hand, agriculture has some advantages if the choice of strategy is appropriate. This and two other related points deserve attention.

First, the flexible nature of agricultural production in terms of factor proportions and input divisibility can be counted as a favorable element for borrowing advanced technologies in agriculture. In manufacturing, the more rigid factor proportions that are technically required often operate as a decisive factor. Thus technologies of a capital-using type must often be adopted even though they are out of keeping with the economic situation of follower countries where labor supplies are extremely flexible. But in agriculture, the current inputs, such as seeds, fertilizers, and insecticides, are all highly divisible; they can be used with different scales of farm operations without differences in efficiency. Thus they do not demand radical changes in farm organization. Furthermore, as previously observed, use of these inputs can be increased efficiently with a complementary increase in the labor input per unit of land. If the above interpretation of the thesis of borrowed technology is accepted for the case of agriculture, it offers theoretical support for the proposition that the positive aspects of Japan's experience can be reproduced in other East Asian countries.

The second point to be emphasized is that the term "reproduction" should not be taken to mean that technologies are borrowed outright without modification. Rather the term implies that the foreign experience becomes the basis for guidelines in the choice of an appropriate strategy. As suggested above, this also requires invention and adaptation on the part of follower countries. In this connection, Japan's experience is again relevant in both a positive and negative sense. In the transition period at the beginning of the Meiji Era, the government made an attempt to introduce "western" advanced methods of large-scale farming. Agricultural machinery, implements, and crop varieties were imported to Japan. The strategy was exactly to take full advantage of borrowed technologies developed in advanced countries. This was a failure, except in Hokkaido where farming conditions are more or less similar to those in Western countries. Thereafter efforts were concentrated on increasing the efficiency of the prevailing system of small-scale farming. The so-called "Meiji technology" that was evolved, has been aptly described as a "combination of indigenous know-how and very selective borrowing from the West." Intimate knowledge of the best of traditional farming methods was thus the starting point for agricultural research and extension activities. In general, it is to be noted that appropriate borrowed technology in combination with indigenous achievements can be expected to contribute a great deal to establishing a country's own new system of improved technologies for transforming its traditional agriculture.

The third observation concerns the rich international backlog of technological knowledge that is becoming more promising to farming in the tropical and subtropical regions that are of predominant importance in the contemporary underdeveloped countries. The advances in agricultural science and research techniques provide the basis for rapid technical progress in these regions, but until recently the resources devoted to research directly relevant to the tropics and subtropics have been extremely meager. The large increases in yield and productivity that have been realized for oil palm, cocoa, and other export crops have demonstrated, however, that the potential for technical advance is great. And for the three major food crops that have received considerable attention in recent years—maize, rice, and wheat—the prospects range from good to spectacular. The international backlog of technical knowledge is also of great importance in ensuring the availability at low cost of the key complementary inputs—chemical fertilizers and pesticides. Technical innovations that are continuing to reduce the real cost of nitrogen fertilizers are particularly significant, because this item is likely to bulk large as intensification leads to increased use of purchased inputs.

In a number of Asian countries, the extent to which productivity and output can be increased by exploiting the international backlog of technological knowledge will be influenced strongly by the measures taken to improve control over water supplies. It was, of course, for that reason that we have argued that the limited capital available to the agricultural sector should be used chiefly for expansion and improvement of irrigation and drainage works to the extent that these are essential to increase crop yields. Although satisfactory data on the magnitude of the outlays for irrigation and other infrastructure investments in Meiji Japan are not available, it seems clear that the rural sector made a highly significant net contribution to financing capital formation in infrastructure and in industry and that to a considerable extent this was made possible by the significant increase in factor productivity in Japanese agriculture. Vernon Ruttan has advanced the view that for contemporary underdeveloped countries, a net transfer of resources *into* agriculture is likely to be required because of the massive investment which must be made in irrigation and drainage facilities.[11] We have left aside this important and difficult issue in the present paper. It may be noted in these concluding remarks, however, that the implications of the viewpoint expressed by Ruttan are somber indeed. Rapid population growth not only accentuates the problems of food supply in an underdeveloped country, but also increases the requirements for capital to bring about the transformation of the economic structure that is a necessary condition for sustained growth.

Regardless of one's view with respect to the net flow of resources between agriculture and the rest of the economy, it is clear that the contemporary developing countries in Asia have a great stake in a strategy for technological progress that can achieve the required expansion of agricultural output mainly through more productive and fuller utilization of the on-farm (internal) resources of labor and land. The Japanese

---

[11] V. W. Ruttan, "Considerations in the Design of a Strategy for Increasing Rice Production in South East Asia," paper prepared for presentation at the Pacific Science Congress session on Modernization of Rural Areas, Tokyo, Aug. 27, 1966; see also Ishikawa, *op. cit.,* Chapter 4.

experience demonstrates that the intensification that will make this possible requires a substantial increase in current inputs and will in most instances depend on sizable investments in expanded and improved water control facilities. But this simply emphasizes the great importance of a strategy that leads to a path of expansion involving the lowest possible capital-output ratio. Hence the great importance, in the early phase of development, of fostering "minor" irrigation works for whose construction and maintenance local funds and underutilized farm labor can be mobilized through the inducement effect of central government outlays.[12] Similarly, the Japanese experience underscores the importance of simultaneous efforts to promote yield-increasing innovations so that the return to investment in infrastructure is augmented by the intensification of farming which it facilitates.

APPENDIX NOTE

JOHN COWNIE

In the foregoing paper an economy is said to reach a "turning point" in its transition from agriculture-dependence (Earlyphasia) to a more balanced state (Middlephasia) when the absolute size of the agricultural labor force begins to decline. If certain assumptions are made about the initial distribution of the economy's labor force and about the growth rates of the total and of the nonagricultural labor forces, then the time required to reach the turning point is easily determined.

The following notation will be used:

L labor force

t time

T, N, A subscripts to denote "total," "nonagricultural," and "agricultural" respectively

prime (')   denotes the annual growth rate of the primed variable

The growth rate of the total labor force at any given time is the weighted average of the growth rates of its components:

$$(1) \qquad L'_T = \frac{L_A}{L_T} L'_A + \frac{L_N}{L_T} L'_N$$

---

[12] See Ishikawa, *op. cit.*, pp. 137–53 for an excellent discussion of the choice between major and minor water control facilities and of the workings of the "investment-inducement effect" of central government subsidies or low-interest loans.

The turning point is defined by the condition $L'_A = 0$. Therefore at the turning point

(2)
$$\frac{L'_T}{L'_N} = \frac{L_N}{L_T}$$

Although L'_T and L'_N are not likely to remain constant over extended periods of time, it is useful here to assume that they are fixed and to calculate the time, t_1, which would be required to reach the turning point given this assumption. This procedure provides a relatively simple expression for t_1, and it delimits the ranges within which the solutions for more complicated growth paths would lie.

If L'_T and L'_N are constant over time,

(3)
$$\frac{L_N}{L_T} = \left(\frac{L_N}{L_T}\right)_{t=0} \cdot \left(\frac{1 + L'_N}{1 + L'_T}\right)^t$$

Combining this expression with (2) shows that at the turning point

(4)
$$\frac{L'_T}{L'_N} = \left(\frac{L_N}{L_T}\right)_{t=0} \cdot \left(\frac{1 + L'_N}{1 + L'_T}\right)^{t_1}$$

Therefore,

(5)
$$t_1 = \frac{\log\left(\dfrac{L'_T}{L'_N}\right) - \log\left(\dfrac{L_N}{L_T}\right)_{t=0}}{\log(1 + L'_N) - \log(1 + L'_T)}$$

It is interesting to compare t_1 with the time t_2 required for the economy to reach the point at which the fraction of the labor force in agriculture has declined to one-half of the total. When $(L_A/L_T) = \frac{1}{2}$, $(L_N/L_T) = \frac{1}{2}$ also. Therefore, again assuming that L'_T and L'_N are constant over time,

(6)
$$L_N = \frac{1}{2} L_T$$

(7)
$$(L_N)_{t=0} \cdot (1 + L'_N)^{t_2} = \frac{1}{2}(L_T)_{t=0} \cdot (1 + L'_T)^{t_2}$$

Therefore,

(8)
$$t_2 = \frac{\log\left(\dfrac{1}{2}\right) - \log\left(\dfrac{L_N}{L_T}\right)_{t=0}}{\log(1 + L'_N) - \log(1 + L'_T)}$$

Figure 1

Growth Rates and Changes in Composition
of the Labor Force

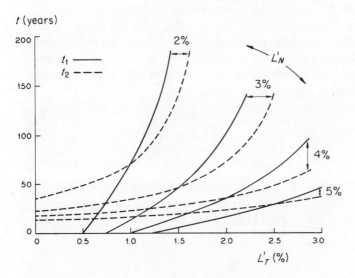

Note: t_1 is the time required to reach the "turning point" at which the agricultural labor force begins to decline in absolute numbers. t_2 is the time required for the agricultural labor force to decline to 50 per cent of the total labor force. In upper diagram t_1 and t_2 are functions of the growth rates L'_N and L'_T, given the initial condition $\left(\dfrac{L_N}{L_T}\right)_{t=0} = .25$

In the lower diagram t_1 and t_2 are functions of the initial composition of the labor force $\left(\dfrac{L_N}{L_T}\right)_{t=0}$ and $\left(\dfrac{L'_T}{L'_N}\right)$, given $L'_N = 4$ per cent.

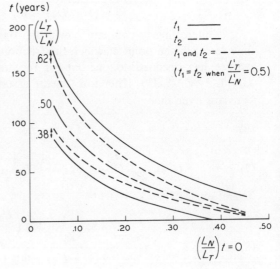

Comparison of 8 with 5 shows that t_2 differs from t_1 only in the first term in the numerator. Thus, for the special case in which L_N is growing at exactly twice the rate of L_T ($L'_T/L'_N = \frac{1}{2}$), the economy reaches the turning point ($L'_A = 0$, with L_A beginning to decline) at the same time that L_A/L_T declines to one half, and $t_1 = t_2$. If the nonagricultural labor force is growing more than twice as fast as the total labor force ($L'_T/L'_N < \frac{1}{2}$), the economy reaches the turning point before the fraction of the labor force in agriculture declines to one half ($t_1 < t_2$). If L_N is growing less than twice as fast as L_T ($L'_T/L'_N > \frac{1}{2}$), the turning point is not reached until after L_A/L_T has declined to one half ($t_1 > t_2$).

Figure 1 illustrates the general nature of these relationships. In the upper panel the assumption is that 25 per cent of the total labor force is in the nonagricultural sector at time zero, and the dependence of t_1 and t_2 on L'_T is illustrated for different values of L'_N. The lower panel assumes a value of 4 per cent for L'_N, and shows the dependence of t_1 and t_2 upon $(L_N/L_T)_{t=0}$ for different values of (L'_T/L'_N).

Comment

T. H. LEE, CORNELL UNIVERSITY

The paper submitted by Professors Ohkawa and Johnston is an excellent and opportune work. With their high professional competence and rich experience in this field, the authors are in an unusually good position to write on the subject. The paper consists of three main parts: (a) a review of the input-output relationship in the long-run pattern of agricultural development in Japan; (b) the identification of the determinants of the possible pattern and direction of agricultural development for the East Asian countries in the future; and (c) the selection of strategies for accelerating the growth of agriculture in these areas in the light of the Japanese experience. The emphasis of the paper is placed on the significant progress of Japan's agriculture within a small-scale farming system and its transferability. Its basic concept, as mentioned by Johnston in another report, is that the growth pattern of Japan's agriculture reveals the importance of the opportunity to exploit the potential of increasing crop yields at a relatively low cost in terms of scarce capital and foreign exchange. The contemporary developing countries have to find such opportunity as Japan has demonstrated before.[1] I have little dissent from this viewpoint. My comments on the transferability of the Japanese model are related to the following unanswered questions posed by the authors in their paper. First, what is a feasible pattern of technological relationships for the East Asian countries to adhere to in transforming their traditional agriculture? Second, what limitations on transferability are imposed by differences in indigenous organizational patterns and beliefs between Japan and these countries? My basic view concerning these two questions is that the contemporary developing countries suffer from their inability to transform traditional agriculture and bring about the major and continuous change in productivity associated with a technologically dynamic agriculture. The crucial fact, as Mellor pointed out, is that introduction of single change in farming practice in such a transitional agriculture will produce small effects on productivity.[2] Several empirical studies on Southeast Asia indicate that within the framework of traditional agriculture, increasing production or crop yields through added labor input seems unlikely to succeed.[3] Considering the available land resource and high population pressure in the contemporary East Asian countries, the possible pattern of land-man ratio in these areas will continue to vary in the future. Japan's experience does not exhibit a path of agricultural development associated with a varying land-man ratio. This implies that the input-output relationships as presented in the paper for any historical period of Japanese agriculture and for the equivalent historical period in the agricultural development of an East Asian country may differ in many respects—even when the period compared is Phase I, and regardless of whether the country undergoes the comparable period now or in the future. Taiwan is broadly thought of as a successful case of the application of the Japanese model to the transformation of traditional agriculture under different initial conditions. The implications of Taiwan's agricultural growth will be useful in suggesting an answer to the above two questions in relation to the modification of the Japanese model.

(1) Theoretically, increase in labor productivity is the most economically efficient way to free a nation's economy of its long-run stagnation and to embark on sustained growth. If we call net output of

[1] Bruce F. Johnston, *Agriculture and Economic Development in Japan: Its Relevance to Developing Countries,* Stanford University, Discussion paper No. 67–3, 1967, pp. 43–44.

[2] John W. Mellor, *The Economics of Agricultural Development,* 1966, chapter 12, pp. 214–19.

[3] *Ibid.,* pp. 136–54.

agriculture Y, the input of labor (man-unit) L, the input of cultivated land D, and the input of capital stock K; then labor productivity, land productivity and the output-capital ratio can be interpreted as $\dfrac{Y}{L}, \dfrac{Y}{D}$ and $\dfrac{Y}{K}$, respectively. The following definitional equations can be specified to show that labor productivity is determined by land productivity and per capita land area of labor and that land productivity is determined by capital intensity and the output-capital ratio:

(1)
$$\frac{Y}{L} = \frac{Y}{D} \cdot \frac{D}{L}$$

(2)
$$\frac{Y}{D} = \frac{Y}{K} \cdot \frac{K}{D}$$

Technological progress and more investment in agriculture are considered to raise land productivity in densely populated areas. Labor productivity in turn, will be raised by the increase in both land productivity and the per capita land-labor ratio or through a sufficiently rapid increase in land productivity under constant or decreasing trends in per capita land area.

The historical growth path of agricultural productivity in terms of labor can thus be defined by the coordinates of land productivity on the vertical axis and per capita land area on the horizontal axis (see Figure 1). Figure 1 shows Taiwan's agricultural development, 1895–1960, in terms of changes in these coordinates. Contour lines through each point indicate iso-labor productivity curves. The direction of the historical path reflects changes in resource endowment, and the level of the iso-labor productivity curves presents the magnitudes of labor productivity in agriculture. Emphasis is not on the presentation of the historical path of agricultural development in Taiwan, but rather on the identification of the strategic factors which raised per capita income or labor productivity.

We have classified the whole growth path, shown in Figure 1, into four cases: (a) the traditional (1895 to 1926–30), (b) the developing (1926–30 to 1936–40), (c) the Malthusian (1936–40 to 1945–50), and (d) the Japanese (from 1945–50). According to our definition, case (a) is apparently the phase of extensive farming in traditional agriculture, the cases (b) and (d) correspond to the phase of intensive farming. Case (d), the Japanese, indicates a relatively constant labor force in agriculture under a constant land area, the experience of Japan in its entire prewar development period. Cases (a) and (b) are the

Figure 1

Growth of Labor Productivity in Taiwan's Agriculture,
1895–1960

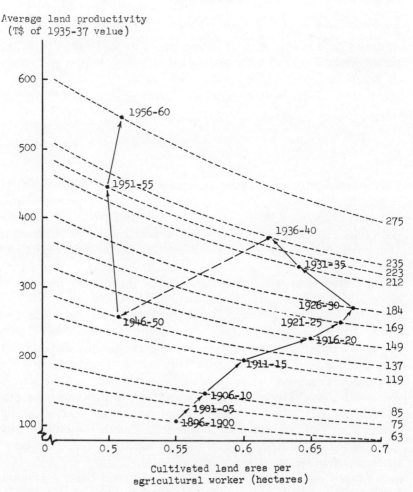

Cultivated land area per
agricultural worker (hectares)

Note: Figure indicates relationship between average productivity per hectare $\left(\dfrac{Y}{D}\right)$ and cultivated land area per agricultural worker $\left(\dfrac{D}{L}\right)$. The product of these two ratios is equal to labor productivity per agricultural worker, i.e. $\dfrac{Y}{D} \times \dfrac{D}{L} = \dfrac{Y}{L}$. For each observation in the figure the corresponding value of $\dfrac{Y}{L}$ can be read off from the isolabor-productivity curve.

Source: T. H. Lee, *Intersectoral Capital Flows in Economic Development of Taiwan,* 1895–1960, unpublished thesis, Cornell University, 1967, Chapter 5.

specific cases that Japan has never experienced. The data in Table 1 are from a recent study by this author.[4]

According to Vanek's classification, case (a) stands for technological change, which is capital-using, while the other cases are of a capital-saving nature.[5] The rate of technological change in terms of land, as seen from column five above, amounted to 0.46 per cent per annum for case (a) and 1.52 per cent and 2.40 per cent per annum respectively for cases (b) and (d). The implications of the case study of Taiwan are twofold: first, a comparatively high elasticity of substitution in case (a) can be thought of as a "big push" investment prior to the transformation of traditional agriculture under the high man-land ratio starting in the late 1920's. This fact tends to disprove the conventional viewpoint on capital allocation, i.e., that agricultural investment should be made complementary to labor input in the pretransformation period. The empirical facts show that heavy investment in land reclamation and irrigation was accompanied by the simultaneous introduction of a new variety of seeds and by technical changes in farming practice. Second, the negative efficiency of capital growth in case (a) has the potential to slow down the growth rate of the national economy as a whole. The heavy investment in irrigation in Taiwan involved large inputs of labor and agricultural materials relative to industrial capital goods inputs.

My comment on the first question is that the technological relationships in the Japanese model are quite different from those of Taiwan and also probably from those of East Asian countries in cases (a) and (b). The strategic heavy investment in irrigation and land improvement experienced by Taiwan will be necessary in the East Asian countries to transform agriculture in the transitional period between the extensive farming and the intensive farming stages.

(2) When viewed solely from the standpoint of the technological requirements of agricultural development; e.g., application of chemical fertilizer, new variety of seeds, etc., Japan's experience is, with some modification, readily transferable to the East Asian countries. However, this statement is subject to severe qualification when Japan's record is reviewed from the standpoint of institutional or organizational requirements for the technological progress. The adoption of new techniques in agriculture generally involves a number of institutional changes. It is

[4] T. H. Lee, *Intersectoral Capital Flows in Economic Development of Taiwan,* 1895–1960, unpublished thesis at Cornell University, Chapter 5.

[5] Jaroslav Vanek, "Towards a More General Theory of Growth with Technological Change," *The Economic Journal,* December 1966.

TABLE 1

Taiwan: Summary of Input-Output Relationships of Agricultural Development in Terms of Land

Cases	Elasticity of sub-stitution	Efficiency of labor growth	Efficiency of capital growth	Techno-logical change rate	Rate of labor increase	Rate of increase in capital	Rate of increase in land productivity
A (Traditional)	0.6436	0.0187	-0.0196	0.0046	0.0044	0.0915	0.0175
B (Developing)	0.4288	0.0110	0.1295	0.0152	0.0107	-0.0051	0.0190
D ("Japanese")	0.4166	0.0070	0.1954	0.0240	0.0070	0.0146	0.0291

dependent on government decisions in many areas, such as the implementation of measures for development, including the effective organization for dissemination of new techniques and for registering farmers' response. Landlords, farmers' organizations, and the market mechanism are the important links in transmitting new techniques to small-scale farmers.

Considering the flexible nature of factor-proportion in agricultural production, the biological nature of the technological process, and the divisibility of input factors that have been developed in the small-scale farming in Japan, the most strategically useful component of Japan's successful record has been the capacity to construct new organizational rules to create a physical and biological environment more in line with farmers' needs and aspirations. The heritage of basic convictions in the present East Asian countries might be incompatible with the organizational rules required by the widespread use of Japan's model. This does not mean that the model is not transferable to the present East Asian countries. But it does mean that the people of East Asia must scrutinize the utility of Japan's experience with their own eyes and fit it into their institutional heritage and value systems.

In conclusion, the following remarks can be made concerning the issues set forth at the outset of this commentary:

1. Viewing the historical growth path of agricultural development in Taiwan, we can understand that agricultural development requires two important measures; (a) creation of growth motivation and (b) sustainment of the growth process. Different policies and criteria of capital allocation are necessary to encourage the above two measures.

2. In densely populated areas, including Japan and the East Asian countries, investment in irrigation facilities, drainage, flood control and land improvement is the primary requirement to motivate the transformation of traditional agriculture. Effective supply of water and appropriate drainage are indispensable to increase land productivity of paddy farming. The policy adopted for financing such investment has to take into consideration the inducement effect of investment on technological change.

3. In the light of point 2, it is clear that water service is an essential input which should be included in the estimate of the agricultural input index. Irrigation facilities must be counted as capital stock in agriculture, a point ignored by Ohkawa and Johnston. Considering that more than 205,000 hectares of paddy land were subjected to new irrigation and drainage in the Meiji period, the omission of water service from the

estimate of the argricultural input index leads to a serious bias. A further investigation on this point will be necessary.[6]

4. The power to sustain agricultural growth is to be sought in the choice of labor-using innovations and in reliance on the market mechanism. The profitability of technical innovations should be looked at from the standpoint of their return to family labor. The policy for development in the periods succeeding the initial heavy investment might better be centered on the measures directed towards the full utilization of land resources. Japan's model will be useful in this case.

5. The proportion of available land and labor in agriculture determines basically the required type of technological change, the measures conducive to development, and the appropriate criteria for capital allocation between sectors. The increase in land productivity results in higher returns to land and higher government revenues from land taxes. Japan's case was deeply influenced by such economic relationships under the labor-using technique. The authors have not clarified the impact of these relationships on the capital transfer from the agricultural sector.

[6] Japan, Ministry of Agriculture and Forestry, *"Meiji Nen-kan Kangai Haisui gigyo Shi-ryo"* (*Statistics for the Irrigation and Drainage Projects in the Meiji Period*), 1929.

The Transformation
of Agriculture in a
Semi-Industrialized Country:
The Case of Brazil

WILLIAM H. NICHOLLS

VANDERBILT UNIVERSITY

*Brazil makes progress at night, when the
politicians are sleeping.*
—POPULAR SAYING

WE BEGIN THIS PAPER with a summary of the first four centuries of Brazilian economic history. During this period there were booms in certain agricultural and extractive products, but until the advent of coffee they failed to lead to permanent and sustained general economic development. We then turn to a review of the modern (post-1900) period, in which the state of São Paulo became Brazil's dynamic center of economic development, with a preeminence that was initially agricultural and later industrial-urban as well. We then arrive at the heart of our analysis, an original piece of research on the interrelationships between industrial-urban development and agriculture during the decade 1940–50, the most recent period for which the necessary detailed basic data as yet exist. We conclude with an appraisal of Brazilian public policy since 1950, with particular reference to its effects on the agricultural sector and the achievement of an integrated national economy.

THE FIRST FOUR CENTURIES:
BOOMS AND RETROGRESSIONS

The discovery of Brazil at the turn of the sixteenth century, began an era during which the eastern coast was regularly visited by various expeditions of the Portuguese and other Europeans. The initial attraction was Brazil wood, from which the new colony derived its name. This wood was the source of a much valued red dye. Foreign competition soon forced Portugal to consider the establishment of permanent settlements to assure its possession of this new land. In 1534–36 the Crown created fourteen hereditary "captaincies" (*capitanias*). These administrative divisions, of which there were ultimately eighteen, were of varying width and continued to the country's then western limits. While many of these *capitanias* languished or progressed very slowly, that of Pernambuco (or New Lusitania) flourished from the outset, thanks to its effective leadership, its greater proximity to Europe, and the rapidity with which the fabulously profitable culture of sugar-cane was established.

The Sugar Boom, 1530–1700

Radiating from Pernambuco's first settlements, the towns of Igaraçu (1536) and Olinda (1537), cane production had by 1600 spread along the entire coast from Salvador (1549) to Natal (1599). The success of this first great European colonial enterprise based on agriculture rather than on precious metals or other extracted products was due, writes Furtado, to a very favorable conjunction of circumstances—the still largely unsatiated demand for sugar in Europe; the relatively advanced techniques that the Portuguese had already developed in cane production in their Atlantic islands and in sugar-making equipment; the merchandising and financial role of the Low-Country merchants (especially the Dutch) who acquired the raw sugar in Lisbon, carried it to Antwerp or Amsterdam for refining, thence distributed it through all of Western Europe, while financing an increasing share of the expansion of productive capacity in Brazil; and the command that the Portuguese had established over the African slave markets, thereby enabling them to solve the severe manpower shortage in the new colony.[1]

[1] Instituto Brasileiro de Geografia e Estatística (I.B.G.E.), Conselho Nacional de Geografia, *Geografia do Brasil*, Vol. III, Rio de Janeiro, 1962, pp. 156–57; Hélio Vianna, *História do Brasil*, Vol. I, São Paulo, 1963 (2nd ed.), pp. 86–89, 69–73, and 118–127; and Celso Furtado, *Formação Econômica do Brasil*, 2nd ed.,

Unfortunately, this very favorable situation was adversely affected by the union of the Portuguese and Spanish crowns in 1580. By this union, which lasted seventy years, the enemies of Spain became the enemies of Portugal as well, and the Brazilian colony was harassed by the British, French, and especially the Dutch. Most important was the Dutch invasion and successful occupation of the entire northeast coast from Sergipe to Natal and Fortaleza during 1630–54. Only the colonial capital of Salvador escaped their prolonged control. The principal economic consequence of this incursion was the establishment by the Dutch of a competitive sugar industry in the Caribbean. While in Brazil, they had made good use of the opportunity to familiarize themselves with the technical and organizational aspects of sugar production. Thanks to this competition, sugar prices were permanently halved and the volume of Brazilian sugar exports halved as well. Thus, by 1700— Brazil—with a total colonial population of perhaps 300,000 (100,000 Europeans)—and Portugal were undergoing a serious economic contraction.[2]

During its century or more of rapid expansion prior to 1650, however, the Brazilian sugar industry had given the first impetus to settlement of the interior. During this period, virtually all of the land suitable for cane in the littoral of Pernambuco (including modern Alagoas) and Bahia had been incorporated into this increasingly specialized industry. Yet the colonists and their slaves faced a growing need not only for food crops and meat, but also for the oxen, lumber, and firewood so essential to the production and processing of cane. Initially, the perennial lower reaches of the local rivers had not only served the transportation needs of the sugar industry, but also gave access to coastal lands that could provide food and production goods of agricultural origin. However, it was soon recognized that the use of the scarce cane lands for these secondary activities as well was uneconomic, the Portuguese Crown finally going so far as to prohibit cattle production in the

Rio de Janeiro, 1961, pp. 18–22. In the latter remarkable book, Furtado has estimated that, in 1600, the per capita income of the Brazilian population of European origin (constituting 30,000 of a total of 100,000 people) was U.S. $350—much higher than that then prevailing in Europe and not again achieved in Brazil until modern times—and that the profits of the Brazilian sugar industry were sufficient to finance a doubling of its productive capacity every two years (*ibid.*, pp. 58, 60, 91).

[2] Furtado, *op. cit.*, pp. 27–29. While seriously damaging the economy of the relatively long-settled Brazilian colony, the rapid growth of the sugar industry in the Caribbean gave great impetus to the growth of the North American colonies through the development of a triangular trade with the Antilles and Europe, increasingly transported in New England bottoms (*ibid.*, pp. 39–43).

sugar zone. With an almost inexhaustible supply of land to the west, it was only natural that this economic need should be met by settlement of the interior. As such economic incentives began to wane with the contraction of the sugar industry, the political need for improved land communications between Salvador and Recife and the tenuously held northern colonies became more apparent as a result of the long struggle against the incursions of the several European powers. Thus the spread of cattle raising into the interior was encouraged for different reasons at different times. Settlement was fostered by the award of *sesmarias* of land to new settlers.[3]

Meanwhile, the interiors of Ceará and Maranhão to the north had been explored and settled during the seventeenth century, with Salvador and Recife serving as the principal nuclei from which these pioneering activities originated. These bold new penetrations appealed most to colonists without financial resources, who saw in cattle raising an opportunity for a relatively rapid accumulation of wealth from a small initial investment. Cattle are self-reproducing and require a minimal labor force, which the indigenous population could easily and willingly provide. Among these colonists were not only the less privileged immigrants to the sugar capitals of Recife and Salvador, but also, and more important, the *vicentinos* from São Vicente (near present-day Santos and São Paulo), whose lack of remunerative export products and isolation from the mainstream of colonial Brazil had already made of them hardy and restless explorers of the most remote corners of the new land. While the *baianos* and *vicentinos* were settling the interior of Bahia, the north of Minas Gerais, and the more remote interior of Ceará, Piauí, and Maranhão—and putting down the strongly hostile Indian tribes in the process—the *pernambucanos* were active to the north and west of Recife. Besides blazing trails within this comparatively restricted area, they also showed particular interest in the neighboring areas of Paraíba, Rio Grande de Norte, and northeastern Ceará. Somewhat less rapidly and thoroughly, they penetrated the *sertão* (interior) of Pernambuco as far as the São Francisco River. By 1711, a contemporary observer reported more than 500 corrals and 800,000 head of cattle in Pernambuco and its dependencies.[4]

While the human population in the arid *sertão* remained sparse, the advent of cattle herds in the interior led to the establishment of trails for driving cattle and conducting *tropas* of burros. These trails ultimately

[3] *Geografia do Brasil, III,* pp. 156–57, 162; Furtado, pp. 70, 73.
[4] Furtado, p. 75; Vianna, *op. cit.,* pp. 228–31.

converged on Recife or Salvador. At places in the interior where they crossed or merged, usually where there were suitable resting, feeding, and watering grounds, small settlements developed, many of which grew into important cattle markets as well. Juàzeiro in Bahia and Petrolina, Salgueiro, and Arcoverde in Pernambuco are good examples within the *sertão*. More favored, however, were the settlements in the less arid intermediate zones between the *sertão* and the coastal sugar belt. Among these were Feira de Santana in Bahia and the major market towns of the *agreste*—particularly Campina Grande (Paraíba) and later Caruaru, some 100 miles from the coast. Upon such centers converged not only the cattle, dried beef, hides and leather from the *sertão,* but also, such surpluses of staple foods as the sugar zone could absorb. Because its climate was less arid than the *sertão,* the *agreste* itself was the main source of the staple food crops. Unfortunately, the initial impetus that the sugar boom had given to such development in the *agreste* and *sertão* had been markedly reduced during 1650–1700. The result was that the cattle industry increasingly took on a life of its own, moving toward self-sufficiency and economic isolation—with meat providing the principal food, and leather the basic raw material for clothing and most other subsistence needs. This was bound to happen in the more remote interior, far from the colonial population centers. But commercialization of the agriculture even of the *agreste* and closer *sertão* (up to 200 miles from the sea) slowed down greatly and even retrogressed as the sugar industry moved into a phase of economic stagnation and contraction after 1650.[5]

The Gold Boom of the Eighteenth Century

By 1700, Portugal and its Brazilian colony were in desperate economic straits. The value of the Portuguese monetary unit in terms of pounds sterling was one-third of what it had been in 1640. Hence, the discovery of gold in Minas Gerais (then in the *capitania* of São Paulo) at the turn of the new century was a godsend that quickly changed the face of the American colony. In the ensuing gold rush the long poor and isolated southern colonists moved *en masse* to Minas, and much of the redundant slave population of the northeast sugar zone was shifted to the gold fields. The first major spontaneous immigration of Portuguese of limited resources also got underway. Some idea of the importance of this immigration is conveyed by the estimates of Furtado, according to

[5] Vianna, pp. 228–31; Furtado, pp. 75–76, 80–81, 86.

which, in the eighteenth century it totaled 300,000, while the European population increased about ten-fold to perhaps 1,000,000 out of a total of 3,250,000. Unlike the silver mines of Peru and Mexico, the mines of Minas were small-scale and required little capital investment, nor did the slave population ever outnumber the free. As a result, the attractions for men of little or no financial resources were great. The gold rush also created an enormous new demand for food, cattle, and beasts of burden, a demand that far exceeded anything that prevailed during the most prosperous years of the sugar industry. In the northeast, the driving of cattle to the south caused a rapid rise in beef prices, provoking official protests by the sugar interests. But the major beneficiaries of this new market were in the south, whose old but rudimentary livestock industry became extremely profitable for the first time. Central Brazil, São Paulo, and Rio Grande do Sul were revitalized by the burgeoning demand for beef cattle, horses, and mules, while the development of food crops was greatly stimulated in the southern part of Minas (from 1720, an independent *capitania*), São Paulo's Paraíba Valley, and the State of Rio de Janeiro (to which sugar-cane production had already been shifting).[6]

By 1800, the richer and more accessible gold deposits had been virtually exhausted, but the gold boom had exacted a severe toll on the northeast. In particular, the economic and political power that Pernambuco and Bahia had long enjoyed, was greatly reduced. The shift of the colonial capital from Salvador to Rio de Janeiro in 1763 reflected the southward shift of Brazil's socio-economic center of gravity. To be sure, the Crown did not completely neglect the northeast. A royally chartered trading company (1755–78), created to stimulate the development of Maranhão and Piauí, proved to be highly successful, while a second trading company (1761–81) concerned with Pernambuco and Paraíba promoted with considerable success the production of tobacco and cotton and the rehabilitation of the sugar industry. In great measure because of these promotional activities, the northeast was in a position to respond positively to a series of favorable political events: the American Wars of Independence and of 1812 which disrupted England's normal sources of supply of cotton, rice, and tobacco; the French Revolution, whose reflexes in the slave revolt in Haiti brought a new stage of prosperity for the Brazilian sugar industry; and the Napoleonic Wars, which brought the Portuguese royal family to Brazil (1808) and opened its ports to all friendly nations. As a result, during the last decades before independence (1780–1822), when the south was rapidly

[6] Furtado, pp. 86, 89–94.

retrogressing to a subsistence economy following the collapse of the gold boom, the colony's agricultural exports nearly doubled.[7]

While this new period of prosperity in Pernambuco had a precarious base, it undoubtedly helped to stimulate the renewed development of the nearby *agreste*. In this less arid region, strategically located between the humid littoral and the very arid *sertão,* several important towns developed between 1772 and 1811. Henceforth, the *agreste* and littoral were to maintain some continuity in the growth of new urban nuclei, particularly with the spread of cotton culture, while the *sertão* region remained static. Even this sparse population, however, proved to be excessive during the calamitous droughts that frequently ravaged the *sertão,* often decimating both the human and animal inhabitants. Striking on the average about two out of every six years, these *secas* set off enormous migrations which often brought short-term profit as well as long-term population growth to the *agreste* and other areas (such as the Cariri Region) less severely affected. Otherwise, the prosperity of the *agreste* was ever more closely entwined with the economic progress of the littoral, although thanks to its rather broad base of subsistence agriculture, the inland region was somewhat less vulnerable to the vagaries of world commodity markets than was the sugar zone, with its highly specialized export agriculture.[8]

Political and Economic Readjustment, 1800–50

Brazil's declaration of independence in 1822, anticipating the constitutional monarchy formalized in the constitution of 1824, did not meet the wishes of its republican opponents. Of these, the most politically important were in Pernambuco, whose governor sought to enlist the whole northeast in favor of a republican form of government during the Revolution of 1824. This outbreak, like its abortive predecessor, the Revolution of 1817, was successfuly repressed. But the republican sentiment was a factor in the agitation that culminated in the abdication in 1831 of Dom Pedro I in favor of his infant son. In the process the real power passed to the dominant colonial landed class of the littoral. While doctrinaire free-traders, this class was to come increasingly into conflict with the English, who had achieved by treaties in 1810 and 1827 extraterritorial rights and preferential tariffs in Brazil. Initially, the landed interests benefited. Because of the treaties, it was possible,

---

[7] *Ibid.,* pp. 102–04, 107–10; Vianna, pp. 311–16.
[8] *Geografia do Brasil, III,* pp. 166–67, 170–72.

in the exportation of agricultural products, to bypass the onerous entrepôt of Lisbon. At the same time, the treaties made imported goods much cheaper and more abundant and credit facilities much ampler than before. However, with the restoration of peace in Europe and North America, the English gave renewed preference to the tropical products of their Caribbean colonies which, with the increasing suppression of the slave trade, looked upon Brazil's slave-produced sugar as unfair competition. English efforts to put an end to Brazilian slave imports were resented by the sugar interests and by tobacco producers as well, since the slave trade promoted the exchange of Brazilian tobacco for slaves in African markets.[9]

Furthermore, Brazilian producers of agricultural exports were again faced with competition in cotton, rice, tobacco, and even sugar-cane from the Southern United States, whose production, likewise based on slavery, was much more efficient. Because of these developments, the northeast was hard hit by a steady fall in sugar prices and an even sharper decline in cotton prices. Moreover, until the treaty with England expired in 1844, the Brazilian government was powerless to finance itself (and to discourage the high propensity to import) by raising import duties. At the same time the landed interests were politically too strong to permit an export tax. The result was heavy deficit financing and the rapid depreciation of the Brazilian monetary unit, with considerable civil unrest especially in the urban areas where small merchants, public servants, and the military were hard hit. Thus, during the second quarter of the nineteenth century, Brazil desperately needed to expand its volume of exports, especially in the face of a 40 per cent decline in its international terms of trade. Although the Brazilian sugar industry (despite many problems) succeeded in doubling its *quantum* of exports, the money value of those exports increased by only 24 per cent. Cotton exports dropped 10 per cent in volume but 50 per cent in value and, although exports of hides and skins doubled, their value fell by 12 per cent. Little wonder that Furtado concluded that "In Bahia and in Pernambuco, and even more in Maranhão, per capita income must have declined substantially during this period." [10]

The only hopeful development during 1822–50 was the gestation of the coffee boom. Coffee had first been planted in the Amazonian state of Pará in 1727 and quickly spread as far south as Rio de Janeiro. Until the Haitian revolt of 1789, however, it had been produced on a small scale for largely domestic consumption. By 1821–30, both sugar with 32

[9] Furtado, pp. 111–14.
[10] *Ibid.*, pp. 114–16, 126–27, 129–32.

per cent of the total value of Brazilian exports and cotton with 20 per cent still outranked coffee with 19 per cent. However, by 1841–50 coffee easily held first place with 41 per cent, while the shares of sugar and cotton had fallen to 27 per cent and 6 per cent, respectively. In the interim, coffee exports had expanded more than five-fold in *quantum* and more than three-fold in value. Thanks to coffee, the real value of Brazilian exports grew by 40 per cent in the second quarter-century. Even so, Furtado estimated that in 1850, per capita of the free population, it was probably little more than 50 per cent of its 1800 level. Furthermore the increasing rewards of coffee production were concentrated on the region centering on the state of Rio de Janeiro and the Paraíba Valley. In fact, this latter region, in the state of São Paulo, was able to recoup its loss of domestic markets following the collapse of the gold boom in Minas Gerais and to resume population growth.[11] Pernambuco and the northeast, on the other hand, largely escaped the boom.

Coffee Becomes King, 1850–1900

The second half of the nineteenth century saw a vast improvement in the Brazilian economy as a whole but a further deterioration in the economic position of Pernambuco and the northeast. By the 1890's Brazil was producing about 60 per cent of the world's coffee. Coffee now accounted for 64 per cent of Brazil's exports by value, and rubber, thanks to the boom then well under way in Amazonia, for 16 per cent. During the previous half-century, coffee exports had increased by 341 per cent by *quantum* and 742 per cent by value, as compared with 214 and 358 per cent for all exports. (Taking into account a reduction of about 8 per cent in import prices in the interim, the gains in total value of exports become 809 per cent for coffee and 396 per cent for all exports.) This spectacular development provided the basis for an average real growth rate in the coffee region, estimated by Furtado at about 2.3 per cent per capita between the 1840's and 1890's. This was a sufficiently dynamic rate of development to reintegrate much of the subsistence sector of central and southern agriculture into the national economy; the per capita annual real growth rate of the extreme south may have averaged one per cent.[12]

[11] *Ibid.*, pp. 132–33, 128; *Agricultura em São Paulo,* Vol. 8 (August 1961), Table 1, p. 21; I.B.G.E., Conselho Nacional de Estatística, *Anuário Estatístico do Brasil, 1958,* Rio de Janeiro, 1958, p. 234.
[12] Furtado, pp. 163–71.

Because of very favorable developments in tobacco and cocoa exports (the cocoa industry attracted a significant influx of people from the rest of the northeast) the state of Bahia probably brought its per capita exports during 1850–1900 up to the level of the rest of the northeast, although in per capita real income it held its own at best. During the same period, the rubber boom had outpaced even coffee development. In the two decades following the 1870's rubber's share of exports by value grew from 5.5 to 15.8 per cent. For 1900–10 the average was 27.9 per cent. During the period 1850–1900, the per capita annual growth rate of rubber-producing Amazonia was 6.2 per cent, despite the absorption of 260,000 immigrants (followed by approximately the same number during 1900–10), mostly from the northeast. As its high outmigration rates would suggest, the northeastern region did not share in this growing prosperity. During the second half of the nineteenth century, the *quantum* of Brazilian sugar exports had increased by a further 33 per cent, but prices fell by 11 per cent. Cotton exports (despite another brief period of precarious prosperity during the American Civil War, which temporarily exploded cotton's share of total exports from 6 per cent in the 1850's to 18 per cent in the 1860's) increased 43 per cent by volume and 89 per cent by value. In the northeast, decimated by outmigration and disastrous drought, these modest gains in terms of real income were insufficient to check the continued reduction (estimated by Furtado at 0.6 per cent per year) in per capita income during 1850–1900.[13]

The sugar zone of the northeast was also strongly affected by the abolition of slavery in 1888—a step that undermined the political power of the old slaveholding class, even though the backlash of that power was strong enough to oust the able and much loved Dom Pedro II from his throne. In the northeast the economic consequences of emancipation were relatively minor. For most of the freed slaves there was little access to land in the subsistence sector of agriculture without long-distance migration. Most of the lands of the *agreste* and *sertão* had been taken up and were already showing signs of demographic pressure. As a result, virtually all of the freed slaves remained on the sugar plantations at low wages, and there was no significant change in the organization of production or the cost of labor. In the hinterland of Rio de Janeiro, where a slave-based coffee industry had developed, most of the earlier coffee lands had been nearly exhausted by the new crop. Because of their familiarity with coffee production, the freed slaves could command higher wages than their fellow emancipates in the sugar region. But rather than

[13] *Ibid.*, pp. 152–53, 164–65, 168–69, 171.

migrate westward, most of them preferred to take advantage of the abundance of unoccupied land in the hills and mountains of the Rio hinterland and withdrew into the subsistence economy.[14]

At the time of abolition, while slaves still constituted most of the labor force in the monetized sector of Brazilian agriculture, a much larger number of free men made up the vast subsistence sector. Their subsistence plots were generally part of the extensive holdings of a major landowner, whose principal commercial interest, if any, was cattle production. With so much land capable of supporting a large tenant population able to feed themselves with virtually no capital and the most rudimentary techniques, the large landholder's principal reward was not economic but socio-political, with power and prestige proportioned, for example, to the number of votes or the degree of social obeisance he could command. While this subsistence sector provided a great pool of underemployed manpower whose productivity was very low, it was unable to satisfy the rapidly growing labor needs of the coffee region. In part this was due to the strong resistance of the landed *coroneis,* to public migration policy, and partly to the prevailing belief that the subsistence system lacked the work discipline essential to the large, well-capitalized, and intricately organized coffee plantations. In the south, the subsistence sector gradually adjusted its economic organization and productivity in response to the increased incentives to commercialize its output. In the northeast, there was little change, as the region was largely bypassed by the wave of European (largely Italian) and Japanese immigrants attracted to the coffee region through active recruitment and heavy public subsidies.[15]

Brazil in 1900

Brazil's first four centuries (apart from the rise of coffee) may be epitomized by a term recently applied by George Dalton to twentieth-century Liberia: "growth without development." With almost monotonous

[14] *Ibid.,* pp. 159–62.

[15] *Ibid.,* pp. 140–43, 144–49. In support of Furtado, it is interesting to consider trends in the combined populations of the five northeastern states of Ceará, Rio Grande do Norte, Paraíba, Pernambuco, and Alagoas and their capital cities during 1872–1900—a period of heavy migration from the northeast to the Bahia cocoa zone and Amazonia. During 1872–90, the population of the five capitals declined 7 per cent while the remaining populations of these states rose 25 per cent; during 1872–1900, the capitals gained 5 per cent and the remaining population of the states 40 per cent. These data suggest that, despite the effects of the various droughts (especially that of 1877–79) in driving rural people into the cities, such outmigration from the northeast as occurred affected these and other urban centers much more than it did in the hinterlands.

regularity, some agricultural or extractive product—Brazil wood, sugar-cane, gold, cotton, cocoa, rubber—flourished for a time and produced enormous wealth, only to collapse with the exhaustion of the particular resource or the rise of competition from other countries more technically progressive and economically efficient. This economic pattern was accompanied by a speculative and exploitive spirit of "getting what you can while the getting's good," a psychology that accounts for the perennial failure to plow back even a small fraction of large current earnings into the capital improvements and better techniques that might have preserved the income base even within agriculture.

As in the southern United States, use of slave labor tended to favor a static and routinized production system; agricultural prosperity based on export markets fostered an agrarian outlook marked by contempt for industrial-urban life and a willingness to accept indefinitely a dependence on foreign industrial products. Compared to Brazil, however, the U.S. South was a paragon of agricultural development. The Calvinistic ethic of work and thrift and the experimental and progressive spirit that derived from the Age of Enlightenment in which the North American republic was born had left their mark on its plantation owners. With their very different cultural roots, Brazil's men of agricultural wealth preferred to preserve a European enclave on the South American continent, favoring industrial goods of European origin, educating their sons in Portugal, and spending much of their own lives abroad or in the court life of the national capital. When the most propitious time for capital formation in the agricultural lands under their control had passed, they could still maintain a materially satisfactory level of "genteel poverty," at which they could continue to enjoy socio-political prestige and influence.

While the stewards of Brazilian agriculture were playing a passive entrepreneurial role, in effect assuring that capital formation and technical advance in that sector would proceed at too slow a pace to prevent ultimate retrogression, industrialization also languished. Manufacturing of any kind was prohibited during colonial times by the mercantilistic policies of the mother country and until 1844 industrial protectionism was effectively prevented by the privileged trade position officially granted to England in 1810. The efforts made by Viscount Mauá during 1850–70 to diversify the Brazilian economy—through encouragement of the food and textile industries and the development of railroads, ports, and banks—met with only modest success and were viewed with scant sympathy by the agrarian-based power structure. Although Mauá actively sought to check the growing power of the new coffee monoculture, the improvements in the infrastructure for which he was responsible had the reverse effect. With the emancipation of the slaves and the subsequent founding of the Republic (1889), the domestic agrarian political base was substantially weakened. At the same time, Brazil fell into disfavor with England and France, its traditional economic partner and cultural mentor, respectively. In search of an economic model, Brazil turned for the first time to the United States, and, impressed by the increasingly protectionist and nationalistic policies of the Yankees, enacted in 1897 an ultraprotectionist tariff. In the first decade of the Republic there were indications (largely in Rio de Janeiro and São Paulo) that industry was responding favorably to this policy. However, before the decade was over, inflation, widespread speculation, and fraud in the formation of new firms and banks had largely discredited domestic industrial development. Handicapped by the strong consumer preference for manufactures of foreign origin and the inclinations of the new coffee tycoons toward the traditional "free-trade" philosophy, Brazilian industrialization still faced a long uphill battle as the country entered the twentieth century.[16]

THE NEW DYNAMISM:
THE RISE OF SAO PAULO, 1900–60

The nucleus of Brazil's modern economic development, both agricultural and industrial, has been the state of São Paulo. The ever-widening influence of this state has spread to the rest of the south and central west, with increasing repercussions even in the old, but long stagnant and poor regions of the north and northeast. Hence, we must now turn our attention to this developmental nucleus whose fabulously large agricultural surplus eventually became the basis of the general economic development of Brazil. It is this development and particularly the emergence of an industrial-urban complex that gives promise at last of serving as the instrument for modernizing a still largely traditional and static agriculture in the country at large.

São Paulo's Agricultural Development

In 1900, when Brazil's coffee exports by *quantum* were some four times their level of the 1840's, São Paulo already accounted for about 50 per

---

[16] Cf. Dorival Teixeira Vieira, "The Industrialization of Brazil" (unpublished manuscript of 1967).

cent of national production and over one-third of world production. In achieving this position, which was to be further strengthened, São Paulo rose from an unpromising backwardness. The state had been handicapped by sparsity of population, a largely subsistence and capital-poor agriculture, the lack of export experience and facilities, and inadequate transportation. During the nineteenth century, coffee production, which initially had flourished in the state of Rio de Janeiro adjacent to the port and capital city of the same name, gradually spread into the adjoining Paraíba Valley in eastern São Paulo. This slave-based coffee brought rapidly declining physical yields as exploitative techniques led to soil exhaustion, soil erosion, and land abandonment. Thus, coffee seemed to be following the familiar unhappy Brazilian pattern—with every prospect of receiving its *coup de grace* from the abolition of slavery. In fact, coffee might have shared the indifferent destiny of Brazilian agriculture in the second half of the nineteenth century, had it not been for the existence of vast virgin lands to the west, the transportation improvements that made these new lands accessible for exploitation and development, and the more venturesome spirit of the *paulistas* and the new immigrant class.

The opening in 1867 of a British-built railway connecting the port of Santos with the city of São Paulo marked the conquest of the state's only major physical barrier to railway development, the formidable coastal escarpment. This line initiated the railway expansion that was to pace the exploitative but persistent westward march of coffee across the state. By 1886, the center of production was north and northeast of the state capital, and the Paraíba Valley's share of São Paulo's coffee production had fallen to only 20 per cent. Thereafter, coffee expansion proceeded on the basis of *free* labor, attracted from abroad by a well-organized and effective recruitment campaign. Less hampered by tradition, which now weighed heavy upon those older regions that had once prospered under a slave-based agrarian system, the *paulistas* greatly invigorated by this influx of immigrants were at last in a position to turn their pioneer tradition of vigor and venturesomeness to good account. By 1920, coffee production in São Paulo was five times its level of 1886, accounting for 79 per cent of Brazilian output and 61 per cent of world production. Brazil as a whole supplied 75 per cent of world output while depending on coffee for about 76 per cent of its exports by value. With coffee production now centered in the middle third of the state, São Paulo's share of the national population had increased to 15 per cent from 9.7 per cent in 1890.

Production in São Paulo continued to increase and to move westward until 1934, when it stood 80 per cent over 1918, with two-thirds coming from the westernmost third of the state. In this latter year the absolute level of the nation's production reached its historical high. Brazil's century-long coffee boom was approaching its end under the onslaught of world-wide depression, serious over-production, and the temporary suspension of national coffee price-support policies. During 1931–40, Brazil still accounted for 64 per cent of world production and São Paulo for 68 per cent of the Brazilian total. By the early 1950's, after sharp reductions in coffee production in the interim, these figures stood at 50 and 45 per cent, respectively. Production now followed closely the volume of exports, and this was still at its approximate absolute levels of the 1930's. But by now, coffee culture had crossed São Paulo's western borders and had spread southwestward to the virgin soils of the rich (but climatically more hazardous) northern region of the state of Paraná. With the highly favorable coffee prices of the 1950's, production rebounded sharply. By the end of the decade, it reached new all-time peaks far in excess of the increase in exports, creating a serious new surplus situation. In the process, however, leadership in coffee production passed suddenly from São Paulo to Paraná. In 1959 the former's rather moderate increase in production was completely eclipsed by the latter's five-fold increase. As a result, São Paulo's share of Brazilian production averaged only 22 per cent in 1962–64 as compared with Paraná's 48 per cent. By that time, while coffee still accounted for 53 per cent of the nation's exports by value, Brazil's world share had fallen to perhaps 41 per cent.[17] The recent decline in the relative importance of coffee in São Paulo marks the end of a prolonged period of coffee development that undoubtedly played a major role in getting a self-sustaining process of economic growth under way in the state and hence in Brazil. First, exploitative as the process was, it was because of the unrelenting quest for virgin soil for the expansion of coffee production that the entire state was at last completely settled. In the course of this development, an infrastructure and general economic climate were created in São Paulo that also favored the settlement and development of the states to the south, west, and north as they were drawn progressively into its economic orbit. Prior to the development of São Paulo, exploitative agriculture had left few long-run benefits in Brazil. But it enabled this state to establish an economic primacy, first in agriculture and then in manufacturing, that produced lasting fruits for

[17] These historical data on coffee developments are largely based on those published in *Agricultura em São Paulo* (Secretaria da Agricultura do Estado de São Paulo), Vol. 8, August 1961, Table 1, p. 21.

the entire nation. By 1960, São Paulo had 18.3 per cent of Brazil's population. The state still accounted for 23 per cent of the nation's value of agricultural production (down from 33.4 per cent in 1948–52) and produced 57.1 per cent of its value added by manufactures (up sharply from 33.8 and 47 per cent in 1920 and 1950, respectively). Altogether, São Paulo was responsible for 32.3 per cent of the national income, with a per capita income of about U.S. $605, 178 per cent of the national average of that time. That the benefits were beginning to spread to the rest of the country is shown, however, by the fact that São Paulo's advantage in per capita income had been considerably higher (221 per cent of the national average) a decade earlier.

Second, federal policy in regard to the coffee crisis of the 1930's had important, if unforeseen consequences, direct and indirect. Although clearly oriented to the special interests of the politically powerful coffee sector, it acted to stimulate diversification in both agriculture and the general economy. Brazil's price-support policy, under which the equivalent of about one-third of total production during the decade was destroyed, encouraged the loss of world markets to competing countries. However, this effect was partially offset by the similar effects of U.S. cotton price-support policy that gave Brazilian agriculture an incentive to substitute cotton for coffee on a substantial scale. Henceforth cotton resumed its rank as Brazil's largest export after coffee (14.3 per cent of total value in 1931–40, and 8.3 per cent in 1962–64).

Much more important, however, Brazil's coffee-defense policy provided the excuse for a tremendous injection of purchasing power—financed by correspondingly large increases in the money supply—into the coffee economy. The unprecedented magnitude of this expansionary monetary policy had a powerful anticyclical effect. With a sharp drop in commodity imports consequent on the foreign-exchange crisis, the demand for domestic manufactures was greatly stimulated. As a result, during the 1930's, idle resources were effectively turned to the production of agricultural and industrial goods for the internal market, with real increases of 40 and 50 per cent respectively during 1929–37, despite a halving of the value of exports. Investment was maintained at a moderate or better-than-moderate level, fundamental structural changes in the Brazilian economy were begun as agricultural savings were invested in the industrial sector, and dependence on foreign trade as the principal stimulus of national economic development was sharply reduced.

Coming hard on the heels of the Great Depression, World War II gave a more pronounced fillip to domestic manufactures than had

World War I. With foreign competition diminished, importable goods scarce, and a heavy wartime demand for many of its primary products, Brazil was able to reduce coffee stocks to manageable proportions during the 1940's while accumulating large foreign-exchange balances. Although the government failed to act as effectively as it might have to protect these balances, and consequently they suffered considerable dissipation through large-scale imports of consumer goods during 1947–50, industrial (physical) production increased by 40 per cent during 1944–50, with producer goods up 110 per cent and consumer goods 26 per cent.[18]

In 1953, now firmly committed to a policy of promoting import-substituting domestic manufactures, the Brazilian government established an elaborate system of multiple-exchange rates that discriminated against the traditional exports (coffee, cotton, and cocoa) while favoring imports of industrial machinery and producer goods. The purpose was clearly to capture a large portion of the exchange earnings of these agricultural exports for general development purposes, thereby furthering industrial growth under a policy of strong protectionism—a policy that was heavily reinforced by the tariff act of 1957. Brazilian agriculture derived some benefits from subsidized exchange rates on imports of fertilizer and petroleum products. But these gains could scarcely offset the substantial reductions in the domestic prices of agricultural exports and the even harder blow from the steep rise in prices of the other modern agricultural inputs, such as tractors and trucks, in the production of which highly protected domestic industries were an increasing factor. Even this exchange discrimination against coffee was not severe enough, with the abnormally high world price that prevailed in the 1950's, to prevent a very rapid expansion in coffee production in that era. Therefore, although late in the same decade the government was remunerating coffee exporters for only about half their actual foreign-exchange earnings, much of the surplus thus syphoned off was dissipated by the costs of the coffee price-support program. According to Baer, the subsidies more than compensated the coffee producers for the discrimi-

---

[18] Cf. Ruy Miller Paiva, "Contribuição da Agricultura ao Desenvolvimento Ecônomico do Brasil," *Agricultura em São Paulo,* Vol. 8 (August, 1961), pp. 46–49.

In emphasizing the contributions of the coffee-defense policy to Brazil's industrial development of the 1930's, we have followed the "accepted" interpretation of such authorities as Furtado and Baer. However, in a recent article ("A Balança Comercial, a Grande Depressão, e Industrialização Brasileira," *Revista Brasileira de Economia,* March, 1968), Prof. Carlos Pelaez presents strong evidence that this interpretation is substantially overstated or even wrong.

natory coffee exchange rate and contributed significantly to the inflation that had become the principal engine for financing industrialization.

If the government was partially thwarted in its objective of exploiting the agricultural surplus for the financing of industrial development, the fault lay not so much in the objective as in the failure to prevent the non-export (domestic food) sector of agriculture from becoming a serious bottleneck in the developmental process. With per capita physical food consumption increasing by 22 per cent and total population by 45 per cent during 1950–62, the terms of trade had turned in favor of agriculture, primarily because of a lag in the expansion of livestock and livestock products, whose higher managerial requirements and greater dependence on purchased inputs favored an inelastic supply response in the face of their higher income elasticities of demand. This condition resulted in the transfer of part of the savings of the nonagricultural sector to the commercial sector (agricultural middlemen) and large landholders, and a good percentage of this part probably found its way into investments in the nonagricultural sector as well as in land, farm machinery, and other tangible hedges against inflation. With the recent rapid increases in the relative costs of modern agricultural inputs, however, the low priority given by government policy to improving the productivity of domestic food production has discouraged the investment of such savings in the modernization of agriculture. In any case, it appears that the use of inflation as a technique of "forced saving" for financing the industrialization process served to transfer real income from the wage-earning class to the entrepreneurial class through the lag in the rise of real wages (a process that had about run its course by the early 1960's), with the heaviest burden falling on rural cash-wage workers.[19]

That the reallocation of agricultural resources has not been proceeding fast enough to meet the increasing domestic demand for food or the changing composition of the Brazilian diet does not mean that significant changes have not been under way. In 1948–52, coffee still held a marked lead in its contribution to São Paulo's gross farm income (32 per cent) followed by cotton (16 per cent) and cattle (13 per cent). Rice, corn, milk, and sugar-cane together accounted for another 23 per cent. Crops still provided 78 per cent of total income, as compared with only 22 per cent for livestock products. But the stage was now set for an acceleration in the diversification of São Paulo's agriculture. Thus, during the 1950's, coffee's share of gross farm income fell from 32 to

[19] Werner Baer, *Industrialization and Economic Development in Brazil,* Homewood, Illinois, 1965, pp. 48–58, 117–18, 161–62.

19 per cent, cotton's share from 16 to 9 per cent, and rice's share from 8 to 6 per cent. The contribution of cattle production grew from 13 to 18 per cent, actually surpassing coffee in 1960 and 1961. The combined share of coffee, cotton, and rice dropped from 56 to 34 per cent. The combined shares of corn, sugar-cane, potatoes, peanuts, beans, and tomatoes increased from 18 to 28 per cent. Nonetheless, the share of all crops was reduced from 78 to 66 per cent, while the contribution of cattle, milk, swine, and eggs combined showed an increase from 22 to 34 per cent.[20]

Despite these recent changes, São Paulo in 1962 still ranked first among the states in the total output of cotton, sugar-cane, potatoes, bananas, oranges, fowl, and eggs; second in coffee and milk; third in number of cattle and in corn and beans; fourth in rice; and fifth in swine. São Paulo's agricultural economy was at last entering a new, more mature stage with the growth of the state's industrial-urban complex. Finally settled to its western limits, the state was in the process of replacing its previously migratory and exploitative export-oriented agriculture with a more stable and conservative system, oriented more toward supplying the rapidly growing food needs of domestic urban markets and more firmly based on modern scientific knowledge and the use of the purchased agricultural inputs, which the new industrial sector was now in a position to furnish, hopefully at remunerative prices.

Industrial-Urban Development in São Paulo

São Paulo's industrial-urban development lagged several decades behind its agricultural development. The manufacture of cotton textiles, Brazil's pioneer manufacturing industry, was at first concentrated in Bahia and other eastern and northern states. By 1900, however, this industry was centered in the city of Rio de Janeiro. Only after 1914 did São Paulo outstrip Rio in textile production, accounting by 1919 for 36 per cent of Brazil's textile output. In 1907, São Paulo had only 16 per cent of the nation's manufacturing workers: the Federal District (city of Rio) and adjoining state of Rio de Janeiro had 32 per cent. By 1919, these percentages were 34 and 31, respectively, underscoring São Paulo's dramatic strides in the interim. In the latter year, the state produced (by value of production) not only 36 per cent of Brazil's textiles, but also 55 per cent of its transportation equipment, 38–49 per cent of its nonmetallic mineral products, paper and fiberboard, metal-

---

[20] Rubens Araújo Dias, "Renda Bruta da Agricultura," *Agricultura em São Paulo,* Vol. 9 (Jan. 1962), Table II, p. 38.

lurgical products, clothing and shoes; and 22–34 per cent of its hides and leather, beverages, food products, furniture, rubber products, chemicals and drugs, and wood products. Of São Paulo's total value added by manufactures, textile products contributed the largest share (29 per cent), followed by food products (20 per cent), clothing and shoes (9 per cent), and beverages (7 per cent)—for a combined total of 65 per cent.[21]

During 1872–1900, the population of the state of São Paulo increased nearly three-fold and during 1900–1920 it doubled again, increasing the state's share of the nation's population from 8.4 to 15 per cent. During the earlier period, the population of the city of São Paulo jumped from about 31,000 to almost 240,000, doubling again to 579,000 by 1920—with the corresponding shares of the state's population at 3.8, 10.5 and 12.6 per cent in the three reference years. Such a high rate of population growth owed much to large-scale immigration. Approximately 1,765,000 foreign immigrants (nearly half Italian and another third, Spanish and Portuguese) entered the state during 1880–1920, the equivalent of 77 per cent of the state's total population in 1900. Most immigrants whose ocean passage had been paid by the federal or state government were obligated to agricultural employment, but most nonsubsidized immigrants elected to remain in the cities. During the periodic crises in coffee (e.g., in 1902–08), the influx of foreign immigrants declined sharply, but urban growth continued on the basis of increased internal rural-urban migration of the foreign-born as well as native-born population. The large foreign-born component of this internal migration is reflected in the statistics for the city of São Paulo. By 1920 35 per cent of the population was foreign-born as compared with only 16 per cent for the rest of the state.[22]

Up to 1920, São Paulo had also attracted, besides this valuable human capital from abroad, an increasing flow of foreign investment capital directed toward developing coffee plantations (although foreign ownership was never a substantial factor), railways and electrical power installations, and a limited amount of manufacturing. It was during the war years 1914–20 that São Paulo's industrial development received its first major impetus. This happened largely under indigenous business leader-

[21] Cf. Simon Kuznets, Wilbert E. Moore, and Joseph J. Spengler (ed.), *Economic Growth: Brazil, India, Japan,* Duke University Press, Durham, N.C., 1955; especially the chapters contributed by George Wythe (pp. 37–41 and 49) and Stanley J. Stein (pp. 430–40).

[22] Vicente Unzer de Almeida and Octavio Teixeira Mendes Sobrinho, *Migração Rural-Urbana,* Secretaria da Agricultura do Estado de São Paulo, 1951, p. 80; and Kuznets, *et al., op. cit.,* pp. 39–40 and 439–40.

ship, although the representation of foreign-born was probably higher than proportionate. The elimination of foreign competition in the face of the scarcity of industrial goods and shipping—combined with high wartime profits on exports of primary products and with high domestic purchasing power—provided the opportunity, promptly seized, for a considerable expansion of domestic manufacturing. As a result, by 1920 real industrial production in Brazil stood at about 250 per cent of its 1914 level and in São Paulo at about 340 per cent. Even so, in 1920, only 13 per cent of the Brazilian labor force was gainfully employed in "manufacturing," a category in which many small workshops and domestic handicraft operations were included.

The 1920's were not a very propitious period for further Brazilian industrial development. The renewed influx of foreign manufactures was a setback to Brazil's fledgling industries at a time when government policy, while protecting coffee producers to an extent that encouraged substantial overproduction, yielded to a resurgence of "free-trade" sentiment in the country and shunned industrial protection. Nonetheless, a number of large-scale industrial plants (including numerous branch factories of U.S. firms) were established, notably for automobile assembly and the production of electrical appliances, tires, cement, rayon, and corn products. As a consequence, São Paulo's real industrial production may have again trebled during 1920–29, although in 1928–29 it stood at only 50 per cent above its previous peak of 1923.[23]

In the onslaught of the Great Depression Brazilian exports were halved, but because of the protectionist aspects of the sharp drop in foreign exchange, such industrial production as Brazil already enjoyed, was hardly affected. Even at its low point in 1932, it was only 12 per cent below its 1928 peak for Brazil and only 20 per cent below for the state of São Paulo. Thereafter, the vast pump-priming operation associated with coffee-defense policy began to produce results. First, much idle plant capacity was brought into use, with very favorable effects on industrial profits. These made possible the purchase of second-hand machinery at low prices from abroad and subsequent new industrial investment, much of it probably of agricultural origin. Thus, we find that by 1940 Brazilian industrial output was 52 per cent above its 1928 high, while both exports and imports were still one-third below their level of 1926–30. During the period 1928–40, there was a significant increase in the variety of chemicals, metal products, processed foods, textiles, and paper produced, while the production of cottonseed oil and

[23] Baer, op. cit., pp. 15–20 and Table 2–3 (p. 21); and Kuznets, et al., op. cit., pp. 40–41.

vegetable shortening grew in conjunction with expanded cotton culture. Nonetheless, while labor productivity had undoubtedly increased, considerably since 1920, the growth of manufacturing employment had barely outpaced that of the total labor force, the former's share of the latter going from 13 to 14 per cent.

During 1919–39, manufacturing employment in São Paulo more than trebled. The state's share of the national total increased from 30 to 34 per cent and its share of national value added from 34 to 39 per cent. The combined share of value added by the city and adjoining state of Rio de Janeiro had remained constant at 28 per cent. Of the other states, representing secondary centers of industrialization, Rio Grande do Sul had declined in relative importance from 11.5 to 9.1 per cent while Minas Gerais and Pernambuco had shown gains, from 5.6 to 7.8 per cent and from 4.3 to 4.9 per cent, respectively. These four (excluding São Paulo) plus the Federal District (city of Rio) just about maintained their share of 49–50 per cent of the nation's total value added. In 1939 these states plus São Paulo accounted for 89 per cent. The primacy of São Paulo is shown by its contribution to the nation's value added, as follows: by manufactures of transportation equipment, electrical products, mechanical products, and textiles—66–87 per cent; by public utilities, chemicals and drugs, paper, clothing and shoes, furniture, metallurgical products, printing and publishing, and beverages—38–49 per cent; and by tobacco products, rubber goods, and food products—33–34 per cent. During 1919–39, the composition of São Paulo's total value added (excluding construction, public utilities, and extractive industries) had significantly changed. While textiles and food products still contributed 28 and 15 per cent, respectively, their combined share plus clothing, shoes, and beverages, had dropped from 65 to 52 per cent, while the combined share of chemicals and drugs, transportation equipment, nonmetallic mineral products, and metallurgical products had increased from 18 to 31 per cent.

During 1920–40, while the population of the state of São Paulo increased by 56 per cent (as compared with 35 per cent for the whole nation), the population of the city of São Paulo more than doubled to 1,326,261 (its share of the state's population growing from 12.6 to 18.5 per cent). By 1940, with 17.4 per cent of the nation's population, the state had 28.3 per cent of all cities of 10,000 or more (and 31 per cent of the population living in such cities) and 14.1 per cent of the rural population. This continued high rate of population growth had become increasingly a function of internal migration. Most of the 659,000 foreign immigrants (24 per cent Japanese, 22 per cent Portuguese, and

22 per cent Italian and Spanish) which the state received during
1921–46 entered before the more restrictive immigration policies went
into effect after 1930. As a result, during 1920–40, the foreign-born
share of the population dropped from 35 to 22 per cent in the capital
city and from 16 to 9 per cent in the rest of the state. Even in 1940,
however, about 60 per cent of São Paulo's population was still rural
and employed in agriculture. Significantly, the illiteracy rate in São
Paulo was 48 per cent, still relatively high, although the national average was 62 per cent.

With its decided headstart São Paulo was in an ideal position to take
advantage of the Second World War and of the conscious shift of the
Brazilian government to an all-out policy of industrialization that followed in the 1950's. Thus, São Paulo's share of the nation's manufacturing employment, 34 per cent in 1939, increased to 38 per cent in 1949
and attained 50 per cent by 1962; and its share of the nation's value
added increased from 39 to 47 per cent during the 1940's reaching 57
per cent in 1962.

São Paulo may be considered part of a broader industrial complex
that is growing up within the triangle defined by the cities of São Paulo,
Belo Horizonte (Minas Gerais), and Rio de Janeiro. But considered
without São Paulo, this area's share of national value added fell from 36
to 23 per cent during the period 1939–62. At the same time the share
of the state of Rio dropped from 28 to 18 per cent and that of the state
of Minas Gerais from 7.8 to 5.3 per cent. During the same period, the
shares of the outlying industrial centers of Rio Grande do Sul and
Pernambuco also dropped, from 9.1 to 6.7 per cent and from 4.1 to 2.4
per cent, respectively.[24]

By 1962, São Paulo's share of the nation's value added was as follows: by transportation equipment, rubber goods, electrical appliances,
and mechanical products—75–89 per cent; by paper, plastics, chemicals
and drugs, textiles, furniture, metallurgical products, nonmetallic minerals, and clothing and shoes—50–65 per cent; and, by printing and
publishing, food products, and public utilities—41–46 per cent. Of the
six leading industries in São Paulo, transportation equipment now led
with 15.8 per cent of total value added, followed by textiles, down to
14 per cent; chemicals and drugs, 11.7 per cent; metallurgical products,
11 per cent; food products, down to only 9.6 per cent; and electrical
goods, 7.8 per cent. Since 1940, the composition of São Paulo's industrial

[24] The data for 1939 and 1949 are based on the Censuses of 1940 and 1950;
data for 1962 are from annual Industrial Register (*Anuário Estatístico do Brasil,
1965,* Rio de Janeiro, 1965, p. 104 *et seq.*).

production had shifted sharply toward the more skilled, durable-consumer-goods and heavy-producer-goods industries. The combined share of textiles, food, clothing and shoes, and beverages (65 per cent in 1919) fell from 52 to only 28 per cent during 1939–62; and the combined share of wood products, furniture, tobacco products, and hides and leather (10 per cent in 1919) fell from 7 to 4.4 per cent. These eight industries combined, which had accounted for 75 per cent of São Paulo's 1919 value added and still accounted for 40 per cent for all Brazil, accordingly dropped from 59 to 32 per cent in the same period.

By 1949, Brazil was already nearly self-sufficient (imports less than 5 per cent of domestic consumption) in processed foods, beverages, printing and publishing, and textiles. By that time, its domestic manufacture of paper, cement, and iron and steel were already sufficiently developed to require imports of only 18–25 per cent of domestic needs. On the other hand it was still heavily dependent (39–80 per cent) upon imports to meet its requirements for chemicals, machinery, electrical goods, motor vehicles and other transportation equipment, and nonferrous metal products. Ten years later, thanks to a drive to develop import-substituting industries, Brazil had attained virtual self-sufficiency in cement while continuing to import only 12–18 per cent of its paper, electrical products, motor vehicles, iron and steel, and chemicals. While Brazil still imported 57 per cent of its metal-working machinery (down from 69 per cent a decade earlier), it had cut its imports from 58 to 23 per cent for other machinery; from 80 to 37 per cent for nonferrous metal products; and from 60 to 38 per cent for transportation other than motor vehicle.[25]

In an evaluation of this recent period of government-induced industrialization in Brazil, Huddle has noted its high opportunity costs as the seeds of its undoing. It was only with the establishment of the multiple-exchange system and a policy of inflationary financing in 1953 that the government began to exercise a strong direct influence on the progress of industrialization. Under the new exchange policy, favored industries could import capital goods at one-fifth to one-sixth of the exchange cost to other industries while enjoying absolute protection against foreign competitors. The effects of inflation were, in turn, to transfer resources from the rest of the economy to the government, which loaned them to the same favored industries. With other sources of funds for long-term investment (including retained industrial earnings) insufficient, the government during 1953–59 extended to the favored industries heavily subsidized loans in an amount equivalent to the total private fixed-capital

[25] Baer, Table 3-13, p. 75.

formation in all industry during the same period. These public loans averaged 20–30 per cent of the profits of industry as a whole and a much higher percentage of the profits of the favored industries, which may have even reduced their own savings out of profits as a result of the government's generosity.

By the late 1950's, says Huddle, unfavorable factors began to appear. As industrialization widened, the original infant industries had to purchase more and more inputs from new, high-cost industries with unreliable delivery schedules. Furthermore, with agriculture neglected and the prices of agricultural inputs increased, food products began to rise and workers began to demand higher wages, more frequently adjusted for inflation. Efforts to neutralize this development through price controls and export restrictions on food products were unsuccessful and tended to reduce import capacity and to drive up the exchange price of imports. This happened despite a new policy of import-substitution in the automobile-parts industries, a policy whose effects (indirect as well as direct) reduced imports less than appeared on the surface. With this switch in public favor to the automotive industries together with the steady rise in food prices and wages, the nonautomotive industries found themselves in an increasingly difficult financial position. Moreover, the industries favored by the government were increasingly capital intensive, with a strong antiemployment bias that created a hardship for the unskilled, not only in the urban areas, but also in rural regions where workers could hope for nothing better, if they migrated to the cities, than employment in a low-productivity service industry. Huddle concludes that, if the new industrialization strategy of 1957–58 "had been focused instead upon removing disincentives in the agricultural and export sectors, while retaining the incentives earlier given to a broad spectrum of manufacturing industries, the post-1962 stagnation, as well as increasing unemployment and underemployment, might have been averted." [26]

Whether or not Huddle's pessimistic but plausible appraisal of Brazil's recent industrialization policy is fully justified, there can be little doubt that São Paulo was the major beneficiary. During 1940–62, the state's population again virtually doubled. Its share of the nation's population was 18.4 per cent, compared to 17.4 per cent in 1940 and 15 per cent in 1920. The 1950's saw the city of São Paulo finally pass the city of Rio to become Brazil's largest. In 1962 its population of 4,251,000 was

[26] This and the preceding paragraph are a summary of a recent preliminary paper by Don L. Huddle, "Notes on the Brazilian Industrialization: Sources of Growth and Structural Change 1947–1963," Economic Growth Center, Yale University ("Center Paper No. 30"), June 2, 1967 (mimeo.); particularly pp. 18–23.

30.7 per cent of the total for the state, compared to 18.5 per cent in 1940 and 12.6 per cent in 1920. During 1940–50, the number of cities in the state with a population of 20,000 or more increased from 16 to 28. By 1960, rural population was only 37 per cent of the total in São Paulo compared to 60 per cent in 1940 and 54 per cent in Brazil in 1960.

Much of this population growth resulted from internal migration from the poorer states, São Paulo gained some 557,000 native-born in-migrants (approximating the 581,000 lost by the northeastern states of Bahia, Ceará, and Pernambuco) during 1940–50 alone. To some extent this migration was rural-to-rural, with in-migration to the rural areas of São Paulo partially offsetting rural-to-urban migration of persons born in the state. Although the old Federal District (city of Rio) gained 788,000 in-migrants (clearly rural-to-urban) during the 1950's, rural-to-rural migration continued to be important throughout that decade because of the attraction of the remaining agricultural frontiers. Thus the three frontier states of Paraná, Goiás, and Mato Grosso—all within São Paulo's economic orbit—gained close to 900,000 people by net in-migration during 1940–50 and perhaps 2,000,000 or more during 1950–60. This is approximately one-third of the total rural-to-urban migration in Brazil during the two decades. During the same two decades, the northern state of Maranhão may have gained 250,000 or more by in-migration.[27]

The New Problem: Generalizing São Paulo's Development to All of Brazil

Clearly, if the state of São Paulo (with a per capita income of $605 in 1960) were a separate country, it would already be approaching (like Japan) a developed-country status. Unfortunately, as Brazilians have been saying for two or three decades, "São Paulo is the locomotive pulling twenty freight cars"—meaning of course, the other twenty states of Brazil. But the fact that Brazil finally *has* a locomotive, a state whose power is already substantially contributing to the economic development of the whole southeast region which it dominates, represents no mean achievement. The principal remaining problem is that of reducing the wide interregional income disparities. Those are dramatized by the comparisons of Table 1. There it will be noted that in 1960 the eight states constituting the "southeast" region (dominated by the cities in São Paulo and Rio de Janeiro) had 61 per cent of the nation's popula-

[27] Cf. a preliminary benchmark study on Brazilian agriculture by J. Edward Schuh and Eliseu Roberto Alves, mimeo. draft of June 1967, particularly pp. 21–25, and 42 of Chapter 1.

TABLE 1

Brazil: Per Capita Income, Population, and National Income – by Region, 1947 and 1960

Region[a]	Number of States	Percentage of Total Land Area	Population Growth, 1950–60 (1950=100)	Per Capita Income (in U.S. Dollars)						Regional Distribution (percentage of national total)			
				1947		1960			Avge. as per cent of 1947	Popu-lation 1950	Income 1947	Popu-lation 1960	Income 1960
				Avge.	Range[b]	Avge.	Range[b]						
Southeast	8	17.7	141	315	151–742	456	218–989		145	59	79	61	80
Rio–Rio	2	0.5	144	403	225–742	653	323–989		162	9	19	10	18
S. Paulo–Parana	2	5.3	153	380	232–414	547	377–605		144	22	36	25	39
Other	4	11.9	130	207	151–274	296	218–408		143	28	25	26	23
Mid–West	2	22.1	165	126	103–178	211	187–265		167	3	2	4	2
Arid Northeast	8	14.3	122	115	83–142	180	99–204		157	32	16	28	15
Humid North	3	36.9	148	122	74–211	156	116–231		128	6	3	7	3
Brazil	21	91.0[c]	136	225	74–742	340	99–989		151	100[c]	100[c]	100[c]	100[c]

Source: Werner Baer, *Industrialization and Economic Development in Brazil*, Homewood, Ill., 1965, Table 7-7, p. 170.

[a]The several states have been combined into the following regions and subregions: *Southeast* – The old Federal District (city of Rio) and the state of Rio de Janeiro; Sao Paulo and Paraná (the principal coffee states); and Minas Gerais, Espirito Santo, Santa Catarina, and Rio Grande do Sul. *Mid-West* – Goiás and Mato Grosso. *Arid Northeast* – Ceará, Rio Grande do Norte, Paraíba, Pernambuco, Alagoas, Sergipe, Bahia, and Piauí. *Humid North* – Amazonas, Pará, and Maranhao.

[b]Lowest and highest per capita incomes within region.

[c]Excludes four territories with 9 per cent of the land area but only 0.47 per cent of the nation's population.

tion and, with a per capita income of $456, 80 per cent of its national income.

The two frontier states that composed the midwest region, sparsely populated yet clearly within São Paulo's orbit, ranked second with only $210, but, in respect to both population and per capita income, were expanding faster than any other region. As a result, per capita income in the midwest region, relative to the southeast's, rose from 40 to 46 per cent during 1947–60. Much more important in 1960, however, was the "arid northeast," made up of eight states with a per capita income of $180, only 39 per cent of that enjoyed in the prospering southeast region. This clearly disadvantaged region, with 28 per cent of the‵ nation's population, received only 15 per cent of the national income. It was the only major region with a declining share of the population during 1950–60. Finally, the three states of the "humid north" region, largely in the Amazonian rain forest, had in 1960 a per capita income of $156, only 34 per cent of that of the southeast, as compared to 39 per cent in 1947. Even the northeast had succeeded in closing the income gap with the southeast slightly (from 37 per cent in 1947), thanks largely to its low rate of population growth (lowest of the four regions), a consequence of heavy out-migration. The north region's population, on the other hand, grew at a much faster rate, so that even though aggregate income increased, the effects of this gain on per capita income were partially canceled.

In the period 1947–60, five states (including São Paulo) within the southeast region enjoyed increases of 44–49 per cent in per capita income. By comparison the national average increase was 51 per cent. The state of Paraná had an increase of 62 per cent, far above the national average. Paraná doubled its population, chiefly because of large-scale settlement on its rich agricultural frontier. Three states, Minas Gerais, Santa Catarina, and the old Federal District, showed relatively low gains of 33–39 per cent. In both 1947 and 1960, the eight states of the southeast region ranked among the top ten in terms of per capita income. The highest ranking states in 1960 were the old Federal District ($989), São Paulo ($605), Rio Grande do Sul ($408), Paraná ($377), Rio de Janeiro ($323), and Santa Catarina ($306). Only the last two changed rank between 1947 and 1960. In 1947 the two remaining states of the southeast, Minas Gerais ($241) and Espirito Santo ($218) ranked ninth and tenth, while Amazonas (still enjoying the ephemeral wartime rubber boom) ranked seventh and Mato Grosso eighth. In 1960 the two southeastern states ranked eighth and tenth, with Mato Grosso ($265) in seventh and Amazonas ($231) still in ninth place.

In the latter year, Pernambuco led the northeast region with $204, having displaced the Amazonian state of Pará for eleventh place.

With 61 per cent of Brazil's population, the eight southeastern states in 1960–62 had 49 per cent of the nation's agricultural labor force, 62 per cent of its cropland, 91 per cent of its tractors, and 58 per cent of its cattle. They accounted for 65 per cent by value of the nation's crop production and 81 per cent by value of its milk production, and they slaughtered 72 per cent of the nation's cattle and 78 per cent of its hogs. With 82 per cent of Brazil's installed electrical generating capacity and 88 per cent of its personnel engaged in manufacturing, the southeast accounted for 89 per cent of all value added by manufacturing. This group of states had 72 per cent of those engaged in wholesale and retail trade in the nation and they handled 85 per cent of this trade. Thus, by 1960 the states of the southeast region had more or less generally entered into a phase of self-sustaining economic development. Coffee had provided the original impetus (as it was still doing in Paraná) but the subsequent substantial industrial-urban development in São Paulo and Rio de Janeiro had gradually spread to the other states of the region, further strengthening both the agricultural and the nonagricultural sectors.

By 1950 industrial-urban development had already had important favorable effects on agricultural incomes and productivity in São Paulo. This can be demonstrated by an investigation of the period 1940–50, before government policy had substituted a strong element of direction and control for the free play of market forces.

INDUSTRIAL-URBAN DEVELOPMENT AS A DYNAMIC FORCE IN TRANSFORMING BRAZILIAN AGRICULTURE, 1940–50

In 1961, Anthony M. Tang and the author completed a ten-year research project on the effects of industrial-urban development (via the factor markets) on agricultural productivity and income in the Southern Piedmont and the Tennessee Valley. Each of us studied a group of some twenty contiguous counties that had a common historical and cultural background, and that 50–75 years ago had approximately the same dependence on agriculture and roughly the same levels of output per farm worker. Each group was differentiated into counties that had remained largely rural-agricultural (the control group) and those that had since experienced substantial industrialization.

We observed that, during the preindustrial period, initial income differences attributable to differences in "original" physical endowment tended to disappear through factor transfers (particularly labor) despite imperfections in the factor markets. We further observed, however, that over a half century, those counties that experienced differentially higher rates of industrial-urban development also enjoyed increasingly superior capital-labor ratios and labor productivity within their agriculture, while neighboring counties that lacked industrial-urban development also lagged behind on the agricultural side. These findings thus strongly support the view that local industrial-urban development makes an important positive contribution to the efficiency of the local factor and product markets, thereby greatly facilitating the transfer of excess labor from, and of needed capital to, agriculture, within the immediate environs of the growing industrial center.[28]

During 1961–62, I conducted a study of the state of São Paulo along similar lines, using data from the federal censuses of 1940 and 1950. This state, containing the industrial heartland of Brazil, was the natural choice, not only because of the level of nonagricultural development reached, but also because of the length of time over which the development had been going on—presumably ample in this case for the effects on agriculture to become fully apparent. As a substitute for the counties used as subareas in the U.S. study, I used the "twenty-three physiographic zones" distinguished in the 1950 census. Because of the inadequacies of earlier censuses, the analysis was limited to the decade 1940–50. Hopes of adding the decade 1950–60 have so far been thwarted by the long delays in publication of the 1960 census results.

Because it is many times larger than our previous twenty-county study areas, São Paulo has perhaps a somewhat smaller degree of historical, socio-economic, and cultural homogeneity. Much more serious, however, is the effect of the shorter time period. Because the analysis spans only a single decade, it was impossible to compare unindustrialized subareas with industrialized ones on the basis of similarities that existed in the preindustrial era. Hence in the São Paulo study there is no con-

[28] See Anthony M. Tang, *Economic Development in the Southern Piedmont, 1860–1950: Its Impact on Agriculture,* Chapel Hill, 1958; and the summary article, William H. Nicholls, "Industrialization, Factor Markets, and Agricultural Development," *Journal of Political Economy,* Vol. XLIX (August 1961), pp. 319–40.

trol group. Nonetheless, the results proved to be of sufficient interest to warrant presentation in summary form here.[29]

As in our previous analyses, per capita value added by manufacture in 1949 was used as the index of industrial-urban development. The twenty-three physiographic zones were ranked in terms of this index and of a large number of other indexes of nonagricultural development and agricultural and population characteristics in both 1939–40 and 1949–50. The former set of rankings were then systematically correlated with the latter sets.

Industrial Development and
Structural Characteristics of Agriculture

Table 2 presents some of the interrelationships found between industrial development and various structural characteristics of agriculture. Although the comparisons shown by the averages for Brazil and São Paulo are also instructive, being generally consistent with São Paulo's higher level of industrial-urban development, we shall focus our attention upon the rank correlation coefficients for the twenty-three zones *within* São Paulo.

First, in regard to land utilization, we find that in both 1940 and 1950 São Paulo's more industrialized zones had relatively more of both cropland and pastureland than did the less industrialized. Having undergone an earlier agricultural development, and enjoying better market opportunities, they also had relatively less unused arable land and natural woodland. However, these distinctions weakened in most cases during 1940–50, a reflection, in all probability, of the clearing of woodland and the expansion of cropland and pastureland that were underway in the newer (and less industrialized) agricultural zones. (In our Tennessee Valley study, the more industrialized zones also tended to have more improved land—cropland plus plowable pasture— and less woodland; the comparable coefficients were .408 * and −.310, respectively, in 1950.[30]) Second, while there was not a very strong correlation between industrial development and particular *types of farming,* the more industrialized zones did have a significantly greater number (relatively) of livestock-feeding (finishing) farms and farms of mis-

---

[29] The detailed results were presented in a preliminary draft, William H. Nicholls, *Industrial-Urban Development and Agriculture in São Paulo, Brazil, 1940–50,* Nashville, Tenn., Dec. 1962, pp. 254.

[30] Hereafter, the comparable coefficients for the Tennessee Valley (TV) in 1949–50 will be inserted in various places in the text parenthetically and without comment.

cellaneous type and a somewhat less significantly greater number of livestock-breeding and crop-livestock farms with fewer crop farms.

Third, relative to their land resources, the more industrialized zones were not significantly different in number of cattle (TV .317). They did, however, show a consistently greater milk production (again reflecting greater market outlets) in both 1940 and 1950 than the zones of lesser industrial-urban development. While the more industrialized zones had significantly *less* chicken and egg production in 1939–40 relative to land area, this gap had nearly been closed by 1949–50. While poultry production is hardly dependent upon land area, it is probable that the farmers of the more industrialized zones were already less self-sufficient (producing less for home consumption) in 1940, and that the increase in commercial production noted in 1950 reflects the beginnings of their response to urban market demands. This increase was sufficient to offset the previous effect—a trend that probably continued in the 1950's to make the correlation coefficient significantly *positive*. However, the strong tendency for hog production per thousand hectares of cropland to be lower as the zone was more industrial, was only slightly weakened during 1940–50 (TV .459 **).

Fourth, in terms of the amount of cropland devoted to different crops (as measured by total physical production), the more industrial-urban zones produced relatively more coffee, sugar-cane, and cotton, crops on which they depended heavily—and produced relatively *less* of such major subsistence crops as beans, corn (TV −.256), and manioc. The lead of the first three crops was increased during 1940–50, but the inferiority of the latter crops decreased, perhaps because the later-settled, less industrialized zones were beginning to produce those products (and swine) on an increasingly commercial basis. In any case, the zones of greater industrial-urban development showed a much higher value of output per thousand hectares of all farmland than did the less industrialized zones. While the more industrialized zones did not as yet derive a significantly higher percentage of their total farm income from livestock and livestock products (and less from crops) than the more agricultural zones, developments during 1940–50 indicated a trend toward this stage. (In the Tennessee Valley, a marked shift in relative income from corn and tobacco—its major, labor-intensive cash crop— to livestock production took place during 1930–50. In 1949 coefficients in the more industrial countries were −.580 ** and +.580 **, respectively, for the crop and livestock shares of total income, indicating, perhaps, the direction of trends in São Paulo after 1950.)

In general, industrial-urban development was not significantly re-

TABLE 2

Structural Characteristics of Agriculture, Brazil and Sao Paulo:
Selected Indexes with Comparisons between the National and
State Averages, 1949–50, and with Coefficients of Rank
Correlation Between These Indexes and 1949 Per Capita Value
Added by Manufacture for Twenty-three Zones of Sao Paulo,
1939 and 1949[a]

Index Correlated with 1949 Value Added by Manufacture Per Capita	Average 1949–50[b]		Rank Correlation Coefficients	
	Brazil	S. Paulo	1939–40	1949–50
Percentage of all farmland (area) by use				
Cropland	8.2	22.4	.590**	.439*
Pasture	46.3	45.5	.399*	.359*
Unused arable land	14.8	12.4	-.367*	-.400*
Woodland — natural	23.6	13.0 }	-.445*	{ -.192
Woodland — reforested	0.5	1.6		.703**
Percentage of all farms (number) by type				
Livestock-feeding farms	1.4	2.0	—	.360*
Livestock-breeding farms	6.7	5.3	—	.293
Crop-livestock farms	29.0	22.2	—	.266
Crop farms	60.0	65.2	—	-.185
Other types	1.1	1.6	—	.483**
Production per 1,000 hectares pasture				
Milk (thousands of liters)	25.6	59.5	.582**	.513**
Head of cattle (excl. calves and oxen)	342	547	.184	.126
Production per 1,000 hectares of all cropland				
Coffee (tons)	102	203	.392*	.442*
Sugar-cane (tons)	1,200	1,123	.263	.486**
Cotton (tons)	40	105	.256	.258
Rice (tons)	146	174	.061	.120
Manioc (tons)	578	53	-.298	-.215
Corn (tons)	349	278	-.342	-.160
Beans (tons)	65	23	-.504**	-.394*
Eggs (thousands of dozen)	9.7	10.2	-.426*	-.033
Chickens	3,871	3,027	-.606**	-.179
Hogs (excluding pigs)	676	379	-.658**	-.607**
Value of farm output per 1,000 hectares farmland	n.a.	$31,267	.638**	.584**
Total value of output per farm	n.a.	$2,683	.658**	.638**

(continued)

TABLE 2 (continued)

Index Correlated with 1949 Value Added by Manufacture Per Capita	Average 1949–50[b]		Rank Correlation Coefficients	
	Brazil	S. Paulo	1939–40	1949–50
Percentage of total farm income from				
Crops	n.a.	81	.311	.107
Livestock	n.a.	19	-.311	-.107
Farmland per farm (hectares)	112.5	85.8	.200	.084
Percentage of all farms with farmland of				
Less than 2 hectares	7.9	1.3	.052	.230
2–99 hectares	84.2	85.5	-.160	-.151
Greater than 500 hectares	3.7	2.7	.286	.340
Greater than 5,000 hectares	0.22	0.09	-.005	-.144
Percentage of all farmland (area) in farms of				
Less than 2 hectares	—	—	—	—
2–99 hectares	16.6	24.7	-.077	-.268
Greater than 500 hectares	62.1	46.8	.130	.200
Greater than 5,000 hectares	26.7	10.9	-.168	-.354*
Percentage of farmland in largest 5 per cent of farms	68	57	.009	.066
Percentage of all farms (number) with cropland of				
Less than 2 hectares	25.4	6.1	n.a.	.061
Less than 100 hectares	99.4	97.5	n.a.	-.602**
Greater than 1,000 hectares	.01	.04	n.a.	.544**
Percentage of all farms, "large scale" farms by type				
All	9.5	17.6	n.a.	.520**
Crop-livestock	1.3	3.2	n.a.	.506**
Crop	4.7	12.6	n.a.	.279
Livestock	3.5	1.8	n.a.	.014
Percentage of all farms (number) operated by				
Hired administrator	5.6	7.9	.695**	.633**
Owner	75.2	64.6	.334	-.068
Cash-renter	9.0	24.0	-.309	.141

(continued)

TABLE 2 (concluded)

Index Correlated with 1949 Value Added by Manufacture Per-Capita	Average 1949–50[b]		Rank Correlation Coefficients	
	Brazil	S. Paulo	1939–40	1949–50
Percentage of farm labor force supplied by				
All male workers	59.3	73.5	.476**	.302
Operator-family workers (males)	31.5	34.7	-.567**	-.388*
Permanent wage employees (males)	10.9	27.1		.629**
Resident share-croppers (males)	6.9	10.1	.605**	.085
Nonresident share-croppers (males)	1.9	0.9		.296
Temporary wage workers (males)	19.1	10.5	-.145	-.458*
Number of farm workers per farm	4.41	5.76	.583**	.483**
Value of field machinery per farm	$29	$91	.683**	.579**
Motorized vehicles per 1,000 hectares of cropland				
Field tractors	0.37	0.75	.420*	.400*
Motor trucks	1.29	2.18	.412*	.366*
Percentage of all farms (number) by type of power				
Animal	26.9	53.2	–	.405*
Animal and mechanical	0.3	1.2	–	.369*
Manual only	72.9	45.6	–	-.471*

Source: Brazil's General Censuses of 1940 and 1950.

[a]The statistical significance of the correlation coefficients is indicated at the 1 per cent level (**) and 5 per cent level (*).

[b]National and state average for each index. Units as indicated except that all values are in U.S. dollars, converted at the rate of 30 Cruzeiros per dollar.

lated to the *size distribution of landholdings*. The more industrial zones did show a more marked differentiation in size extremes, with relatively more farms of very small size (less than 2 hectares) and of large size (greater than 500 hectares). But, if we take land area into account, we find that these zones had less land held in huge (greater than 5,000 hectares) farms. There was no relationship between industrial development and concentration of land ownership, although if *cropland* only is considered, industrialized zones had relatively fewer farms with less than 100 hectares and relatively more with more than 1,000 hectares. In any case, the farms of the more industrialized zones were more intensively utilized, with significantly larger proportions classified' by the census as "large-scale" farms (requiring rather modest minimum absolute levels of cropland and livestock numbers) and as "large-scale" crop-livestock farms, although the same was not true for "large-scale" crop or livestock farms.

While by far the most common *farm-operator* in all parts of São Paulo was the landowner (whether operating the unit through share-cropper subunits or as a single unit with his family and cash-wage workers), the moderate but nonsignificant tendency in 1940 for the more industrialized zones to have relatively more owner-operated farms and fewer renter-operated farms (TV .337 and −.337) had completely disappeared by 1950. However, the more industrialized zones in both years had relatively many more farms operated by hired administrators, suggesting a higher rate of landlord absenteeism and a more commercialized operation.

The tendency of industrial-urban development to bring with it a more highly mechanized and commercialized agriculture is reflected by the *changing composition of the farm labor force*. Thus, in 1940, the more industrialized zones clearly showed a heavier dependence upon male labor, probably reflecting the more mechanized nature of their agriculture. The subsequent weakening of this relationship is perhaps attributable to the extent to which manual operations declined even in the less industrialized zones. Otherwise, the most notable difference between the more and less industrialized zones was the former's much heavier relative dependence in 1950 on permanent (monthly or full-time) cash-wage employees and (reflecting the greater scarcity of casual labor in an industrial-urban zone) lighter relative dependence on *temporary* cash-wage day labor. While the more industrialized zones were not yet less dependent upon share-croppers than the more agricultural zones, this relationship probably turned significantly negative during the 1950's as more and more large landowners abandoned cropping on shares for a system in which the entire landholding was operated as a single unit with considerable farm machinery and cash-wage workers. The weakening of the tendency for the more industrialized zones to draw a smaller proportion of their farm-labor force from farm-operator families than did the zones of lesser industrialization may reflect the fact that, as tractor-drawn machinery has displaced animal equipment and the hoe, landowners have proved more willing to participate personally in field operations.

It is also interesting to note that, while there was no significant difference between the zones of greater and lesser industrial-urban development in *average size of farm,* as measured by area of farmland (TV .000), the more industrialized zones in São Paulo had more farm workers (TV .326) and a higher value of farm machinery (TV .184) and total output per farm (TV .433 *) than the less industrialized. The more industrialized zones also had significantly more field tractors (TV .475 *) and motor trucks per 1,000 hectares of cropland. In all of these respects, however, the strength of the relationship diminished somewhat during 1940–50, reflecting the ever-widening influence of the growing urban centers, with its favorable effects in terms of intensity of land use and the degree of mechanization. Even in 1950, however, São Paulo's more industrialized zones had (relatively) a significantly greater number of farms using animal equipment or animal and tractor draft-power, with relatively fewer farms whose techniques were still wholly manual.

The Impact of Industrialization on the Local Capital Market

Let us now turn to those indexes most closely related to capital resources and to the efficiency of the local capital market in transmitting some of the benefits of industrial-urban development to the capitalization of the nearby agriculture (Table 3).

First, the data indicate that São Paulo's zones of greater industrial-urban development enjoyed distinct advantage in the per capita value of total payrolls and capital (both fixed and inventory capital) in their nonagricultural sector. They also had, even more than their counterparts in the Tennessee Valley, higher per capita bank deposits (TV .729 **) as well as higher per capita bank loans. The more industrialized zones also had a superior infrastructure (as measured by railroad density) and greater human capital as the result of greater investments in primary education (TV −.671 ** for illiteracy rate in 1930) and public health (TV −.200 for infant mortality rate). Their

TABLE 3

Local Capital Market, Brazil and Sao Paulo: Selected Indexes with Comparisons between the National and State Averages, 1949–50, and with Coefficients of Rank Correlation between These Indexes and 1949 Per Capita Value Added by Manufacture for Twenty-three Zones of Sao Paulo, 1939 and 1949[a]

Index Correlated with 1949 Per Capita Value Added by Manufacture	Average 1949-50[b]		Rank Correlation Coefficients	
	Brazil	S. Paulo	1939–40	1949–50
Nonagricultural sector, per capita				
Total payrolls	$16.3	$38.5	.939**	.930**
Fixed capital	55.9	123.4	n.a.	.936**
Inventories	30.0	61.3	n.a.	.751**
Bank deposits	49.5	99.8	n.a.	.840**
Bank loans	42.6	74.1	n.a.	.594**
Kilometers of railroad per 1,000 sq. km. land area	4.4	29.6	n.a.	.863**
Percentage foreign-born				
Total population	2.3	7.6	.518**	.406*
Farm operators	6.3	25.7	.501**	n.a.
Percentage of males 10+ completed primary school	15.0	27.2	n.a.	.856**
Percentage of population 5+ illiterate	57.3	40.4	-.879**	-.896**
Crude rate of stillborn births, 1939–42	n.a.	2.45	-.433*	n.a.
Infant mortality rate, 1939–42	n.a.	175	-.290	n.a.
Persons employed per establishment				
Manufacturing	16.5	23.1	.799**	.701**
Wholesale trade	7.1	8.7	.826**	.597**
Retail trade	2.1	2.3	.740**	.737**
Agriculture	4.4	5.8	.583**	.483**

(continued)

TABLE 3 (continued)

Index Correlated with 1949 Per Capita Value Added by Manufacture	Average 1949–50[b]		Rank Correlation Coefficients	
	Brazil	S. Paulo	1939–40	1949–50
Value of output per establishment				
Manufacturing (value added)	$19,867	$34,470	.880**	.933**
Wholesale trade (sales)	143,660	228,500	n.a.	.334
Retail trade (sales)	8,580	13,477	.755**	.747**
Agriculture (gross output)	n.a.	2,683	.658**	.638**
Value of capital per establishment				
Manufacturing (fixed capital)	19,277	30,617	.880**	.933**
Wholesale trade (fixed capital)	5,923	7,577	n.a.	.334
Wholesale trade (inventories)	28,703	46,437	n.a.	.611**
Retail trade (inventories)	3,057	4,677	.410*	.607**
Agriculture (fixed capital)	n.a.	7,762	.657**	.575**
Capital per person employed				
Manufacturing (fixed capital	1,168	1,325	.375*	.044
Wholesale trade (fixed capital)	835	869	n.a.	−.299
Wholesale trade (inventories)	4,050	5,327	n.a.	.620**
Retail trade (inventories)	1,480	2,021	.308	.430*
Agriculture (fixed capital)	n.a.	1,348	.059**	.468*
Horsepower per person employed in manufacturing	2.14	2.30	n.a.	.154
Output per person employed				
Manufacturing (value added)	$1,204	$1,492	.493**	.488**
Wholesale trade (gross sales)	20,263	26,217	.516**	.519**
Retail trade (gross sales)	4,157	5,820	.770**	.742**
Agriculture (gross output)	n.a.	466	.592**	.479**
Value per hectare all farmland of				
Crop & livestock production	n.a.	$31.3	.638**	.584**
Land and buildings	$20.6	61.2	.685**	.658**

(continued)

TABLE 3 (continued)

Index Correlated with 1949 Per-Capita Value Added by Manufacture	Average 1949–50[b]		Rank Correlation Coefficients	
	Brazil	S. Paulo	1939–40	1949–50
Value per hectare of cropland all				
Crop production	n.a.	$113.3	.194	.396*
Fertilizer purchased	$1.00	$2.80	n.a.	.538**
Insecticides purchased	0.47	1.22	n.a.	.416*
Harvested output (kg/ha.)				
Coffee	790	720	n.a.	-.401*
Rice	1,390	1,250	n.a.	.034
Potatoes	3,540	5,220	n.a.	.289
Cotton (unginned)	440	630	n.a.	.179
Corn	1,250	1,250	n.a.	-.164
Sugar-cane (thousands)	26.9	36.1	n.a.	.442*
Beans	630	550	n.a.	.168
Percentage of pastureland in planted pasture	13.9	42.7	n.a.	.068
Milk production per cow milked (liters per year)	484	621	n.a.	.520**
Per farm value				
Land and buildings	$2,323	$5,247	.687**	.588**
Livestock and machinery	n.a.	2,515	.580**	.209
Crop production	n.a.	2,177	.623**	.549**
Milk and eggs	n.a.	215	.607**	.598**
Animal production	n.a.	292		.089
Land per farm worker (hectares)				
All farmland	25.5	14.9	-.251	-.629**
Cropland	2.10	3.34	.110	.259
Cropland and pasture	13.9	10.1	.233	.489**
Capital per farm worker				
Land and buildings	$527	$911	.660**	.663**
Vehicles and workstock	32	48	.344	.703**
Productive livestock	n.a.	220	.175	-.177
Field machinery	7	16	.603**	.418*
Stationary machinery	5	8		.517**
Value, all nonrealestate capital	n.a.	292	.428*	-.140

(continued)

TABLE 3 (concluded)

Index Correlated with 1949 Per-Capita Value Added by Manufacture	Average 1949–50[b]		Rank Correlation Coefficients	
	Brazil	S. Paulo	1939–40	1949–50
Value of production per worker				
Crop production	n.a.	$378	.550**	.445*
Milk and egg production	n.a.	37	n.a.	.411*
Animal production	n.a.	51	n.a.	−.135
Rural dwellers per room (average)	1.23	1.17	n.a.	−.493**
Rural housing amenities; percentage with				
Electric lights	1.4	3.9	n.a.	.685**
Piped water	3.6	12.7	n.a.	.781**
Toilet apparatus	10.4	21.8	n.a.	.672**

Source: Brazil's General Censuses of 1940 and 1950.

[a]The statistical significance of the correlation coefficients is indicated at the 1 per cent level (**) and 5 per cent level (*).

[b]National and state average for each index. Units as indicated except all values are in U.S. dollars, converted at the rate of 30 Cruzeiros per dollar.

higher percentage of foreign-born population (TV .646 **) was probably also an asset in both the urban and rural sectors, since this element of the population could be expected to bring with it levels of education, skills, and motivation above those of the native-born population.

It is clear that, as late as 1949–50, the average manufacturing establishment in São Paulo was relatively small scale and the average agricultural establishment (at least in number of workers) fairly large scale. However, the size of establishment—whether measured by number of workers, capital, or output—in São Paulo's more industrialized zones, was on the average greater not only in manufacturing and in retail and wholesale trade, but also (although to a somewhat lesser degree) in agriculture as well. The advantage of the industrial zones in average size of establishment did tend to decline in most instances during 1940–50, notably in agriculture. The principal exception was manufacturing, in which establishment size as measured by capital and output (but not number of workers) was relatively larger in the more industrialized zones in 1950 than in 1940, suggesting some shift toward more capital-intensive types of manufacturing. However, if we look at capital per worker, we find that a moderately higher value had prevailed in 1940 in manufacturing in the more industrialized zones, but that this difference had disappeared by 1950, a finding confirmed by the alternative physical measure of motive force (horsepower) per manufacturing worker. In contrast, capital per worker was significantly higher in the industrial zones not only in wholesale and retail trade but also in agriculture (TV .615 **). This lead in capital per worker had strengthened in retail trade although it had weakened in agriculture during 1940–50. Nonetheless in 1950 as well as in 1940, labor productivity (output per worker) was significantly higher in the manufacturing sector of the more industrialized zones, perhaps because of their greater human capital. The same was true in wholesale and retail trade and in agriculture (TV .525 **), although the productivity advantage of agriculture in the more industrialized zones weakened somewhat during 1940–50.

The fact that the zones of greater industrial-urban development generally enjoyed larger capital resources (and higher labor productivity) undoubtedly reflects their large debt to the earlier successful development of nearby agriculture. The agricultural sector in turn had benefited from the availability of more capital resources (probably on more favorable terms as well) consequent on the proximity of the growing industrial-urban centers. That the agriculture of São Paulo's more industrialized zones did benefit is supported by most of the remaining, more detailed indexes presented in Table 3.

First, the more industrialized zones had a significantly higher value of output per hectare of all farmland. This was reflected (along with the stronger nonagricultural demand for land) in higher per hectare farmland values. The same zones also had a higher value of crop production per hectare of cropland, although the lead was less pronounced than was the case for all farmland. This relationship was due partly to the fact that, while still at very low levels, the per hectare expenditures for fertilizer (TV .445 * for all farmland) and insecticides were significantly higher in the more industrialized zones. Even so, the soils in the latter had been heavily depleted in the westward march of coffee in the state, a depletion still reflected in their significantly lower coffee yields in 1950. The yields of sugar-cane (which was being produced in São Paulo by the most modern techniques) and to a lesser extent of potatoes (much of which crop was produced by relatively advanced techniques, particularly in conjunction with irrigated rice production in the Paraíba

Valley), did tend to be higher in the more industrialized zones. In rice, cotton, corn, and bean yields, however, these zones were no more than holding their own in 1950—although this was no mean achievement in light of the virgin tracts just then coming under cultivation in the highly agricultural western frontier zones. However, in view of more recent improvements in techniques (particularly in irrigated rice and cotton), the more industrialized zones may have shown a relative advantage in these latter crops by 1960.

Second, in value of livestock production per hectare of pastureland, the more industrialized zones had a relative advantage only in milk production. While the state of São Paulo had by 1950 already gone a long way in substituting more productive planted pastures for low-quality natural pastures, there was no significant difference between the more and less industrialized zones in the proportion of planted pastures or (as we saw earlier) in the number of cattle per thousand hectares of pasture. However, in the light of their greater investment in the dairy breeds (primarily Holstein) and greater amounts of purchased feed rations in response to a growing urban demand for milk, the more industrialized zones did have a strong relative advantage in milk production per cow milked and in milk production per thousand hectares of pastureland.

Third, for the average farm of the more industrialized zones, investment in both real estate (land and buildings) and nonreal estate (livestock and machinery) was significantly greater than for the average farm in the less industrialized zones (TV .711 ** for real estate capital). However, both relationships weakened during 1940–50, suggesting that the relative increase in land values and nonreal estate on the recently settled agricultural frontiers was at least temporarily outpacing that in the older agriculture of the more industrialized zones. The weakening of the second relationship was especially marked—the relationship was no longer significant in 1950—although this change may to some extent reflect the fact that our efforts to estimate the *value* of livestock (not reported by the 1950 census) were not sufficiently accurate. The average farm of the more industrialized zones did, however, produce a greater value of both crops and livestock—although with the latter most of the value was apparently derived from the livestock products (milk and eggs) rather than from the sale of the animals. This relationship was somewhat less strong in 1950, perhaps again because of inaccuracies in our estimates of gross value of production (particularly of animals) based on the physical data (excluding values) of the 1950 census.

More important, although subject to the same errors of estimation for 1950, were the resources and output of the average farm worker in the several zones. In 1940, the physical land resources that the average farm worker had to work with were not significantly different in the industrialized and nonindustrialized zones. By 1950, however, there was distinctly less total farmland per worker in the more industrialized zones. Nevertheless, perhaps because of increasing intensity of land use and the increasing substitution of animal and mechanical power for labor, the average farm worker in these zones actually had more crop and total productive (crop and pasture) land to work with in 1950, by which time this relationship had become highly significant. In value terms, however, the more industrial zones showed more real estate investment per farm worker, a pronounced lead that was almost the same in 1940. While the more industrialized zones also showed a moderately greater nonreal estate investment in 1940, this lead had disappeared by 1950, largely because of the (estimated) livestock components. Nonetheless, both in 1940 and 1950, there was significantly more farm (field and stationary) machinery per worker in the more industrialized zones, although there was some decline in the latter's advantage during the decade as farm mechanization spread to the zones of lesser industrialization. In per worker investment in vehicles and work animals, on the other hand, the superiority of the more industrialized zones became distinctly greater during 1940–50, undoubtedly because of their earlier use of motor trucks, facilitated in turn by somewhat better highways and mechanical service facilities. Finally, the superiority in crop production per farm worker in the industrialized zones, while somewhat weaker than in 1940, was still moderately strong in 1950 as was per worker production of milk and eggs. Once again, however, per worker income from animal production (assuming our estimates were accurate) in these zones was not significantly different from that of the more rural-agricultural zones.

Our last indexes of capital investment relate to housing. Housing is usually a consumption good under urban conditions. However with production and family living more closely interrelated in the rural sector, housing (particularly worker housing) is considered a "nonproductive" part of agricultural investment. While São Paulo's rural housing was in general not only more crowded but also lacking in the amenities of modern life, the rural (like the urban) housing was significantly better in the more industrialized zones. Thus, in 1950 rural housing, as measured by the average number of persons per room in the more industrial zones, was significantly less crowded. (In urban housing, no such advantage existed.) The rural domiciles of the more industrial zones also showed (despite small absolute differences) a strong superiority over the less industrialized zones in extent of piped water, electric lights, and toilet facilities (TV .729 ** for rural level of living index).

Our findings from analyses of the impact of industrial-urban development on agriculture, via the local capital markets, in the Tennessee Valley and the State of São Paulo were surprisingly similar for both areas. However, one important difference should be noted. In São Paulo, the per worker value of farm capital was less closely related to industrial development in 1950 than in 1940, whereas in the Tennessee Valley the comparable coefficient steadily increased from 1900 to 1950, the period in which most of its industrial-urban growth took place. Perhaps this difference is largely attributable to the fact that, during 1900–50, both capital and labor flows in the Tennessee Valley were between the rural and urban sectors, while in São Paulo as late as 1940–50 they were in considerable part from the older to the newer *rural* zones. (During 1890–1910, our Tennessee Valley study area did experience a somewhat similar phenomenon. Some of its most rural counties temporarily prospered and attracted considerable in-migration on the basis of lumbering and coal-mining, a process about as exploitative as that more recently followed by the expansion of agriculture in São Paulo's western frontier zones.) Such cross-currents in factor flows within São Paulo tended to obscure the rural-urban relationships. Part of the reason for this lies in the fact that agricultural settlement had only been completed recently. In the Tennessee Valley where the settlement process had long since ceased, these relationships had become more clearly drawn. With the settlement completed as of about 1950, it seems reasonable to expect that the influence of industrialization on agriculture in São Paulo will approach more closely to that already observed in the Tennessee Valley, even with the antiemployment bias of the artificially stimulated industrialization that became a factor in São Paulo after 1950.

Industrialization and the Local Labor Market

Finally, let us consider those indexes most closely related to local labor resources and to the efficiency of the local labor market in relieving the problem of low agricultural incomes and low farm-labor productivity by facilitating the transfer of excess farm labor resources to nonagricultural employment. Most of these indexes are presented in Table 4, although certain of them (particularly those on per worker capital or output) in Table 3 could just as appropriately have been placed in Table 4. Where there is such an overlap, such as in capital per worker, the previous entry was concerned with factors affecting the numerator of the index, whereas we are here concerned with the factors affecting the denominator.

In Table 4, we first find that the more industrialized zones (as measured by 1949 per capita value added) were also far more urban and less rural (TV .806 ** and —.806 **), with far higher population densities (TV .748 **). They also had far higher per capita wholesale and retail sales (TV .651 ** and .818 **) although their advantage in these indexes weakened somewhat during 1940–50, especially in wholesale trade. (The latter trend is more easily understood in the light of the fact that in São Paulo farm products accounted for 39 per cent of wholesale sales and food products for 18 per cent more. Much of the wholesale trade, therefore, involved the assembly of agricultural products in the more rural areas.) Nonetheless, during 1940–50, the more industrialized zones not only greatly strengthened their lead in percentage of male workers in the secondary (manufacturing and construction) industries (TV .938 **), but also further strengthened their lead in employment in the tertiary (service) industries, with the subgroup "commodity trade" showing the greatest increase (from .682 ** to .783 **). At the same time, of course, the more industrialized zones showed relatively fewer males gainfully employed in the primary (agricultural and extractive) industries (TV —.788 **), a relationship that was strongly marked and increasing.

Reflecting their generally higher labor productivity (Table 3 above), the more industrialized zones also had significantly higher annual wages per worker in all nonagricultural employment and in manufacturing (TV .802 **), but again this lead was weaker in 1950 than 1940. Female participation in the labor force was also considerably higher in the industrialized zones in terms of all employment and manufacturing (TV .905 ** and .460 **), although in agricultural employment, these zones had relatively lower female participation. In educational achievement, in terms not only of completion of primary school (Table 3) but also completion of the middle school (TV .708 **) and university courses as well, these zones also enjoyed higher indexes. With a predominantly white population in the state as a whole, São Paulo had a moderately larger (relatively) white population (TV —.325) in 1940, but this factor disappeared during 1940–50.

As noted earlier in (Table 3), the more industrialized zones also led in foreign-born population (TV .646 **). There were, however, distinct

TABLE 4

Population and Labor Market, Brazil and Sao Paulo: Selected Indexes with Comparisons between the National and State Averages, 1949–50, and with Coefficients of Rank Correlation between These Indexes and 1949 Per Capita Value Added by Manufacture for Twenty-three Zones of Sao Paulo, 1939 and 1949[a]

Index Correlated with 1949 Per Capita Value Added by Manufacture	Average 1949–50[b]		Rank Correlation Coefficients	
	Brazil	S. Paulo	1939–40	1949–50
Per capita value added by				
Manufacture	$35.3	$94.4	.922**	1.000**
Wholesale sales	74.3	166.6	.873**	.719**
Retail sales	61.4	111.8	.848**	.810**
Residential classification of population; percentage				
Urban	25.0	39.9	.910**	.928**
Suburban	11.2	12.7	.469*	.515**
Rural	63.8	47.4	−.799**	−.890**
Population density per sq. km.	6.1	37.0	.786**	.742**
Percentage of gainfully employed males in				
Primary industries	65.8	47.8	−.726**	−.839**
Secondary industries	13.7	22.6	.599**	.872**
Tertiary industries	20.2	29.5	.727**	.748**
Per worker annual earnings in				
Manufacturing (nonadmin.)	$350.4	$404.9	.679**	.550**
Wholesale trade (nonadmin.)	678.9	785.8	.666**	.103
Retail trade (nonadmin.)	278.6	327.2	.737**	.572**
All nonagricultural (all)	307.7	437.7	.892**	.719**
Percentage of male population of 10+ completed				
Middle school	2.74	4.78	n.a.	.800**
University	0.80	1.20	n.a.	.724**
Females as percentage of labor force in				
Manufacturing	16.3	21.2	n.a.	.658**
Agriculture	26.5	21.4	−.454*	−.302
All sectors	20.7	18.6	n.a.	.898**

(continued)

TABLE 4 (continued)

Index Correlated with 1949 Per Capita Value Added by Manufacture	Average 1949–50[b]		Rank Correlation Coefficients	
	Brazil	S. Paulo	1939–40	1949–50
Ethnic classification of population (percentage)				
White	61.7	85.6	.395*	.198
Italian	n.a.	3.0	.782**	n.a.
Portuguese	n.a.	2.2	.586**	n.a.
Spanish	n.a.	1.7	.649**	n.a.
German	n.a.	0.5	.210	n.a.
Japanese	n.a.	1.8	-.073	n.a.
Percentage of population by religion				
All Noncatholics	6.5	9.3	n.a.	-.223
Protestant	3.3	3.5	n.a.	-.187
Spiritualist	1.6	2.7	n.a.	.158
Jewish	0.1	0.3	n.a.	.671**
Orthodox	0.1	0.3	n.a.	.529**
Moslem	0.01	0.02	n.a.	.090
Buddhist	0.3	1.4	n.a.	-.144
Female fertility Twelve and over, bearing children				
Percentage bearing live children	n.a.	55.9	-.792**	n.a.
Average number children per mother	n.a.	5.1	.211	n.a.
Percentage of total male population in age range 0–4	16.4	14.6	-.594**	-.518**
Crude birth rate	43.7	31.8	-.437*	-.686**
Crude death rate	20.6	14.3	-.517*	-.599**
Crude natural increase	23.1	17.5	-.137	-.140
Net immigration rate, 1940–50	n.a.	+6.7	n.a.	-.116
Rate of population growth, 1940–50	126.0	127.3	–	.035
Population, all ages; male – female ratio				
Nationwide	99.3	103.6	-.213	-.290
Rural	104.1	111.7	n.a.	.253
Urban	89.8	95.6	n.a.	-.072

(continued)

TABLE 4 (concluded)

Index Correlated with 1949 Per Capita Value Added by Manufacture	Average 1949–50[b]		Rank Correlation Coefficients	
	Brazil	S. Paulo	1939–40	1949–50
Population, age range 20–39				
Male-female ratio	96.4	105.7	−.109	n.a.
Percentage of male population	28.7	31.0	.307	n.a.
Percentage of female population	29.6	30.7	.546**	n.a.
Population, age range 40–59				
Male-female ratio	107.0	116.1	−.265	n.a.
Percentage of male population	13.8	14.4	−.047	n.a.
Percentage of female population	12.8	13.0	.056	n.a.

Source: Brazil's General Censuses of 1940 and 1950 and various federal and state publications on vital statistics.

[a]The statistical significance of the correlation coefficients is indicated at the 1 per cent level (**) and the 5 per cent level (*).

[b]National and state average for each index. Units as indicated except all values in U.S. dollars, converted at the rate of 30 Cruzeiros to the dollar.

differences by nationality. In 1940 these zones had relatively the largest numbers of people of Italian, Spanish, and Portuguese birth, but their percentages of Japanese- and German-born population were not significantly different. The Italian-born population has been particularly outstanding in the development of the city of São Paulo. The Portuguese- and Japanese-born have shown a stronger preference for agriculture, and are prominent in such small-scale operations as fruit and vegetable growing near the major cities. Lately the Japanese have been moving in increasing numbers into the urban centers or have joined the Syrian-Lebanese to become one of the two major ethnic groups participating in the assembly and first processing of farm products in the more rural zones. Comparable data at the local level were not available in 1950, although data on religious preference in the latter year (despite the predominantly Catholic affiliation of the Italians, Portuguese, and Spanish) are a partial substitute. While there is some evidence [31] that Brazil's small Protestant minority has as a group, attitudes more favorable to hard work and thrift than the predominant Catholic population, São Paulo's more industrial zones if anything tended to have relatively fewer Protestants and noncatholics. As for other religious minorities, the more industrial zones showed a significantly larger (relatively) population of the Jewish and Orthodox faiths (the latter including most of the Syrian-Lebanese), but no significant differences in relative numbers of Moslems (Syrian-Lebanese) and Buddhists (Japanese). In the Tennessee Valley, the Presbyterians and Quakers played a leading role in local industrial development.

More important for present purposes are the various rather fragmentary indexes of vital statistics, migration, and age-sex distribution that are presented in Table 4. First, we observe that as early as 1940 São Paulo's more industrialized zones had much fewer females (relatively) who had borne one or more live children (TV $-.620$ **). While this index perhaps reflects a later age of marriage and higher incidence of spinsterhood, it was not matched by longer run lower fertility rates, since the average number of children per mother (TV $-.762$ **) was if anything higher in the more industrialized zones. That the latter index was not very reliable for São Paulo is suggested by the fact that the percentage of the total (male) population in the age class 0–4 was lower to a marked degree in the more industrial zones in 1940 and (to a somewhat lesser degree) in 1950 as well (TV $-.549$ **). The latter relationship is further confirmed by the finding that the crude birth rate for 1939–42, after adjustment for underregistration of births, was significantly lower in the more industrialized zones, a tendency that was further strengthened for the decade as a whole (1940–50 average). However, since the crude death rates (unadjusted) for the same dates were also lower to a marked degree in the more industrialized zones, the effect on the crude rate of natural increase was such that in neither period did the industrial zones tend to have significantly lower rates of natural increase (TV $-.605$ ** in 1940).

While the state of São Paulo's net in-migration during 1940–50 amounted to 6.7 per cent of its average population of that decade, it is curious to learn that the net in-migration rate or rate of population growth (TV .842 ** and .735 **) of the state's zones of greater indus-

[31] Emilio Willems, "Protestantism as a Factor of Culture Change in Brazil," *Econ. Dev. and Cultural Change,* Vol. III (1955); and "Protestantism and Culture Change in Brazil and Chile," *in* W. V. D'Antonio and F. B. Pike (ed.), *Religion, Revolution, and Reform: New Forces for Change in Latin America,* New York, 1960.

trialization did not differ significantly from those of lesser industrialization. Clearly the growth of the urban population of São Paulo (largely in its industrial zones) during 1940–50 required a substantial rate of net in-migration. It is possible that much of this was short-distance (intrazonal) rural-urban migration. At the same time much of the interstate movement was probably rural-to-rural, attracted by the state's rapidly developing agricultural frontier areas. In any case, given the peculiar circumstance of uncompleted agricultural settlement, the less industrialized zones still tended to have net in-migration rates comparable to those of the zones of greater industrial-urban development.

To what extent were these migratory movements sex- or age-selective? For São Paulo as a whole, the male-female ratio for the population of all ages in 1950 indicates that the rural areas with net *in-migration* had gained relatively more males and those having net *outmigration* had lost relatively fewer males, while the net *in-migration* to urban areas had involved relatively more females. Among our twenty-three zones within São Paulo, however, the rural population of the more industrial zones had relatively more males, but this factor was so moderate as to be statistically nonsignificant, while there was virtually no difference in male-female ratios in the urban populations of the more and less industrialized zones. If alternatively we look at the 1940 population in the age range 20–39 (the most productive), the indication is that earlier in-migration to the state had been slightly male-selective, but that within the state there was no difference in terms of the male-female index between the zones of greater and lesser industrialization.

However, the more industrialized zones showed a moderately higher percentage of their total male population—and a significantly larger population (relatively) of females—in the 20–39 age range, suggesting that for these zones previous in-migration had been age-selective for both sexes. This means that the more industrialized zones had tended to attract from the less industrialized (or from other states at a rate higher than the less industrialized) both males and females as they reached adulthood. (The comparable relationships found in the Tennessee Valley— −.746 **, .788 **, and .878 **, respectively—were much stronger, however.) For the age-class 40–59, however, the relative male and female populations did not differ between the zones of greater and lesser industrial development. The more industrialized zones did, however, show lower male-female ratios, which suggests that (insofar as not attributable to higher life expectancy among women who have survived the child-bearing years) still earlier in-migration had brought relatively more females.

Let us return for a moment to the two indexes that are most important to the present analysis: per worker farm capital and farm output. We have already noted that in 1950 São Paulo's more industrialized zones enjoyed higher per worker farm capital (.468 *) and higher per worker farm output (.479 **) than did the less industrialized—results similar to those (.468 * and .479 **) found in our study of the Tennessee Valley. Thanks to the longer historical span of the earlier study and the existence of a control group, we could with more or less certainty trace a cause-and-effect relationship (at least for 1900–50) in which industrial-urban growth influenced agricultural development by improving the efficiency with which the capital, labor, and product markets functioned. While the degree of association between industrialization and the agricultural indexes in São Paulo was approximately the same, it is not yet possible to assess cause and effect with similar ease on the basis of a single decade.

Furthermore, an improvement in per worker farm capital or per worker farm output can come about through increased capital or more remunerative product markets (the numerator) or through a reduction in the farm labor force (the denominator), or all in combination. While the Tennessee Valley area experienced all three types of adjustments, the most important undoubtedly was the reduction in the size of the labor force, both through local occupational shifts and outmigration and through the declining fertility rates associated with urbanization. In São Paulo, while similar adjustments of a substantial nature were also evident, as yet none of these latter indexes of labor adjustment has been as closely related to industrial-urban development as in the Tennessee Valley. In part, this result probably reflects a greater efficiency in the operation of the national labor market in the U.S. and the existence in this country of more adequate nonfarm job opportunities (because of which, even the Tennessee Valley study area suffered as a whole considerable net *outmigration*) than in Brazil. Furthermore, unlike the Tennessee Valley, São Paulo is itself the mecca in which most of the nation's surplus farm population must be absorbed. The above result, however, is probably attributable in much greater part to the fact that São Paulo's expansion of nonagricultural employment was in 1950 still far from sufficient to absorb the large rural surplus, while its own agricultural frontiers (and those in neighboring states) were still capable of attracting much of the surplus population of the older agricultural regions. The fact that the differential advantage of São Paulo's more industrialized zones in per worker farm capital and output *weakened* substantially between 1940 and 1950 undoubtedly reflects the competition from this agricultural frontier which, despite its lack of industrial-urban development, offered sound inducement to, and attracted considerable amounts of, not only labor but also capital in purely agricultural development.

The comparable, largely agricultural counties of the Tennessee Valley (being much older) were clearly overpopulated by 1950. These counties needed even higher outmigration rates as well as substantial outside capital if their small-scale, labor-intensive farms were to be reorganized on a more productive basis. Undoubtedly, some of São Paulo's older zones were facing a similar problem insofar as they had lagged behind other zones in industrial-urban development. But, with the old and new agricultural zones grouped indiscriminately in our analysis under the heading, "less industrialized," the effects of industrial-urban development on agricultural incomes and productivity—particularly on such important population characteristics as fertility rates, migration rates, and age-sex structure—were considerably obscured for the decade 1940–50. That our results were nonetheless so similar during that period for São Paulo and the Tennessee Valley, despite such important differences in circumstances, underlines the importance of further industrial-urban development as a factor in transforming Brazilian agriculture. As settlement of the frontier zones is completed in the states of Paraná, Mato Grosso, and Goias—as it has been in São Paulo since 1950—conditions will approach more closely to those in which the Tennessee Valley found itself several decades earlier. It will then become more evident that even these new areas cannot, without industrial-urban development of their own, avoid the rural overpopulation and the agricultural undercapitalization that already plague the northeast and other older and stagnant agricultural regions of the country.

Summary

We may conclude from this analysis of São Paulo that (abstracting from the countereffects of an agricultural frontier that has not yet disappeared), local industrial-urban development—by facilitating the flow of capital into, and the flow of labor out of, agriculture—had by 1950, already exercised an important influence in raising the incomes and productivity of nearby farmers—an influence that has probably been considerably strengthened during the subsequent eighteen years.

On the *capital* side, São Paulo's industrial-urban development during the 1950's increased personal incomes and savings, thereby raising the total resources of the local banking and credit institutions, while creating a greater demand for income-elastic foods and other consumer goods. The nearby agriculture clearly benefited from these changes, which facili tated investments in land improvement, the development of more profitable capital-intensive enterprises (particularly milk, poultry and eggs, and specialty crops), the raising of capital-labor ratios, and an increased scale of farming operations—all of which increased farm output and incomes per worker relative to those in the (older) zones of lesser industrial-urban development. The nearby agriculture also benefited from the favorable effects of increasing population density and of the expanding tax base within the urban-oriented infrastructure, which improved both the quantity and quality of electricity, railroads and highways, education, and health facilities available to the nearby rural people.

On the *labor* side, the productivity of farm labor was raised by nearby industrial-urban development, not only because of concomitant higher rates of capital formation in agriculture, but also because of the greater facility with which excess farm labor could move into higher-income, nonfarm employment. Furthermore, farms located near industrial-urban centers could use the labor that remained in agriculture more productively. Thanks to their greater access to nonreal estate capital and to more favorable markets for local products, they could concentrate on more land- and capital-intensive products that utilized farm labor more fully, with a resultant rise in productivity that sufficed to cover the now higher opportunity cost of farm labor as determined by nonfarm wage levels.

In all probability all of these effects strengthened after 1950, but it is likely that they did so at a slower pace than they might have, given the shortcomings of public policy, in particular the government's allocation of the real resources that it succeeded in capturing through its system of multiple-exchange rates and its inflation-derived forced-savings policy of 1953–64. We shall conclude this paper with a brief and somewhat speculative appraisal of how Brazilian agriculture fared under the national public policies of this more recent period.

BRAZILIAN AGRICULTURAL DEVELOPMENT SINCE 1950: THE EFFECTS OF FORCED-DRAFT INDUSTRIALIZATION ON AGRICULTURE

Relative to Brazilian agriculture generally, the agriculture of São Paulo must have gained most (or suffered least) from the official policy of forced-draft acceleration of the growth of the industrial sector during

1953–64. Clearly, the state of São Paulo was the major beneficiary of the resources that the government allocated to industrial development. To a lesser extent the state also benefited differentially from the resources diverted to subsidized imports of tractors (discontinued in 1960 in favor of a domestic tractor industry), fuels, and fertilizers (discontinued in 1964) and to coffee price-supports. The farmers of São Paulo therefore must have received substantial direct and indirect benefits from the new policies, primarily through the resultant favorable effects on the urban demand for farm and food products.

From a financial point of view, however, these benefits were rather ephemeral and, from the standpoint of encouraging fundamental resource adjustments and increased efficiency in agriculture, were even less satisfactory. This was because of the unfavorable effects of public policy on employment. First, the particular capital-intensive industries that were promoted kept farm wages relatively low even in the more industrial zones, as in-migration outran remunerative nonfarm job opportunities. Second, the heavy import subsidies in effect for a time on certain agricultural inputs favored excessive mechanization. This mechanization received further stimulus from the tendency to invest agricultural savings (apart from those put into agricultural land, driving up land values) in farm machinery as a convenient hedge against inflation. This is scarcely a useful practice from the standpoint of optimum allocation of resources.

To be sure, the perceptive farm manager could detect that the terms of trade (insofar as middlemen were not capturing the benefits) were turning in his favor, particularly in the livestock-products sector, and many began to shift their resources accordingly. Unfortunately, however, these improved terms of trade reflected the government's continued neglect of agriculture, a neglect that took the form of insufficient and badly administered agricultural credit, research, and extension services. The coffee price-support policy was *not* an effective substitute. It did help to spread some of the benefits of economic growth to São Paulo's less industrialized frontier zones and to a much greater degree to the northern section of the state of Paraná. While it may have stimulated industrial development in these areas, the coffee price support policy may also have been biased against employment in agriculture, insofar as coffee land was diverted to planted pasture under the stimulus of changing relative prices, public production-control measures, and most of all, unfavorable weather. In any case, if the resources allocated to the coffee price support policy had been devoted to improved agricultural services, many more improvements in the allocation of agricultural resources would have resulted than actually did.

Lacking these improvements, São Paulo's agriculture has since 1950 made far less progress in raising its productivity, particularly in the far more complex and less familiar livestock sector, than it might otherwise have done. Livestock and livestock products are income elastic. For most producers laboring under inefficient production techniques, higher relative prices did not mean greatly increased profits. Therefore the supply of such income-elastic products was much less price-elastic than it should have been, while the supply schedule was shifting downward slowly if at all. This problem was further compounded by the increasing resort to consumer food-price controls as an anti-inflation measure while the prices of important agricultural inputs (upon the increased purchase of which, modernization of the livestock industries so much depended) rose unrestrained. The recent end to subsidies on fuel and fertilizer imports (an anti-inflation measure) and the increasing abandonment of cheap foreign sources of other major agricultural inputs in favor of strongly protected domestic sources have also increased the difficulties of transforming and modernizing Brazil's still relatively backward agriculture as well as of promoting the spread of mechanization insofar as this is economic at still low farm wage rates. (In fact mechanization was already economically justifiable with the price structure that prevailed in 1963, at least in some areas of southern Brazil.)

Our emphasis on the livestock rather than the crop sector of Brazilian agriculture may appear excessive, in view of the fact that the Brazilian diet still depends predominantly on food products of vegetable origin. Furthermore, crop production in Brazil (including most of São Paulo) is still largely based on technically backward methods. The generally low physical crop yields have, if anything, tended to decline, insofar as the initially high yields of virgin land on the frontiers have failed to offset the declining yields in the older agricultural areas, which have lagged in increasing their use of fertilizer, improved seeds, insecticides, and other modern agricultural inputs. However, to an increasing extent— even in the northeast—I have found that farmers are not only profit-motivated, but are also eager to accept such improved techniques if they have adequate technical assistance in their effective use and if the relative prices of farm products and purchased inputs make such improvements pay financially. In any case, since 1950 agricultural progress has enabled food-crop output to expand at a rate sufficient at least to maintain constant (though not lower) relative prices to urban consumers. Even this was a relatively satisfactory performance, considering the fact that Brazil's rate of population increase had risen to 3 per cent per year during 1950–

60, while the urban population was expanding at 5.4 per cent per year.

Thus far, this achievement in the crop sector probably owes more to relatively elastic supply functions for the major staple crops, given an abundance of cropland, than to higher productivity. Furthermore, on the demand side, the pressures of urban population growth have been less strongly augmented by the additional element of income elasticity of demand. Of the traditional staple foods of vegetable origin, those for which the highest elasticities in the *urban* sector were found in 1962–63 were products of wheat (0.36)—of necessity largely imported—and rice (0.21). Beans, corn meal, and manioc flour had elasticities close to zero. (Relative to the rural sector, the urban sector had a much higher per capita consumption of wheat and potatoes, a slightly smaller consumption of rice, and, a far smaller consumption of beans, corn, and manioc; the urban sector also consumed more oranges and vegetable oils per capita but less sugar and bananas.) The only vegetable products with urban income elasticities *higher* than wheat (0.36) were oranges and bananas (0.64–0.74), vegetable oils (0.55), and potatoes, margarine, and manioc root (0.40–0.48); the only livestock products with elasticities *less* than wheat were powdered milk (0.35), sundried beef (0.15), lard (0.08), and salt pork (−0.04).[32] Nonetheless, with the prospect of

[32] Fundação Getulio Vargas, Instituto Brasileiro de Economia, *Projeções de Oferta e Demanda de Produtos Agrícolas para o Brasil,* Rio de Janeiro, January 1966, pp. 37 and 44. Comparable data are also presented (p. 45) for the rural sector (0.40 for all foods as compared with 0.55 in the urban sector). It is interesting to note that, for most categories of food, the income elasticity of demand was lower in the rural sector than the urban sector, suggesting (insofar as the results do not reflect the greater difficulties of collecting the basic data) the generally easier accessibility of the food supply to the lower-income rural population. The only significant exceptions—elasticity higher in the rural area— were found for lard and salt pork (*toucinho*), rice 0.33, wheat products 0.41, and potatoes 0.59. Except for potatoes, the rural elasticity was 0.50 or more only for butter 1.09, cheese 0.68, eggs 0.57, and fresh beef and fresh milk 0.50 each.

Comparable data were also shown for three regions—the south, the east, and the north-northeast—the ranges in elasticities for *all foods* being from 0.62 to 0.50 (urban) and from 0.44 to 0.36 (rural), with the north-northeast the highest and the south lowest in both sectors. The urban north-northeast had the largest number of foods with elasticities exceeding +1.0—cheese 2.33 and chickens 1.91; wheat flour, margarine, and fresh pork 1.23–1.39; and fresh milk, potatoes, wheat pastes, oranges, and butter 1.00–1.10. Other high-ranking products were eggs 0.95 and canned meats, powdered milk, bananas, fresh beef, and canned fish 0.71–78. Only manioc flour had a negative elasticity −.10. The *urban south* had a much shorter list of products with elasticities greater than +1.0— chickens 1.45, butter 1.26, cheese 1.11, and canned fish 1.05; or between +0.7 and +1.0—pork 0.93, fresh fish 0.83, canned meats 0.81, and fresh beef 0.79; while three of its products, lard, corn meal, and manioc flour, had *negative* income elasticities of −0.10 to −0.11.

continued rapid growth of the population, both total and urban, and with the best agricultural land at last taken up, there is a growing necessity (as well as an increasing economic opportunity) to modernize crop production, particularly in the older and less remote agricultural regions. Even more urgent, with the low *price* elasticities of demand for most staple food products, is the expansion of storage facilities. Such facilities permit the stabilization of crop supplies (and prices) for the benefit of both farmers and consumers. If all these improvements are to come about, the Brazilian government must commit substantially more resources to the public agricultural agencies serving the long-neglected food-crop-producing sector than it heretofore has.

Even so, it is Brazil's livestock sector that stands in the greatest need of stimulation and development, and, therefore, of public assistance. The fact that the relative prices of livestock products have *increased* substantially in recent years reflects both the technological backwardness of the livestock sector and the evident desire of the urban consumer to substitute livestock products for cereals as his income rises. While geographically the most widespread agricultural enterprise in Brazil, beef-cattle production remains perhaps the most backward and traditional sector of agriculture. Even with its high degree of inefficiency, however, the Brazilian cattle industry has thus far managed to produce beef cheaply enough to enable even the nation's poorest to eat much more meat than most of the world's poor. Nonetheless, the rate of cattle increase in Brazil was only half that of population growth during 1950–60 in the face of very high income elasticities: 0.72 in the urban and 0.50 in the rural sector. While improved transportation probably increased the proportion of fresh-beef output available in the urban centers, these facts make it clear that a vast improvement in the efficiency of beef production—through better breeding stock, more effective disease

The rural north-northeast (Brazil's poorest sector) had few products with income elasticities of +0.70 or higher (wheat flour 2.01, potatoes 1.80, butter 1.25, and eggs 0.73) but a somewhat larger number between 0.50 and 1.00 (cheese and wheat bread 0.63; whole milk and wheat pastes 0.56−0.57; and rice, edible manioc root, and salt pork 0.52−0.53). However, it had the longest list of products with *negative* income elasticities. Barely negative were beans and vegetable oils ranging *minus* 0.01–0.03; slightly more negative were dried milk, oranges, (dried) fish, and corn meal, *minus* 0.08–0.10; and highly negative were the traditional sundried beef −0.72 and the crude plantation-produced staples of the back-country sugar-cane industry, brown sugar cake −0.35 and aguardente −1.13. For the *rural south,* only butter 1.03 and cheese 0.70 had elasticities greater than +0.70; three between 0.50 and 0.70 (lard 0.68, fresh beef 0.59, and brown-sugar cake 0.63); and only molasses and manioc flour had *negative* elasticities, *minus* 0.16–0.17.

control, improved pastures, and more adequate forage crops—is urgent if prospective domestic demand is to be met. (Although it is generally regarded as unlikely that Brazil will become a significant exporter of beef products in the foreseeable future, the country certainly has the potential, given sufficiently radical improvement in the productive efficiency of its huge cattle industry.)

Needs and opportunities are also great in the production of milk, poultry, and swine. Brazil's dairy industry faces very high urban income elasticities for its milk products (cheese 1.38, butter 1.21, and fluid milk 0.76) but, even in the major urban milksheds—where milk producers are following many improved practices—annual production per cow averages only about 2,500 lbs. for animals with considerable Holstein blood and about 1,000 lbs. for Brahma (Zebu) animals. (The lowest ranking U.S. states, Mississippi and Louisiana average about 3,400 lbs.) Brazil's poultry industry (facing income-elasticities of 1.31 for fowl and 0.70 for eggs) is, in general, even less well organized. Finally, swine production (with a very favorable urban income elasticity for pork)—despite much good Duroc stock, relatively good disease-control practices, and good feeding practices—still requires per hundred pounds of output (under the best conditions) 35 per cent more physical input (in corn-equivalent), including the breeding stock, than U.S. farmers had achieved as early as 1910–14. Yet, with a very large total output of corn (whose yield has increased significantly in the south with the rapid adoption of hybrid seed) and manioc—both of which have income elasticities near zero or even negative in human consumption— Brazil has a very good potential for achieving an efficient commercial swine industry. In places where market opportunities exist, there is already a surprisingly large number of milk, pork, and even poultry producers who are following many of the improved practices of their American counterparts. In general, however, the lack of adequate and reliable public technical assistance, compels the Brazilian producers to tackle managerial problems of enormous complexity on a purely empirical basis. So long as such assistance continues lacking, the increasing desire of Brazil's urban consumers for these products will be frustrated by the highly inelastic (and very slowly downward-shifting) supply schedules in these important industries.[33]

[33] For a detailed documentation of these matters, for crop as well as livestock production, see the series of reports on seven major agricultural regions, now being issued by the Graduate Center for Latin American Studies, Vanderbilt University, under the general title: William H. Nicholls and Ruy Miller Paiva, *Ninety-Nine Fazendas: The Structure and Productivity of Brazilian Agriculture,* 1963.

Toward an Integrated National Economy

While the close observer of Brazilian agriculture can find good reason to be critical of the backwardness of its production techniques, there is, on balance, much reason to be optimistic, provided that the Brazilian government does its part in lending agriculture a helping hand. Much of this optimism must rest on the progress that Brazil has made since 1940, toward a single integrated market for farm products and agricultural inputs. Thus far this movement has taken place primarily within the midwest and southeast regions dominated by the development centers of São Paulo and Rio, but today it is spreading over the northeast as well.

What is perhaps most remarkable is that Brazil, despite the most inadequate transportation and communication facilities, remained politically unified during the four centuries that elapsed before it began the process of effective economic integration. This feat of preserving the consciousness of nationhood over so vast a territory bodes well for the future of Brazil, since, of all Latin American countries, it has the greatest potential (in terms of "extent of the market") for realizing the economies of large-scale manufacturing.

As we have already seen, this relatively modern phenomenon of internal economic integration began with the march of coffee westward from Rio de Janeiro and through São Paulo, an expansion intimately bound up with railway development. As railways were extended, large, highly-capitalized and well-managed coffee plantations were established; marketing and financial intermediaries emerged; and São Paulo's coffee economy became well integrated into the national and even the world economy through transportation, storage, and standardization facilities which soon constituted a highly sophisticated marketing system. However, so thoroughly did coffee dominate the economy of southern Brazil that, in spite of indirect benefits from railway construction, food crops and livestock products for the growing internal market lagged far behind coffee in the efficiency of their production and marketing. To be sure, local assembling and processing firms were gradually developing along the railways, but standardization of product was minimal, storage capacity grossly inadequate, local transportation primitive, and the railroads themselves woefully unsatisfactory, particularly for livestock and fresh meat. As a consequence, in São Paulo and to a greater degree in the rest of the south, there was much physical waste and little incentive for expanding commercial farm production, while the prices of farm products differed widely between regions and showed extreme fluctuations both seasonally and year-to-year.

Commerce between the south and north of Brazil was extremely difficult, relying almost exclusively on sea and river transportation. Coastal shipping was inefficient and expensive and river transportation, by and large confined to the Amazon Basin, was subject to seasonality in certain areas. These shortcomings made the northeast, which imports from southern Brazil much of its wheat and rice and—in its frequent drought years beans, corn, and other staples—especially vulnerable to adversity. Within the northeast, railways were less developed and integrated than in the south, with most transportation between interior points by donkey trains and cattle drives, and between the coastal cities by sailboat. Certain strategically located towns came to serve as the major central markets receiving most of the farm products of the hinterland and then channeling them into the major urban centers, these operations being conducted in regular street fairs.

During the last two decades, however, this picture of a primitive and ineffective system of marketing has begun to change significantly, largely because of recent highway development and the rapid growth of truck transportation. The transformation was, of course, most striking in the south where it affected many sleepy old provincial towns within 100 miles of the city of São Paulo. Although they received their initial developmental impetus from the railroad extending from that metropolis, these towns were nonetheless only tenuously integrated into the regional economy until recently when they were linked to the state capital by major arteries, largely paved. While local farm-to-market roads remained underdeveloped, truck transportation grew in importance because of its advantages in speed, flexibility, and reliability over the less costly but poorly equipped and hopelessly administered public railway system.

As a result of these improvements in transportation in conjunction with burgeoning urban demand for food products, the southeast is fast approaching the achievement of a well-integrated regional economy for both food products and agricultural inputs. The independent truck owner-operator has become Brazil's modern pioneer. He is introducing an important new competitive element into the local assembling, transportation, and distribution of food products, while assuring farmers improved access to the important manufactured farm inputs that constitute his return load. Along with the independent trucker, we have that other remarkable catalyst in the modernization of agriculture in the southeast, the ubiquitous traveling salesman from São Paulo. Some of the most valuable agricultural extension work in Brazil is being done by the sales representatives of private firms as they push the sales of such products as protein supplements, insecticides, vaccines and veterinary medicines, chemical fertilizers, motors and pumps, and improved seeds.

In several southern states, a network of state agencies has been established to supply farmers with seeds, vaccines, fertilizers, and other farm supplies at subsidized prices. But despite their price advantages, these agencies have not wrested the market from private firms, which continue to compete on the basis of higher quality or better quality control. (Except among the Japanese, agricultural cooperatives have played a very minor role.)

Storage capacity for cereals (much of it public) has also been expanded considerably in the southeast. But even apart from its frequent diversion to accommodate coffee surpluses, this storage capacity still remains below desirable levels for purposes of supply and price stabilization. Storage, grading, and standardization have been developed further for rice than for most other food products, but in general remain at an inferior stage, handicapping the development of price reporting, specification buying, warehouse warrants, commodity exchanges and futures trading—devices essential to modern marketing and to the implementation of price support policies such as have long since been in effect in Brazil's coffee industry. Even so, considerable progress in cereal marketing has been underway in southern Brazil. With urban expansion, the commercial production of perishable products has been growing up rapidly around the major cities. Chief among these products are milk, poultry and eggs, and fruits and vegetables. Indeed such areas as the Paraíba Valley (between the cities of Rio and São Paulo with excellent highway and railroad connections to both) are now undergoing the same kind of agricultural rehabilitation—with increasingly sophisticated marketing and production techniques—that New England experienced, as the increasingly important advantages of favorable location gradually overcome the drawbacks of poor or incompletely recovered soils and unfavorable topography. In such local processing operations as cotton-ginning and rice-hulling, considerable excess capacity is now common. This encourages local price agreements, which are especially hard on the small farmer who does not have (as his large-owning neighbor often does) substantial interests in such local commercial enterprises. Once again, however, the growth of the trucker-buyer as a factor is probably having an ameliorative effect on these local monopolies. At the retail level, neighborhood food stores continue to be small-scale, high-margin marketing units. They are, however, subject to the competition of not only the traditional, primitive, ambulatory street markets still popular even in Rio and São Paulo—a competition still relatively severe because so many of the marketeers, lacking better job opportunities, are willing to work for very low net wages—but also of chain stores and supermarkets. The growth of these

latter reflects the increasing number of automobiles and home refriger-
ators and even the slowly worsening scarcity of domestic servants in the
largest cities.

Thus, it is clear that in São Paulo, for a half a century in the vanguard
of Brazilian industrial-urban development, the single integrated market
for both farm commodities and farm inputs (including labor) began.
Today the extent of that market has spread beyond the borders of the
state, and with the cities of São Paulo and of Rio as its centers, has
continued to expand, until it now embraces most of the southeast and
even much of the frontier midwest.

By 1964, with only 2.9 per cent of the national territory, the state of
São Paulo had 18.8 per cent of the nation's mileage in public roads
(federal, state, and the equivalent of county) and the eight-state southeast (as defined in Table 1), with 17.7 per cent of the land area, had
66.9 per cent of such roads, whose total extent was about 340,000 miles.
Over three-fourths of the nation's public roads were low-quality and
casually maintained county roads but, even of these, São Paulo had
21.2 per cent and the southeast 70.2 per cent. These high figures reflect
the greater density of rural populations in the southeast. Undoubtedly,
they also reflect the willingness of local political units in that part of the
country to accept responsibility for land communications of a class
which, in much of the rest of Brazil, are ignored as mere "trails" and
left out of the statistics. Of the nation's 76,400 miles of federal and state
roads—by far the most important for long-distance communication—
São Paulo had 10.7 per cent (of which, 37 per cent paved) and the
southeast 55.3 per cent (of which, 20 per cent paved). The 44.7 per
cent remaining for the vast balance of the national area was only 9.1
per cent paved.[34] Even so, within the southeast region, it is already possible to drive on paved highways from the city of São Paulo (via Rio)
to Salvador in the northeast, to Brasília to the north, almost to the
Uruguayan border to the south, to Maringá in the north of Paraná to
the southwest, and to several points on São Paulo's western borders for
connections with roads serving the major agricultural regions in southern
Mato Grosso. The city of Rio is linked with this system via São Paulo
and also has all-paved connections with Salvador, Vitória, Belo Horizonte, and Brasília. The importance of this recent highway development
to regional economic integration can hardly be exaggerated.

Improved transportation is the principal instrument in the economic
fusion that is beginning to take place between the north and northeast

[34] These and subsequent highway statistics are computed from data presented
in *Anuário Estatístico do Brasil, 1965*, p. 246.

and the dynamic southeast of Brazil. The 1940's saw the creation of one of the world's oldest and most extensive networks of airways, bringing for the first time the remotest corners of the nation into effective communication with the center. In 1960 came the nearly overnight creation of the new federal capital, Brasília, in the interior. This undertaking was an act of sheer economic madness from whose short-run fiscal and monetary consequences Brazil has still not fully recovered. From a broader historical perspective, however, the establishment of the new capital is probably justified as a great integrative measure, of key importance in peopling the nearly empty interior and in linking all parts of this continental nation into a single economic entity. The most important short-run benefit from Brasília has been the initiation of the arterial highways needed to connect the city with the rest of Brazil. A new system was constructed by paving old roads in the southeast and by blazing new roads in the interior. Of the 14,400 miles of federal highways now open to traffic outside of the southeast, a large percentage owes its existence to Brasília. Of course, the establishment of a new capital was not logically required for this highway construction. It is difficult, however, to imagine any other imperative for the rapid execution of this ambitious program in a nation whose outlook is still essentially coast oriented. While only about 10–12 per cent of these new federal highways are paved, they are all-weather roads which are attracting a rapidly growing volume of truck traffic. The consequence is that, with Brasília tied to the major cities of the north and northeast, these regions are at last enjoying effective land communication with São Paulo, Rio, and the whole southeast as well.

The effects have already been remarkable. As the new federal highways are being completed to the north, northeast, and west of Brasília, human settlement and the agricultural development of the hinterlands are increasing apace. The manufactures and farm products of the southeast are moving in large volume by truck to the northeast, and both primary products and human migrants make up the return traffic. Many of these migrants are bound for the newer agricultural regions where farm labor is relatively scarce and well remunerated, and where well-organized farm-labor markets exist to meet the joint needs of the migrants, truckers, and agricultural employers. It is true that long-distance truck transportation, although highly competitive, is still relatively expensive, especially for south-north traffic. Hence, improving the efficiency and lowering the cost of coastal shipping are essential to the process of national economic integration, and recently, significant efforts have been made in this connection. (The extent to which similar efforts are appropriate for the railway system is more problematic—given its present sad state and the huge capital outlay that creation of an effective and efficient system would require.) Even so, the beneficial effects of highway development in the midwest, north and northeast have already been substantial. Almost everywhere in Brazil, agricultural products of every description have gained in value because of greater access to markets, and a vast variety of consumer goods manufactured in the southeast are now widely available in the street fairs and stores of the most remote towns. In the northeast, the greater availability of manufactured products —and the lower truck tariffs for return trips to the south—are a great stimulus for the monetization and commercialization of agriculture. The social benefits that have come from the cheap rubber-thong sandal and transistor radio have also been substantial.

Within the north and northeast, the anticipation of improved roads has created a transportation revolution even before the expectations have been fulfilled. On the local level, trucks are rapidly displacing donkeys, bringing such comparatively remote states as Maranhão, Piauí, and the whole vast interior into effective communication with the major regional capitals of Belém, Fortaleza, Recife, and Salvador. The result has been growth in marketable surpluses of staple food products. While crop and livestock production techniques remain primitive and almost entirely manual, they are receiving a stimulus to modernization through the spread of trucking. As part of the return loads brought back by truckers, manufactured farm inputs as well as feed concentrates and improved breeding stock are finding their way increasingly to the more remote areas.

The prevailing structure of agriculture and land-tenure arrangements in the northeast is to a great extent reflected in the structure of the region's local farm-product markets. Cattle production (and in the major urban milksheds, milk production) are typically the principal interest of the large landowners, who reserve most of the available pasturelands, forage crops, and crop residues for their own account. Because they have more capital and knowhow at their disposal, these large producers (particularly when urban outlets for milk are good) are most likely to improve their techniques in livestock production. In crop production— largely delegated to tenant families (under varying arrangements) using almost completely manual techniques—improved production practices are seldom found, except where the landowner reserves a substantial part of his cropland for direct operation with cash-wage labor, some mechanization, and—although this is rare—somewhat better, purchased inputs. By either system the large landowners concentrate rather considerable quantities for sale. This produce comes more often from purchases of the tenant's product and from crop-shares received for the use of the plantation's own processing facilities (especially in sugar-cane and manioc) than from explicit land rents, which in many cases in the northeast are surprisingly low. Thus they have substantial bargaining power both in the acquisition and the sale of their produce. Today it is a common practice for the landowners to truck their products, either to the nearest towns, in whose assembling and first-processing enterprises they often have a commercial interest, or (generally in hired trucks) direct to major urban markets.

Small independent farmers, of which there are relatively few in most regions, often depend on their large neighbors for facilities to process their produce as well as for its purchase or transportation. However, the increasing prevalence of independent truckers or trucker-buyers is improving their bargaining power. Small farmers fortunate enough to live near major market towns usually sell directly in the large street fairs, bypassing the middleman at the cost of one or two days' absence from their farms each week. In such areas small farmers are found in larger numbers, often with their own primitive processing equipment. (In certain more remote areas, where the alternative of occupying free public lands still exists, many families prefer to work on large holdings. There is a great complex of social as well as economic reasons for this, but undoubtedly the small farmer's more limited access to market outlets and farm-processing equipment is a factor.)

More generally, it is clear that the marketing structure of the northeast is inferior to that of the south. Its much greater dependence on major street fairs reflects the comparative lack of standardization, a deficiency that makes purchase by inspection mandatory. Processing facilities are fewer, less efficient, and less competitive, and waste of byproducts is greater, particularly in cattle slaughter. In a region characterized by frequent and often disastrous droughts, storage facilities are still quite inadequate even for seasonal price stabilization. Fewer farmers have easy access to the purchased farm inputs necessary to agricultural modernization. Frequently public agricultural services are inaccessible, making efficient use of the inputs difficult or impossible, and even where possible, too expensive for most farmers because low volume demand for such inputs keeps their price up. Nonetheless, even within the northeast, one can perceive at least the beginnings of regional (and national) economic integration and a more efficient marketing system as transportation improvements and regional urban growth proceed apace.

In addition, the increasing toll of outmigration has tended to unite the citizenry (including even the large landholders) of many provincial towns in the necessity of local industrialization to keep their young people at home.

Finally, the federal government, both through the large regional development agency (SUDENE) and directly, is at last making a major effort, administrative and financial, to improve the infrastructure of the northeast, particularly its highways, education, and electric power. It is also trying to help the area catch up in the race for economic development, promoting industrialization primarily through very generous income-tax exemptions to private enterprise for building new plants in this disadvantaged region. The problems of establishing economically viable industrial plants in the northeast are still formidable, and one can easily find arguments against using scarce capital resources there, rather than in the still only partially developed southeast. However, on balance, it would appear that the time has arrived for the southeast to be thrown back largely upon its own resources (except that public support of measures for raising its agricultural productivity should continue, with readjustments for better balance). Undeniably, the policy of subsidization must be wisely administered. (The recent establishment of an automobile assembly plant in Recife gives the optimist pause on that score.) However, the northeast's indirect subsidization of the south at the price of the neglect of its agriculture and the loss of its sons—consequences of a public policy that hit that largely rural area harder than any other— has perhaps continued too long. In the northeast, even more than in the southeast, planning for industrial development should aim above all for greater nonfarm employment, and should probably give full consideration to the agricultural resources—particularly in the form of a high potential productivity in raw materials—with which the region is endowed. A balanced industrial-development program will also require much additional public investment in the northeast's agricultural agencies (especially those concerned with research) as well as in primary education and public health.

A Concluding Parable

Although the northeast's Golden Age in the preindustrial era came to naught, São Paulo and the southeast have clearly entered their own Golden Age of self-sustaining economic development. It seems not unreasonable to expect that they can expand this prosperity to encompass

fully the rest of Brazil. As Brazil continues to enlist the economic assistance of the more advanced nations in this endeavor, it would appear
quite appropriate for these other nations to insist, as a *quid pro quo,*
that Brazil's richer regions lend a helping hand to the poorer. The
paulista of today, aware of his undisputed energy and present economic
superiority, has a tendency toward excessive provinciality and egocen-
tricity. These attitudes are untrue to the pioneering tradition of the
paulistas, whose leading role in the exploration and settlement of an
entire nation could well be paralleled within the very different context
of current development.

Perhaps the *paulista* should reevaluate the appropriateness of his joke
that São Paulo is the locomotive pulling twenty freight cars—the other
states. Certainly this was accurate enough when that locomotive was
Coffee, and for a time it remained accurate even when a stronger locomotive (Industry) was added. Somewhere along the line, however, the
older locomotive was put on a siding where, though it was no longer
pulling anything, someone kept its steam up. Meanwhile, the newer
locomotive pulled faster than ever. The accelerated movement was due
in part to the excellence of the engineer (a *paulista,* of course) but, in
even greater part, to the fact that half of the cars (the north-northeast)
had been uncoupled and their contents removed and used to fuel the
Industrial locomotive—and, occasionally, the old Coffee locomotive as
well! When the *paulista* (with his southern neighbors close behind) became aware of the rapidly increasing gap between his own train and the
abandoned cars at a standstill far to the rear, he was faced with a difficult choice. He could try to forget them, he could back up, or he could
look for a second locomotive and engineer for the stalled cars. While
debating the alternatives, he made a new discovery: Someone had added
a caboose (Agriculture) to each train, with the one on the rear train
much heavier and considerably more in need of new ball-bearings and
axle-grease. What should he do?

In our story, at least, the *paulista* found for the second train another
engineer and a locomotive of the Industrial type at least half as good as
his own, filled up the empty cars, and—substituting additional competent
engineers and pusher-locomotives of the Agricultural type for the drag
of the two cabooses—arrived at a wholly successful solution. Shouldn't
one hope for as much in the Brazilian reality of today?

Comment

G. EDWARD SCHUH, PURDUE UNIVERSITY

Nicholls' paper is in four parts. In the first part he discusses the repeated booms and retrogressions that characterized the first four centuries of Brazilian history. In the second part he turns to the rise of São Paulo since the beginning of the twentieth century. In the third he examines the role of industrial-urban development in transforming Brazilian agriculture in the decade 1940–50, and in the fourth and final part he surveys Brazilian agricultural development since 1950.

I have chosen to direct most of my attention to part three. Here we find the heart of his analysis in what Nicholls has indicated is an original piece of empirical research on the interrelationships between the industrial and agricultural sectors of the Brazilian economy.

Before turning to this, however, I would like to compliment Professor Nicholls on an excellent job of integrating a great deal of empirical knowledge and background material into a fascinating story of the development of Brazil. Professor Nicholls is most knowledgeable on the Brazilian agricultural sector. He has gained this knowledge through an extensive study of the Brazilian literature as well as empirically, through his continuing research activities on the country. He approaches the wealth of empirical data at his fingertips with the aid of a broad analytical framework that enables him to integrate and synthesize these data in a most effective way. As a result, his work is full of fruitful insights.

The first part of the paper treats the repeated booms and retrogressions of the first four centuries of Brazil's history. Although they played a major role in the shaping of modern-day Brazil, none of these periods of strong economic activity were self-sustaining nor did they lead to self-sustaining development. The perplexing problem to the development economist, of course, is why?

Nicholls speculates as to possible reasons for this. In part he feels that the cycles themselves resulted in a speculative and exploitive spirit of "getting what you can while the getting's good," with a perennial failure to plow back even a small fraction of large current earnings into the capital improvements and better techniques which might have preserved the income base even within agriculture. In addition, he suggests as important factors: (1) the static and routinized production system which arose because of the dependence on slave labor, (2) an unwillingness to protect local industry with tariff walls, (3) an agrarian philosophy that viewed industrial-urban life with contempt, and (4) the very strong orientation of the Brazilian settlers to their European homeland—in contrast to their North American counterparts. These factors were complicated by the outright prohibition of manufacturing by Portugal during the colonial period and the effective prevention of industrial protectionism at a later date by the privileged trade position given to England.

After this long series of booms and busts, however, one boom finally led to the development of an industrial-urban complex which appears to have the potential for putting Brazil on the road to self-sustaining growth and development. What is the explanation for this? Once again, the boom was of agricultural origin, and in its early phases it did not seem to be greatly different from the previous cycles. Nicholls once again provides insights into the factors that made the difference.

He argues that the existence of vast virgin lands for continual exploitation of coffee, the transportation improvements that made these lands accessible, and the more venturesome spirit of the *paulistas* and new immigrant class were contributory factors lacking in the earlier cycles. Perhaps of more importance, he suggests, was the recognition of the validity of industrialization as a goal, a willingness to imitate the industrial protectionist policies of the United States, and a series of fortuitous events, such as the two world wars, that stimulated the development of domestic industry. Industrial development was facilitated by policies designed to siphon the surplus from the agricultural sector into industrialization.

In a capsule, then, agriculture served as the *base* for Brazil's rapidly growing industrial sector. For a long period this industrialization was evolutionary, but in the last two decades it has been largely government induced. It is highly concentrated in the state of São Paulo, and this high concentration has led to large regional disparities in per capita income levels, despite the fact that subsequent industrial-urban growth has been spreading into other states.

In the next section of his paper Nicholls addresses himself to the problem of how this rather highly concentrated development can be transmitted to the remainder of the country. This is the basis of part three of his paper in which he examines the role of industrial-urban development in transforming the agricultural sector.

At this point there is a significant shift in the investigative approach. Whereas previously he had emphasized the role of agriculture in the development of the industrial sector, the author now turns to a discussion of how industrial-urban development affects agriculture.

The Industrial-Urban Hypothesis

The analytical framework that Nicholls uses in this part of his paper is based on the conception of Dr. Schultz, as expounded in his book, *The Economic Organization of Agriculture.*[1] Schultz was concerned with two aspects of the agricultural development of an already mature economy, that of the United States. The first of these was the tendency for agriculture to experience secular low-income problems as the country developed. This he explained on the basis of (a) the low-income elasticity of demand for farm products, (b) labor-saving technological change in farm production as elsewhere in the economy, (c) farm-product-saving technological changes in the marketing and consumption sectors, and (d) the high fertility rate of farm relative to nonfarm people. These factors require a continual adjustment of the labor force out of the agricultural sector, and the mechanism by which this is accomplished in a market economy is through low relative incomes for farm people.

The second aspect of agricultural development that concerned Schultz was the spatial difference in labor incomes within the agricultural sector. Most obviously significant, of course, was the fact that the poverty problems of U.S. agriculture had significant regional dimensions. On investigation it turned out that the low income factor connected with U.S. agriculture was concentrated in the South, and was not characteristic of the agricultural sector as a whole.

To explain this Schultz developed a theory of spatial development that has come to be known as the industrial-urban hypothesis. Briefly summarized, this hypothesis is as follows: (a) economic growth in a country occurs at different locations and at different times, (b) the centers of growth are primarily industrial-urban in composition, (c) the existing economic organization functions best at or near the center of a particular matrix of economic development and also in those agricultural zones situated favorably in relation to such a matrix.

Thus, the income level of agriculture in a community which experiences industrial-urban growth can be expected to increase relative to that in a community which does not experience such growth. Moreover, because of a spatial adjustment lag, the closer a community is to an

---

[1] Theodore W. Schultz, *The Economic Organization of Agriculture*, New York, 1953.

industrial-urban center, the higher would be the income level of agriculture in the community.

Schultz goes on to argue that there are three factors accompanying industrial growth which create regional income disparities:

(1) An increase in the proportion of the population engaged in productive work.

(2) An increase in the productivity of the labor force, from such factors as increased investments in education.

(3) A reduction in the impediments to factor-price equalization, or a reduction in the imperfections in the factor and product markets faced by agriculture.

This hypothesis has been tested in the United States economy by Ruttan,[2] Nicholls,[3] Tang,[4] Sisler,[5] Bachmura,[6] Sinclair,[7] and Bryant.[8] The results of these studies have not been uniformly favorable to the hypothesis, and as a result the theory has been refined and extended to a more general framework.

The results, in brief form, are as follows: Ruttan, Nicholls, and Tang, each of them working with the Southeastern United States, found the data to be consistent with the hypothesis. Bachmura obtained similar results for the lower Mississippi Valley, as did Sinclair for the South as a whole. Sisler and Bryant, extended the analysis to include the total United States and found the hypothesis to be lacking. Sisler found that the hypothesis was borne out by the data from east of the Mississippi, but not by the data from west of the Mississippi. Bryant, using a larger analytical frame of reference and a different set of data, obtained results similar to those of Sisler. He found that east of the Mississippi River, the closer a county is to an industrial complex and the larger the complex, the higher are the earnings of farmers. However, the reverse is true in the

[2] V. W. Ruttan, "The Impact of Urban-Industrial Development on Agriculture in the Tennessee Valley and the Southeast," *Journal of Farm Economics* 37:38–56, February 1955.

[3] William H. Nicholls, "Industrialization, Factor Markets, and Agricultural Development," *Journal of Political Economy* 69:319–340, August 1961.

[4] A. M. Tang, *Economic Development in South Piedmont, 1860–1950,* Chapel Hill, 1958.

[5] D. G. Sisler, "Regional Differences in the Impact of Urban-Industrial Development on Farm and Nonfarm Income," *Journal of Farm Economics* 41:1100–13, December 1959.

[6] Frank T. Bachmura, "Migration and Factor Adjustment in Lower Mississippi Valley Agriculture: 1940–50," *Journal of Farm Economics* 38:1024–42, November 1956.

[7] Lewis S. Sinclair, "Urbanization and the Incomes of Farm and Nonfarm Families in the South," *Journal of Farm Economics* 39:510–516, May 1957.

[8] W. Keith Bryant, "Causes of Inter-County Variations in Farmers' Earnings," *Journal of Farm Economics* 48:557–577, August 1966.

divisions west of the Mississippi. Hence, the hypothesis not only failed for the western part of the United States, but a relationship was found which operated in the opposite direction to that postulated.

In understanding the Schultz analytic method and Nicholls' application of it, it is important to put them both in their proper frame of reference. Schultz was writing from the standpoint of a mature economy, as most of us would define it, but an economy in which there were substantial regional income disparities within the agricultural sector. He was not concerned with the problem, currently receiving so much attention in developing countries, of how agriculture can be made more productive so that it can contribute to the industrial development of the country.

Nicholls, in the present study, also examines the part of an economy on its way to development; one in which a strong industrial sector is in place, and in which wage rates are much higher than can be obtained in the agricultural sector. When this fortunate situation exists, the question arises, "How can the gains from industrial development be distributed on as wide a base as possible?" In the U.S. economy, the work of Nicholls and others has led us to argue that *local* economic development programs should be tied to nearby growth centers. The important point to recognize is that under these circumstances the problems encountered are quite different from those connected with the agriculture of most of the underdeveloped world.

With this as a background, I would like to consider three aspects of the analysis in part three of Nicholls' paper:

The Direction of Causality

The frame of reference of the analysis is such that causality flows from industrialization, as a process *exogenous* to agriculture, to the agricultural sector. Nicholls does admit, however, that the cause-effect relationship between industrialization and the agricultural indexes in São Paulo is not at all clear. I would agree. In fact, I would argue strongly for a reverse direction of causality.

The Tennessee Valley, where Nicholls successfully used the industrial-urban hypothesis to show what was taking place, offered a set of conditions greatly different from those in the state of São Paulo. In the Tennessee Valley, the agriculture at the beginning of the study period was largely stagnant. The process of industrialization was imposed from the outside, and came largely as an exogenous shock to the system. Clearly this had an impact on the agricultural sector, and the *a priori* evidence on the direction of causality was rather clear.

The case of São Paulo is quite different, however. The state ranks high in agricultural resources. The agricultural sector has been dynamic and growing rapidly, with rather large increases in total factor productivity over time. Moreover, the evidence from numerous sources is that agriculture contributed heavily to the development of the industrial complex of São Paulo. Not only did the government transfer substantial capital from agriculture to industry through an ingenious use of multiple exchange rates and outright confiscation of exchange earnings, but agricultural entrepreneurs also invested rather heavily in the industrial sector. This was very important in the period covered by Nicholls' study. At the present time, some seventeen years later, it is my impression that the net flow is still from agriculture to industry, although there may be some areas of the state in which the direction is opposite. This makes me question whether causality can be assumed to run in the direction that Nicholls has postulated.

The Role of Increased Efficiency in the Factor and Product Markets

In their work on the Southeastern United States, both Tang and Nicholls have stressed the third set of factors accompanying industrial growth as originally stressed by Schultz—these can be summarized as follows: that industrial growth reduces the imperfections in the factor and product markets faced by agriculture and hence raises farm income per worker. Nicholls has carried this over to his Brazil work and argues that what is happening is a reduction in the imperfections in the markets.

Keith Bryant [9] has argued rather effectively that the role of imperfections has been overemphasized in these analyses. He demonstrates that in the case of the United States many of the observed relationships can be understood as a straight-out influx of capital from the industrial sector and that no appeal need be made to the reduction of imperfections in the markets. On the contrary, he argues, the evidence on a reduction in market imperfections is simply not there.

In addition, he maintains that the effect of industrial-urban development on agriculture is in large measure a question of *agglomeration*. The literature on agglomeration emphasizes the effects of economies of scale, localization economics, and urbanization economies on firms in industrial-urban complexes. The counterparts in the agricultural case are as follows:

[9] W. Keith Bryant, "Industrial-Urbanization and the Spatial Distribution of Income in Agriculture," Proceedings, *Workshop on Income Distribution Analysis*, North Carolina State University, June 1966.

(1) The expansion of the nonfarm labor markets increases the numbers and kinds of jobs available to prospective migrants. This speeds up the migration process as the opportunity cost of labor rises and thereby forces the reorganization of agriculture.

(2) A similar set of forces works in the credit market, with more credit at lower interest rates being made available to agriculture.

(3) The local demand for farm products grows as the urban population expands. At some point the market is large enough so that local agriculture can operate at a lower average cost—either because of increased specialization or because of the realization of economies of size.

(4) With the agglomeration, more social-overhead capital is provided. This means roads, which lower transportation costs, and improved educational facilities, which increase labor mobility and raise labor productivity.

These are the same kinds of factors that turn up in Nicholls' discussion. But it is important to recognize that they do not necessarily imply a reduction in market imperfections.

The Policy Implications

Nicholls' paper is somewhat disappointing in its failure to distill out the policy implications of his findings. One is led by implication to believe that industrialization may be important in transforming or modernizing the agricultural sector. Yet I doubt very much whether this is the solution in most underdeveloped countries. It seems to me that the development in many cases has to start with the agricultural sector, where most of the resources are, and proceed to raise the productivity there so that the resources for industrialization become available.

To make the issue clear, I would pose the question: "Where should we put the next $1 million of developmental resources for the northeast of Brazil—in agricultural research and extension, or in industrialization?"

Agricultural Planning: The Peruvian Experience

HYLKE VAN DE WETERING

IOWA STATE UNIVERSITY, AMES

THE ROLE of the agricultural sector in the economic growth of Peru is complex. The Peruvian government has pursued a protectionist policy with respect to domestic industrial production, but has preferred to rely on international suppliers in the case of wheat, beef, and dairy products. It is the national policy to provide the urban consumer with a low-cost food basket. In those instances in which domestic supply cannot meet domestic demand at prevailing market prices, the central government has followed a general policy of duty free imports.

Total public expenditure in agriculture through the budget of the central government averaged 930 million soles for 1964 and 1965.[1] Fiscal revenues from agricultural export taxes and import duties on agricultural inputs and capital goods averaged 725 million soles for

NOTE: The author served as a member of the Iowa Mission to Peru. He acted as advisor to the Agricultural Sector Planning Office (OSPA) of the Ministry of Agriculture and as technical director of a study on long-term demand and supply projections of major crop and livestock products sponsored by the Agricultural University of LaMolina, the United States Department of Agriculture (USDA), the Agreement on Technical Cooperation in Statistics and Cartography (CONESTCAR) and the National Planning Institute (INP). The author would like to acknowledge his indebtedness to his many Peruvian associates, in particular Carlos Amat y Leon, Rafael Otero M., and Jose Salaverry Ll. of the Agricultural University at LaMolina, Walter Petrovitch H. of the INP, Mario Cuneo M., Dr. A. Angulo A. OSPA and Roberto Valverde P. of the Agricultural Development Bank.

[1] Republic of Peru: Ministerio de Hacienda, *El Presupuesto Funcional de la República*, Lima, Peru, 1964 and 1965.

these years.[2] The above figures, in conjunction with figures for earlier years, show that producers of export crops have contributed the major share of the financial resources that the public sector allocated for agricultural development. Such funds were used principally in the promotion of food crop production.

The imposition of duties on food imports could generate sufficient revenue to double the financial resources currently allocated to agriculture. Our study shows (see Table 11) that if such funds were used exclusively in the promotion of domestic production of cereals, tubers, beans, and pulses, the productivity index of these food groups could increase by about 4 per cent per year. The funds currently projected available for the promotion of these food groups are so small that they fall short of inducing a 1 per cent increase in over-all productivity.

The Peruvian government has done little to encourage the expansion of export crops; in fact the principal export crops (cotton, sugar, and coffee) are subject to taxation, while food crops are not. Export crops generated 35 per cent of the gross value of agricultural production in 1964.[3] Prior to 1960 the value of production of export crops expanded at a rate of 8.3 per cent per year, but in the early 1960's this rate slowed down to 2.9 per cent because of increasing competition in slowly expanding international markets and worsening cost-price relationships at home.[4] The relative stagnation in the agricultural sector in the last few years stemmed principally from the slow rate of growth of the agricultural export sector. The above loss of potential export earnings was not critical, because of the rapid expansion of export earnings in minerals and fishmeal products.

The Ministry of Agriculture has traditionally favored a policy of expanding acreage in food crops at the expense of acreage in export crops. About 65 per cent of the land in food crops is grown by operators who farm less than 5 hectares.[5] Consequently the public sector in agriculture has chosen to work with small producers, an effort that in recent years has been intensified through the agrarian reform program. Commercial producers have been reluctant to shift toward food crops for

[2] Ministerio de Hacienda, Instituto Nacional de Planificación [INP] Dirección del Sector Público, *Recaudación de Impuestos y Otros Recursos,* Lima, Peru, 1967. (private communication)

[3] Convenio de Cooperacíon Técnica Estadística y Cartografía [CONESTCAR], *Estadística Agraria Perú 1964,* Lima, Peru, 1965, pp. 34–36.

[4] Republic of Peru: Ministerio de Agricultura, Oficina Sectorial de Planificación Agropecuaria [OSPA] *Diagnostico Agropecuaria,* Lima, Peru, 1966, p. 35.

[5] CONESTCAR: *Muestreo Agropecuario Nacional 1964,* Lima, Peru, 1967. (private communication)

immediate human consumption or for animal use because of the very limited domestic markets for these commodities. Production of feed grain for use in the livestock industry is of very limited importance in Peru, partly because domestic livestock production is not competitive with imports and partly because the periodicity in internal-cost inflation and devaluation makes it difficult to obtain long-run commitments from commercial producers to specialize in food grains or livestock production.

Existing price controls and enabling legislation are spread among national and municipal authorities and are designed almost exclusively to favor the urban consumer, thereby eliminating the price incentive to the domestic producer and defeating the public expenditure on agricultural research and extension.[6] Although the government has repeatedly expressed its concern about the slow rate of growth in domestic food production, the financial resources made available to the agricultural sector through the budget of the central government have remained a small and constant proportion of the total budget.

In more general terms, the Peruvian government in its effort to transform the nation into a modern industrial society is faced with the fact that its objectives for the agricultural sector conflict with those for other sectors. Cheap food increases the real income of urban wage earners and helps to expand fishmeal and mining exports. On the other hand, the marked rural poverty of the central and southern Sierra could gravitate into an explosive social disequilibrium unless many landless peasants are given a subsistence base. A stable exchange rate, in the face of internal cost inflation, provides a low-cost food basket for the urban consumer but may well dampen the expansion of export crops that could be used to finance capital imports for industrial development. Most important of all, the expansion of social services, transport, and energy development severely strains available public budgetary resources.

It is difficult to say at which stage of economic development the urban sector can afford a transfer of income to the rural sector. It is a decision that cannot be made in terms of economic efficiency only, but must rest on considerations of equity as well. Agricultural planners in Peru typically think that the latter should outweigh the former, but they do not have the power to reduce income and land distribution inequities more than marginally.

[6] Geoffrey Shepherd and Dale B. Furnish, *The Economic and Legal Aspects of Price Controls in Peruvian Agriculture,* Iowa Universities Mission to Peru in cooperation with the Agency for International Development, Lima, Peru, 1967, pp. 25 ff.

Because of a lack of technical expertise, the planning concept was limited to drastic changes in institutional structure or output targets. Neither had much relation to available public resources or other considerations such as political, technical, and historical feasibility. The first draft of the 1967–70 agricultural development plan did not go beyond a statement of general objectives justified in terms of observations on existing deficiencies in production, consumption, marketing, credit, etc., with little quantification of these deficiencies or attempt to establish their interconnection.[7] In constructing a planning methodology the learning process proved to be frustrating and very time consuming. The constant need to produce a preliminary planning document precluded the possibility of a systematic or comprehensive approach or of executing a broader economic analysis of the projected performance of the agricultural sector than contemplated by the planners.

In Peru the bulk of public expenditure in agriculture does not go directly into the creation of products, but into either the acquisition of knowledge or the redistribution of land. It is funnelled through some twenty agencies, each with its own special objectives and all competing for scarce financial and technical resources.[8] Most agencies have several regional offices, creating thereby an administrative structure that in theory is well adapted to handle the diversified needs of the agricultural producer in various parts of the country. In practice it has been very difficult to assess the product-creating effect of the various agencies, even in those few cases where the agency is directly concerned with the expansion of land resources or the improvement in the productivity of existing land. It is clear therefore that the product-investment nexus is not easily ascertainable in Peru.

Since most planning models are based on an implicit causality between investment and production and the control choices that can be derived therefrom, they may not be readily applicable to the case of Peru. I suspect that the Peruvian situation is rather typical of both developed and underdeveloped countries. In the latter the importance of public expenditure in agriculture can easily be overrated in relation to the impact of legislative, fiscal, monetary and price policies. In fact, an examination of the factors contributing to agricultural growth in Peru in the period 1950–64 would, on balance, give little reason to impute positive importance to either public expenditure or the set of

[7] Ministry of Agriculture, OSPA, *Peru's Agriculture: Summary of Diagnosis, Objectives, Strategy and Policy,* Lima, Peru, 1966.

[8] Oficina Nacional de Reforma de la Administración Pública, *Diagnostico y Reformas por Sectores, Sector Agrícola,* Lima, Peru, 1967, p. 355.

measures taken by the public sector relative to agriculture. The impact of planned public expenditure in agriculture is likely to remain relatively modest compared to autonomous increases in production or to those induced through expanding internal and external markets.

Agricultural planners in Peru are typically somewhat impatient with the role of free markets in achieving a satisfactory rate of growth in agricultural production. A more activist approach is preferred, putting great emphasis on public investment in agriculture. To the extent that such investment can be redirected at will, it is expected to play an important role in redressing regional imbalances in agricultural progress. Economic growth in other sectors has been largely restricted to the urban and coastal zone. The government has relied heavily on public expenditure in agriculture as the main instrument in achieving a more equitable pattern of development. Consequently both agrarian reform and promotion of agriculture were forcibly redirected to zones with the lowest economic potential.

In most underdeveloped countries the bulk of the increase in production is achieved through expansion of the land base rather than through yield increases. Peru is no exception. The Ministry of Agriculture, as well as the semiindependent public sector in agriculture, is staffed almost exclusively by technicians who received their academic training in the life sciences. This explains the widely held professional opinion that increased production is most readily achieved through increased yields. Agricultural planners are of the same background and have not fully adjusted to the need to consider a broader range of planning variables such as irrigation, colonization, and price policies.

The idea of planning implies that the planner may reasonably consider a number of alternatives. To the extent that agricultural planning focuses on the role of public expenditure in agriculture such planning is concerned with maintaining a reasonable degree of flexibility with respect to the total amount of expenditure made available for agricultural development from the budget of the central government or external sources. But, in fact, agriculture's share of the national budget throughout the period 1951–65 has been small and virtually constant.[9] It is true that public expenditure has grown more rapidly than the gross domestic income but, for public investment in agriculture to have a

[9] International Bank for Reconstruction and Development, *The Agricultural Development of Peru, Part 2, Detailed Report* (report of a mission organized by the Food and Agriculture Organization of the United Nations and the International Bank for Reconstruction and Development at the request of the government of Peru), Washington, D.C., 1959, p. 35; and *Presupuesto Funcional de le República,* Lima, Peru, 1958–65.

measurable impact upon agricultural growth, it must show a much sharper acceleration. The most important annual budget decisions are those that create new activities within the budget. It is essentially this component that gives some flexibility between years. Since such activities usually refer to new institutional activities (e.g., the creation of CONAP, CONESTCAR, ONRA, OSPA),[10] they are not variables that readily enter into a quantitative model of economic growth. Most growth models are relatively strong on behavioral relationships between major macroeconomic variables, but are relatively lacking in those variables that enter into public revenue and expenditure accounts, the structure of internal and external public debt, and the balance of payments. If a growth model is to be used for planning purposes, ideally it should provide suggested courses of action for the principal instrumental variables entering into the public accounts. In a second stage, the aggregated public accounts must be decomposed on a sectoral basis and subsequently on an agency basis. Presumably, there is an infinite number of ways to decompose a given total between the various public accounts. In practice the momentum of existing programs will, in the main, dictate the method of sectoral decomposition of planned total public expenditure. Peruvian agricultural planners have focused their attention almost exclusively on the role of public expenditure in relation to agrarian reform and the improvement of rural income levels in the Sierra, to the detriment of either commercial agriculture or the urban consumer.

The easy and arbitrary manner in which normative positions are taken with respect to both the ends and means of agricultural planning in Peru is very disconcerting to a visiting foreign adviser. At the same time, to assume that past policies are the norm for the future is equally dangerous. Paradoxically therefore, it is no simple matter to ascertain the objectives of agricultural planning. For example, it is not clear whether the government aims to tax private urban consumption expenditure to support agricultural development, or whether the agricultural sector is to be taxed in an indirect manner to support urban industrial development. A reading of the National Development Plan [11] would suggest the former, but a consultation of existing legislation [12] and budget allocations would suggest the latter.

[10] Corporación Nacional de Abastecimientos (CONAP), Convenio de Cooperación Técnica Estadística y Cartografía (CONESTCAR), Oficina Nacional de Reforma Agraria (ONRA), Oficina Sectorial de Planificación Agropecuaria (OSPA).

[11] Ministerio de Hacienda, INP, *Plan de Desarrollo Económico y Social 1967–1970,* Lima, Peru, 1967, p. 127.

[12] See, El Congreso de la República Peruana, *Ley de Creación del Ministerio de Agricultura No. 9711,* Jan. 2, 1943, Tit. 1; El Congreso de la República

Agricultural planners, perhaps because of their background in the life sciences, have been reluctant to study the financing of agricultural development. This emphasizes the need for agricultural economists with experience in macroeconomic analysis. Where a national planning institute exists, the above information can be adopted instead of having to be generated first hand. On the other hand carrying out the financial and macroeconomic analyses within the agricultural planning office would have the advantage of strengthening the stature of planners who in a hierarchichal sense take their directives from planners interested in more global objectives.

The financial resources available to the agricultural sector on current account are allocated principally through the budget of the central government. For many agencies this is the only source of funding. Other agencies derive considerable revenue from earmarked tax revenue. All the larger agencies in agriculture derive a considerable part of their revenue on capital account. External debts are important for the agencies in charge of agricultural credit, promotion, irrigation, and colonization. Internal debts are important principally for the agrarian reform agency and agricultural development bank. Given the limited availability of these resources much of the desired acceleration of the land reform process will depend on the possibility of attracting international financing.

To date, revenue and expenditure accounts are only partially available to the agricultural planners. The construction of such a set of accounts is a painstaking process complicated by the fact that expenditure and revenue data are itemized for control purposes rather than for programming or functional purposes. From a pragmatic point of view, the budgeting and the program evaluation processes are the most important and time-consuming components of agricultural planning. In both these areas substantial improvements in methodology are needed. Both budgeting and evaluation should order accounting data in such a way that a cost and output estimate can be assigned to the various proposed activities of the agency. The establishment of programming offices within each

Peruana, *Ley de Promoción y Desarrollo Agropecuario del Pais, Especialmente la Producción de Articulos Alimentosos y Normal Abastecimiento No. 16726,* Oct. 27, 1967 (general dispositions); Dale B. Furnish, *Investigaciones Legales de las Estructuras de Comercialización Agropecuaria en el Perú: Trigo;* and *Un Análisis de las Leyes Sobre el Ganado y la Carne en el Perú,* Iowa Universities Mission to Peru in cooperation with the Agency for International Development, December 1967; Raul L. Munoz Cabrera, *Investigaciones Legales de las Estructuras de Comercialización Agropecuaria en el Perú: Aceite y Grasas Comestibles,* Iowa Universities Mission to Peru in cooperation with the Agency for International Development, Lima, Peru, 1967 (unpublished).

agency has been only partially successful in reshaping agency accounts. In practice the programming offices have played an important role only in formulating the preliminary budget requests submitted to the Ministry of Finance. The constant scarcity of funds has put the programming offices under considerable pressure to overestimate the impact of their proposed activities and to underestimate the cost of carrying these activities out. Since the fiscal situation is so variable between years, few agencies document their needed financial resources beyond next year's budget request. Consequently, the problem of how to finance agricultural development on a longer run basis has never been studied in detail.

In the absence of functionally classified public expenditure data, no substantive generalization can be made about the cost of transforming traditional agriculture. Theoretical studies of agricultural development focus on the endogenous variables and their logical interrelationships. Certain exogenous variables like population, the subsistence wage rate, or technological progress have also been considered, but little or no attention has been given to instrumental variables. Yet, the main focus in agricultural planning should be precisely on instrumental variables corresponding to individual decision-making units. The reasons for this are as follows. First, planning necessarily takes place in a decentralized system where decision makers at the lower levels do not necessarily think in terms of the same performance concepts as decision makers at the top levels. Second, the performance concepts maximized at the lower levels of the hierarchy may be in direct conflict with over-all objectives. It is of course the function of the planners to resolve such conflicts. In a centralized planning system this would be carried on by decree. In the Peruvian decentralized situation it would have to be done through persuasion, a method with little chance of success under present conditions. Formally, the issue can be resolved through casting the planning process in mathematical form and optimizing a social welfare function. However, there is not enough agreement on the role of agricultural development in Peru to permit weighting of objectives.

Taking the above observations as a point of departure, we decided that the preliminary agricultural development plan should limit itself to determining in a systematic manner the feasible rate of growth, rather than the optimal rate of growth or optimal allocation of public expenditure.

To determine the feasible rate of growth in agriculture we studied the major exogenous and endogenous variables in agricultural development. The specific variables considered were population, gross domestic income, public revenue and expenditure accounts, balance of payments, exchange rate, indexes of land productivity, trends in land use, agricultural labor force, intermediate inputs used in agriculture, prices paid and received by farmers, agricultural taxation, agricultural credit, proposed public land expansion and productivity programs (including their financial requirements), and other public expenditure in agriculture. The above variables were used to develop three alternative hypotheses concerning the rate of growth in agricultural production. By estimating the growth in demand, decomposed by region and rural and urban areas, we obtained targets that domestic development in supply had to meet if reliance on imports were to be reduced.

An increase in domestic supply comes about through an increase in either cultivated acreage or yield levels. In the Ricardian theory of economic growth an increase in cultivated acreage, barring technological progress, is associated with decreasing average yield levels.[13] In our study we assumed that yields were independent of the expansion in the land base since too little is known about the quality of Peruvian soils under actual and proposed cultivation.[14] Historically, cultivated acreage in food and export crops grew at the same rate as population, and it seemed reasonable to project a continuation of that tendency in the period 1967–70, allowing for a decrease in cultivated acreage in export crops. Total cultivated acreage was decomposed simultaneously by individual crops and by groups of crops in three regions (see page 435). Given the projected increase in cultivated acreage we considered the feasibility of the projected increases for each region. For this purpose the land use limits as given in the preliminary land inventory [15] and the proposed public investment in irrigation and colonization were consulted.

With respect to yield increases we explored three hypotheses. Under the first hypothesis the general yield index would increase at its historical rate, that is, zero per cent per year. Under the second and third hypotheses the general yield index was to increase annually by one per cent and two per cent, respectively. The projections were carried out in two stages. First, the general productivity hypothesis was adopted, and then the indexes of yields by groups or crops or individual crops were determined simultaneously by regions (see pages 422–23). The projected increases in yields were separated into two components, those induced by agricultural research and extension programs, and those due to autonomous

[13] H. Barkai, "Ricardo on Factor Prices and Income Distribution in a Growing Economy," *Economica (New Series)*, Vol. 26, pp. 240–250, August 1959.

[14] Oficina Nacional de Evaluación de Recursos Naturales [ONERN], *Capacidad de Uso de los Suelos del Perú*, Lima, Peru, 1965.

[15] J. C. Paez, *et al.*, Diagnostico Agrario, Ministerio de Agricultura, Servicio de Investigación y Promoción Agraria [SIPA], Lima, Peru, 1964 (mimeo.).

developments not related to activities in the public sector. The latter are captured in the main by a projection of trends in past yields. We also took account of the fact that induced productivity increases modify the past trends in yields. The projected yield levels for 1970, according to the three hypotheses, were compared with the impact that planned productivity programs [16] are expected to have in 1970. From this comparison it developed that the proposed programs, if fully funded, would be barely sufficient to accelerate the general yield index by one per cent per year (see Table 11).

Given the respective hypotheses relative to expansion in acreage and yield improvements, it is a simple matter to compute the projected expansion in production. Using enterprise budgets from the Agricultural Development Bank [17] and the Agricultural Promotion and Research Service [18] we computed the necessary labor requirements and intermediate inputs corresponding to the various production hypotheses. A previous detailed analysis on population growth by regions and by rural and urban areas yielded a provisional estimate of the growth in the agricultural labor force by regions. The projected growth in the available labor force was closely balanced with the projected labor requirements according to the production hypotheses.[19] Because of the limited acceleration in productivity and the typically low values for the input elasticities, commercial inputs like fertilizer and pesticides were projected to grow at approximately twice the rate of growth in production. Domestic, installed, manufacturing capacity can adequately cope with the projected expansion in commercial inputs. Subsequent sections deal in detail with the foregoing observations.

PROJECTED PERFORMANCE OF
THE ECONOMY

During the period 1950–64 the Peruvian economy grew at a rate substantially higher than the average for Latin America. The gross domestic

[16] See, Ministerio de Agricultura, SIPA, *Proyectos de Incremento de la Producción 1967–1970: de Papa; de Cereales-Avena-Quinua-Trigo-Cebada; de Arroz; de Maíz; de Menestras,* Lima, Peru, 1967.

[17] Harry Higgins and Roberto V. Piedra, *Zonificación y Sectorización Territorial—Costos Básicos de Producción Agrícola 1965,* Oficina de Planificación, Banco de Fomento Agropecuario del Perú, Lima, 1966 (mimeo.).

[18] Paez, *op. cit.*

[19] It was assumed that yield-increasing techniques would not be labor increasing.

income doubled between 1950 and 1964.[20] The principal factor permitting such rapid growth was the rapid expansion of fishmeal and mineral exports. The dollar value of exports tripled between 1950 and 1964. Since 1950 public investment and expenditure has absorbed an increasing share of the gross domestic product (GDP), reaching 16.5 per cent of final demand in 1964. At the same time, the stability of the exchange rate in the presence of a moderate but continuous decline in the domestic purchasing power of the Peruvian sol periodically eroded the profitability of agricultural and industrial exports. This erosion was an important factor in the most recent devaluation (September 1967).

The growth in GDP between 1950 and 1964 was accompanied by substantial changes in its sectoral composition. During this period the industrial sector increased its relative share from 15.6 per cent to 19.3 per cent, while that of the agricultural sector diminished from 25 per cent to 17.4 per cent.[21] The agricultural sector and the population grew virtually at the same rate; all other sectors grew at least twice as fast. Per capita income increases, except for the agriculturally employed segment of the population, were well above the minimum designated desirable at the Punta del Este meetings of 1961. The contrast between a viable economic future in urban-based occupations and the relative stagnation of per capita earnings in agricultural employment led to an accelerated migration of rural dwellers to the cities. But the growth of industrial activity with its related service complex was largely restricted to the Lima metropolitan area. Economic growth in Peru, therefore, was unbalanced among sectors and among regions. Population movements between census years reflect this increased dualism of the Peruvian economy. We project that for the period 1960–70 the rate of growth of the urban population in the coastal area will be at least 4.8 per cent per year, while the annual rate of growth of the rural population in the Sierra is not likely to exceed 0.9 per cent for the same period. The mobility of Peru's most ample resource, unskilled young labor, will continue to be a major factor in transforming the traditional economy. Official planning documents, however, reflect the belief that economic growth should be shared more equitably among regions and between urban and rural population groups. Therefore, public investment and expenditure plans call for a juxtaposition of the expected resource allocation on the basis of a complementary relationship between growth in private and public activities. Under this principle the "Plan de Desarrollo

[20] Ministerio de Hacienda, INP, *La Evolución de la Economía en el Período 1950–1964,* Vol. I, Lima, Peru, 1966.
[21] *Ibid.,* Vol. 3.

Económico y Social 1967–1970" [22] gave first priority to public investment projects related to agricultural activities in the central and southern Sierra.

The Peruvian industrial sector (excluding mining and fishmeal) is primarily oriented towards internal final demands. To meet these demands it relies heavily on imports of intermediate goods, capital goods, and raw materials. A rapid and sustained rate of growth in this sector is possible only with an equally dynamic export sector. Although the Peruvian export sector is diversified, it is nevertheless restricted to raw materials, such as fishmeal, cotton, sugar, and mineral exports. Reduction in export earnings has caused a reduction in industrial growth. To the extent that public revenue relies heavily on import duties and transaction and profit taxes, it tends to be reduced with decreases in industrial activity. Pursuit of a countercyclical or expansionary economic policy during recessions would lead to a sizeable budget deficit that would have to be financed externally or through domestic inflation. The Peruvian government prior to 1963 followed the conservative alternative of trying to adjust expenditures to revenues.

In more recent years the government has pursued an expansionist policy in the public sector. Expansion was most rapid in health, education, communication, and transportation. Savings on current account decreased rapidly. Prior to 1962 a large share of capital expenditure was financed by means of savings on current account. Subsequently, savings on current account decreased rapidly as the growth in public revenue failed to keep pace with the growing pressure of current expenditures. This brought about an increased dependence on foreign public capital, which means of course a growth in the public external debt with increased future interest and amortization payments. Recent projections by the National Planning Institute indicate that, in the event of a decline in copper prices, amortization and interest payments will exceed the traditional upper limit of 15 per cent of export earnings.

If high levels of public investment are to be maintained, the government will have to slow down the growth of current expenditure and generate additional tax revenue in order to meet the financial needs of the growing capital accounts. Tax revenue increases were less than proportional to public expenditure and investment. To meet the growing financial demands of public expenditure and investment it has been fiscally expedient to increase indirect taxes notably import duties. With the growing amortization and interest payments on the foreign public debt, the need for internal financing of public investment will increase and the case for tax reform will strengthen.

[22] *Plan de Desarrollo Económico y Social 1967–1970.*

The principal variables of the public accounts also enter into the national income accounts and balance of payments accounts; for example, the national income, balance of payments, and the public sector accounts are interdependent systems of economic variables. Because of the interdependence of the major macroeconomic accounts a macroeconomic model must be designed to provide the required consistency among the accounts and must be supplemented by projections of the complete balance of payments and public sector accounts. A comprehensive forecast of the performance of the economy must be made to provide agricultural planners with an estimate of the probable financial resources available (historically the proportion of financial resources made available to public agencies in the agricultural sector through the central budget has averaged below 3 per cent), the expected rate of growth in per capita income, and a good indication of whether or not devaluation of the domestic currency should be taken into account.

The Peruvian national development plan is based upon projections of the major macroeconomic variables and the principal components of the public expenditure and investment accounts. The plan lists as general objectives the attainment of increased production and productivity, a more equitable income distribution, increased employment, and reduced dependence on external financial assistance and export markets. Simple historical projections revealed that the above objectives were mutually incompatible unless a strongly accelerated capital formation could be financed out of savings on current account. Taxes as a proportion of gross domestic income would have to increase sharply, mostly at the price of reduced growth in urban consumption expenditure. Imports of durable consumer goods would have to be decreased very substantially as would imports of intermediate inputs and raw materials after domestic industries were established. The establishment of domestic industries would entail a very sharp initial rise in capital goods imports, but these would level off after a five-year period. Under the plan the agricultural sector would receive priority, first, because its rate of growth lagged well behind the other sectors, and second, because expansion of agricultural production was considered the principal means by which rural income levels could be raised. The plan does not detail the economic and legal studies or the investment projects that support the feasibility of the broad strategies sketched in the above paragraphs. It is consistent, however, in that, within an integrated system of national income and public-sector accounts, certain variables can be predetermined if a corresponding number of variables can be adjusted accordingly.

In the light of past experience the supposed flexibilities in the composition of imports, capital formation, and public revenue are doubtful.

The National Planning Institute did not execute or sponsor studies that might have shown how the required flexibility could be brought about. The plan, therefore, presents little more than a normative projection of important macroeconomic and fiscal variables.

Within the Peruvian planning system the agricultural planning office (OSPA) takes its broad directives from the National Planning Institute (INP), but serves simultaneously as an advisory arm to the Ministry of Agriculture. In the latter capacity OSPA had to decide whether the projected income growth and public investment program of INP were sufficiently realistic. The rapid rate of growth in per capital income forecast by INP would, particularly when skewed towards the rural population, accelerate the demand for domestic and imported foods considerably. This in turn would justify a considerable public investment in agriculture, particularly in those regions where the population was predominantly rural. On the other hand, if income growth was relatively low and restricted to the urban areas, as it historically has been, and if the government were forced into an austerity program and devaluation, then both the expansion of demand and the priorities of public expenditure in agriculture would be drastically altered.

Agricultural planning cannot reach an acceptable level of reliability without considerable preliminary research. In Peru few of the necessary basic economic studies have been made, or at least are available. Few opportunities exist to carry out basic research within a planning office, where data must be available at short notice.

The work of the USDA/CONESTCAR contract team was designed to fill, in a modest way, the above gap. This group carried out comprehensive studies producing population, income, price, demand, yield, acreage, and import-export projections as well as Engel curves and gathering data for price elasticities. The agricultural planning office produced corresponding studies on required labor and nonlabor inputs, the required public credit, the required public investment and expenditure that corresponded to three comprehensive groups of supply projections, and the projected availability of public finances for the agricultural sector.

To make projections of the major macroeconomic variables, one of the Thorbecke-Condos macroeconomic models was used.[23] The variables

[23] Erik Thorbecke and Apostolos Condos, "Macroeconomic Growth and Development Models of the Peruvian Economy," in Irma Adelman and Erik Thorbecke (ed.), *The Theory and Design of Economic Development,* Baltimore, 1966. The authors present three alternative models; the one employed in the present study is identified as "Model A." The model was reestimated using 1963 constant price time series.

included in the model are presented below with their corresponding symbols:

X = gross domestic income (GDI)

X^d = disposable GDI

Z = terms-of-trade effects

C = total consumption

C^p = private consumption

C^g = public consumption

I = total gross investment

I^p = private gross investment

I^g = public gross investment

M = total imports of goods and services

E = total exports of goods and services

T = total tax revenues

T^d = direct tax revenues

T^i = indirect tax revenues

It should be noted that GDI is being used instead of GNP or gross national income.[24] This is justified by the importance of the terms-of-trade effects in the past evolution of the Peruvian economy and by the relatively small magnitude of net transfers.

The symbol Z refers to the terms-of-trade effects, defined as the product of the terms-of-trade index and the value of exports at 1963 prices, taking the existing terms-of-trade index in 1963 as a basis and measuring deviations either positive or negative from the 1963 level. Symbolically:

$$Z = \left(\frac{Px_n}{Px_o} \div \frac{Pm_n}{Pm_o} - 1 \right) Qx_n \, Px_o$$

where Px_n and Px_o refer to the unit value of exports in year n and in the base year respectively; Pm_n and Pm_o refer to the unit value of imports in year n and in the base year respectively. Qx_n refers to the volume of exports in year n.

[24] The relationships defining each of these concepts are: $GDI = GNP + Z +$ Net transfers and $GNI = GDI +$ Net transfers.

The model describes the structure of the economy by means of nine equations (for nine endogenous variables) of which four are identity equations defining X, X^d, I and T^i, respectively, and the remaining five are behavioral equations. C^p is regressed on disposable GDI, C^g on total tax revenues, and total tax revenues on GDI. The private investment function depends on exports (E_{-1}) and the terms-of-trade effects (Z_{-1}) both lagged one year. Thus, private investment is determined completely exogenously by the export sector. As the builders of the model point out, "This appears to be a reasonable hypothesis in the case of Peru, given (a) the relative importance of the export sector; (b) the very highly capital-intensive nature of the export sector; and (c) the virtual absence of a domestic capital goods producing sector." [25] Finally, imports are regressed on total consumption and total gross investment. The structural model is presented below:

(1) $X = C^p + C^g + I^p + I^g + E + Z - M$

(2) $X^d = X - T^d$

(3) $I = I^p + I^g$

(4) $T^i = T - T^d$

(5) $C^p = c_o^p + c^p X^D$

(6) $C^g = c_o^g + c^g T$

(7) $I^p = i_o^p + i_e^p E_{-1} + i_z^p Z_{-1}$

(8) $M = mo + m_c(C^p + C^g) + m_i I$

(9) $T = t_o + t_x X$

Equations 1–4 are identities, and 5–9 are the postulated behavioral equations. The variables determined within the system of equations (endogenous variables) are X, X^d, I, T^i, C^p, C^g, I^p, M and T. The predetermined or exogenous variables are E, Z, I^g, T^d, and t_o, where the last three may be catalogued as potential policy instruments in the hands of the government.

The basic data used in the estimation of the model were taken from the INP national income accounts. Values are given in millions of soles at constant 1963 prices. The five behavioral equations were estimated on the basis of a sample consisting of yearly observations for the period 1950–65. Once estimated, the nine equations were solved for the endogenous variables in terms of the exogenous variables. The results are presented in Table 1. The reduced form shows explicitly how the value

[25] Thorbecke and Condos, *op. cit.*, p. 190.

of each endogenous variable is affected by each of the exogenous variables. Each coefficient appearing in the reduced form should be interpreted as the amount by which the respective endogenous variable will change with a one-unit variation in the corresponding exogenous variable. The high responsiveness of X to changes in the export sector variables is reflected in the relative magnitudes of the multiplier effect of a unit change in E and Z and that of I^g. This shows an important linkage between export growth and income growth.

The model appears to describe the evolution of GDI relatively well, since it signals all turning points correctly. It does show, however, a tendency to overreact to changes in the export sector. This is particularly clear for the recession of 1957–58 and the subsequent export boom of 1959–61. These overreactions are largely explained by the model formulation in which investment is solely dependent upon current and lagged exports earnings. Substantial private mining investments occurred precisely in the years in which the model overreacts. For example, in 1953–54 the Marcona mining complex was brought into production, followed by the Toquepala copper mines in 1957–58. The relatively poor prediction of GDI in 1965 and 1966 can be explained for the most part by the very large public foreign capital inflows for those years.

Similar developments must be allowed for when the model is used in projecting the major macroeconomic variables. Projections of the endogenous variables are linear combinations of the projections of the exogenous variables, in our case exports, the terms of trade, public investment, and direct tax revenue. It might have been possible to use the projections of the National Development Plan for this purpose. We did not do so because we felt the INP projection to be too optimistic.

The Peruvian export sector is quite diversified. In 1965 nine primary products accounted for 95 per cent of the total value of exports. (Agricultural exports constituted 23 per cent of all exports in 1965.) With the recent devaluation, cotton exports can be expected to increase moderately because of the drastic increase in the price-cost relationship for that crop. In the case of sugar and coffee, world production will continue to exceed world consumption for some years to come. Apart from this, there is the fact that Peru's foreign markets for these two products are in economically developed countries with low income elasticities and low population growth. Such markets offer little prospect of rapid expansion. A more detailed treatment of individual products may be found elsewhere.[26]

[26] René Vandendries, *El Comercio Exterior y el Desarrollo Económico del Perú,* Iowa Universities Mission to Peru in cooperation with the Agency for International Development, Lima, Peru, 1967.

TABLE 1

"Reduced Form" of the Thorbecke-Condos Model A

Endogenous Variables	Exogenous Variables						
	E	Z	E_{-1}	Z_{-1}	I^g	T^d	Constant Term
X	2.871	2.871	0.930	0.791	1.204	-1.416	21,697.43
X^d	2.871	2.871	0.930	0.791	1.204	-2.416	21,697.43
I	0	0	0.772	0.657	1.000	0	2,895.43
T^i	0.558	0.558	0.181	0.154	0.234	-1.275	-842.68
C^p	1.675	1.675	0.542	0.461	0.702	-1.410	22,894.54
C^g	0.537	0.537	0.174	0.148	0.225	-.265	-2,825.17
I^p	0	0	0.772	0.657	0	0	2,895.43
M	0.342	0.342	0.559	0.476	0.724	-.258	1,267.36
T	0.558	0.558	0.181	0.154	0.234	-.275	-842.68

We project that from 1966 to 1971 exports will accelerate annually from 3.5 per cent in 1967 to 4.5 per cent in 1971. A cumulative rate of 8.2 per cent is projected for 1972 and after, when, as anticipated, the Cerro Verde, Cuajones, and Michiquillay mines become productive.

The terms-of-trade effect was estimated by projecting export and import prices. Export prices characteristically have shown large fluctuations without a definite trend, but import prices have grown steadily. Export prices increased after the recession of the developed economies in the late 1950's and increased to a very high level in 1966 chiefly because of copper prices. We think this trend will level off. Import prices have risen at an average rate of 1.4 per cent per year, and we assumed that they will continued to grow at that stable rate.

Table 2 presents the projected values of the endogenous variables. The annual rate of growth in disposable income is projected at 3.4 per cent between 1966 and 1970, thereafter to accelerate rather sharply. The variables included in the model are not sufficient to project the public sector accounts. On the revenue side they omit nontax revenue and the capital account. On the expenditure side they omit current and capital transfers and the amortization and interest payments on the public debt.

Revenues on capital account were projected separately.[27] Nontax revenue was estimated through a linear regression for the period 1950–64. The total revenue projected for 1970 equals 31.7 billion soles (Table 3). Total public expenditure, by definition, equals total revenue.

From past performance agriculture can be assumed to be a relatively constant proportion of total public expenditure. On this basis public expenditure in agriculture can easily be predicted within a relatively narrow range. We considered three possible percentages. A pessimistic projection would allocate 2.8 per cent of public expenditure to agriculture. At the other extreme, we did not expect this allocation to exceed 3.3 per cent. The intermediate figure, 3 per cent, was thought to be the most probable. Under these hypotheses total public resources available to the agricultural sector in 1970 would range from a low of 889 million soles to a high of 1,047 million soles (see Table 4). The percentage composition of public expenditure within agriculture in 1970 was set equal to the percentage composition of 1966. This yielded a first approximation of projected financial resources available by activities in 1970.

[27] On basis of information furnished by the Dirección de Macroeconomía of INP.

TABLE 2

Projected Values of The Major Macroeconomic Variables, 1966–75

(in millions of soles at 1963 prices)

Variable	1966	1967	1968	1969	1970	1971	1972	1973	1974	1975
X	102,175.5	108,420.9	111,545.1	114,118.6	117,154.7	120,018.6	126,574.2	133,808.7	141,544.9	149,796.3
X^d	98,676.9	104,526.9	107,436.9	109,784.3	112,582.1	115,794.5	121,388.5	128,233.9	135,522.0	143,353.9
I	22,058.4	23,905.8	25,494.5	26,435.2	27,605.2	28,912.7	30,173.0	32,207.8	34,410.0	36,777.2
T^i	11,322.2	12,142.3	12,536.2	12,811.0	13,163.6	13,586.3	14,383.6	15,402.7	16,490.3	17,646.8
C^p	67,815.9	71,229.7	72,927.8	74,297.7	75,930.3	77,804.9	81,069.2	85,063.9	89,334.4	93,887.2
C^g	12,251.7	13,421.7	14,006.1	14,489.0	15,057.9	15,706.8	16,822.6	18,177.9	19,627.2	21,173.0
I^p	17,811.3	19,233.1	20,355.5	20,782.3	21,273.1	21,821.8	22,443.1	23,783.0	25,227.2	26,767.7
M	21,667.0	23,448.2	24,723.5	25,555.1	26,575.6	27,724.8	29,133.6	31,141.9	33,304.6	35,621.6
T	14,820.8	16,036.3	16,644.4	17,145.3	17,736.2	18,410.3	19,569.5	20,977.5	22,483.2	24,089.0
C	80,067.6	84,651.4	86,933.9	88,786.7	90,988.2	93,511.7	97,891.8	103,241.8	108,761.6	115,060.0

TABLE 3

Projected Revenue of The Public Sector by Major Sources, 1966–70

(in millions of 1963 soles)

Revenue Categories	1966	1967	1968	1969	1970
Total revenue	26,418.2	28,358.9	29,592.1	30,318.3	31,738.5
Current account	18,669.8	19,954.6	20,662.6	21,310.8	21,995.4
Direct taxes	3,498.6	3,894.0	4,108.2	4,334.3	4,572.6
Indirect taxes	11,322.2	12,142.3	12,536.2	12,811.0	13,163.6
Nontax revenue	3,849.0	3,918.3	4,018.2	4,165.5	4,259.2
Capital account	7,748.4	8,404.3	8,929.5	9,007.5	9,743.1
Public foreign capital inflow	5,916.0	4,774.0	5,715.0	5,007.0	5,364.0
Repayment of development loans	667.4	700.7	735.7	772.5	811.1
Public internal debt	1,165.0	2,929.6	2,478.8	3,228.0	3,568.0

TABLE 4

*Public Financial Resources Projected for the Agricultural Sector
in 1970, According to Three Public-Expenditure Hypotheses*[a]

	Percentage of Public Expenditure in Agriculture		
	2.8	3.0	3.3
Agrarian reform and colonization	173.4	185.8	204.3
Agricultural research, extension and development	129.2	138.4	152.3
Irrigation	146.5	156.9	172.6
National fertilizer corporation	132.1	191.5	155.6
Agricultural development bank	207.1	221.9	244.0
Other	100.3	107.5	118.3
Total public resources in agriculture	888.6	1,002.0	1,047.1

[a]Based on projected public expenditure in 1970 of 31,738.5 million
soles (at 1963 prices).

POPULATION GROWTH

Peru can be divided into three natural regions—the Coast, the Sierra,
and the Selva. The composition and growth of population have been
very different among these regions. The Sierra and Selva are predominantly rural, whereas the Coast is predominantly urban. The rapid
growth of population in the first two regions has been fed by a sizeable
emigration from the Sierra. Employment opportunities and per capita
earnings are very different between these regions, in both the agricultural
and nonagricultural sectors. Labor productivity in industrial and related
activities is increasing substantially faster than in agriculture. Consequently, the differences in per capita income between the urban and
rural population will increase rather than diminish. Such differences,
although undesirable, are virtually permanent in a structural sense.

The stated objective of the agricultural development plan is to
increase rural incomes in the Sierra through increasing yields of basic
food crops. However, financial resources projected available fall short

of permitting more than a one per cent increase in yields of basic food crops. From the foregoing it follows that the increase in per capita rural incomes cannot exceed a moderate annual percentage, unless the current rate of rural-urban migration is at least maintained. A detailed computation of agricultural labor requirements by regions (for projected developments in crop and livestock production) revealed that the current rate of growth in rural population is almost exactly balanced by the projected rate of growth in labor requirements. The projected rate of growth in labor supply is net of migration. Using cross-sectional data we found a fairly close relationship between the level of agricultural productivity and the daily wage rate.

Any retention of agricultural labor supply, not related to labor requirements, will therefore lower the labor productivity and earnings of the agricultural worker. Almost inevitably the gap between the per capita incomes of the urban and rural population will increase. Peruvian planners do not want the public sector to play an entirely passive role in this process. The agrarian reform program is directly aimed at solving the problem of rural poverty. Until now, this process has been slow because the government, by law, cannot appropriate without adequate compensation. Projected available funds for land reform do not permit an acceleration of this fundamental program.

Population projections were carried out in two stages. Official projections were available for urban and rural population,[28] but not for population growth by natural regions. With respect to national population, demographers feel that the decline in mortality rates has entered a stage of deceleration. Nevertheless the average mortality rate for 1980 is projected at less than half the current rate of 14.2 per thousand. During the period 1940–61 the average rate of female reproduction was 3.2. There is no agreement among demographers on the future course of this critical determinant of population growth. The officially adopted population projection anticipates a decrease in the birth rate from 4.41 to 3.81 in the late seventies. Growth of total population is projected at 3.1 per cent annually during the next decade. This is certainly the lowest estimate admissible.

Because of the insufficiency of vital statistics in Peru it proved impossible to establish conclusive differences between urban and rural mortality rates. From 1961 census data, it was determined that rural

[28] See, Ministerio de Hacienda, INP, Dirección Nacional de Estadística y Censos, *Boletines de Análisis Demografico: No. 1—Población del Perú* and *No. 3— Población Urbana y Rural del Perú,* Lima, Peru, 1964–65.

fertility rates were considerably higher than urban fertility rates. Therefore, the projected decrease in the average national rate of fertility could
only be sustained by projecting a balanced decrease between urban and
rural fertility rates, although there are no *a priori* reasons supporting
a decrease in rural fertility rates. The rates of rural-urban migration
were estimated through an intercensal comparison. They show an
acceleration between the two census years. To avoid the risk of obtaining
too rapid a rate of urbanization, current rates of migration were assumed
to remain constant for the next twenty years. The resulting projected
annual rate of growth in rural population equalled 1.1 per cent as
compared to 4.27 per cent for the urban population. Comparatively
minor increases in migration rates would reduce the rate of rural population growth to zero.

The composition of the population by three natural regions was
obtained on the basis of the census of 1940 and of 1961. Changes in
composition among regions between the two census years were assumed
to be linear and yielded the projected composition in 1970. Total projected population could then be distributed among regions. Changes in
composition between urban and rural population for a given region were
assumed to be linear between 1940 and 1961. Using the projected
composition for 1970, we distributed the projected total for each region
according to rural or urban areas (see Table 5). These projections
indicated a very rapid urbanization of the coastal region. A later, independent estimate for the Lima metropolitan area reinforced this observation. Initially, however, we lowered the rate of urbanization on the
Coast because of an anticipated shortage in the agricultural labor force.
Consequently, the projected rate of growth in rural population tends to
be biased upwards, and is larger than the official projection.

TABLE 5

Projected Population Growth for Urban and Rural Areas
by Regions, 1960–70
(annual geometric rates)

	Coast	Sierra	Selva	Republic
Urban	4.8	2.5	5.8	4.1
Rural	2.9	1.0	3.9	1.8
Total	4.4	1.3	4.5	3.1

DEMAND PROJECTIONS

The dualistic pattern of economic growth in Peru has created a striking heterogeneity among regions and population groups in respect to the principal factors that determine demand. A demand forecast based on average national parameters would introduce a systematic error. Thus, for example, domestic demand for traditionally imported food products projected from disaggregated data is larger than if aggregate data are used. This error was avoided by disaggregating the forecast.

In the more-developed countries regional differences in per capita income are relatively small. Both the rural and urban population have equal access to a wide variety of food products. This tends to create a homogeneous consumption pattern throughout the country. In Peru, however, the rural population consumes a substantial proportion of what it produces. Generally a few staple crops constitute the bulk of the rural diet, e.g., rice on the Coast, tubers in the Sierra and bananas in the Selva.

Largely on the basis of secondary information [29] we obtained twenty-five typical household consumption profiles distributed by regions and population groups. We found that the differences in per capita consumption between the urban and rural population were large for food groups except for cereals (see Table 6). A regional comparison of per capita consumption of food groups yielded differences of a similar order. The heterogeneity with respect to individual foods was even more striking. However, urban consumption patterns tend to be fairly homogeneous among regions.

The average blue-collar and white-collar family in Peru spend close to 55 per cent of family income on food. We estimated that the urban expenditure-income elasticity for all food equalled 0.8, a relatively high figure when compared with results obtained in other countries. The multiplicity of qualities and forms in which food is marketed con-

[29] See, Carlos Collazos Chiriboga, *et al.*, *The Food and Nutrition Situation in Peru*, República del Perú, Ministerio de Salud Pública y Asistencia Social, and Interamerican Cooperative Service of Public Health, Lima, 1960; Ministerio de Hacienda—*Plan Regional para el Desarrollo del Sur del Perú, Patrones de Consumo en las Ciudades de Arequipa y Cuzco*, Vol. XV, Lima, Peru, 1959—INP, Dirección Nacional de Estadística y Censos, *Encuesta Sobre las Condiciones de Vida de la Familia en: Lima-Callao, Arequipa, Huancayo, Chiclayo e Iquitos, Abril 1964–Marzo 1965* (resultados finales), Lima, Peru, 1966 (private communication); and CONESTCAR, *Hoja de Balance de Alimentos 1964*, Lima, Peru, 1967.

TABLE 6

Indexes of Per Capita Consumption of Major Food Groups by Urban and Rural Areas in Three Natural Regions and Over-all, 1964

(total consumption in Republic = 100)

	Coast			Sierra			Selva			Republic		
	Urban	Rural	Total	Urban	Rural	Total	Urban	Rural	Total	Urban	Rural	Total
Cereals	118	99	114	100	100	100	58	39	45	109	92	100
Tubers and roots	47	44	46	100	162	145	15	116	86	61	137	100
Beans and pulses	62	92	69	110	85	92	128	341	277	80	118	100
Fruits	91	43	81	–	99	28	291	705	580	105	95	100
Vegetables	112	54	99	276	54	113	63	12	27	155	49	100
Fats and oils	190	117	174	141	21	55	40	34	36	167	39	100
Dairy products	146	79	131	226	6	68	9	73	54	162	26	100
Meats	136	87	125	154	37	70	142	167	158	142	61	100

tributes to substantial price differentiation between income groups. Quantity-income elasticities are therefore substantially smaller than expenditure-income elasticities. The primary data underlying the econometric analysis of a number of household expenditure surveys were made available by the Ministry of Health and the Dirección Nacional de Estadística. A family of Engel curves was estimated for every basic commodity for each of the twelve cities for which data were available. Surprisingly, the double-logarithmic curve ranked above the other possible expenditure-income relationships in terms of a weighted criterion that included the coefficient of determination, the additivity property of individual product relations into group expenditure curves, and the additivity of individual product elasticities into a weighted group average. Constant-expenditure elasticities imply that the percentage composition of household expenditure changes with increasing per capita income. Nevertheless, when we made a detailed comparison for Lima between the household expenditure data of 1934 and 1964, we found that the percentage composition of the blue-collar and white-collar food budget had changed very little.[30] To assume that real income per capita had not risen for these numerically important income groups seemed unduly pessimistic. The difference must rather be sought in compensating changes in prices for food relative to nonfood.

A more precise formulation can be obtained as follows. With a double-logarithmic demand function the proportional rate of growth in food consumption will be a linearly weighted function of the proportional rates of growth in food and nonfood prices and per capita income in current prices. The weights are the respective price and income elasticities. From the above relationship the proportional rate of growth in food expenditure is easily derived by adding the proportional rate of growth in the price of food. Given that the expenditures on food and nonfood have increased at equal rates the following relationship must hold

$$p_f = \frac{1 + e_f + e_{nf} + E_f}{1 + e_f + e_{nf} + E_{nf}} p_{nf} + \frac{E_{nf} - E_f}{1 + e_f + e_{nf} + E_{nf}} y$$

where e indicates a direct price elasticity and E an income elasticity. The subscript f refers to food and the subscript nf to nonfood products. The lower-case letters p and y indicate the proportional rates of growth prices and per capita income, both in current prices. For Lima the total-expenditure elasticity on food equalled 0.79 and the

[30] The detailed data of the 1934 household expenditure survey were made available by the Dirección Nacional de Estadística y Censos.

TABLE 7

A Complete Scheme of Direct and Cross-Price Elasticities

| | Prices | | Expenditure Elasticities |
	Food	Nonfood	
Food quantities	−.70	−.09	0.79
Nonfood quantities	−.31	−.91	1.22
Budget proportions	.51	.49	1.00

direct-price elasticity for all food equalled −0.7. The percentage of the total expenditure on food for Lima is 51. Thus, given that the weighted sum of the expenditure-income elasticities must equal unity, it follows that the expenditure-income elasticity for nonfood equals 1.22. No direct estimate of the price elasticity of nonfood was available, but this parameter can be deduced from the interrelationships that must hold among the direct and cross-price elasticities within a complete system of such parameters (Table 7).[31]

Substituting the appropriate parameters in the former formula gives

$$p_f = .3\,p_{nf} + .7\,y$$

In a purely inflationary situation food prices, nonfood prices, and per capita income in current prices should all increase proportionately and not affect the allocation of total income between food and nonfood expenditure. Since the complete scheme of elasticities was elaborated on the assumption that the consumer is not subject to money illusion, the above-derived equation should possess a similar quality. The reader may verify that if $p_f = p_{nf}$, then $y = p_f = p_{nf}$. When referring to personal disposable income the consumer price index for Lima-Callao has usually been suggested as the proper deflator. When considering the food and nonfood items we find that in the period 1950–54 to 1960–64 the consumer price index of food increased at 8.2 per cent annually, whereas the price for nonfood increased at 5.3 per cent annually. Suppose that real per capita incomes have increased for the blue- and white-collar workers in the Lima-Callao area over the years. This means that

[31] Ragnar Frisch, "A Complete Scheme for Computing All Direct- and Cross-Demand Elasticities in a Model with Many Sectors," *Econometrica*, Vol. 27, pp. 177–196, April 1959.

per capita income in current prices must have increased more than the weighted sum of the indexes of food prices and nonfood prices, i.e., we have respectively

(1) $$p_f = .3 \, p_{nf} + .7 \, y$$

(2) $$p_f > p_{nf}$$

(3) $$y > .51 \, p_f + .49 \, p_{nf}$$

Since above equations are expressed in proportional growth rates we can write another equation, 2b from equation 2, as follows: $p_f + d = p_{nf}$, where d is the difference in the proportional rates of growth of nonfood prices and food prices respectively. If food prices have increased faster than nonfood prices, d should be negative. Similarly equation 3 can be transformed into an equality by adding a parameter z

(3b) $$y = .51 \, p_f + .49 \, p_{nf} + z$$

If real per capita income has increased, the parameter z should be positive. After substituting equations 2b and 3b into equation 1 we obtain

$$z = - .92d$$

For the period 1950–54 to 1960–64 d equalled approximately -2.9, and consequently real per capita incomes in the Lima-Callao area must have increased at 2.7 per cent annually for that same period.

Consumption patterns for the Lima metropolitan area are such that a quantity-weighted index will give proportionately larger weights to tubers, fruits, and vegetables, all of which are minor expenditure components of the typical blue-collar and white-collar food budget. On the other hand, an expenditure-weighted index will give proportionately larger weights to meats and milk products, although in terms of quantities bought both groups are small relative to tubers, cereals, fruits, and vegetables. Since the retail price of meats and milk products is determined in international markets, an expenditure-weighted index for Lima-Callao is dominated by imported food products, particularly beef. On the other hand, a quantity-weighted index is dominated by domestically produced food.

The quantity-weighted index has increased less than the expenditure-weighted index. In other words, prices of domestically produced foods increased less on the whole than prices of imported foods between 1950–54 and 1960–64. The domestic price of the latter is determined by the strength of the Peruvian Sol relative to the U.S. dollar and by the price trends, in terms of U.S. currency, in international markets. Trends in the dollar price of imported foods are best measured by taking the ratio of the value of food imports in current dollars to the value of imports expressed in 1963 dollars. This ratio has been virtually constant for the period 1950–64. Consequently, domestic increases in the price of imported foods stemmed principally from the periodic devaluations of the Sol (i.e., in 1953, 1957, 1958, and 1967). On the other hand, price increases for domestically produced goods reflect a purely inflationary component coupled with the effects of shifts of the aggregate demand and supply curves for domestic food. If, after separation of the inflationary component, the price of domestically produced food should show a long-run tendency to increase, it could be argued that the rate of growth in demand for domestic food, at given prices and marketing margins, was larger than the rate of growth in supply of domestically produced food. Evidently the proper choice of what represents the "purely inflationary component" is of critical importance in the above calculation.

When we take the consumer price index for Lima-Callao as equivalent to the purely inflationary component, we know that the consumer price index for domestically produced foods has increased between 7.3 and 8.2 per cent annually in the period 1950–54 to 1960–64. This range indicates a relatively small, but systematic increase in the deflated price of domestically produced food since the latter index rose more than the over-all consumer price index. The observed price increase may stem from increased marketing margins or lagging domestic production not compensated by imports. A comparison of the index of farm prices received for food and livestock products [32] and the Lima-Callao consumer food price index, indicates that, whereas the former index increased at 5.3 per cent annually between 1951–55 and 1960–64, the latter increased at 8.2 per cent annually between 1950–54 and 1960–64. The difference between these estimates is so large that it raises serious doubts as to the accuracy of the observations on farm prices received for food and livestock products. Ignoring the preliminary evidence on the growth of marketing margins, we will assume that the increase in the consumer price of domestically produced food was due to lagging domestic production. The direct price elasticity for all food in the Lima-Callao area was estimated to be -0.7. An increase of $.9 \times .7 = 0.63$ per cent in the growth rate of the domestic supply would have eliminated the observed increase in the deflated price of food.

[32] Ministerio de Hacienda, INP, Dirección Nacional de Estadística y Censos, *Indices de Precios al Consumidor–Lima Metropolitana–Callao*, Lima, Peru (published quarterly since 1935).

Thus, on the whole, it can be argued that, except for those commodities for which imports supplemented lagging domestic production, domestic supply must have responded adequately to domestic demand. This is true for corn, rice, barley, tubers, roots, fruits, vegetables, poultry meat, eggs, pork, and mutton. With the recent rate of growth in population at close to 3 per cent annually, and the demand for food quite elastic in respect to both income and price, the effective aggregate demand for food must have grown at least at 4.5 per cent annually. The above analysis would thus cast doubt on a large body of professional opinion within the Peruvian public sector which considers agricultural supply to be a major bottleneck in economic development, at least insofar as urban food provision is concerned. It also brings into question the accuracy of agricultural production statistics (and their derived consumption series), since they indicate a virtual stagnation in domestic food crop production in recent years. A passive supply projection using the more recent historical series (last six years) tends to be very gloomy with respect to the projected performance of the agricultural sector. When it takes into account a larger historical series (from 1950, for example), the projected performance is considerably more optimistic, but still underestimates the independently calculated rate of growth in demand.

According to our projections the GDI will increase at an annual rate of 5.1 per cent between 1960–64 (average) and 1970. The bulk of this income formation is projected as restricted to the urban areas. Growth of rural per capita income is primarily determined by the growth in value of agricultural production. We did not use historical rates of rural income formation but preferred a supply hypothesis that assumed a one per cent general productivity increase in agricultural production per hectare per year. Even so, rural per capita incomes are projected to increase only slowly, being virtually stagnant in the Sierra. The above projections are not very optimistic, because they offer little hope of having a measurable impact on rural poverty, particularly in the southern and central Sierra.

The Agricultural Planning Office (OSPA) drew up a set of comprehensive supply projections that showed a marked acceleration in gross agricultural production for food crops in general and for the Sierra in particular. These projections rationalize the philosophy behind the National Development Plan. The projections are not consistent, however, with a regional equilibrium of commodity flows. The considerable acceleration in rural demand would concentrate on those products in which supply would expand relatively least (livestock products, fruits, and vegetables). On the other hand rural demand would expand least in those products in which supply would expand relatively most (tubers, roots, cereals). Rural consumers would compete with urban workers for a limited domestic supply of livestock products, fruits, and vegetables, using as payment the marketable surplus in tubers, roots, and cereals. The Sierra would become a net importer of livestock products and a net exporter of cereals—a reversal of traditional commodity flows.

We did not have the necessary price-quantity relationships to work out the precise equilibrium solution. For the larger cities the direct price elasticity for all food equalled -0.8. The direct price elasticity for cereals was -0.4 and for tubers and roots -0.7. Commercial margins for farm products are a multiple of the on-farm value. Consequently market demand at the farm level is quite price inelastic for crops like tubers, roots, and cereals. The projected surplus over home consumption and urban demand would actually yield a decreasing cash income. Undoubtedly, this would tend to defeat the government's effort to expand production beyond an economically justifiable limit. Table 8 presents the projected annual growth rates in per capita GDI used in the demand projections.

Table 9 presents the projected cumulative annual growth rates in quantitative demands for various food groups by the rural and urban population in each of the four regions between 1960–64 and 1970. It can be seen that the demand for food will grow almost explosively in both the coastal region and Selva, while the Sierra registers a substantially lower expansion. For the Republic, as a whole, demand in almost all food groups will expand at a rate well beyond 4 per cent per year. The agricultural sector must have a considerable capacity to expand production if it is to meet this challenge. Because of the pattern of income and population growth, the demand for the staple food crops of

TABLE 8

Projected Growth in Per Capita Gross Domestic Income,
Urban and Rural, by Regions, 1960–64 (average) to 1970

(annual geometric rates)

	Coast	Sierra	Selva	Republic
Urban	3.9	1.8	2.7	3.2
Rural	2.0	0.5	2.0	1.0
Total	3.5	0.9	2.2	2.1

TABLE 9

Projected Cumulative Growth in Demand by Food Groups for The Rural and Urban Population, in Three Natural Regions, 1960–64 to 1970

(in per cent per annum)

Commodity Group	Coast			Sierra			Selva			Republic		
	Urban	Rural	Total	Urban	Rural	Total	Urban	Rural	Total	Urban	Rural	Total
Cereals	6.2	3.7	5.8	3.3	1.3	1.8	6.6	5.2	5.8	5.3	1.8	3.6
Tubers and roots	3.2	3.7	3.3	3.3	1.2	1.8	3.4	4.2	4.2	3.2	2.1	2.5
Beans and pulses	6.4	4.5	5.8	3.3	1.2	2.4	6.8	4.9	5.1	4.9	2.7	4.0
Fruits	8.7	5.4	7.8	4.2	1.8	4.2	6.9	4.3	4.6	6.8	4.4	5.6
Vegetables	7.4	5.1	7.2	3.6	1.4	2.9	8.1	5.3	8.4	5.6	2.3	4.8
Fats and oils	6.6	3.1	6.1	3.7	1.3	2.6	7.6	4.6	5.4	6.1	2.5	4.6
Milk and dairy products	7.8	4.8	7.5	3.1	1.5	2.2	8.3	5.9	7.8	6.9	2.3	5.6
Meats	7.8	4.6	7.4	2.4	0.1	1.1	8.0	8.0	8.0	6.5	3.6	5.4

the Sierra grows relatively the least, while the demand for the typical food crops of the Coast and Selva will grow relatively the most. Consequently, in agricultural promotion programs consideration might well be given to a reallocation of resources determined by future deficits in domestic production. This would almost certainly increase the proportion of public expenditure allocated to the Coast, an increase that would be in the interest of the urban consumer. On the other hand, increased allocation of public expenditure in the Sierra is the only active instrument available to the government to alleviate rural poverty. Whether public expenditure should be used to promote urban or rural interests is essentially a political decision. In the past the government has tried to satisfy both the urban consumer and rural food producers. We predict a continuation of that compromise.

Projection of Land Productivity

Except for export crops, average yield levels have been virtually constant between 1950 and 1964. Percentage changes in annual productivity fell within a range of 0.5 per cent around a zero average. Considering that agricultural statistics in Peru contain a large error of observation, it would be defensible to maintain that neither group of crops showed significant productivity increases. This fact conditioned our assumptions concerning possible increases in the future. We consider that within the period 1960–64 to 1970 productivity increases cannot reasonably exceed a cumulative rate of 2 per cent per year. Individual crops may exceed this rate, as may groups of crops, but the rate of growth in the aggregate yield index will fall within the upper limit of 2 per cent. Indeed, it might have been more realistic to accept the historical rate of increase of close to zero per cent. The aggregate yield index and its components show, however, a relatively low value for the mid 1950's when compared to either the early 1950's or early 1960's. A yield index for the years 1956–64 would show an over-all productivity increase equal to approximately one per cent per year.

Reporting of agricultural statistics does not involve a direct field-sampling of yield levels. Estimates by districts for basic crops were reported annually by part-time field investigators. Both the number of field reporters and the means of transporting them were limited in relation to the magnitude of the task. Communicaton between workers in the field and in the Ministry of Agriculture lacked feedback. Certain obvious errors were corrected after receipt of field data but no trend analysis, comparisons with previous years, or secondary sources were consulted in constructing the final series. Since the field staff was subject to a high rate of turnover and received little guidance or material support from headquarters in Lima, year-to-year reports show fluctuations that are unacceptable by any criterion. Aggregation of district data into departmental data still gives unacceptable results. A correlation analysis of yield trends between departments produced coefficients of determination very close to zero. A correlation analysis of yield trends between crops within the same department also gives nonsignificant results.

Analysis of each series at the departmental level was therefore not possible. Nor did we think that detailed considerations of each year at the national level would be useful. Instead, we choose to compare the beginning and ending five-year periods of the fifteen-year series 1950–64. We felt that a wider historical perspective was more likely to reveal true long-term trends. Standard linear-regression analysis on the same data resulted in coefficients of determination that, in the majority of cases, were not statistically significant, confirming implicitly that no statistically significant trends would be detected. In many cases, trend coefficients were obtained that indicated either rapid productivity increases or decreases. Despite their magnitude such coefficients would have been acceptable under the hypothesis that the true trend coefficient equaled zero.

The simplest hypothesis, for projection purposes, was that, for the majority of the eleven basic crops, yield productivity had not increased between 1950 and 1964 and that the next ten years would see a continuation of this stagnation. (For a few crops known to have been characterized by continuous adoption of yield-improving varieties and commercial inputs, a discretionary productivity increase could have been determined.) We did not seriously consider adopting this simple hypothesis because it appeared too pessimistic for use in long-term projections.

There remained two alternatives: (1) to take the basic data seriously and devise a method of analysis that would filter out the erratic nature of the data, or (2) to consult with agronomists and other experts and compile, in some systematic manner, their views on the probable improvements in yield levels. We explored both alternatives but adopted alternative one. In a series of meetings sponsored by the Agricultural Planning Office (OSPA),[33] technical experts of the Ministry of Agriculture set down their views on probable short-run yield improvements. These experts were drawn principally from the Agricultural Research,

[33] Ministerio de Agricultura, OSPA, *Previsiones del Desarrollo de la Oferta y de la Demande de los Productos Agropecuarios 1967–1970,* Lima, Peru, 1967 (mimeo.).

Extension, and Development Service (SIPA), the Office of Land Reform and Colonization (ONRA), the Agricultural Credit Bank (Banco de Fomento Agropecuario) and various organizations representing producer interests. The estimates presented by these technicians were uniformly optimistic. There are two explanations for this. First, many of the experts tended to confuse yield potential with probable yields. Their personal experience was mostly with experimental yield improvement, and it proved to be impossible to translate this knowledge systematically into a forecast of actual yield improvements. Second, some of the estimates were undoubtedly influenced by the desire to get additional funds for their respective agencies' growth. This created pressure to overestimate program impacts and to underestimate the costs of carrying out stated objectives.

As a substitute for the above procedure we explored three general yield hypotheses, i.e., the yield index of the eleven basic food crops was assumed to increase respectively at zero, 1, or 2 per cent per year. The projections were carried out in two independent stages. The first stage was the selection of one of the above three general productivity hypotheses. The second stage consisted in projecting the component crops of the yield index. Once the general yield index is selected, these component projections can be used to compute the projected yield level of individual crops or the projected yield index of groups of crops.

The important feature of this method is that once the general productivity hypothesis is chosen, all yield levels are simultaneously determined. This does not mean that all yields will increase proportionately. On the contrary, some will increase substantially more than the average, while others may actually decrease. However, all individual crop yields are assumed to vary positively in accordance with the magnitude of the general productivity hypothesized. Hence, under the 2 per cent general productivity hypothesis all crop yields will increase faster (or decrease less) than under the one per cent hypothesis. There is good reason to be suspicious of any long-run productivity increase exceeding a rate of 4 per cent per year for any particular crop. For groups of crops the long-run productivity increase cannot reasonably exceed 2–3 per cent per year. On the other hand, with a great many crops using a minimum level of commercial inputs, one should be skeptical of long-run productivity decreases exceeding more than 2 per cent per year for particular crops or zero per cent for groups of crops.

With the method of simultaneous projections adopted, it was not necessary to invoke the above qualitative considerations. Projected rates of yield increases all fell within preestablished limits. While the projected yield increases may have a margin of error, we think it the best possible estimate in view of the nature of the basic data.

Division of Peru into three regions based on ecological criteria—the Coast, Sierra, and Selva—is also useful for analyzing the development of agricultural supply in the last two decades. Yields for the same crop have increased at different rates in the three regions, and are likely to continue to do so for the next ten years. The explanation must be sought in the radical differences between these regions in respect to socio-economic conditions, natural productivity of the land, transportation costs, and government involvement in agriculture. Most of the above differences have a persistence that will carry them well beyond the horizon of the development plan.

There are activities such as agricultural extension and development, agrarian reform and agricultural credit that are in the domain of public policy and can therefore be redirected at will. However, the Peruvian government has not disposed of the necessary funds, nor even chosen to reallocate what funds are available, in such a fashion that increases in productivity of the existing land base would be maximized. In our projections we assume a continuation of that choice, since the need for productivity increases will continue to be small relative to the social necessity of agrarian reform and to competing activities in irrigation and colonization. On balance, therefore, a historical projection is likely to capture the principal effects of the conditions that influence land productivity. Furthermore, the strategic issues in agricultural development planning and foreign aid are centered around the relationship of cost of productivity increases to cost of land expansion. In this study, national production was estimated as the sum of independent projections in yield and acreage, where possible, on a regional basis.

Yield levels were first projected at the national level only. The national yield projections were then translated into projected yield levels by natural regions. The three general hypotheses as to projected increases in over-all productivity at the national level could then be translated into a set of specific yield projections for eleven basic crops by three natural regions (see Table 10).

Table 11 is based upon the detailed project plans of the agricultural promotion service (SIPA) for the year 1970.[34] From this it can be seen that the land area involved in extension programs is approximately 8 per cent of the projected total cultivated area for that year. The area per farm unit subject to extension will average 1.2 hectares, indicating that the extension effort is to be directed largely towards small farmers. If

[34] See, SIPA, *Proyectos de Incremento de la Producción 1967–1970.*

TABLE 10

Projected Growth in Yields Per Hectare of Eleven Basic Crops by Natural Regions, 1960–64 to 1970, According to Three General Productivity Hypotheses[a]

(in per cent per annum)

	Coast			Sierra			Selva			Republic		
	H_1	H_2	H_3	H_1	H_2	H_3	H_1	H_2	H_3	H_1	H_2	H_3
Tubers and roots												
Potatoes	2.5	2.9	3.9	-0.7	0.5	1.5	–	–	–	-0.5	0.6	1.6
Sweet potatoes	3.6	4.6	5.1	2.1	3.1	3.1	0	0	0.6	3.3	4.2	4.7
Manioc	-1.1	-1.0	0	-0.6	-0.1	0.4	-2.6	-2.2	-1.6	-2.2	-1.8	-1.4
Cereals												
Wheat	1.6	1.1	2.9	-0.1	1.1	2.1	–	–	–	-0.1	1.1	2.1
Barley	-1.1	-0.6	0.9	-1.5	-0.4	0.6	–	–	–	-1.5	-0.4	0.6
Corn	2.2	2.6	3.9	-0.2	0.6	1.6	-0.9	0	1.0	1.1	1.7	2.9
Rice	-0.2	0.8	1.8	1.3	1.3	1.3	0.6	1.6	2.6	-0.1	0.9	2.0
Beans and pulses												
Beans	1.8	1.8	2.1	1.3	1.4	2.5	-0.3	0	0.7	1.2	1.4	1.9
Horse beans	0.4	1.4	2.2	–	–	–	–	–	–	0.4	1.4	2.2
Industrials												
Cotton	1.4	1.6	1.8	2.1	2.3	2.7	-2.4	-2.7	-2.8	1.4	1.6	1.7
Sugar cane	1.1	2.8	3.5	–	–	–	–	–	–	1.1	2.8	3.5

[a] H_1, H_2, and H_3: zero, 1, and 2 per cent, respectively, annual increase in productivity per hectare over planning period.

TABLE 11

Projected Impact of Agricultural Productivity Programs on Yield Levels by 1970

Basic Food Crops	Land Area (thousands of hectares)			Yield Per Hectare (kilos)			On-Farm – Value of Productivity Programs (millions of 1963 soles)
	Without Promotion	With Promotion	Total	Without Promotion	With Promotion	Weighted Average	
Cereals							
Corn	396.7	39.4	436.1	1,534	2,519	1,600	67.6
Rice	96.4	13.8	110.2	4,103	4,759	4,185	19.8
Barley	179.0	7.1	186.1	907	1,794	941	10.1
Wheat	142.7	7.9	150.3	976	1,856	1,018	12.3
Quinua	20.3	2.9	23.2	994	1,596	1,069	5.1
Total cereals	835.1	71.1	905.9	1,588	2,770	1,669	114.9
Tubers and roots							
Potatoes	262.6	26.9	289.5	5,678	9,485	5,996	159.6
Sweet potatoes	12.4	0	12.4	15,736	–	15,736	–
Manioc	64.8	0	64.8	9,602	–	9,602	–
Oca-olluco	29.6	0	29.6	2,933	–	2,933	–
Total tubers and roots	369.4	26.9	396.3	6,484	9,485	6,662	159.6
Beans and pulses							
Beans	49.1	6.8	55.9	1,046	1,393	1,088	9.0
Broad beans	34.8	2.0	36.8	1,214	1,774	1,244	2.1
Horse beans	1.0	2.8	3.8	1,052	1,544	1,415	6.1
Peas	25.1	0.9	26.0	1,173	1,572	1,187	1.0
Chick peas	7.5	0.7	8.2	758	994	778	1.0
Lentils	2.3	0.3	2.6	934	1,288	975	0.5
Total beans and pulses	119.8	13.5	133.3	1,101	1,470	1,138	19.7
Total basic food crops	1,324.3	111.5	1,435.5	2,910	4,233	2,998	294.2

Source: Ministry of Agriculture: Servicio de Investigacion y Promocion Agraria (SIPA), "Proyectos de Incremento de la Produccion" (varios productos), Lima, 1967.

these programs are not carried out, the yield level of cereals projected for 1970 would have to be lowered by 5 per cent, that of tubers and roots by almost 3 per cent, that of beans and pulses by a little over 3 per cent and that of all basic food crops by 3 per cent. Since 1960–64 is the base period of the above projection, the induced acceleration in yield increases through public productivity programs is less than 0.5 per cent annually. In terms of 1964 farm prices the additional farm value produced in 1970 would equal 294 million soles.

The financial resources projected necessary to carry the programs out in 1970 equal 162 million soles in terms of 1964 prices (see Table 12). These figures suggest that the cost and return relationships in productivity programs are satisfactory. Additional food production can therefore be obtained in a straightforward manner through funds allocated in agricultural research and extension. The Peruvian government however has not put a high priority on this objective.

In order to achieve an annual 2 per cent increase in the yield index of eleven basic crops, approximately 460 million soles would have to be allocated to the agricultural research and extension service in 1970. Available expenditure in 1970 for all programs of the Agricultural Extension and Research Service (SIPA) is projected to be within a range of 130–150 million soles (see Table 4). However, only a fraction of this will be allocated to cereals, tubers, roots, beans, and pulses since the momentum of other existing programs will also have to be maintained.

TABLE 12

Projected Financial Resources Required in 1970 to Achieve Productivity Levels According to Stated General-Productivity Hypotheses

(in millions of 1964 soles)

Projected Public Expenditure	Cereals	Tubers	Beans and Pulses	Total
Required to achieve Hypothesis 2	125.8	75.8	4.9	206.5
Required to achieve Hypothesis 3	276.7	160.1	23.1	459.9
By Agricultural Extension Service	77.7	47.8	36.1	161.6
Available	–	–	–	52.5

TABLE 13

*Projected Financial Resources Needed for Eight Productivity
Programs of The Agricultural Extension and Research Service by 1970*

(in millions of 1964 soles)

	Total	Adminis-tration	Investi-gation	Exten-sion	Crop Develop-ment	Livestock Develop-ment
Cereals	77.7	14.7	18.4	30.9	13.2	—
Tubers	47.8	8.3	9.3	17.4	12.7	—
Beans and pulses	36.1	5.5	7.4	11.6	11.7	—
Fruits	51.5	9.1	19.1	11.2	12.0	—
Vegetables	14.0	2.0	2.5	4.2	5.3	—
Poultry	30.7	4.1	3.0	8.7	0.7	14.2
Beef and milk	55.2	7.1	15.0	3.0	2.0	28.2
Sheep and Alpaca	24.4	3.5	2.9	7.4	0.7	10.0
Total products	337.5	54.4	77.4	94.5	58.3	52.3
Total SIPA	462.3	74.6	106.1	129.4	79.9	71.7

Source: See Table 11.

The financial resources required by all of the planned programs of
SIPA in 1970 would equal 462 million soles (see Table 13). Cereals,
tubers, beans and pulses constitute only 35 per cent of the total SIPA
budget. Since the financial resources available for SIPA will probably not
exceed 150 million soles, the proposed programs cannot be executed
on the scale originally planned. Assuming a proportional cutback in all
programs, the expenditure available for those in cereals, tubers, beans,
and pulses is projected not to exceed 52.5 million soles, indicating that
allocated public expenditure is too small to have a notable impact on
productivity improvement. Of the total funds available to SIPA approximately 28 per cent are put into extension, the rest being used for research, development, and administration. On a regional basis plans are
for approximately 40 per cent to be allocated to the Sierra, 24 per cent
to the Selva, and the remaining 36 per cent to the Coast (see Table 14).
As projected,[35] the allocation of funds among programs, activities, and

[35] Ministerio de Agricultura, SIPA, Oficina de Planeamiento, Programación y
Presupuesto, *Gastos Según Programas Por Departamentos, Julio 1962–Junio 1966*,
Lima, Peru, 1967 (memorandum submitted to the Agricultural Sectoral Planning
Office).

TABLE 14

*Projected Percentage Composition of Expenditure on
Extension and Development Programs by Regions in 1970*

	Coast	Sierra	Selva	Republic
Administration	27.2	39.5	33.3	100.0
Research	14.0	44.6	41.4	100.0
Crop development	74.0	21.3	4.7	100.0
Livestock development	27.9	41.4	30.7	100.0
Extension	36.1	52.3	11.6	100.0
Total	35.1	40.9	24.0	100.0

Source: See Table 11.

regions is not necessarily optimal, because of the extent to which such allocations are necessarily governed by political and professional interactions. We are now completing a regional linear-programming model for potatoes in order to determine the optimum allocation of public investment funds consistent with (1) a maximum increase in production for a given total public expenditure in extension and development programs, and (2) projected changes in demand, supply, and costs of production. By comparing the actual allocation with the optimal allocation we hope to obtain a dollar estimate of the potential monetary benefits foregone under the present allocation. The recently introduced Agricultural Promotion Law calls specifically for land use zoning along the foregoing lines. By systematically executing similar studies on other crop and livestock programs we hope to obtain a more rational allocation of agency funds among the various programs. However, this still leaves unsettled the strategic planning decision concerning the balance between administration, research, development, and extension.

PROJECTED LAND EXPANSION

The land and water available in Peru are adequate to the needs of domestic production. Other Latin American countries, however, possess a much more accessible agricultural-resource base than Peru. Agricultural land under cultivation in 1964 equalled 2.1 million hectares. Half of this was in the Sierra, one-third in the Coast, and the rest in the Selva.[36] The land/man ratio in Peru is low when compared to other countries, developed or underdeveloped. One of the first tasks of the Agricultural Planning Office (OSPA) was to elaborate an inventory of land expansion projects. This was released by the Peruvian government as part of a plan to increase cultivated area by one million hectares by 1975.[37] There does not appear to be a strong need for such a drastic increase. In fact the rate of actual land expansion created through public investment is lower now than in the preceding fifteen years.[38] We feel that the concept of land/man ratio must be interpreted very cautiously. In itself, it does not indicate land scarcity or land surplus.

Livestock contributes only 25 per cent to the gross value of agricultural production. Sheep, hogs, and poultry are of minor importance. Most of the cattle and sheep are raised and fattened on the natural pastures of the Sierra highlands. Only the poultry industry has created a derived demand for feeds such as corn, but this crop must compete with the byproducts of rice, wheat, and cotton. Apart from export crops, cultivated land in Peru produces crops destined for direct human consumption. A relatively small acreage is therefore sufficient to meet the needs of domestic demand.

The land/man ratio is a fairly stable coefficient for a given country. This coefficient is subject to a secular trend, which while it cannot always be easily explained, is certainly predictable. Cultivated land expands because there is a demand for food and industrial crops. Whether this demand is generated domestically or externally makes little difference. The demand is met either through productivity increases on existing land or through expansion of the land base. In most underdeveloped countries increased demand for agricultural products has been met traditionally through expansion of the land base. Peru is no exception. Large areas, particularly in the Selva, have only recently been explored, and a land inventory for Peru is of necessity subject to constant upward revision. Coupled with the absence of hard knowledge about unexplored areas, there exists the uncertainty about the agricultural potential of traditional production areas. The report of a recent study by ONERN on Puno mentions that the agricultural potential of the *Altiplano* for crop use has been considerably underestimated.[39]

[36] CONESTCAR, *Estadística Agraria Perú 1964*, Lima, Peru, 1965.

[37] Ministerio de Agricultura, OSPA, *Inventario de Proyectos para Incrementar el Area Cultivada en un Millón de Hectareas*, Lima, Peru, 1965.

[38] José A. Salaverry Llosa, *Superficie Agropecuaria—Uso Actual y Potencial*, CONESTCAR, Lima, Peru, 1967 (mimeo.).

[39] ONERN, *Programa de Inventario y Evaluación de los Recursos Naturales del Departamento de Puno*, Vol. 5, Lima, Peru, 1965.

It is generally conceded that Peruvian agricultural statistics underreport the actual acreage under cultivation, particularly for the Sierra and the Selva.[40] Even in the coastal area land growth has been considerably underestimated, and it is only in the last two years that comprehensive cartographic surveys have revealed true land use. It is not therefore a question of whether Peru's land potential is exhausted, but rather of whether, in meeting growing demand, economic conditions will dictate a new trend towards productivity increases or a continuation of the former pattern of new land development. The public sector can have an influence in determining which direction will be taken, but it cannot by its own efforts insure the final outcome in terms of production achieved.

With respect to the land/man ratio there is an historical trend from which we decided not to deviate too radically. A geometric projection taking 1953 and 1962 as base years would have put the land/man ratio for the eleven basic crops at 0.1385 in 1970. The actual value adopted equals 0.1272 (see Table 15). This more conservative estimate resulted from the following considerations. The area for industrial crops in the coastal region has shown a considerable slowing down in its rate of expansion; in fact we project this area in 1970 to be slightly smaller than its 1960–64 average size. On the other hand, coastal population is growing well above the national average. This will cause a rapid expansion in the market for domestically grown food crops in the coastal region, an expansion accelerated by adverse market conditions for export crops. Hence, it seemed reasonable, in view of the substitution of food crops for cotton in land utilization, to set the land/man ratio for food crops in the coastal region at slightly below the indication of its historical trend. On the other hand, there was no need to deviate from the historical trend in regard to cotton, whose falling land/man ratio reflects a considerable decline of the relative importance of this crop.

Cultivated acreage in the Sierra is almost exclusively allocated to food crops. Certain valleys produce a substantial quantity of products that are consumed in the urban centers of the coastal region and the Sierra.[41] Nevertheless, in the absence of statistics on interregional trade movements, it seemed prudent to assume that in the Sierra cultivated acreage would expand almost proportionally to population. This puts no undue

[40] See Eduardo Watson Cisneros, *Situación de las Estadísticas Agropecuarias en el Perú*, CONESTCAR, Lima, Peru, 1964; and Shane Hunt, *Peruvian Agricultural Production 1944–1962*, Report submitted to the National Income Accounts Division of the Central Reserve Bank of Peru, Lima, 1963.

[41] Ministerio de Agricultura, SIPA, Oficina de Estudios Economicos, *Abastecimiento y Promedio de Precios de Productos Agrícolas en las Campānas Agrícolas 1956–1965*, Lima, Peru, 1966.

TABLE 15

Historical and Projected Land/Man Ratios by Regions
(in hectares per person)

Land/Man Ratio	Coast			Sierra			Selva			Republic		
	1951–55	1960–64	1970	1951–55	1960–64	1970	1951–55	1960–64	1970	1951–55	1960–64	1970
Total population into:												
Total transitory crops	.1245	.1206	.0889	.1738	.1701	.1698	1.0366	1.1152	1.1030	.1508	.1438	.1272
Food crops (except fruits & vegetables)	.0486	.0479	.0457	.1727	.1687	.1695	.8827	.9811	1.0409	.1221	.1132	.1069
Industrial crops (except coffee)	.0759	.0727	.0432	.0011	.0014	.0003	.1539	.1341	.0621	.0287	.0306	.0203
Rural population into:												
Total transitory crops	.4302	.4982	.4099	.2411	.2459	.2556	1.3785	1.5511	1.5986	.2644	.2810	.2712
Food crops	.1681	.1977	.2107	.2396	.2438	.2551	1.1738	1.3645	1.5086	.2141	.2213	.2280
Industrial crops	.2621	.3005	.1992	.0015	.0021	.0005	.2047	.1866	.0900	.0503	.0597	.0432

strain upon known, available land resources. Given the fact that agricultural statistics tend to underreport actual acreage in production, the adopted estimate is conservative.

In the Selva cultivated acreage is determined almost wholly by regional population growth. The export potential of the Selva in food crops is dubious and historically has been nonsignificant. The construction of new penetration roads, notably the Carretera Marginal, will foster a great deal of spontaneous and government-directed colonization. Therefore, even with the high rate of population growth in the Selva region, it appears quite feasible to maintain historical land/man ratios, except in cotton. Using the above independent regional considerations, we computed the dependent national average. In the ratio for food crops we found an almost linear decrease, but there was a drastic reversal for industrial crops when the projected period (1960–64 to 1970) is compared with 1951–55 to 1960–64.

In the foregoing determination we were guided by the growth in total population by regions, and we expressed implicitly that the three natural regions of Peru are, on balance, self-sufficient with respect to production of the eleven basic food stuffs included in our study. This is only approximately true with respect to the urban population but substantially true for the rural population, as the regional consumption and production patterns of the above crops show.

Given that the Sierra region is predominantly noncommercial in food crop production and, on balance, has tended to have reduced yield levels, it appears reasonable that the cultivated acreage in that region should increase at a rate not less than that of rural population. Census data show that a very high proportion of the rural population, almost regardless of age, is classified as agriculturally active.[42] In other words, the agricultural labor force in the Sierra is nearly identical with its rural population. The land/man ratio projection (with respect to the rural population) adopted for the Sierra can be seen to correspond closely to its historical tendency. The populations of both the coastal region and Selva have rapidly become more urban. *Ceteris paribus,* the land/man ratio when divided into rural population will tend to increase. This tendency is less for the Coast than for the Selva because of the stagnation in export crops.

Until 1962, statistics on cultivated acreage were collected and published by the Dirección de Economía Agraria, an entity within the Min-

[42] Ministerio de Hacienda, INP, Dirección Nacional de Estadística y Censos, *Sexto Censo Nacional de Población, 2 de Junio 1961, Resultados de Primera Prioridad,* Lima, Peru, 1964.

istry of Agriculture. The Agricultural Census of 1961 [43] revealed considerable differences between the estimates of the DEA and those of the Ministry of Agriculture, and this led to a complete revision of the Census estimates. In 1963 a cooperative agreement was signed between the Ministry of Agriculture and the Agricultural University at La Molina creating CONESTCAR.[44] This office was charged with reporting agricultural statistics, executing periodic agricultural censuses, and doing the cartographic work basic to crop area estimation. The DEA did not publish estimates for 1963, but CONESTCAR obtained provisional estimates by means of a linear regression on the DEA 1959–62 series. A subsequent subsample of the census data led to comprehensive revisions in many series for the period 1960–64.[45] Data for 1965 and 1966 have not yet been published. The 1964 revisions, for such basic food crops as potatoes and corn, are a compromise between the low census estimates and the higher estimates of the Ministry of Agriculture. Cartographic surveys for the coastal valleys have substantially improved crop area estimation. However, to date, no such substantial improvements have been introduced into the methods of measuring yields per hectare. With respect to the Sierra and Selva region, data reporting has been reorganized since 1964, but it has not necessarily been improved.

In our projections we have made uniform use of the five-year time series published by CONESTCAR in its *Estadística Agraria 1964*. Time series prior to 1960 are identical to those used by the National Planning Institute in elaborating national income accounts. These series were prepared by the Planning Office in the Ministry of Agriculture in the light of the results of the 1961 Census and of additional information made available from the Caja de Depositos, SIPA and the Superintendencia de Abastecimientos.[46] It is evident that the adjustments are somewhat arbitrary since they were made after the fact and on the national level only. With the existing acreage-reporting system, it is virtually impossible to measure reliably (i.e., within a 3 per cent margin) increases in cultivated acreage. Observations are necessarily fairly gross. A comparison of acreage reports from SIPA and CONESTCAR for the same region shows little or no directional correlation.

Our work on demand has given us good reason to believe that the current CONESTCAR series for the period 1960–64 underestimate the

[43] Ministerio de Hacienda, INP, Dirección Nacional de Estadística y Censos, *Primer Censo Nacional Agropecuario,* Lima, Peru, 1965.

[44] Convenio de Cooperación Técnica, Estadística y Cartografía.

[45] CONESTCAR, *Muestreo Agropecuario Nacional,* Lima, Peru, 1964.

[46] Ministerio de Agricultura, Oficina de Planeamiento, Comisión Análisis de Tendencias del Desarrollo Agropecuario, *Anexo Estadística,* Lima, Peru, 1965.

actual expansion in domestic agricultural production for that period. Projections to 1970 based upon these series tend to be unduly pessimistic and have given rise among foreign and Peruvian economists to an undue tendency to consider the agricultural sector stagnant. The last figures published by the DEA related to 1962, and the first original figure emanating entirely from CONESTCAR will relate to 1965. Apart from the difficulty of reporting relatively small changes in acreage between years, there is the problem of establishing a comprehensive base estimate. The diverse and scattered nature of cultivated acreage in Peru is such that only a comprehensive aerographic survey could provide the necessary base. For fully 70 per cent of the cultivated acreage of Peru such an estimate is still lacking. Crop area estimation for 1965 must therefore be guided by previous results, with a good chance that in the process of "guestimating" many small figures, the aggregated total will show surprising stability. Without the comprehensive 1964 publication of CONESTCAR the present projections would have been difficult if not impossible. It is equally true, however, that no matter how efficiently and comprehensively elaborated, bad field data will produce information of doubtful value independently of its level of aggregation.

Climatic factors in Peru are a very important and much ignored determinant of cultivated acreage. They affect all crops, if not equally, certainly to a considerable extent. The availability of water in the coastal region depends on precipitation in the Sierra where a drought inevitably creates scarcity of water for irrigation in the former region. A three-year moving average of annual discharges of the fifteen major rivers along the Peruvian coast revealed a remarkably consistent seven-year cycle. The relationship between inadequate precipitation and cultivated acreage is quite direct, e.g., for rice in the coastal region and for potatoes in the Sierra. While cyclical climatic factors are so marked that they affect all crops to some extent, it does not necessarily follow that they determine long-run trends in acreage or overshadow such trends as a factor in food supply projection. If this were so, a projection of supply would be dependent upon an accurate long-range weather forecast. Nevertheless, in the years covered by the Agricultural Development Plan a cyclical increase in water availability in the Sierra and in the coastal region is projected. Hence, the rather optimistic production projections of the plan might be borne out because of essentially exogenous developments.

Year-to-year fluctuations in reported acreage are relatively large. A standard linear or geometric regression yields coefficients of determination which, while statistically significant, are too low to be acceptable for forecasting. Other series (e.g., fruits and vegetables) constructed by

the Ministry of Agriculture on the basis of judgment yield higher coefficients of determination, but were excluded from the present analysis.
Because components of the projections were unreliable, nothing could be
gained by grouping individual projections, summing the groups and obtaining a group total. The total estimated acreage might accidentally
yield a land/man ratio in line with historical trends, but this could not
be guaranteed. Second, even if the total estimated acreage behaved according to expectations, this would not guarantee that its components
would. Such a guarantee could be made only if a simple trend analysis
consistently revealed high coefficients of determination. Since our ideas
on projected total acreage were relatively firm, we adopted a method for
imposing a restriction upon the total cultivated acreage by regions by
simultaneously determining the historical evolution in the composition
of acreage by groups of crops, and crops separately.

The projections, then, took place in two independent stages: the first,
to determine the total acreage, and the second to determine the composition of the total acreage. Hence, we could introduce a number of
hypotheses on land development and rapidly calculate the acreage of
each crop, by region, using the independent estimate on composition.
The composition of cultivated acreage within a given region has remained
remarkably stable over the years; in other words expansion of cultivated
acreage has been roughly proportional for all crops.

To obtain a more exact idea of the trends governing the relative composition of crop acreage we adopted the following procedure. Individual
crops were put into groups. The cereals group comprised rice, corn,
wheat, barley, quinua, and cañahua. The bean and pulse group comprised beans, horse beans, broad beans, chickpeas, peas, and lentils. The
tuber and roots group comprised white and yellow potatoes, sweet potatoes, manioc, oca, olluco and mashua; and the industrial crops group
sugarcane, cotton, and tobacco. Projections for coffee, fruits, and vegetables were not included as part of the simultaneous acreage projections.

The acreage of each crop and each group of crops was listed for the
quinquennium 1951–55 and the quinquennium 1960–64, using adjusted
DEA data for the first period and CONESTCAR data for the second.
The acreage of each crop was listed separately by regions as well as by
the national total. Then the percentage composition of each group within
a given region was determined. The national totals were not computed,
since the composition of these totals in the set of projections is derived
from separate projections of total acreage and its composition by regions.
To obtain two points for projections we computed the average composition for each of the two above-mentioned five-year intervals. In each case

the sum of the components must equal 100 per cent. Assuming the composition of acreage to change linearly, it follows that by a simple linear extrapolation, the 1970 composition can be determined. Given the projected total acreage for a food group, it is then very simple to compute the projected acreage for each crop.

The above procedure for separate crops can also be applied to groups of crops. It has the advantage of permitting the analysis of composition to be carried out separately from projecting the total cultivated acreage grown. In general, accuracy in the projection of total cultivated acreage is more critical to the over-all conclusions of the study than accuracy in the projection of acreage of any single crop. The method used allowed us to concentrate on the strategic decision concerning the projected man/land ratio and to use this as an imposed condition within which group- and crop-acreage estimates were accommodated. No conventional methods of statistical analysis were used in acreage projections, primarily because time series data in Peru are subject to error. We could have applied traditional regression analysis on the relative composition of acreage. While individual percentage trends might not necessarily sum to 100 per cent, a number of trials indicated the differences to be very small.

Table 16 indicates that the average annual expansion in land under cultivation between 1960–64 and 1970 should equal 37,680 hectares. Approximately 35 per cent of this expansion is projected to take place

TABLE 16

Projected Average Annual Increase in Cultivated Area by Crops in the Three Regions, 1960–64 to 1970

(in thousands of hectares)

Crop	Coast	Sierra	Selva	Republic
Cereals	7.73	9.17	2.86	19.76
Tubers and Roots	0.56	6.16	3.46	10.18
Beans and Pulses	2.07	1.64	0.63	4.34
Fruits	1.84	0.45	2.22	4.51
Vegetables	0.81	0.64	0.06	1.51
Total food crops	13.01	18.06	9.23	40.30
Industrial crops	-3.22	0.17	0.43	-2.62
All crops	9.79	18.23	9.66	37.68

in the coastal region. We believe that, because of the substantial elasticity in the use of available land resources, the projected increases in both the Sierra and Selva could take place without major direct public investment. Between 1950 and 1964 land under cultivation in the coastal region expanded by 273,000 hectares.[47] Irrigation of newly created land accounted for 75,000 hectares. An almost equal expansion was achieved by improving the irrigation systems on existing land. Water storage and utilization of underground water permitted an increase in cultivation of 85,000 hectares. River defense work, drainage projects, and small irrigation projects created an additional 35,000 hectares.[48] The figures on newly irrigated land and improved land do not include many small private projects.

Virtually all large-scale irrigation projects and improvements in the irrigation systems of adjoining valleys were financed by the public sector. The costs of building or improving irrigation systems were relatively low. A detailed study of the expenditure accounts of the Ministry of Development revealed that for fifteen completed large-scale coastal irrigation projects the installed cost per irrigated hectare equalled 22,000 soles (in 1963 prices, see Table 17). Improvements of existing irrigation systems cost on an average 6,500 soles per hectare (in 1963 prices). The average period of construction for these fifteen projects was eleven and four-tenths years.[49] Public investment in irrigation has fluctuated considerably because of the tendency to initiate projects in bunches.

Nevertheless, public investment in irrigation has shown a marked tendency to decline in relation to total public investment and even more so in relation to total government expenditure. Future irrigation works will all be large scale and their estimated cost per hectare, including the improvement of existing irrigation systems, will vary from 40,000 soles per hectare to 26,000 soles per hectare depending on the proportion of new and improved land (see Table 18).[50]

McGaughey's studies on the profitability of proposed irrigation projects show that with an annual rate of discount of 10 per cent, the resulting benefit-cost ratios are less than 1.8 and as low as 0.6. A first comparison with benefit-cost ratios obtained in productivity programs indi-

[47] Llosa, *op. cit.*

[48] Mario Cúneo Mimbela, *Plan de Desarrollo Agropecuario—Programa Irrigación,* Ministerio de Agricultura, OSPA, Lima, Peru, 1967.

[49] José A. Salaverry Llosa, *Inversiones en Obras, Estudios, Irrigaciones y Mejoramiento de Riego 1944–1966,* CONESTCAR, Lima, Peru, 1967 (mimeo.).

[50] Stephen McGaughey, *Evaluación de Proyectos, Información Requerida, Criterios y Prioridades,* Iowa Universities Mission to Peru in cooperation with the Agency for International Development, Lima, Peru, 1967 (mimeo.).

TABLE 17

Area and Construction Costs of Completed Coastal Irrigation Projects

Project	Area (in hectares) Planned New	Planned Improved	Realized New	Realized Improved	Project Cost[a]	Cost Per Hectare[b] New Land	Improved Land
Canal Internacional	1,500	—	1,120	—	21.5	19.2	—
Margen Izquierda Rio Tumbes	2,300	—	2,300	—	6.0	2.6	—
San Lorenzo	45,000	31,000	33,000	31,000	815.6	30.0	5.0
Canal Huallabamba	3,400	—	2,550	—	4.3	1.7	—
Derivacion Chotanochancay	—	60,000	—	18,000	190.0	—	10.6
La Esperanza	8,000	—	2,250	—	13.6	6.1	—
El Imperial Canete	8,156	—	6,117	—	200.0	32.7	—
Represa Turpo-Chinc	—	25,000	—	12,500	7.0	—	0.6
Represa Anacocha	—	23,600	—	11,800	2.1	—	0.2
Cabeza De Toro	6,500	—	4,875	—	15.5	31.8	—
Choclococha	—	26,000	—	10,300	190.1	—	18.5
La Joya	12,000	—	7,500	—	194.2	25.9	—
La Ensenada-Majia	2,000	—	1,500	—	26.5	17.7	—
Caplina	2,500	—	750	—	0.3	0.4	—
Canal Azucarero	2,500	—	750	—	3.7	5.0	—
All fifteen projects	88,856	165,600	51,712	83,600	1,690.3	22.2	6.5

Source: Jose Salaverry Llosa, *Inversiones en Obras, Estudios, Irrigaciones y Mejoramiento de Riego, 1944–1966,* CONESTCAR, Lima, Peru, 1967.
[a]In millions of constant 1963 soles.   [b]In thousands of constant 1963 soles.

TABLE 18

Area and Construction Costs of Proposed Coastal Irrigation Projects

| Projects | Proposed Area (hectares) | | | Construction Cost Per Hectare (1965 soles) | |
	Total	New	Improved	Individual	Weighted Average
Large irrigation					
(1) Olmos	86,751	86,751	–	49,300	–
(2) Choclococha	36,500	8,500	28,000	25,900	–
(3) Tumbes	19,460	12,315	7,145	28,900	–
(4) Moquequa	6,750	3,080	3,670	49,300	–
(5) Majes	57,000	57,000	–	64,900	–
Small irrigation					
(6) Pampa Dorada	1,185	1,185	–	105,800	–
(7) Majes	3,310	1,780	1,530	77,600	–
(8) Camana	1,815	210	1,605	26,700	–
(9) Tamba	2,270	505	1,765	30,000	–
(10) Ibera	880	880	–	23,000	–
(11) Chococo	1,523	–	1,523	18,600	–
(12) Anaura	1,175	–	1,175	6,400	–
(13) Huansocolla	925	–	925	15,000	–
All projects	219,544	172,206	47,338		47,304
Alternative project groups					
A (no's 1–3)	142,711	–	–	–	40,500
B (no's 1–3; 8–13)	151,301	–	–	–	39,900
C (no's 7–13)	11,900	–	–	–	37,300
D (no's 2,3,8–13)	64,550	–	–	–	26,037
E (undetermined)	–	–	–	–	–

Source: Stephen McGauhey, *Iowa Universities Mission to Peru,* Lima, 1967.

cates that a dollar of public expenditure on improving yields will give the greater return.[51] However data on cost and returns for productivity programs are not yet as reliable as similar data for irrigation projects. We are fairly certain that the stated returns on productivity programs are too optimistic. On balance, therefore, one cannot recommend public investment in productivity programs over irrigation projects with any degree of certainty. However, there are secondary considerations that favor productivity programs. The programs are divisible and can be located anywhere in the Republic, whereas irrigation projects are tied to a specific location in the coastal region and have a long gestation period. Irrigation projects require a substantial commitment of public investment over a considerable period of time. Because of the large initial capital requirements of such projects and the limited internal sources of finance for them, the Peruvian government will have to rely on external financing if it wants to pursue a vigorous land expansion policy in the coastal region. International agencies have financed a large number of feasibility studies in recent years, but have been reluctant to finance the foreign exchange cost of any large-scale project.

Public investment projected available for irrigation activities in 1970 equals 157 million soles. Assuming that most feasibility studies will have been completed by 1970, substantially all funds will be available for newly irrigated or improved land. At the average cost of 30,000 soles per hectare for current projects in their terminal stages, the projected funds would create an additional 5.3 thousand hectares of cultivation in 1970. Since irrigated land is at least double cropped, the projected increase will bring a minimum of 8,000 hectares under cultivation. Water storage, underground water utilization, and small irrigation projects could easily generate another 3,000 hectares of cultivation in 1970. The projected total increase of 11,000 hectares offsets the needed increase of 9,800 hectares in cultivated land in the coastal region.

PROJECTED FEASIBLE GROWTH IN PRODUCTION

Given the projected yields and acreages by crops and regions, it is a simple matter to determine the projected rates of growth in production (see Table 20). We used 1964 farm prices as specified by regions in

[51] See pp. 426–27 and Delbert A. Fitchett, *Investment Strategies in Peruvian Agriculture: Some Recent Experiences in Development Planning,* Memorandum prepared by the Rand Corporation for the Agency of International Development, Santa Monica, California, 1967.

TABLE 19

Total Public Expenditure on Land Expansion Activities in the Coastal Zone, 1950–65

(millions of constant 1963 soles)

Year	Total	Irrigation	Improvements	Drainage	River Defense	Dams	Ground Water	Studies
1950	85.0	79.0	2.0	–	0.7	–	–	3.3
1951	203.7	199.4	–	–	0.5	0.1	–	3.7
1952	191.8	183.8	1.4	–	1.4	0.1	–	5.1
1953	187.4	172.8	7.4	1.1	0.2	0.6	–	5.3
1954	54.0	42.9	5.5	1.5	0.4	0.4	–	3.3
1955	101.9	98.8	0.9	0.8	1.3	–	–	0.1
1956	142.3	123.0	1.4	3.5	2.5	6.6	–	5.3
1957	160.4	106.0	4.4	0.6	–	45.8	0.2	3.4
1958	170.6	153.9	1.8	–	10.0	–	0.2	4.7
1959	59.4	40.3	17.8	–	0.3	–	–	1.0
1960	13.5	6.5	–	–	6.2	–	–	0.8
1961	9.3	1.1	4.8	–	1.2	1.2	–	1.0
1962	42.3	20.6	14.9	4.6	0.5	0.6	–	1.1
1963	84.8	38.3	0.2	2.0	0.4	–	–	43.9
1964	97.5	55.5	2.6	1.9	0.5	4.2	2.8	30.0
1965	139.6	79.2	6.6	3.8	2.0	–	–	48.0

Source: See Table 17.

TABLE 20

Projected Growth in the Value of Agricultural Production by Groups of Crops for the Three Natural Regions, 1960–64 to 1970, According to Three Yield Hypotheses

(cumulative annual rates)

	Coast	Sierra	Selva	Republic
Hypothesis 1 – 0 yield increase per year				
Food crops	4.4	1.3	4.1	2.6
Industrials	0.6	3.4	3.6	1.3
All crops	1.9	1.4	5.0	2.0
Hypothesis 2 – 1 per cent yield increase per year				
Food crops	4.9	2.3	4.6	3.3
Industrials	1.0	3.4	3.6	1.5
All crops	2.3	2.3	5.2	2.6
Hypothesis 3 – 2 per cent yield increase per year				
Food crops	7.0	3.0	5.7	4.2
Industrials	2.2	3.5	3.6	2.4
All crops	3.9	3.0	5.8	3.4

the *Estadística Agraria 1964* to determine the growth rates in value aggregates.

The value of all crops produced in the Republic is expected to grow between 2 and 3.4 per cent annually, barring exogenous factors such as major devaluations and the effects of the weather cycle. Projected public funds for agricultural research and promotion will not be sufficient to attain a yield increase of 1 per cent per year (hypothesis 2). Hence, food production is expected to grow at approximately 3 per cent per year. Both the Coast and Selva are projected to achieve substantial rates of growth in food production, but in the Sierra expansion in food crop production is not expected to exceed 2 per cent annually.

In general the rates of growth in food production tend to be very close to the projected rates of growth in population by regions and for the Republic. Unless public investment in agriculture is increased beyond projected levels, food production will continue to expand at about the same rate as population growth. Prior to 1960 traditional export crops were the most dynamic component in the growth of agricultural pro-

TABLE 21

Projected Increase in the Level of Agricultural Production
Between 1960–64 and 1970

(millions of 1964 soles)

	0 yield	1 per cent yield	2 per cent yield
Yield effect	185	561	1988
Acreage effect	1626	1626	1626
Total increase	1811	2187	3614

duction. We project a reversal of that situation for the period 1960–70. It should be kept in mind however that the devaluation of 1967 has resulted in a change of the cost-price relationships in the export sector. Hence, beginning in 1968, production of exports will be larger than previously anticipated. This might raise the projected rate of growth in export production for the period 1962–70 to 3.5 per cent.

It can be seen from Table 21 that the bulk of the increase in the value of agricultural production will be forthcoming through land expansion rather than through yield increases. Currently projected productivity programs could permit an increase of 90 million soles beyond the minimum expected increase of 185 million soles. But of the 162 million soles required for these programs we expect only 50 million to be available.

Apart from the acceleration in productivity, it is expected that the major part of the increase in agricultural production will be forthcoming from the Coast and will be in food crop production (see Table 22). It

TABLE 22

Projected Percentage Composition of the Increase in Value of
Crop Production between 1960–64 and 1970
According to an Average of Yield Hypotheses 1 and 2

	Coast	Sierra	Selva	Republic
Food crops	38.6	25.8	11.0	75.5
Industrials	13.0	1.1	10.4	24.5
Total	51.6	26.9	21.4	100.0

is expected that the recent devaluation will accentuate the importance of the coastal region as a contributor to agricultural growth, because of the anticipated acceleration in export production.

PROJECTED INPUT REQUIREMENTS

In a systematic approach toward determining agricultural input requirements the classical factors of production, land, labor, and capital, as well as commercial inputs must be considered. In certain cases other physical factors impose narrower constraints, for example, water availability on the Coast and transportation facilities in the Selva. In the Peruvian case there is a substantial elasticity in the availability of land, labor, and capital (including those of manufactured origin).

It is only in the last two years that a systematic attempt has been made to study the effect of commercial inputs upon yield levels under empirical conditions. Data obtained for the southern Sierra indicate that a moderate application of a balanced fertilizer will, on the average, double the current yield level for potatoes and cereals (see Table 23). The distributions of response coefficients are characteristically skewed to the

TABLE 23

Characteristic Response Coefficients[a] Obtained Under Empirical Conditions with Uniform Levels[b] of Fertilization in the Southern Sierra, 1966

Crop	Number of Observations	Mode	Median	Arithmetic Average	Average Increase in Yield Per Hectare (kilos)
Potatoes	1038	1.50	1.43	2.18	4894
Corn	773	1.50	2.31	1.83	846
Wheat	151	1.50	1.73	2.04	798
Barley	322	1.50	1.76	1.83	736

Source: Data supplied by Corporacion Nacional de Fertilizantes.

[a]Response coefficient is yield per hectare obtained without fertilizer divided by yield per hectare obtained with fertilizer.

[b]Application equals 50-30-50 for potatoes and 51-30-0 for cereals.

right, so that the average exceeds the median. The most frequent response coefficient indicates that recommended fertilization increases current yield levels by half. When the average-response coefficient was used, the benefit-cost ratio of the fertilizer application equalled 9.1 for potatoes and 2 for cereals. However the typical, or most frequent, benefit-cost ratio was 4 for potatoes and 1.1 for cereals. It follows from the foregoing data that, for a substantial number of producers, fertilization of cereals offered no economic incentive, whereas the fertilization of potatoes was generally profitable. To the extent that supervised credit is an essential component of public productivity programs, the figures indicate that a substantial number of producers will not be able to repay their credit, even though on the average the program results in substantial productivity increases. Traditionally, public agricultural credit has been extended with a view to sound banking principles rather than to the objective of increasing land productivity. A shift towards the latter objective in credit availability is a prerequisite for the success of productivity programs in food crop production.

Preliminary input-output relations for the principal crops were obtained by the Agricultural Planning Office from comprehensive cost-of-production studies by SIPA [52] and the Agricultural Development Bank.[53] Both studies specified typical costs of production according to yield levels. For a given projected yield level the corresponding input structure was determined through graphical interpolation. This assumes that in achieving a higher yield level producers will follow the established cultivation practices corresponding to that level. The expansion path in input use is therefore not necessarily optimal in the sense that the producer minimizes his cost for a given output. An increase in yield is generally obtained through a number of qualitative changes, such as the simultaneous introduction of improved seed and fertilization. Therefore a producer effectively changes his production function while moving towards higher yield levels. Such shifts in the production function can frequently be effected at very little money cost to the producer. Therefore it has been found rather consistently that the average cost of production is declining with higher yield levels. Using the projected yields by crops and by regions according to three general productivity hypotheses, we computed the required outlay in terms of fertilizer, pesticides, seed, equipment, and labor. From Table 21 we find that hypothesis three gives a yield-increasing effect of 1,803 million soles over hypothesis one (3,614 minus 1,811). Comparing the input requirements

[52] Paez, *op. cit.*
[53] Higgins and Piedra, *op. cit.*

TABLE 24

Projected Annual Cumulative Growth Rates in Input Requirements,
1962–70, According to Supply Hypotheses 1 and 3

| | Crops | | | | | |
| | Food | | Industrial | | Total | |
Input	Hyp. 1	Hyp. 3	Hyp. 1	Hyp. 3	Hyp. 1	Hyp. 3
Fertilizer	6.8	12.0	−1.4	.6	3.3	6.9
Pesticides	5.8	8.9	1.2	4.4	3.3	6.5
Seed	3.1	4.8	−2.8	−1.6	2.7	4.3
Equipment	3.5	3.7	−3.6	−3.6	1.0	1.1
Labor	3.8	3.8	−3.1	−3.1	1.1	1.1

for hypotheses one and three, we found that the above increase of 1,803 million soles could be obtained for an additional outlay of fertilizer, pesticides, and seed totalling 357 million soles. The marginal benefit-cost ratio to the producers would therefore equal 5.1. Table 24 presents the projected annual growth rates in input requirements according to supply hypotheses one and three. Since hypothesis one is likely to be exceeded by a small margin only, the projected rate of growth in demand for commercial inputs will not exceed 4 per cent annually. On the other hand the growth rate in labor requirements equals only 1.1 per cent annually. This figure corresponds exactly with the officially projected rate of growth in the rural population.

Comment

WALTER P. FALCON, HARVARD UNIVERSITY

Professor Van de Wetering's paper is a contribution to the literature on agricultural planning. As recent surveys by Gittinger and Ojala have indicated,[1] there are few available source materials on how developing

[1] J. P. Gittinger, *The Literature of Agricultural Planning,* National Planning Association, Washington, D.C., September, 1966, and E. M. Ojala, "The Program-

countries have actually formulated their plans for the large and difficult agricultural sector. Therefore, this detailed and thorough presentation of the Peruvian approach should be most helpful to practicing planners and to teachers of planning.

There are two aspects of the paper in particular that elicit comment. The first is Van de Wetering's explicit treatment of the relationship between agricultural planning and the over-all macro framework. Indeed, this entire volume, which stresses the broad interactions, is a refreshing change from earlier "fundamentalist" literature. The second appealing feature is his technique, which can be characterized as emphasizing consistency, efficiency, and sensitivity.[2] Van de Wetering's continued concern with commodity and regional balances and with the sensitivity of results to varying assumptions is highly commendable.

In spite of these considerable merits, several aspects of the paper left me uneasy. One of the major difficulties, especially for readers who are not intimately familiar with Peru, is in distinguishing "what was" from "what should have been." Quite clearly, Van de Wetering was an insider in the process and hence his description of what took place is first-rate. Rarely, however, does he take issue with the methodology that was used or the conclusions that were reached. Thus it is impossible to tell whether or not he personally agrees with all of the main themes in the paper. (The strong equity-over-growth bias that runs throughout is a good case in point.) My major comments and criticisms, therefore, may be on issues which were outside the control of the planners (e.g., Van de Wetering) and perhaps of the entire agricultural ministry. Yet they should have been addressed in the paper.

The most serious of these issues is the question of priorities. Specifically, the absence of any discussion on priorities is the main defect of the paper. The significant priorities involve not only intersectoral questions, e.g., agriculture versus manufacturing, but intrasectoral issues as well, e.g., export crops versus domestic food crops. To a large extent my comments will focus on these matters. To a lesser extent they will raise questions about agricultural policy which also received only summary treatment in the paper.

In terms of general approach, I believe it fair to characterize the Peruvian formulation as highly autarkic. Self-sufficiency in food seems to have dominated the entire planning effort to 1970, and the effects

ming of Agricultural Development," in H. M. Southworth and B. F. Johnston (ed.), *Agricultural Development and Economic Growth*, Ithaca, N.Y., 1967, pp. 548–586.

[2] See D. E. Bell, "Allocating Development Resources," in C. J. Friedrich and S. E. Harris (ed.), *Public Policy, IX,* Cambridge, Mass., 1959, pp. 84–106.

of an increased agricultural growth on the expansion of exports appear to have been minimized. This seems a bit curious, especially in light of several of the author's own statements. Exports appear to have played an important role, especially for the agricultural sector. Since, in addition, export crops grew at more than 8 per cent annually prior to 1960, and since fishmeal exports are currently less encouraging, it seems questionable whether the discrimination against export crops through export taxes and through relative neglect in terms of planned inputs is the correct strategy. In any event, it would have been useful if Van de Wetering had discussed this rather crucial priority issue, because virtually all of the projections in his paper are dependent upon it.

A second interesting feature of the Peruvian approach to agricultural planning is its strong demand orientation. In this context, a comparison between Peruvian and (say) Indian and Pakistani planning could not be more striking. For in the latter countries, the planning has started with inputs and the supply potential in agriculture, and has then related this growth in agricultural output to various macrovariables such as GNP, exports, etc. In the Peruvian case, however, projections were begun with the assumption of growths in regional income and population. Through the extensive use of income elasticities, commodity projections were made on a regional basis. These estimates were then conceived of as being what was "required" from agriculture.

In principle, there need be little cause for concern or comment as to whether agricultural planning begins with demand or supply considerations. That both are important and must be analyzed is obvious. In practice, however, there are several aspects of this particular demand formulation that caused me concern. First, there are suggestions, often quite explicit, that not only should the country as a whole be self-sufficient for the major commodities, but that each of the regions should be as well. Van de Wetering states, for example (page 420), that "in agricultural promotion programs consideration might well be given a reallocation of resources determined by future deficits in (regional) domestic production." Surely this is carrying the autarkic and regional-balance priority too far. Surely the possibility of solving imbalances by fiscal rather than production means ought to have been discussed more fully. (One might even argue that one of the principal objectives of agricultural planning in Peru ought to be increased economic integration of the regions.) Probably it is this demand orientation and methodology that explain why the principal attention, as noted above, is on food crops rather than on export commodities. Second, it is obviously difficult in this formulation to estimate the growth in per capita incomes, especially for the more rural areas, until there is some estimate of the growth of agricultural output. This reconciliation never comes about, at least not explicitly, within the paper. Third, the what-is-required-from-agriculture approach may have been a contributing factor in leading the Peruvian planners to focus on "feasibility" rather than "optimality" for agriculture, *i.e.,* ". . . the preliminary agricultural development plan should limit itself to determining in a systematic manner the feasible rate of growth, rather than the optimal rate of growth or optimal allocation of public expenditure" (page 394). This is not to say that supply considerations do not enter, but they are brought in at a very late stage and then only in deciding whether the various regional demands can be met. And nowhere in any real sense are there discussions of farmer acceptance of various programs, of increasing innovation in rural areas, and of other general problems of production within a decentralized decision-making framework.

A third feature of the Peruvian plan is the size and structure of the public program for agriculture. By international standards the 3 per cent total spent on agriculture is *very* low.[3] Indeed, to have struggled with the lengthy discussion of the macromodel only to find that the maximum range of public expenditure to be considered for agriculture was 2.8–3.3 per cent was a little like finding the baby gone with the bathwater. In short, this narrow range eliminated at the outset a number of the more interesting comparisons. It would have been most interesting, for example, to have known what a 5 or a 10 per cent allocation might have meant for agriculture and what effect this would have had in turn on the more macrovariables.

Given this 3 per cent total, and given the sizeable proportion of funds committed for land-expanding activities, the author is undoubtedly correct in stating that "public expenditure is too small to have a notable impact on productivity improvement." His discussion highlights the problems, not only of a small total, but also of a governmental bias for extensive rather than intensive approach. In this regard, Peru seems typical of many of the developing countries.

Even with the limited financing for yield-increasing programs, however, I would have liked to know more about how the various productivity programs (especially research and promotion service) were assessed and how each was expected to contribute towards the increased output shown in Table 11. In particular, additional information on the

---

[3] In Pakistan, for example, approximately 15 per cent of the development expenditure goes to agriculture directly. If "irrigation" also is included the proportion is raised to about 25 per cent.

choice of the "input package" would have been interesting for comparative purposes. The recent literature which has stressed physical complementarity among agricultural inputs has argued an important principle. But what a country or an agricultural ministry does in "package selection" when faced with financial, administrative, and organizational shortages seems to me to be the crux of the agricultural planning function.[4] On this point the discussion is brief, although Van de Wetering's major point, *viz.,* that the proposed agricultural program, regardless of how allocated, is much too small to alter significantly the future pattern of agricultural productions, comes through clearly.

Finally, the paper as presently cast is primarily concerned with the setting of targets. Unquestionably this is an important aspect of planning. But planning ought, in my opinion, primarily to be a framework for policy making. And on the important policy questions Van de Wetering says relatively little. How, for example, is the switch from export to food crops to be accelerated? Through price incentives? Input subsidies? Tax policy? To ask for further discussion and analysis of these policy questions after the lengthy and detailed material already presented by Van de Wetering may be unkind; yet I am sure he would agree that the policy aspects of a plan are far more important for its success than is the setting of targets.

Notwithstanding the above comments, this paper does add significantly to one aspect of the literature on planning. In large part, the comments that I have put forth simply ask for additional analyses or take as variables certain parameters that Van de Wetering, as an insider, may have found as fixed.

[4] For further discussion on this point see J. W. Mellor, "Production Problems and Issues in Agricultural Development," *Journal of Farm Economics,* December 1966, pp. 1195–1202, and this writer's comments thereon, pp. 1207–1209.

INDEX

Abaca. *See* Raw materials.
"Accounting" effects of increase of exports on gross domestic product, 67–73
Accounting matrix
  for South African study, 87–89
  for West African study, 78–81
Adelman, Irma, 118, 118*n,* 136*n,* 159, 164, 174*n,* 201, 400*n*
Africa
  commercialized and subsistence sectors of, 5
  cultivation of new lands in, 6
  urbanization of, 60
  See also South African pilot study; West Africa; West African pilot study.
African slaves, 161
  and Brazilian economy, 318
  and gold boom, 315–316
  and sugar boom, 312
  See also Slavery.
Agglomeration effect, 384–385
Agrarian reform in Peru, 388–389, 391, 409. *See also* Land reform.
Agrarian society, 9, 130
Agrarian stagnation. *See* Agricultural stagnation.
Agricultural Census of 1961 (Peru), 433
Agricultural cooperatives
  in Brazil, 372
  in mainland China, 260
Agricultural credit
  and agricultural development, 394–395
  in Eastern Europe, 255–256
Agricultural Credit Bank (Peru), 422
Agricultural development
  and causes of stagnation, 131–138
  and gap between microanalysis of production functions and global approach, 12

and growth of nonagricultural sector, 22
historical sequence model of, 9
and improved inputs, 12
and industrialization. *See* Industrialization.
multisectoral approach to, 12
and new policies and criteria, 309
in Peru, 203–209
regional model in. *See* West African Pilot Study
East African study as model of, 92–93
and spatial-equilibrium models, 115–116
"turning point" in, 300–303
and world economic development, 95–96
of West African region. *See* West African pilot study.
Agricultural Development Bank (Peru), 396, 445
Agricultural development model, 75–87, 116–118. *See also* Models.
Agricultural exports
  average unit value of, 32
  dependence of developing world on, 5
  of developing countries, 7–8
  from less-developed countries to developed countries, 55–57
  See also Exports.
Agricultural extension services. *See* Extension services.
Agricultural inputs. *See* Fertilizer; Inputs; Irrigation; etc.
Agricultural investment. *See* Investment.
Agricultural labor force. *See* Labor force.
Agricultural output. *See* Output.
Agricultural planners
  and agrarian reform, 392
  in Peru, 390–391

Japanese immigrants in Brazil, 359, 372
Jasny, Naum, 242n
Jews, role in industrial development of
São Paulo, 360
Johnson, D. Gale, 242, 244n, 247, 247n
Johnston, Bruce F., 7, 10, 279n, 280n,
284n, 286n, 287n, 295n, 303,
304n, 309, 447n
Jones, Edwin, 262n, 263n
Jorgenson, Dale W., 9, 134n, 219n
Jorgenson-classical thesis, 135, 136n,
164
Jorgenson "trap" case, 135n
Juàzeiro (Brazil), 315
Jute. See Raw materials.

Kahan, Arcadius, 244n
Kaneda, Hiromitsu, 280n, 286n, 297n
Karcz, Jerzy F., 10, 240n, 241n, 243,
244n, 248, 258n, 265, 269, 269n
Karlik, Jiři, 257n
Kelly, Ruth, 178n–179n
Kenaf, 72
Kenya, cereal exports of, 40
Kindleberger, 148
Klatt, Werner, 262n
Korbonski, Andrzej, 248n, 258n
Korea, agricultural output of, 7
Kornai, 125
Kristensen, 48
Kumar, T. Krishna, 109n
Kuvshinov, I. S., 250n, 251n
Kuznets, Simon, 242n, 330n, 331n

Labor force
and agricultural development, 394–
395
of Argentina
and demand for food, 181
in pre-1930 period, 176
of Brazil, 321, 339
and cattle industry, 314
and coffee boom, 324
during sugar boom, 312
of East Asia, 290–291, 295
in Eastern Europe, 251–252, 271
engaged in investment in overhead
capital, 136
exploitation of, 152–153
growth rate, turning point in, 300–
303
immigration to Argentina, 176n
imported, 161, 164

in India and Japan, 293
and industrialization, 346–347, 354
and Japanese agricultural development, 284–285, 289–290
and land improvement, 288
in open agrarian society, 142–146
participation of women in, 270
of Peru, 210–211, 396, 409
ratio to land, 159–160
reallocation of, 133, 135–136
role of, 131–132
subsidized and taxed, profit rate and,
151–154
transfer out of agriculture, 180–181,
355–356, 381
of two functional economic areas of
equal population, 112
in USSR, 246–248
See also Labor productivity; Labor
surplus.
Labor market
and functional economic area, 110
and industrialization, 355–363, 385
Labor productivity
in Brazil, 332
equations for, 305–306
in India and Japan, 293
and industrialization, 340, 352, 356,
385
and Taiwan's agricultural growth, 306
See also Productivity.
Labor substitution, capital intensification and, 296
Labor surplus, 131–132
and marketing facilities, 146n
in open agrarian economy, 155–156
Labor-intensive methods, 147
Labor-land ratio, 159–160
in East Asia, 295
Labor-using innovations, 310
Land
percentage socialized in Eastern Europe, 250–251
in West African study, 85
withdrawal of, 181n
Yugoslavian acquisition of, 258
Land availability
in Brazil, 324
during coffee boom, 321
for cereal cultivation, 41
in East Asia, 278–279, 290
in East Asia and Japan, 292–293
and prices, 25